# MICHAEL POLANYI

*A Critical Exposition*

SUNY Series in Cultural Perspectives
Antonio T. de Nicolas, Editor

# MICHAEL POLANYI

*A Critical Exposition*

*Harry Prosch*

STATE UNIVERSITY OF NEW YORK PRESS

Published by
State University of New York Press, Albany

© 1986   State University of New York

For information, address State University of New York
Press, State University Plaza, Albany, N.Y., 12246

Library of Congress Cataloging in Publication Data

Prosch, Harry, 1917–
    Michael Polanyi : a critical exposition.

    (A SUNY series in cultural perspectives)
    "Bibliography of Michael Polanyi's writings"—P.
    Bibliography: p.
    Includes index.
    1. Polanyi, Michael, 1891–      I. Title.
II. Series.
B945.P584P76   1986        192        85-27849
ISBN 0-88706-277-6
ISBN 0-88706-276-8 (pbk.)

10  9  8  7  6  5  4  3  2  1

*To John Brennan*

# Contents

## Part IV—*Evaluation*

# Acknowledgments

My thanks to Professor John C. Polanyi and to Routledge and Kegan Paul, Ltd., for their permission to include in my Bibliography Professor Polanyi's complete list of his father's scientific papers, which appeared originally in *The Logic of Personal Knowledge, Essays Presented to Michael Polanyi on his Seventieth Birthday 11th March 1961* (London: 1961), pp. 239–47.

I should here express my gratitude to the following publishers also for their permission to quote so copiously from their books and journals:

University of Chicago Press
Oxford University Press
American Psychological Association
Journal of the British Society for Phenomenology
Special Collections, The University of Chicago Library
Peter Smith, Publisher
Pergamon Press

My thanks also to Professor Thomas A. Langford, who first provided me with a bibliography of Michael Polanyi's nonscientific writings. This bibliography enabled me to begin my reading of these publications and also provided a basis for my own extensive further research into his writings, which has finally resulted in what I trust to be the complete bibliography of Polanyi's publications, which appears in this book. Professor Langford told me that he was indebted to Professor Richard Gelwick for the list he sent me. So I wish to take this opportunity to thank Professor Gelwick also for at least indirectly starting me off.

I want to thank Professor Marjorie Grene for many helpful discussions of Polanyi's views and of the issues upon which we both feel he shed so much light. Her help was invaluable; but she is not to be blamed for what I here say about Polanyi. I know she disagrees with some of it.

I would thank John Brennan (to whom this book is dedicated) were it not that "thanks" would be too weak a word to use. In any case, now I cannot, because of his shocking and untimely death. There is such a mutuality in what friends give and take from each other that "thanks" are never needed. The sun came up on many of our discussions about the man for whom we mutually had so much respect and, I would add, whom we seemed to understand, together, so well. I have wanted often, since my friend's death, to seek the security of his confirmation for the things I was saying in this book.

I wish to thank Skidmore College, and especially the Faculty Research Committee and Deans Edwin Moseley and Eric Weller, for being most helpful during the years I have been working on this book, in allowing me leaves and in giving me grants from time to time that covered the expenses involved in my research, such as typing costs and particularly the costs of bibliographical research at the university libraries of Chicago, Columbia, Brown, and the State University of New York at Albany, and at Union College, Union Theological Seminary, New York City Library, and the Library of Congress. I also wish to thank the British Museum in London and the Bodleian Library at Oxford for granting me the use of their resources.

The research staff of the library at Skidmore College was indefatigable in their efforts to help me, and my gratitude to them is boundless.

Last but not least, my thanks to my typist, Mona Clear, for her patience and endurance during these years.

Skidmore College
Saratoga Springs, New York
September 3, 1985

# Introduction

This book had its origin in a sabbatical leave I spent with Michael Polanyi in Oxford, England, during 1968–69. I had come as an interested but rather critical spectator, intending to assess coolly what this strange interloper into philosophy was doing, and to analyze his thought into its fundamental grounds and principles. I left a fellow participant in an active effort to develop an adequate contemporary philosophy, wholly convinced that Polanyi was on to something tremendously fundamental, sound, and healthy for the modern mind, but not yet wholly convinced that he had got it all perfectly straight.

I had already begun writing this book toward the end of this stay with him. He himself interrupted my work on it twice, however: once when he asked me to share a Visiting Professorship with him at the University of Chicago and then later when he asked me to help him bring out in the form of a book what proved to be his last series of lectures. By this time his advanced age made it necessary for that work with him to be more that of a collaborator than of an editor or an assistant; by the time we got started on the book he was no longer able to write. Accordingly, in the preparation of our text, I made every effort to stick as closely to the very words of his unpublished lectures and of his other published works as continuity, coherence, and the development of a book with its own internal integrity permitted; nevertheless I tried to say nothing in it to which I myself could not subscribe in some legitimate sense. Accordingly the book, *Meaning,* was published under both our names. Its final written form was my work; but, as I tried to make clear in the Preface and in the Acknowledgments, the ultimate origin of everything in it was Michael Polanyi. To the best of my knowledge and understanding there is nothing in it that is not wholly consistent with his own views, even if he may never himself have made some of the statements in the book—at least not in the precise way in which they are there expressed. He himself read all the manuscript and accepted it, not I am sure, as the great book *he* would have written, but as the best that could be done under the circumstances.

Since *Meaning* enlarged the scope of what Polanyi had published before and introduced some new and far-reaching notions, it was necessary to incorporate all of these also into this book of my own about his thought. His interruptions therefore doubly delayed the completion of my work. This book will, I hope, further my ultimate purpose of assisting the development of an adequate contemporary philosophy. Its immediate goal, however, is to provide a critical exposition of the thought of Michael Polanyi, under the supposition that such a work will at this time best further my ultimate purpose. I believe that no one other than Polanyi has in recent years been so assiduous in ferreting out and criticizing those attitudes, beliefs, and working principles that have debilitated the modern mind by undermining its trust in its own higher capacities; nor has anyone else offered more pregnant suggestions for a truly new philosophic position free from these difficulties. Efforts at an adequate philosophy for our time should then, it seems to me, begin with a thorough digest of what Polanyi has done.

Polanyi's concerns were decidedly contemporary. His general notions about the scope and function of philosophy, however, harked back to Socrates or at least certainly to Plato. The question, Plato's Socrates had declared, was whether he should be a physician or a servant— whether he should continually try to improve the minds and souls of his fellow citizens, or try to serve their existing tastes and interests. And he indicated this question was the same as asking whether he should be a philosopher or a politician.

No doubt most contemporary politicians are still making the same choice that Socrates' interlocutor, Callicles, advised him to make, for his own safety, namely, to be the servant of his fellow citizens. It is not at all clear, however, that most contemporary philosophers, especially those in the Anglo-American sphere, are still making Socrates' choice, to be physicians to the minds of their fellow citizens. But they are not all making Callicles' choice either. Rather they seem to be thinking of philosophy as a theoretic study of some sort, or possibly as the development of a set of analytic skills, rather than as a practical art devoted to improving the soul.

Perhaps it would carry us too far afield to enter into the pros and cons of this very fundamental issue at this point. Before finishing this book, however, the reader should have found this issue somewhat clarified. He may even have found that the physician-philosopher, Polanyi, has converted him, if he had before been of the opinion that a philosopher should not attempt to be a physician. To Polanyi this conversion could be the same thing as having effected a cure, since one of the symptoms of what ails the modern mind is, for Polanyi, precisely the denial by the modern mind that its reflecting more deeply can cure its ills. Rather, the modern mind tends to assume that its "ills," to the extent it would use such a term at all, are caused by essentially external or nonreflective economic, social, or environmental factors, and/or by internal psychoses or neuroses—resulting indeed in mistaken, nonadaptive, attitudes and beliefs, but by no means caused by such mistaken ideas. Rather, the causes of neuroses and psychoses are again most often referred to external circumstances, either to organic malfunctioning, external to conscious mental processes, or to external circumstances under which one has lived in a family or a society. Therefore the cure is also thought to be effected by external applications either of various drugs or surgical operations or of various shocks administered to the patient, either physically, or psychically "on the couch" as when one is suddenly forced by the manipulations of the psychiatrist to see some unpleasant facts about attitudes he has been attempting to conceal from himself.

On the other hand, the reader may find that Polanyi has not at all converted or cured him. But he may still have come to a better understanding of why he refuses to be converted or cured. For Polanyi, even this self-knowledge would constitute some measure of success!

To a physician-philosopher, philosophy is not merely an academic pursuit. It is, rather, a way of life. For if the soul can be improved by reflection, then a physician of the soul who does not live by what he presumably understands, yet is trying to get others to understand and to live by, must surely be suspect, even to himself. So philosophy for Michael Polanyi was not merely an academic pursuit. His life and character were living illustrations of his own philosophic views. He was a walking refutation of the charge that philosophers always build mansions, and then live in hovels beside them. Those who knew him knew this was not true of him. In an important sense his life grew out of his thought, as his thought grew out of his life.

But his life and character are not my major concerns in writing this book. It is not a biography—not even an intellectual biography. Only a few words about his life are therefore needed, I believe, to grasp the meaning and significance, the thrust, of his thought, as he himself saw it.

He was born in 1891 in Hungary and began his professional career there as a physician in the commonly accepted meaning of the term, a medical doctor, in the Austro-Hungarian army during World War I. He had chosen the medical profession over his real love, chemistry, because he feared that he might be denied a University appointment in view of the fact that his family was Jewish. However, the call of chemistry was too powerful and after the war he took the chance and began a second career as a physical chemist at the Kaiser Wilhelm Institute in Berlin.

It was a great era in German science, and Michael Polanyi found himself associating with such men as Fritz Haber, Erwin Schrödinger, Max Planck, and Albert Einstein. But during the early 1930s, when the shadow of Adolph Hitler began to engulf all of Germany, Polanyi felt it necessary to leave. The Germany he knew and respected was unquestionably disappearing. Moreover it became clear to him that his own life itself might soon be in jeopardy. Accordingly he went to England with his wife and two sons and joined the University of Manchester there as Professor of Physical Chemistry. After a number of years in this post, however, he exchanged this Chair for that of Professor of Social Studies.

Something that rarely happens in the contemporary world was taking place. A well-established professional man was graduating to a new profession. Indeed, this was his second change of profession. But this time the change came after many years of successful and significant work in the profession he was leaving—in fact, after having spent what would normally be called his best years in it. Actually, he did combine work in both professions for a time, publishing works of note in each. His last scientific paper appeared in 1949; but he had also been publishing in economics and in what would have to be called philosophy since 1935.

The history of this shift in his interest cannot be rehearsed in detail here. But a brief outline will probably be helpful and should suffice. Polanyi had long been critical of the extreme positivistic view of science, a view most popular in his younger days, but which even now exerts influence upon modern thought, not only as a philosophy of science but in many other ways as well. The intellectual connection of positivism with nihilism and of nihilism with the ruthless political movements of the left and the right in his day became ever clearer to him. As they did, the importance and intellectual respectability of holding firm beliefs on the ideals essential to science and to a free society—and an acknowledgment of their interconnection—also became ever more clear to him.

Polanyi found himself increasingly involved in questions and problems regarding the relation of science to society and, in general, in problems of the social sciences, especially of economics, largely because he found it necessary to investigate thoroughly the socialist insistence upon a centrally planned economy as a substitute for the market mechanism of private capitalism. But it was also becoming ever clearer to him that nothing short of a complete overhaul of the current philosophic views of science and of knowledge could dispel the threat to freedom— indeed, their threat to science itself—from the prevailing authoritarian and utilitarian social and intellectual movements. Popular thought seemed to imply that only scientific theories were capable of verification (i.e., of proof), and that moral or ethical or political or religious ideals and principles were essentially unprovable, mere matters of emotional preference. No one seemed to see the extent to which not only the existence of a free society, *but also the existence of this presumably verifiable science itself,* rested upon freely held beliefs in ideals and principles that not only could not be proved, but could not even be made wholly explicit. It seemed to him that no one saw that the unprovability of these beliefs did not render them intellectually unrespectable or unworthy of being held. It therefore appeared to him necessary to show people, philosophers included, why and how this was so.

In this way the philosopher Polanyi gradually emerged. He found a voice for his message in articles published in a great variety of periodicals and in a small book, *Science, Faith and Society,* and finally in 1958 in a magnum opus entitled *Personal Knowledge.* From then on he continued to publish numerous articles and several additional books and monographs, as well as to conduct seminars and to lecture at universities and at conferences in various parts of the world. His retirement from the University of Manchester was followed by two years as a Research

Fellow at Merton College at Oxford, where he lived and continued to write until his death in 1976. His influence had a slow but steady growth, especially in America, unfortunately not as much among philosophers (who have in general either ignored him or discounted his importance as a philosopher) as among sociologists, economists, psychologists, scientists, and theologians.

I hope to be able to show to my own doubting colleagues in philosophy that his key term, "personal knowledge," which sounds to many something like "square circle," is a very meaningful and important term when understood in the context of his whole philosophy, and that moreover, in its proper meaning, it is not even a startling innovation. It refers to a commonplace that most people, perhaps even most philosophers, already know. Yet Polanyi's work should not be regarded as unimportant or trivial on the grounds that he has labored to bring forth and defend only an obvious truth which everyone already knows at least implicitly.

The status of what he has brought forth is, I think, similar in this respect to what Kant brought forth. Kant rightly held that the fact that rational moral discourse could be shown to have proceeded always under the guidance of the categorical imperative did not render trivial his work in bringing this principle to our attention. Indeed, he held that if this principle were not already involved in everyone's moral thought, he would have been proposing merely a creation of his own mind, with no claim to anyone else's attention and consequently no claim to adequacy as a universal principle. If the term "critical" applied to a philosophy, therefore, means only that the philosophy attempts to bring to our attention the categories and principles we do in fact all use in making our judgments—and the limitations these put upon our knowledge—then Polanyi is also, with Kant, a critical philosopher, in spite of the fact that he subtitled his *Personal Knowledge* "Towards A Post-Critical Philosophy." As we shall see, by this subtitle he meant to call attention to a very significant difference between the *kind* of limitations on our knowledge recognized by Kant's critical philosophy and those recognized by his own. This was a difference in kind that must have great significance for our views concerning ourselves, our social organizations, and the nature of what *is,* that is, for our views of nature and the universe, our ontology and metaphysics. We shall find what we can rightly call knowledge in Polanyi's terms will seem to us less absolute, perhaps, than what we could rightly call knowledge in Kant's terms. At the same time we shall find it to be more extensive and significant.

Most important, our study will also show that Polanyi, in his role as a physician-philosopher, was mainly concerned with trying to cure the modern mind of what ails it. But, of course, since no one can talk about sickness without at least implying certain criteria for health, we will also be bringing out what his criteria for a healthy soul were. Whether what he said about this, as well as about other questions, turns out to be cognitively convincing must, of course, be left to the personal judgment of his readers. There is no proof in such matters that is not a proof personally to or for a particular person. But, as he reminded us, the same thing is true of *all* cognitive judgments, although it is quite frequently forgotten in our day in the case of some of them. He was saying, in other words, that no cognitive judgment can ever be rendered wholly explicit, but that the meaning, and indeed the acceptance, of all such judgments must depend ultimately upon some elements known only tacitly by a mind in action. This is even true, as he did not flinch from saying, of this very basic judgment itself that he was making—the judgment that all cognitive judgments are personal ones.

Many philosophers have stolen a glance into the infinity of mirrors set up by the reflexive character of personal judgment. Some have forthwith become skeptics and some have become absolutists of one kind or another. Polanyi tried to show us how we can avoid both these alternatives and yet continue to face the intraversable infinity of personal judgments with an equanimity born neither of skeptical despair nor of escape into an Absolute. In a formal sense the unique epistemological position that he was led to by these concerns lies at the heart of his philosophy; but in a more ultimate sense it does not. For he was not exploring epistemology or ontology simply because they are there, i.e., for their own sake, much less because such explorations are erudite academic exercises calculated to win him a place in the profession. He was exploring them because he believed such explorations are essential at this time in order to restore the health of the modern mind. To lose sight of this overarching aim in his philosophy would be (as some have done) to misunderstand much that he has written and also to demand from his thought further detailed inquiries and concerns that were irrelevant for him, irrelevant because not essential in resolving the problems that made his thought necessary and that shaped it into the form he gave it.

He obviously subscribed, therefore, to the basic principle that significant philosophy deals at all times and places with the most pressing general problems existing in the intellectual climate of its own time and place. Yet his subscription to this basic principle should not mislead us into confusing his thought with the pragmatic philosophy of John Dewey. It is true enough that he shared with Dewey the notion that significant thought begins with problems; but the impetus propelling a mind toward both a recognition and a solution of its problems was not for him the itch to restore ongoing activity, but rather a passion to attain comprehensive and meaningful wholes in any situation in which one is involved. The psychology from which he took his bearings, in other words, is quite different from that from which the American pragmatists took theirs. Instead of seeing organisms as primordially blind activists, gradually structured into going concerns through frustrating problematic situations by these organisms' own efforts to achieve a restoration of activity, he saw organisms as primordially meaning-seeking centers, already oriented toward the goal of finding or attaining structurally ordered holistic entities both within and without themselves, whether or not these ordered wholes were needed to restore ongoing activity. He freely acknowledged his debt to the Gestalt psychology of his day, just as the pragmatists freely acknowledged their debt to the functionalist psychology of theirs. But this difference from the pragmatists in where Polanyi entered philosophy, made, as we shall see, a considerable difference in where he came out.

Bearing in mind, therefore, the manner in which Michael Polanyi understood the nature of philosophy and the purpose he believed it to have, I have organized this book on his philosophy around the notion of what he thought ails the modern mind and how he thought it can be cured. This plan appears to break naturally into the Parts of this book, which I have called Diagnosis, Prescription, Treatment, and Evaluation. In each of the first three parts I intend to try to restate his position relative to that topic as fully and accurately as I understand it, together with his reasons for holding this position. I have avoided a chronological or historical approach in presenting his views on these matters, because I wish to do for Polanyi's work something which no one has yet done, not even Polanyi himself. I want to show how the various subjects and areas he had taken up belong together in terms of his fundamental objectives.

In addition I had originally hoped to show at the same time how Polanyi's thought could be of use in resolving some of the problems which current thought seems to find most difficult. I finally decided, however, not to try also to accomplish this latter task, because I feared the manuscript would become far too long. Not only would I have had to show, from examining the pressing and controversial problems in the contemporary literature on epistemology, how his views could shed some real light upon these issues; but I would have had to do this also with regard to the literatures in each of the many other areas of thought that he discussed. So I confined myself to the task of showing simply from Polanyi's own texts how, in his own intentions, the several facets of his varied work held together.

Accordingly, in these three Parts I held to a minimum my own defense of his views and arguments, and my criticisms—as well as those which others might make—and simply tried to report accurately just how Polanyi himself defended them. I thought such straightforward reporting would then allow my readers to judge for themselves whether his own arguments for his several theses were persuasive or, if not, where they might find it necessary to take issue with him.

In regard to Evaluation, the last Part, I limited myself to dealing with a number of people basically sympathetic to Polanyi's views, but who seemed to me to differ with aspects of his thought. The only critics who I have discovered take issue with his most basic positions do not seem to me to understand these positions, and so are all but worthless in providing any telling objections to his fundamental principles. It is my hope that this work may help philosophers understand the meaning and strength of Polanyi's basic contentions so that, if he is fundamentally wrong at some point, critics may be able to show just how and why what I have shown to be his reasons for this view are inadequate. Of course adequacy in this case cannot be assumed to mean beyond any *conceivable* doubt, since we are dealing with a philosopher who contends that no position can be established so absolutely. Adequacy can only mean beyond any *reasonable* doubt. For he never claimed his philosophy to be adequate in any other way.

But in the end, of course, the final evaluation of his work must be of his efforts to play physician to the modern mind, and I attempt such a final evaluation. An evaluation of this kind clearly proceeds from the point of view of philosopher-as-physician. Whether or not he would have found it entirely acceptable, it is, I trust, the kind he might have found relevant and congenial.

# PART I

## *Diagnosis*

# CHAPTER ONE

# Indications of Malaise

Many people today suspect that something ails the modern mind. They point to the unparalleled scope and destruction of the two world wars of our century, to the collective insanity that kept them going long beyond any advantages that could have been hoped for by either side. They point to the unprecedented tyranny and mass exterminations of our totalitarian nightmares, both of the right and the left, and to the Nazis' supreme effort at genocide. They also cite our continued stock-piling of nuclear weapons, even after our capacity to destroy all life on earth several times over has been attained. And to our failure to grapple with the problems generated by our own offal—the waste products (including now, of course, radioactive materials) that are polluting our air, earth, and water, even the vast oceans. There are also the continuing festering sores of racisms and of religious fanaticisms and bigotries, the self-destructive drug culture, and increasing fraudulence in politics, business, the professions, and even academic circles.

It is true that some of these dismal features of our own century may only be contemporary versions of the sorts of trouble and imperfections mankind has always been subject to, and that a widening of our historical perspectives might lead us to take a somewhat brighter view of our own times. Nevertheless there is quite a catalogue of horrors, and surely no one could be blamed for wondering whether or not some screws might be loose somewhere in our mental machinery.

Michael Polanyi was decidedly less inconoclastic with respect to contemporary life than are most of our current prophets of doom. However, he too was taken aback by much of what man had wrought upon himself in our time. In 1970 he reflected upon the fact that our two world wars and our totalitarian regimes had killed (up to then) something like fifty million people, as well as destroyed the major cities of Europe as centers of culture and learning—cities such as Vienna, Berlin, Leipzig, Prague, Moscow, Budapest. We have destroyed, he pointed out in a lecture in 1967, much of what the liberal movement in Europe had accomplished in the preceding two centuries: a united cultural domain sharing in an intellectual, artistic, and moral progress of surpassing richness.

He recalled how a combination of scientific enlightenment and moral idealism was still firmly supporting this great European culture in the first part of this century. Our minds were at home, he said, in all the ideas and arts of Europe and we could travel anywhere freely without passport and settle down without permit.[1] It was obviously a place of much more cosmopolitan outlook and mentality than now eixsts. No doubt the contrast between Europe at the beginning of the century and now was strikingly obvious to a man of Polanyi's age and mode of life.

All things change and pass away, of course. But the strange thing about the passing of the Europe that once was is that the free cultural and cosmopolitan aspects of what it was are still what the intellectuals of Europe really want and need—and yet, as we shall find him pointing out, it was the intellectuals of our century themselves who played the largest part in destroying those very things that they needed and that were already theirs. Such operative perversity as this must lead one to suspect the operator's mental health, a mind blind to that which it wants and needs (and even in a sense to what it knows), and which proceeds on a path toward its own destruction, may surely be suspected of suffering from obsessions that are pushing it to such nonadaptive behavior.

The destruction of the Europe that Polanyi looked back to was well underway in the later 1930s. The First World War had had its disastrous effects, the Stalinist and Hitlerian horrors were already being laid upon much of Europe, the Great Depression with its mass unemployment and hardship had begun and its end was not yet clearly visible, and the

Second World War, which would round off the destruction, was just around the corner. However, it would be a few years yet before that particular symptom of our insanity would overwhelm us. But there were other symptoms at the time and some of them became evident to Michael Polanyi. He referred to them in the Preface of his 1940 collection of essays, *The Contempt of Freedom,* as the "prevailing progressive obsessions."[2] Let us follow his efforts to uncover these prevailing obsessions, since it was these that first led him to believe that the modern mind was not well.

One of the symptoms that most early concerned him and that seemed to him to point to the presence of some sort of obsession, was one that might appear to us today to be a fairly mild disturbance compared with what has since come to haunt us. However, it is not unrelated to our present troubles, as Polanyi showed. This symptom, of course, was one most likely to come to the attention of a scientist. It was the concerted movement in England in the 1930s to deprive science of its autonomy and to make it responsible to society and for its welfare. There still exists, of course, the threat of a revival of this movement in our day under the tremendous burden of problems that have resulted from unrestrained scientific inquiry.

Polanyi thought that the general public (who must, in the end, foot the bill one way or another for scientific teaching, inquiry, and growth) would be tempted to ask that science be deliberately oriented toward discoveries useful to the general public—or at least that science be restrained from discovering what could possibly harm the public. The public therefore, he held, would always need educating as to the desirability of supporting free inquiry, if free inquiry were to continue to exist.

But what seemed unhealthy to him about the movement to control science was that it was an intellectual movement—which moreover included many scientists! Polanyi felt that intellectuals, especially scientists, should really know better than to support social control over science. They surely knew that freedom to pursue those inquiries that seemed most likely to the inquirers themselves to uncover theoretically interesting and important truths, not merely practical inventions, was the life-blood of science.

He could not help but feel, therefore, that an obstruction of some sort must be blocking their view, that they were failing to see this connection. His suspicion became even stronger as it became clear to him that very few of his fellow-scientists who stood with him against the planning of science knew how to argue against it. Apparently even *their* vision was being blocked. At best they could only offer the weak utilitarian argument that free, or "pure," research would simply result eventually in greater usefulness to man. This was a weak argument, not because it was not true, but rather because it tacitly accepted the premise that science ought to be subject to utilitarian evaluation. It was not therefore a defense of free scientific inquiry, as such. By its terms, free science might be abandoned at some point, should some doubt arise that it would, under particular circumstances, contribute better than planned inquiry to desirable practical ends.

Polanyi pointed out in his Preface to the Torchbook edition of his major work, *Personal Knowledge,* that the

> enquiry of which this volume forms a part started in 1939 with a review article on J.D. Bernal's *The Social Function of Science.* I opposed his view, derived from Soviet Marxism, that the pursuit of science should be directed by the public authority to serve the welfare of society. I held that the power of thought to seek the truth must be accepted as our guide, rather than be curbed to the service of material interests.[3]

Polanyi continued to address himself to this issue in a number of talks and in articles and letters published during the 1940s. Most of these communications he gathered together and had reprinted, with some additions and revisions, as Part One of *The Logic of Liberty* in 1951.[4] How he diagnosed the difficulty that lay behind the symptoms and what he prescribed for the disease will appear later in this book. At this point we are concerned only with pointing to those symptoms of sickness which he saw at the start of his inquiries.

Polanyi saw in those early days another sign of illness, one often closely related to the utilitarian view of science. It was the tendency of intellectuals to flirt with Marxist and other proposals for planned cultures. Polanyi saw that intellectuals, as such, had no need for a planned culture. It would work against the professional interests of scholars, artists, historians, literary men, philosophers, theologians, and other professionals. In no case would they be able to do their work on orders from above—from public officials acting in accordance with an overall plan for culture. In other words, Polanyi already saw at that time what many intellectuals have only after some years painfully discovered in Eastern Europe.

Why then were these intellectuals so interested in such a proposal? From what they were saying, their interest appeared to Polanyi to stem from a general and all-pervasive moral dissatisfaction with the whole apparatus of a capitalist economy—profits, businessmen, markets, prices, buying and selling, and the crassness, greed, self-centeredness, impersonality, and ugliness of modern industrial civilization. They wished to see this supplanted by an ideal system in which the work of the world would be performed for the good of all, that is, according to a plan for social betterment, instead of in the helter-skelter, piecemeal, haphazard way it was being performed—largely in response to selfish interests, with the lucky or more powerful appropriating the lion's share of the benefits for themselves.

Attacks upon the system of individual capitalism, and on the market through which it worked, were unquestionably given a special urgency in the times in which Polanyi was writing by the existence of the chronic unemployment that had prevailed, at least in Europe, since the First World War, culminating in the Great Depression of the 1930s. People's faith that the system, with all its moral faults, actually worked was being given a series of severe and protracted jolts. Yet Polanyi thought that it was not simply the existence of chronic, even severe, unemployment that lay at the bottom of dissatisfaction with a "free" economy, i.e., an unplanned one, but rather the much deeper moral and spiritual rejection of such a system. And in this rejection Polanyi thought he detected obsessions and irrationalities.

That workers whose lives were being made intolerably uncertain by the constant threat of unemployment should turn upon the system under which this unemployment seemed to be the order of the day was hardly surprising. But much of the dissatisfaction with the present order of the economy came from intellectuals, from people not under these immediate threats and whose professional life would derive little benefit from scrapping the system. Those who needed cultural freedom most in order to get along with their chosen work formed the bulk of those most obsessed with the notion of curtailing it through adopting a planned economy. It was clear to Polanyi that the planned economy these people envisaged would also involve a planning of the whole culture, since all human activities must use economic resources. This notion of a planned culture was also, however, actually already embraced by most proponents of a planned economy, since they usually proposed that a planned economy would create a more decent culture, not merely one of greater material advantages. Thus if intellectuals were indeed aiming at the planning of a culture then, of course, this aim would also demand control of the economy. A planned economy and a planned culture entailed each other. They were two sides of the same coin. But intellectuals' minds were apparently blocked from seeing the noose into which they were asking their necks be put.

Polanyi found that social planners also failed to see something else, something much more decisive in respect to this issue, namely, that the noose they were asking for, although quite capable of strangling their own professional lives, was only a paper noose with respect to what it was supposed to accomplish—that is, that planning a whole modern economy was as impossible to bring off as it would be for a cat to succeed in swimming the Atlantic Ocean. Even the neoclassical economists seemed to be unable to see this simple fact. Polanyi saw that Von Mises, Von Hayek, Frank Knight, all seemed to be supposing that a real choice of economic systems existed—that people could really have a planned economy, if they were willing to give up freedom. In other words, these economists were rejecting planning because it would, they supposed, eliminate freedom, not simply because (as they, of all people, should have known) it was economically impossible. Thus Polanyi saw that even those who wished to defend free economic institutions found themselves apparently, for some reason, powerless to deal clearly and rationally with the problem.

Proponents of planning also seemed to be overlooking what should have been for them the fact that the existing culture—corrupt as it was supposed to be—had apparently been good enough to produce a formulation of what the standards of a good culture are. Marx had said about ethics that men have known for two thousand years, at least, what they ought to do: namely, that they ought to do unto others as they would have them do unto them. The trouble was, as he put it, that no one had been able to do this under the economic, political, and social conditions that had existed up to now. So the conclusion was, apparently, that all these conditions must be swept aside to make way for other conditions that would enable men to live according to this great ethical principle. But, if what Marxist theory also said about the genesis of all ideas (including the ethical) was true, namely, that ideas are all mere products of our economic systems, it was surely strange that no one apparently was noticing that throwing out the capitalistic bath water might also be eliminating the ethical baby. So neither proponents nor opponents of a planned economy seemed to be thinking very clearly, even in their own terms. Although each side pretended to a thoroughgoing objectivity about the whole question, there seemed to be more passion than reason in what they were all saying. Some factors surely must *not* be meeting the eye.

Polanyi addressed himself to this confusion of the modern mind about its economic institutions and their relation to freedom and culture in a number of articles written in the latter 1930s and during the 1940s. Many of these he gathered together to form the second part of his *The Logic of Liberty*.[5]

But there was yet another obsession of the modern mind of which Polanyi became aware in those days. He implied its existence in a short note published in 1936 in the *Philosophy of Science,* entitled "The Value of the Inexact."[6] He argued that chemical concepts had always been fascinating to him, as opposed to physical ones, because they showed "the great value of inexact ideas." He held (obviously against the tendencies of the time) that it "was easy to prove that no completely exact statement can be of any value in natural science." But he noted that applying the argument to physics "always appears to be a combination of far-fetched trivialities and sophistry." However, he thought it was the matter-of-fact situation in chemistry. Such terms as "relative stability," "affinity," "tendency," "inclination," and "general expectations" are used as descriptions of chemical behavior and are, he held, obviously quite inexact. Moreover "there is not a single rule in chemistry which is not qualified by important exceptions." The character of a substance, he claimed, is as complex as the features of a physiognomy. And chemistry is the "art" of being aware of "these complex attitudes of matter." Should chemists ever allow themselves, he said, to be "frightened by the physicists into abandoning all vague methods and to restrict themselves to the field where exact laws (. . . supposed to be such by physicists) pertain, the development of chemistry would . . . be stopped dead."

By comparison with descriptions in physics, he held, descriptions of chemical substances and the art of dealing with them lie quite near to human behavior and to the art of "commanding" human behavior, about which, he maintained, it would also be "supremely unreasonable" to claim that vital knowledge could be attained by precise measurements and mathematical treatment.[7] However, he acknowledged that such "supremely unreasonable" claims were being made. In the matter of human behavior, too, men were busy claiming to embrace certain principles of exactitude, in spite of the fact that they seemed to know these did not fit their subject matters and problems, for they did not restrain themselves in their inquiries strictly to these avowed principles of exactitude.

The recognition of modern man's penchant for exactitude—for precise statements—and the recognition of the fact that science and more fruitful general thought actually function by quite different principles, gradually came to be of central interest to Polanyi and, under the rigorous further study and development he gave them, finally took their place in his thought as two of the keys needed to understand what caused the sickness of the modern mind and what the possibility was for its cure.

CHAPTER TWO

# The Causes

Sometimes the causes of a disease are discovered through closer analysis of one of its symptoms. This is especially true if the disease is basically functional. Two of the symptoms we have discussed in the first chapter appeared to Michael Polanyi to share something fundamental, an irrational hankering after a planned society—irrational, because actually harmful to the further exercise of the profession of those intellectuals who desired it. This hankering thus seemed to him to flow from an obsession for some overriding social purpose of such a kind that it required a planned society. But, as Polanyi clearly saw, this requirement of a planned society entailed in the end some brand of totalitarianism, which, in both the means that evidently had to be used to bring it into existence and those that had to be used to maintain it, seemed to him to require a ruthlessness that only a nearly pathological fanatic would be able to muster. So for this reason too this hankering seemed pathological to Polanyi.

In 1941 he wrote:

The attack on science is a secondary battlefield in a war against all human ideals. And the attack on the freedom of science is only an incident in the totalitarian assault on all freedom in society. This attack is entailed in . . . demanding unconditioned support of scientists for the rise and continued rule of the right kind of political power.

. . . This doctrine . . . calls for unlimited violence in order to achieve the establishment of desired changes in the social structure and rejects all obligations to truth or humanity which might obstruct its own set purpose.[1]

He then went on to explain why such restrictions on freedom were not required by a liberal society and what sort of change in the outlook of people inspired them to have recourse to such drastic measures.

Liberal society, by maintaining various systems of dynamic order, entrusts its fate largely to forces beyond its control. . . . The faith that society may confide itself to a variety of principles, which guide systems of co-operation by individual adjustment, is the faith of Liberalism. . . .

Suppose society decides to abandon the pursuit of largely uncertain ends and to take its fate wholly into its own hands, directing its course entirely towards definite and specific immediate aims: then the structure of society must be changed accordingly. . . . No respect for law, or even humanity or truth, must interfere with the immediate good of society which is thus defined and entrusted to the State. No individual has any justification to act independently under a State which alone knows the whole plans for the future welfare of the community.[2]

When the general aspirations that have operated vaguely and pluralistically in a free society have been replaced by specific social aims, Polanyi pointed out, powerful emotional forces are set in motion, and then men's hopes,

withdrawn from where they dwelt in many dimly perceived expectations, are now focused entirely on the single concrete task set by the State. Such faith is narrowed down to the point of idolatry and intensified to the pitch of fanaticism. It produces a curious type of fanaticism, deriving its strength from the destruction of all ideals; combining fanatic passion—in an entirely novel way—with hardheaded, biting cynicism.[3]

And the attitudes and actions that these fanatics must espouse then also become clear.

> Any motive that goes beyond the fulfillment of directions from above can be tolerated only as a residue of private life and must be branded as unsocial or disloyal if it should attempt to pursue aims of any wider significance. There must be left no more independent witnesses, or judges, or scientists, or preachers, or painters, musicians, play-wrights, journalists, historians, economists, or even doctors, law-yers, or clergymen; no independence of unions, professional associa-tions, congregations, or even sports clubs can be tolerated; the validity of all laws, of science, of the arts, or religion must be suspended and their substance declared subject to summary review by the State.

> . . . But the destruction to be undertaken . . . is so vast, and the lingering feelings of respect for the intellectual and moral treasures hitherto cultivated, as well as for the men who would defend them, is still so strong that only disciples steeped in fanaticism will be able to suppress their own scruples and wield the weapon of terror with sufficient effect. The party members educated in unscrupulous fa-naticism is [sic] an indispensable factor in the making and mainte-nance of the Totalitarian State.[4]

All this seemed quite plain to Polanyi on the basis of what had already taken place in Europe by 1941 and what was still taking place there. But its explanation was not so obvious. The problem appeared to be twofold: where such fanatics came from, and how they could meet with so many sympathizers in our day—and find that so many nonsym-pathizers were either apathetic or else, if opponents, confused and weak.

Polanyi had himself, of course, seen his own free and enlightened Europe transform itself within half a lifetime into the nightmares of Stalinism and Hitlerism. As a member of the educated intelligentsia, he had seen this first-hand as a participant in the sciences, the arts, and the literature of this period and in its aspirations, its speculations, its hopes and fears. He said that he recalled the shock when "the possibility first dawned upon us" during the slaughter of the First World War "that progress might fail us, that we may actually be witnessing the destructon of Europe."[5]

Looking back, therefore, upon the thought of that earlier period and at its subsequent stages, he began to find clues for developing his "diagnosis of the pathological morality of our time."[6] One of these clues was an anomaly in what perhaps was the most attractive philosophy for the intelligentsia in the early twentieth century: Marxism.

Marxism quite obviously made great claims to being "scientific." The Marxists seemed to mean by this that other socialists before them had only been Utopian dreamers, muddling along with moral concepts and ideals, such as "rights" and "freedom" and "justice," whereas Marxism simply gave a factual historical and economic analysis of the situation. And this showed scientifically that capitalism was due to perish soon from its own "contradictions" and that the workers would take over, disencumbering the private capitalists of their private capital and turning them all into workers, after which there would, of course, be only one class. Socialized distribution would then come into being alongside the already socialized production and there would be, could be, no more class conflicts.

No moral ideals were included (it was said) anywhere in Marxist theory or in its predictions. It was all very scientific, very objective, very detached. Only, Polanyi noticed, if you scratched such a purely scientific and objective Marxist, he bled moral passion profusely. It seemed quite apparent to Polanyi, therefore, that the moral dimension that the Marxist regarded with such explicit scepticism and complete contempt was all the time seething underneath and turning him into a fanatical, dedicated, and self-sacrificing *proponent* of the changes that he ostensibly held were simply immanent in the world. And the presence of this moral fervor seemed to have no relation at all to whether he was or was not a member of the proletariat. In fact, as a European intellectual—which he often was—it was hardly possible for him to be a proletarian.

Now this might have been merely amusing and another example of Hume's contention that the errors in philosophy were only ridiculous, not dangerous (as contrasted with those in religion), were it not for the fact that this dedicated Marxist was prepared to adopt the most violent means to further the end for which he felt so much urgent passion—even though he claimed it was scientifically inevitable. Not only was he prepared to lie, cheat, and steal—even from his friends and comrades—or even kill, if the Revolution (or those in control of the Party) seemed to require it, but he was also prepared to accept, in the Soviet Union, a regime of almost unspeakable tyranny—indeed he was fully prepared to contribute himself to that tyranny. Bukharin bore false witness against himself, thereby assisting in condemning himself to death, rather than jeopardize the Revolution by discrediting the Party through showing that the charges against him were fraudulent. Greater love of tyranny surely has no man than this: that he is prepared to lay down not only his life for it, but his personal integrity as well. Nor can any greater tyranny over the human mind be conceived than that it could succeed in requiring a man to love it this much. There had indeed been many tyrannies before, Polanyi noted, but never had their victims reveled in them. Something curious and out of the ordinary was surely afoot. There was a supreme dedication to social purpose involved in commitment to this tyranny, as to an ideal, but there was also a seemingly incompatible element involved in this commitment, "a fanaticism," as Polanyi put it, "bitterly hostile to all ideals; combining fanatic passion in an entirely novel way—with hard-headed . . . cynicism."[7]

By the middle forties, in his *Science, Faith and Society,* Polanyi, in a passage paralleling the remarks about totalitarianism quoted above, gave evidence of his discovery of a further dimension to the problem. Instead of accounting for the transition from the liberal to the totalitarian society as the abandonment of generally perceived and vague expectations in favor of specific and immediate social ends, he explained the transition by tracing the pragmatic consequences of the abandonment of belief in "spiritual realities."

We arrive at the following theory of totalitarian government. In order that a society may be properly constituted there must be competent forces in existence to decide with ultimate power every controversial issue between two citizens. But if the citizens are dedicated to certain transcendent obligations and particularly to such general ideals as truth, justice, charity, and these are embodied in the tradition of the community to which allegiance is maintained, a great many issues between citizens . . . can be left . . . for the individual consciences to decide. The moment, however, a community ceases to be dedicated through its members to transcendent ideals, it can continue to exist undisrupted only by submission to a single centre of unlimited secular power. Nor can citizens who have radically abandoned belief in spiritual realities—on the obligation to which their conscience would have been entitled and in duty bound to take a stand—raise any valid objection to being totally directed by

the state. In fact their love of truth and justice turn then automatically . . . into love of state power.[8]

It is apparent that Polanyi here sees totalitarianism as following, in
practical logic, from a radical abandonment of belief in such ideals as
truth, justice, reason, and morality. But this cannot be the whole story,
because it is clear from what has been said above about the Marxist's
underlying moral drives that he both has and has not abandoned belief in
these "spiritual realities." He has ostensibly, but not in fact. This ambivalent state of mind Polanyi came to call "moral inversion"—a "condition in which passions for high moral purposes operate only as the
hidden force of an openly declared inhumanity."[9]

Although touching upon this phenomenon only briefly in *Science,
Faith and Society,* he had set it forth rather clearly in his 1945 article,
"Science and the Modern Crisis."[10] He did not name it "moral inversion," however, until 1950, in his article "The Logic of Liberty."[11] After
this he used this term repeatedly in his writings, inasmuch as it became
for him the key symptom of what ails the modern mind, the analysis of
which, he found, was to yield the proximate cause or causes of its
affliction.

The lines his inquiry were to take were laid out by his reflection that
if moral inversion involved hidden moral passions then two things had to
be explained: where the moral passions came from and why they had to
be hidden. The moral passions, Polanyi speculated, originated with
Christianity. He reminded us that speaking at all of moral passions was
something new. Morality had been mostly defined as a composed state
of mind. From antiquity to the present, he said, moral demands had
continued to be most generally conceived of as curbs upon our passions,
not originators of passions. Perhaps he said, only one record of an
outbreak of moral passion in ancient times exists: that of the Hebrew
prophets. And even this outbreak, he pointed out, was not primarily
moral but religious. But, he held, the Messianic religious passion of these
prophets, reinforced by the apocalyptic messages of the New Testament,
contributed to the Messianic rebellions that occurred in Central Europe
from the eleventh to the sixteenth centuries. Following Norman Cohn's
*The Pursuit of the Mellenium,* Polanyi held that these "chiliastic outbursts"
were inspired by Pope Gregory VII's moral reforms. This pope's efforts
to purge the Church resulted in popular revolts against the clergy. These
rebellions combined a moral dimension with a religious one. Polanyi

believed that the master ideas behind these upheavals "could be conceived only in a Christian society, for they assailed the spiritual rulers of society for offending against their own teachings. Rulers who did not preach Christian ideals could not be attacked in these terms."[12] Purity of heart, a simple unselfishness, and an unbounded love of one's fellow men are difficult things to demand of rulers. But, if these rulers are Christian, it seems they must preach them; and then, at some point, they may be attacked for the want of them.

It was here for the first time, said Polanyi, that moral passions unknown in the ancient world made their appearance in our civilization, passions for moral reform which, because of their coupling with religious zeal, were imbued with a strength and fervor not before possessed by moral aspirations, and which actually moved their bearers in the direction of a fierce immoralism.

Polanyi accounted in this way for part of what he meant by moral inversion: the presence of moral passions so strong as to move those who hold them toward an immoralism in the means they adopt to satisfy these passions. But it is also essential to the meaning of moral inversion that these passions be hidden. Even though these first instances of moral passion were not really hidden to their possessors, they did, Polanyi held, possess the germinal possibility of becoming somewhat obscured.

> Since no society can live up to Christian precepts, any society professing Christian precepts must be afflicted by an internal contradiction, and when the tension is released by rebellion its agents must tend to establish a nihilistic Messianic rule. For a victorious rising will create a new centre of power, and as the rising had been motivated by Christian morality, the new centre will be beset by the same contradictions against which its supporters had risen in rebellion. It will, indeed, be in a worse position, for its internal balance will not be protected by any customary compromise. It can then hold on only by proclaiming itself to be the absolute good: a Second Coming greater than the first and placed therefore beyond good and evil. We see arising then the "amoral superman," whom Norman Cohn compares with the "armed bohemians" of our days, the followers of Bakunin and Nietzsche.[13]

Polanyi claimed therefore that there is inherent in moral passions a tendency to draw a veil over them, because of the practical need to rationalize exemptions from moral restrictions upon the use of power if those who are imbued with these passions are ever to be ruthless enough to do to their societies what their moral passions are urging them to do. But this tendency is only a potentiality. Polanyi had also to explain how it became an actuality in our day.

Modern moral passions have, of course, lost their religious connections. They have moved from distinctly religious thought and concern into the civil and secular. So it was necessary for him to explain first how they made such a move into the secular, bringing their zeal with them, and then how they managed to conceal their operations from those whose lives they were, in fact, directing.

The attempt to explain how they made such a move led Polanyi to the second cause of modern moral inversion—the first having been simply the Messianic legacy of Christianity. The origins of this second cause, he found, lay in the scientific revolution of the seventeenth century. This revolution supplied us, he pointed out, with the supreme axiom of eighteenth century rationalism: the rejection of all authority.[14] The early scientists, from Bacon through Newton, were all agreed that knowledge must be built up from observations and experiment and that nothing of the traditional views should be accepted without sceptical and critical scrutiny—not merely dialectical or discursive scrutiny, but a running of the gauntlet of observation and controlled experimentation.

Thus the notion of a complete and perfect objectivism came into being and has continued down to our day as the ideal that is supposed to be the guide of science and thus of all reliable knowledge. All personal and subjective elements came to be regarded as disturbances to the attainment of this perfect objectivity. Every effort therefore had to be made to eliminate them. This ideal is perhaps too prevalent and too well-known in our own day to require much discussion. As we shall see, it is one of the biggest contributing factors, in Polanyi's view, to our contemporary madness and was for many years the object of his most extensive attacks.

Scientific objectivism, in its most simple and straightforward sense, holds (1) that there are objective states of affairs, that is, that something is the case "independently of our minds," which it is our business to come to know; and (2) that the method of careful and accurate observation of immediately given sense data, without reference to our personal participation, our wishes, wants, values, hopes, fears, or expectations, is of the utmost importance; and (3) that the final arbiter of scientific theory is a crucial experiment with all factors carefully controlled, an experiment that can subject our theory to an acid test because it results in the observations or lack of observation of sense data predicted on the basis of the theory. It was sometimes put, notably by Charles Saunders Peirce (in the days before the Positivists), that this method was designed to let Nature, herself, speak to us. We had only to listen—and look.

Apologists for this objectivist view of science have upon occasion admitted, of course, that this may not have been exactly the way any scientist had ever actually gone about his work. But noting that scientists did not operate exactly in this manner was never regarded by proponents of the view as to the point. They held that logic was logic, whether anyone ever followed it or not. To the extent that other factors actually entered into the picture, they were taken to be merely some of the unavoidable disturbing psychological factors, inevitably present because we are only animals with feelings and desires, and so not perfect inquisitional machines. Nevertheless it was thought that theories that finally came to be accepted would be ones that had stood up under these formal criteria and that had the personal factors originally entangled with them gradually ground away as more and more scientists engaged in testing them. It was supposed, theoretically, that what should eventually emerge from the operation of the scientific method must be perfectly objective knowledge.

The foregoing is indeed only a very rough and generic sketch of what has been meant by objectivism in science. Exactly what the hard and fast logical structure of scientific inquiry is has been the subject of much inquiry, continuing into our day and generating considerable controversy. But, regardless of what the exact logical structure of science may be, the important point is that philosophers of science and most proponents of science have thought for many years that there must be such an exact logical structure. For this was thought to be essential to the ideal of objectivity itself, since objectivity is thought to require perfect detachment from all subjective factors, and only logical structures could be so detached. However difficult it might be to attain such pure objectivity and perfect detachment—and indeed its proponents have always admitted it was quite difficult—one could not claim to have attained knowledge unless one had attained such detached objectivity. And the historical upshot, when all these views resulted in (and issued from) a new philosophical position called Logical Positivism, was that those inquiries or beliefs that could not by their very nature be established in a detached logical manner through the methods of science came to be relegated by philosophers of this persuasion to some other status than that of "knowledge." That by these standards values of all sorts would ultimately be so relegated should be fairly apparent.

These views lay tacitly in the minds of many men long before the Logical Positivists made them explicit. Indeed they are still widely held, either explicitly or tacitly, in intellectual circles even after the demise of Logical Positivism. "Value-free" social science and the behaviorisms in our day only try to explain causally the *facts* about such values as are held. In the interest of "objectivity" they claim no capacity to deal rationally with the possible value of holding them.

In the 60s certain philosophers of science did indeed begin to question whether or not what Hilary Putnam then called the "received view on the role of theories"[15] had got things wholly right. Among the better known of these were Norwood Hanson,[16] Paul Feyerabend,[17] Thomas Kuhn,[18] and Stephen Toulmin.[19] These philosophers raised serious questions about various aspects of the "received view" and made some rather radical suggestions for changes in it; but they left untouched the ideal of objectivity in knowledge. For they thought that the "received view" (including the correspondence theory of truth connected with it) was unable to show how science achieved true objectivity. But this seemed to mean for them that there were problems either with the received view or with science, not with the notion that knowledge ought to be objective. The bottom line of each of their criticisms—and also of the criticisms by those who later arose to refute their proposals—was that a given position or view did not successfully explain how the knowledge claims in science can really be objective.

Let us take Frederick Suppe for example. Frederick Suppe claims to be in the minority of contemporary philosophers of science, because he dares to call into question the utility of maintaining the "so-called K–K thesis," which, he says, the vast majority of philosophers of science (even Kuhn and Feyerabend) either explicitly or tacitly assume. This thesis in effect says "that one cannot know that P [is the case] unless one knows that one's claim to know that P [is the case] is correct."[20] In other words, one must know that he knows.

My purpose here is not to get into all of Suppe's reasons for wishing to call the usefulness of this thesis into doubt. I only want to show that, in abandoning the K-K thesis, Suppe might surely seem to be one philosopher of science who is abandoning the ideal of objectivity, since he is abandoning the thesis that one only has knowledge if, when he knows that P, he also knows that his reasons for holding that P are correct. For surely holding this thesis must mean that one needs to recognize his view to be completely and explicitly objective, i.e., that none of his reasons are personal or subjective. They are all logically relevant, sound, and conclusive, that is, objective. Yet even Suppe, it turns out, in abandoning this K–K thesis, does not give up the ideal of objectivity. Suppe seems to hold that because the methodologies used by science for evaluating the truth of putative knowledge claims are admittedly fallible (we know, historically, that sometimes these methods have yielded wrong results), we have to separate these fallible methods from a standard of what knowledge is that is independent of them. Why do we have to? Suppe says we must do so, "if we are to allow the canons of rationality for assessing knowledge claims to evolve *without compromising the objectivity of knowledge.*"[21]

It turns out that Suppe simply wants to remove from any particular scientific judgment the necessity of such a judgment's always being truly objective, by placing such full objectivity instead safely out of harm in sort of an ideal (always aimed at or intended?) independent of any historically particular evaluation made by science. Objectivity then becomes exemplified only in the growth in sophistication and efficiency of the methods of science—not as the methods themselves exist at some point in the past, present, or future states of science.[22]

The objectivity of knowledge must never be compromised for him. Somehow, somewhere, in some way—metaphysically, or historically in the development of science—we must hang on to it. "Epistemic relativism," he says, "wherein changes in canons of rationality amount to changes in what counts as knowledge, making knowledge be whatever a science accepts and allows to enter its domain," must be avoided, "since it destroys the objectivity of scientific knowledge in precisely the ways Kuhn's and Feyerabend's accounts do."[23]

The notion that "what counts as knowledge" must be true and detached objectivity seems to be, I think we must say, still very much the basic creed of epistemologists and philosophers of science, whatever their critiques of each other. Therefore Polanyi's contention that the modern mind is fatefully enamored with such an ideal is not at all passé. It was not merely the Positivists of his day and those who espoused the "received view" who were so enamored with detached objectivity. It is still our own contemporaries in the natural sciences, the social sciences, psychology, and philosophy who have these ideas entrenched in their thinking. The philosophers, it is true, are having difficulty showing to each other's complete satisfaction just how objectivity *is* involved in the knowledge claims in science; but the ideas that science is, in fact, a source of objective knowledge and that what "knowledge" *means* is strict objectivity, they apparently do not dream of giving up.

An accompanying dichotomy of facts and values is fairly widespread. Hardly anyone today supposes that values are objective, and thus, of course, values are quite generally rejected as possible objects of knowledge. Perhaps the pervasive attitude toward values is best instanced by my beginning students who almost universally seem to think that everyone has "their" own moral values, just as they have their own preferences in foods, clothes, sexual orientations, and pop music. These students' own moral values, if they have any, they often tend to hold on to by no other means than Peirce's method of tenacity.

But in the beginning of scientific rationalism men were ignorant of its logical consequences for moral knowledge. The new rationalism was originally combined with a world view that was, Polanyi said, "expected to set men free to follow the natural light of reason, and thus put an end to religious fanaticism and bigotry. . . . Humanity would then advance peacefully towards ever higher intellectual, moral, political, and economic perfection."[24]

Polanyi showed, however, that what he called the "legacy of Christ" haunted almost from the start this rosy picture painted by the Enlightenment. He observed that even before Condercet gave expresion to this expected development of "universal progress," Rousseau had challenged its hopes. "He declared," said Polanyi, "that civilized man was morally degenerate, for he lived only outside himself, by the good opinion of others. He was a 'hollow man,' an 'other-directed person,' to use terms which were given currency two centuries later."[25] And Rousseau laid the rise of this degeneration precisely "to the progress of the human mind." This progress, he claimed, had produced inequalities and consolidated them by the establishment of property. Man's original virtue had been corrupted and he had entered slavery. "Here," said Polanyi, "is moral fury attacking all that is of good repute, all accepted manners, custom, and law, exalting instead a golden age which was before good and evil."[26]

As Polanyi saw it, although Rousseau's wet blanket did not smother the fires of optimistic hope for the future, his argument and his rhetoric poured into the channels of rationalism a fierce passion for humanity, in fact for all the supreme hopes of Christianity—and thus also for the eventual charges of fraud and hypocrisy, and the disillusionment that has followed. For, although rationalism had torn these high moral hopes from their dogmatic religious framework, they did not perish, but immediately moved over and attached themselves—incongruously, of course—to science and reason. Polanyi thought that without this infusion of Christian fervor dwelling in the hearts of most Europeans and exemplified by Rousseau, Voltaire's vision of mankind purged of its religious follies and fanaticisms and settling down to cultivate its gardens might have come true. So the *philosophes* failed to establish the age of quiet enjoyment which was supposed to follow upon mankind's release from bigotry and religious zeal. Instead, they induced a violent tide of secular social dynamism, which was indeed to spread many benefits for humanity, but which also was to degenerate into a fanaticism fiercer than the religious furies these *philosophes* had laid to rest.[27]

Polanyi was not claiming that Rousseau was the historical cause of all these fanaticisms and furies. His point rather was that Rousseau was able to anticipate "in three respects the inherent instability of the rationalist ideal of a secular society." He saw (1) that this ideal entailed an unrestrained individualism, demanding absolute freedom and equality, for there were no authorities in the rationalist ideal, and (2) that this ideal necessitated a society under popular government—but one exercising absolute power, since under this new rationalism there were no "natural laws" to restrict the exercise of the General Will, and (3) that this ideal involved an amoral individualism asserting the rights of a unique, creative personality against the morality of a discredited society. Rousseau might as well have said: "against the morality of any existing society," since any society, as Polanyi pointed out, is bound to be discredited if judged by moral perfectionism. And so moral perfectionism is bound to mean that the individual becomes a law unto himself and is unable to recognize the legitimacy of the traditional morality of the society in which he exists. To all effects and purposes, therefore, the moral perfectionist becomes not merely *amoral*, but actually *immoral*; for he acts as he pleases. The transplantation of this "romantic immoralism" onto the national scale finally turned what had only been the simple Machiavellian and *realpolitik* expediency of States into a romantic notion of an exalted nationhood functioning "rightly" as a law unto itself. Such a notion is, Polanyi added, "admittedly strange to Rousseau's cosmopolitan outlook, yet this too was largely prefigured by his thought."[28]

These implications that Rousseau so early was able to see in rationalism have been borne out by subsequent history, Polanyi observed. That they were actually thought of ahead of their time suggests, he said, that they were true logical consequences of their antecedents, viz., of sceptical rationalism combined with the fervor of secularized Christianity.[29] Let us see in the next chapter just how Polanyi thought these developments did prove to be the paths of history.

# CHAPTER THREE

# The Pathogenesis

Just how the logical consequences of the rationalist ideal that Rousseau perceived in fact worked themselves out in history can be seen rather clearly. Michael Polanyi indicated that this could be spelled out by inquiring into how moral inversion, although its causes emerged earlier in England, proceeded rapidly toward totalitarianism on the Continent, but not at all in England or North America.

It was Milton and Locke, Polanyi held, who first formulated liberalism. Their argument contained two points. (1) Freedom from authority was demanded so that truth might be discovered. (2) Tolerance of opinions was demanded on the basis of philosophic doubt. Locke first formulated this second argument as a political doctrine. He held that we can never be so sure about the truth of our religion to have a warrant for imposing it on others.[1]

Locke's argument therefore says that since it is impossible to demonstrate which religion is true, we must admit them all. The general principle seems to be that we must not impose beliefs that are not demonstrable. If we were to apply this general rule to ethical principles, Polanyi inferred, we would find that, unless we can demonstrate some of them with certainty, we ought to tolerate fully any instance of their total denial. But it turned out that, in terms of the scientific objectivism that was becoming the general way of thinking, ethical principles cannot be demonstrated. How can one prove scientifically, Polanyi asked, the obligation to tell the truth or to uphold justice and mercy? Since no ethical principles can be proven, it would seem to follow from the general principle that a system of mendacity, lawlessness, and cruelty would have to be accepted as an equal alternative to one involving any sort of ethical principles. But of course, a society in which unscrupulous propaganda, violence, and terror prevailed would offer no scope for tolerance either, and so "the inconsistency of a liberalism based on philosophical doubt becomes apparent: . . . freedom of thought is destroyed by the extension of doubt to the field of traditional ideals," specifically because it is these traditional ideals (truth, etc.) that alone can uphold a right to freedom of thought.[2] Yet, although the logic of the basic principles begun by Locke and Milton would seem to contain no limitations preventing their extension to the destruction of freedom of thought itself, such destruction did not occur in Anglo-American areas, whereas it did on the Continent.

Actually, Polanyi said, such a consummation was prevented in the Anglo-American sphere by an alogical reluctance to pursue the accepted philosophic premises to their ultimate conclusions.[3] This reluctance was probably due, he said, to the distinctive religious character of Anglo-American liberalism. Philosophic doubt was applied only to secure equal rights for all religions—not to secure equal rights for irreligion.[4] Polanyi noted that Locke specifically excluded atheists from this tolerance.[5] At least implicitly amoral beliefs were thus also excluded. This sort of scepticism, a "scepticism kept on short leash," was hardly a menace to moral principles, he held. Another restraint on Anglo-American scepticism arose, he noted, from the fact that the establishment of democratic institutions took place in England and America at a time when religious beliefs were still strong, indeed dominant. These institutions (such as the American Constitution) gave effect to the moral principles that underlie a free society, and it was at least tacitly, and often explicitly, thought that the rights so implemented came from God. The tradition of democracy embodied in these institutions then proved strong enough (partly because of their supposed religious support) to uphold in practice the moral standards of a free society against any question that might arise about their intellectual credentials—their "proof."[6] Also, Polanyi reminded us, it was even pretended in the Anglo-American sphere, through philosophic hedonism, that these particular ethical principles could be scientifically demonstrated. This empty pretension, turned out to be a very salutary myth, he maintained.[7]

All these restraints were absent on the Continent. The movement there was antireligious from the start, having had to oppose itself to the authority of the Catholic Church, and it therefore imposed no restraint on sceptical speculations. Nor were standards of morality embodied in traditionally established democratic institutions on the Continent. Therefore, when a feudal society, dominated by religious authority, was attacked by radical scepticism, there emerged a liberalism unprotected by either a religious or civic tradition against destruction by a logical extension of the philosophic scepticism to which it owed its origin. What this meant, in a word, was that Continental thought was forced to face up to the fact that the universal standards of reason could not be philosophically justified in terms of the sceptical attitude that had initiated the rationalist movement, whereas Anglo-American thought was not required to attempt their justification in these terms.[8]

Polanyi pointed out that various substitutes were found for the standards of moral conduct which thus fell into disrepute on the Continent. These substitutes were derived from the contemplation of individuality. The case for the uniqueness of the individual challenged the world to judge an individual by universal standards. Any individual could be a creative genius and so could claim to be a renewer of all values and thus incommensurable with any. This claim came to be extended eventually to whole nations. Each nation had its own unique set of values which could not be criticized in the light of a supposed universal reason. A nation's obligation could only be to realize its own powers—which it anyhow was set to do. There could be no moral reasons, therefore, for any nation, in following its destiny, to allow any other nation to stand in its way.[9]

If one applied this claim of Romanticism about the supremacy of uniqueness to single persons, Polanyi said, one arrived at a general hostility of the individual toward society, as exemplified in the anticonventional and almost extraterritorial attitude of the Continental bohemian. If one applied it to nations, however, one arrived at the concept of a unique national destiny that made a quite contrary claim upon individuals, namely, a claim to the absolute allegiance of all its citizens to the State. A national leader, in this way of thinking, very neatly combined the advantages of both. He could stand entranced in the admiration of his own uniqueness, while identifying his personal ambitions with the destiny of the nation lying at his feet.[10]

But Romaniticism, Polanyi held, was originally only a literary movement and a change of heart rather than a worked-out philosophy. Its counterpart in systematic thought was constructed by Hegel. Hegel, said Polanyi, clad Universal Reason "with the warm flesh of history. Declared incompetent to judge historic action, reason was given the comfortable position of being immanent in history. . . . Identified with the stronger battalions, reason became invincible; but unfortunately also redundant."[11] This remark, of course, tends to trivialize Hegel's thought. The "stronger battalions" are stronger, for him, only because they are those advancing the interest of reason in achieving Mind's self-recognition, i.e., freedom, during a particular era of history. It is probably true, however, that many of those who were influenced by Hegelian thought began to think more or less along chauvinistic lines, and that this helped turn the modern mind from judging historical situations rationally to judging rationality historically, as Polanyi seemed to think it did.

The next step then, of course, was to point out the redundancy of reason and to complete its disestablishment. Marx and Engels, in their own terms, turned Hegelian dialectic "right side up." The "stronger battalions" must, they held, be recognized simply as the makers of history in their own right, not as the mere servants of an immanent Reason. Reason, for the Marxists, should be regarded as only an apologetic merely rationalizing the conquests of the "stronger battalions." History must therefore be viewed as simply the outcome of class conflicts, not the continuous triumph of reason, nor as legitimately subject to unhistorical, i.e., "pure," rational judgment

In ordinary words, Polanyi said, what Marxism means is that, as new technical equipment becomes available from time to time, different sorts of productively necessary elements become more important, and so it becomes necessary to change the legal order of property in favor of the new class that happens to be in control of such elements. And this is invariably achieved by overthrowing the hitherto dominant class. Socialism, itself the mere result of one such violent change, would, of course, necessarily, automatically, bring this succession of violent changes to a close, simply by resulting in the classless society. Therefore, Polanyi said, what had been regarded previously as rationally defensible "eternal truths, such as Freedom, Justice, etc." were placed by this doctrine in a very doubtful position. The socialist revolution would take place, it held, without reference to them. For, in this view of things, they are not revolutionary ideas. They had been called into being historically (although not necessarily deliberately) by the propertied class to soothe their consciences as exploiting rulers and to bemuse the suspicions of the exploited. And there is also no clear place left for them in the classless society, since everything in the realm of ideas comes to be understood in Marxism as a mere product of class interest, and the class interests that had given birth to these moral ideas would no longer exist.[12] This complex theory provided, therefore, a substitute for the discredited standards of human conduct.

Developing along parallel lines, Polanyi continued, the legacy of romantic nationalism was also gradually transposed into purely materialistic terms. Wagner and Valhalla indeed affected Nazi imagery, and Mussolini gloried in recalling ancient Rome. But the effective idea of Hitler and Mussolini, Polanyi claimed, was not these notions of romanticism, but their classification of nations into "haves" and "have-nots"— on the model of Marxist class war. The actions of nations were in this view not determined by right or wrong nor susceptible of being judged by these standards. And so a second kind of substitute for moral standards of human conduct was developed, a much more hard-headed and cynical one. Those nations in possession of the world's goods, it was claimed, preached peace and the sacredness of international law, because such law sanctioned their holdings. But such a code of peace and international law obviously could not be acceptable to empty-handed but virile nations. These nations would rise and ruthlessly overthrow the degenerate capitalistic democracies that had become dupes of their own pacific ideology, which had been intended originally only to bemuse the underdogs. So the Fascist texts ran very much like the Marxist, only applied to "class" war between nations instead of between economic classes of people within them. "Romanticism," wrote Polanyi, "had been brutalized and brutally romanticized until the product was as tough as Marx's own historic materialism."[13]

So, Polanyi summed up, the self-destruction of liberalism on the Continent was brought to its ultimate conclusion. The replacement of moral ideals by philosophically less vulnerable, because more basically animal, objectives was carried out in all seriousness. Human appetites and human passions were actually substituted for reason and for the ideals of man in this framework of thought.[14]

Such then were the philosophic notions and half-notions that Polanyi thought guided the revolutions of the twentieth century. These were logically rooted in the antiauthoritarian and sceptical formula of "liberty." And they were themselves antiauthoritarian and sceptical in the extreme. They even set men free from obligations to truth and justice! Begun in the name of reason, they ended by reducing reason to a caricature of itself: to a mere rationalization of conclusions predetermined by desire and eventually to be secured and held by force. Man was to be recognized hereafter as the maker and master of what had before been his ideals, no longer their servant. Polanyi held that the foundation of liberty was thereby destroyed. If thought and reason are nothing by themselves, if they are only the effects of social causes, then it is meaningless to demand that thought be set free. This, said Polanyi, is the meaning of meaninglessness.

And so, he thought, the stage was set and the plot established by these philosophies. It was only necessary to find actors who would be willing and fully prepared to act upon these thoughts. They were ready and waiting, he claimed. They were the nihilists.[15]

Polanyi reminded us that the word "nihilist" was popularized by Turgenev in his *Fathers and Sons*, published in 1862. His student, Bazarov, is an extreme individualist without any interest in politics. The next nihilist in Russian literature also shows no such interest—Dostoevski's Raskolnikov in *Crime and Punishment* (1865). Raskolnikov wants to know why he should not murder an old woman, if he wants her money. Bazarov and Raskolnikov are both experimenting privately with a life of total disbelief. Their scepticism is a clear outgrowth of a supposedly scientifically based materialism. It is, however, only private. But only a few years later, Polanyi tells us, we see the nihilist transformed into a political conspirator. The terrorist organization, the Narodniki (Populists) had come into being. Dostoevski portrayed the new type in his later novel *The Possessed*. By this time the nihilist has become an ice-cold businesslike conspirator, closely prefiguring, Polanyi said, the ideal Bolshevik, whom he saw represented on the Moscow stage in the Stalin period. He maintained this resemblance is not accidental, the whole code of conspirational action–cells, secrecy, discipline, ruthlessness, known as the Communist method, was taken over by Lenin from the Narodniki.[16]

Old, honest Bentham, said Polanyi, would not have disagreed with any of the philosophic views expounded by Bazarov. But he and other sceptically minded English and Americans merely used such philosophies as a mistaken explanation of their own conduct, while their actual conduct was determined by their traditional beliefs. The difference was that the nihilist Bazarov and his kind took such philosophies seriously and tried to live by their light alone.[17]

The moral of this tale would seem to be: If like the Anglo-Americans, you have only a faulty philosophy to live by, then hypocrisy and casuistry, and maybe rationalization—or just plain stupidity—become your virtues and saving graces. Of course, moral perfectionism could not but condemn and scorn such qualities as these. On the Continent, therefore, Anglo-American belief in the traditional ideals was either laughed at or regarded as outright hypocrisy. For these nihilists evil became more honored than virtue; for hypocrisy was (somehow) the worst of sins. And, of course, outright evil could hardly be accused of hypocrisy.[18]

Polanyi explained the transition from the apolitical to the political nihilist by pointing out that at the first or private stage of nihilism the nihilist tries to live without any beliefs, obligations, or restrictions. But the solitary nihilist is unstable. Starving for social responsibility, he is susceptible to being drawn into politics, provided he can find a political movement based on nihilist principles. Such a movement, whatever else it might be directed toward, would adopt a creed of political violence and would be interested in smashing the existing order. Thus the European revolutionary "dramatists" turned for their players to those nihilists who had been converted from extreme individualistic nihilism to political nihilism. For such people could be enlisted in the service of the fierce and narrow political creeds needed by the plots that these creeds had created.[19]

Marxist materialism, it thus turned out, "had all the attractions of a second Enlightenment" to these players, Polanyi observed, "taking off and carrying on from the first anti-religious Enlightenment, and offering the same intense mental satisfaction." Those accepting it "felt suddenly initiated to the real forces actuating men and operating in history; to a reality that had hitherto been hidden to them and still remained hidden to the unenlightened, by a veil of deceit and self-deceit." A future of unbounded promise seemed to be opened. They acquired a sense of moral superiority and "righteousness fiercely intensified paradoxically by the mechanical framework in which it was set."

Here was a scientific Utopia relying for its fulfillment only on violence, and therefore one that nihilists could eagerly embrace, for it satisfied at once their need for violent and destructive action, and their repressed moral feelings, respectably masked by a pseudo-scientific, hard-boiled "realism" that brooked no hypocritical, soft-headed talk of "ideals" of "justice," and that therefore also satisfied their philosophic scepticism. Their sense of righteousness, said Polanyi, having lost its cognitive backing, became reinforced instead by a calculated brutality, born of scientific self-assurance that only force and matter truly existed. The basic desires of men and their class interests had only then to be turned loose, they thought, in order to usher in the millenium, which existed in their minds as a curious cross between a dialectical synthesis of opposites and an equilibration of natural forces. In such a view existing moral codes could only be snares and cheats, and therefore could be (in fact, ironically ought to be) zestfully done in. So, said Polanyi, "there emerged the modern fanatic, armoured with impenetrable scepticism." And the power of Marxism over such a mind "is based on a process exactly the inverse of Freudian sublimation . . . *moral inversion*. The morally inverted person has not merely performed a philosophic sub-stitution of moral aims by material purposes, but is acting with the whole force of his homeless moral passions within a purely materialistic framework of purposes."[20]

It is owing to this peculiar moral and intellectual appeal which we have just observed operating in Marxism, said Polanyi, that "Nihilism had served as a cultural leaven throughout the past two centuries." This movement of rebellious immoralism, which produced in France the bohemian and in Russia the revolutionary intelligentsia, Polanyi main-tained also "found an even wider outlet in the German Youth Move-ment." It comprised millions of young men and women by the end of the First World War. It dedicated itself in 1913, at its famous congress on the Hohe Meissner Mountain, "to a fervent 'inner truthfulness,' con-demning existing morality as a bondage imposed by a corrupt society and affirming instead the romantic values idealized by Nietzsche, Wag-ner, and—more recently—Stefan George." Polanyi said he remembered "no instance in which this youth movement protested the rise of Na-tional Socialism, while there is evidence it amply contributed to the ranks of Hitler's supporters. The same romantic nihilism spoke . . . through Oswald Spengler" on the rise of Hitler to power in 1934: "Man is a beast of prey. . . . Would-be moralists . . . are only beasts of prey with their teeth broken. . . . Remember the larger beasts of prey are *noble* crea-tures . . . without the hypocrisy of human morals due to weakness."[21]

Therefore Polanyi claimed that

> Nazi fanaticism was rooted in the same conviction of the irrelevance
> of moral motives in public life that Marxism expressed in terms of
> historic materialism. . . . Fascists believed with Marx that such
> moral appeals were but rationalizations of power. Hence their con-
> tempt of moralizing and their moral justifications of violence as the
> only honest mode of political action.[22]

This then, concluded Polanyi, "is the convincing power of an inversion by which scepticism and moral passions reinforce each other in
acting on minds whose moral convictions are hamstrung by scepticism."[23] We must recognize, warned Polanyi, "that these ideas are
highly stable and seductive. . . and that their power is not due simply to
an evocation of evil instincts, but is gained by satisfying in its own
manner the same ideals which we ourselves hold and which we are
defending against their attack."[24]

But *are* "we" defending them? In an address at the University of
Toronto in 1967, Polanyi brought the views outlined in these last two
chapters, which he had originally developed to account for the growth of
the totalitarian movements of our century, to bear upon our own present
situation.

He pointed out that when faith in the unlimited progress of nineteenth century liberalism "collapsed in the mud-filled trenches of
France" in the First World War, "the doctrines of Nietzsche and Marx
swept through the brains of Europe's intellectual elite, and these, the
'armed bohemians' of the Continent, massacred liberty and drowned it
in blood."[25]

And then Polanyi asked what *we*, the Anglo-Americans, have said
about this in our universities. We have continued furthering, he charged,
the academic movements that even before the war were leading in the
very direction that continental Europe had taken: the positivism that
"had set out to eliminate all metaphysical claims to knowledge," the
"behaviorism . . . which was to lead on to cybernetics, which claims to
represent all human thought as the working of a machine[,] Sigmund
Freud's revolution . . . reducing man's moral principles to mere rationalization of desires," and "scientistic" society with its "programme

of explaining human affairs without distinction between good and evil."
We have continued all these, he claimed, and so we have gone on leaving
"our true convictions . . . without theoretical foundation."[26] Our de-
fenses of the free society, when they existed at all, have been confused
and weak.

We too, he said, have in effect renounced the ideals of the nineteenth
century, although we did not drown them in blood. We have rather, he
remarked, "choked them in cotton wool." History, he thought, will not
celebrate our performance, but it may still recognize that these academic
games may have "kept us faithful at heart to the ideals." But he raised
some doubt about even this, because of the effects of our teaching upon
our own youth. To be sure, many of our young people, he said, still
seem to have generous impulses, and yet perhaps

> our morally neutral account of all human affairs has caused our
> youth and educated people in general to regard all moral professions
> to be mere deception or self deception. . . . For once we learn to
> regard all established rules of moral conduct as mere conventions,
> we must come to suspect our own moral motives and thus our best
> impulses are silenced and driven underground. Such self-suspicion
> does torment our age and particularly much of our youth, allowing
> them only destructive forms of moral manifestations, that alone are
> safe against self doubt. "I'm interested in anything about revolt,
> disorder, chaos, especially activity that has no meaning. It seems to
> me to be the road to freedom." Such a program (of a popular
> songwriter) appeals to the conscience of our youth, for it is safe
> against suspicion of hypocrisy.[27]

Nihilism moving on toward moral inversion is thus, according to
Polanyi, not a pathological state of mind that Western man has already
gone through, but one in which he is still deeply involved. It therefore
remained for Polanyi a major symptom of what ails the modern mind.
Its causes are still operative in us: (1) a scepticism born out of the
objectivist ideal of knowledge, and (2) the moral passions for Messianic
purity and social perfection, born out of the secularization of the hopes
and aspirations bequeathed us by Christianity. The diagnosis still fits, for
the patient is still suffering from the same symptoms. The problem of
prescription and treatment which Polanyi was busy working out for the
last twenty-five or thirty years of his life, if Polanyi is correct, still
requires our efforts if we are ever to be free to "cultivate our gardens."

Toward the end of his article, "History and Hope," he told us, pointing to the Hungarian Revolution and the tendencies in the Soviet sphere to revolt against accepting falsehoods of all sorts—dishonest paintings and novels, and even theories of Party truth—that there is a demand to revert to the original Enlightenment as it was before the movements of scientism and romanticism had clashed with the new tide of social hopes and then fused with it into mutual destruction. But, he asked, can we revert to the convictions of that time? He indicated that he believed we cannot. We must, he held, go beyond this aim, to escape nihilism, not try to return to the previous state of mind. We must, he said, revise rationalist enlightenment and purge it of its fateful deficiencies. We must realize to the full the logical difficulties of the modern mind and accept these difficulties as our problem.

> We cannot, [he said] build safely on the metaphysical presuppositions of a free society, while holding fast to principles of free thought and free individualism which refuse any commitment to such presuppositions. The modern mind must continue to work its own destruction. . . . so long as it fails to reach a vision of itself— and of the universe around itself—within which the unlimited demands of the modern mind can be seen to require their own framework of intrinsic limitations.[28]

It is this medicine of "intrinsic limitations," which he prescribed to us for our disease, to which we now turn. The limitations are two: those upon our unbridled demands for objectivity and those upon our unbridled demands for moral perfection. The former, we shall see, is the medicine he prescribed to us. The latter is part of the treatment to which we may become capable of responding favorably after the medicine has taken effect.

# PART II

*Prescription*

# CHAPTER FOUR

# A New Epistemology

As we have seen, Michael Polanyi had early diagnosed one cause of the sickness of the modern mind as our presumption that knowledge was achieved only through a detached objectivity. As he saw it, our identification of knowledge with detached objectivity gradually poisoned the confidence we had had in the intellectual bases for our moral convictions, inasmuch as it appeared that a detached objectivity could not discover adequate grounds for such convictions. Along with this loss of confidence also went, of course, a weakening of our active commitment to the ideals that make a free society possible.

The moral inversion that followed in the wake of this weakening, on the Continent, at least, saw many subconsciously begin to pin their unacknowledged hopes for a better society upon a "tough," "realistic" approach that looked down upon overt moral action as hypocritical and/or simple-minded. Since it was presumed that the more elemental interests of men, such as their economic or power needs, would always exist, action based upon such interests came to be thought the only kind of realistic action, inasmuch as it could be counted upon to take place regardless of what people said or thought. What would result from such actions then came to be understood to be merely predicted states of affairs, not at all the normative results of men's principles or intentions.

But, fortunately for their subscribers, the states of affairs that such theories enabled them to predict just happened also to be the very ones their own suppressed moral passions led them to want most. And so, Polanyi thought, men came to believe that plain, animal-like kicking and screaming, devoid of specific moral intention or direction, unfettered by traditional, "hypocritical" moral principles, was the sort of action they should permit themselves, regardless of any pangs of conscience or moral squeamishness that this might cause. Actually, such men reminded themselves, these really would be the actions most people were in the end going to take anyway, and so these were those that were, in fact, going to move history. Why should not one be on the bandwagon rather than under it? Actually, of course, they were on it really because it was going where they subconsciously wanted to go.

Such views as these thus set men free to subvert and destroy the old order of things with all the fervor of their subterranean moral passions. They could enforce the emerging new totalitarian revolutionary order with equal ruthlessness, denying as unscientific and unrealistic the efficacy of moral ideals in human affairs. They scornfully rejected those traditional moral principles that claimed personal rights against either the revolutionary party, or the State when it was finally in the hands of the revolutionary party.[1]

Such was the morbid condition of the contemporary mind, as Polanyi came to understand it. But to what could we turn for a remedy? Could the confidence we once had in the ideals intrinsic to a free and tolerant society be restored? If an obsession for detached objectivity led us to this state of mind, then it seemed clear to Polanyi that we could not find our way out of it until we abandoned this obsession. But surely one could not simply call for its rejection. People could hardly be expected to abandon their firm understanding of the very constitution of knowledge itself without being shown some powerful reasons for doing so.

Polanyi had already presented some reasons for doing so, of course. Almost from the beginning, as we have seen, he had recognized the absurdity of this attachment to detachment. It had apparently always been clear to him that even physics could not satisfy this desire completely. His remarks on the value of the inexact show this. In his early articles upholding the freedom of science, he was basing part of his argument also upon the existence of personal elements, the various beliefs and commitments held by individual scientists, which enabled them to work in the particular ways demanded by the specific projects of their scientific inquiry. Freedom was thus said by him to be essential to the conduct of science, because of the dependence of science upon these personal elements. It was clear to him, therefore, that scientists actually were *not* detached and perfectly objective, no matter what any of them or their apologists might say, and moreover that this very lack of detachment was an impetus to scientific discovery and progress, not in any sense an impediment or an imperfection.[2]

So, through mere reflexive understanding of his own work as a scientist and of the work of his colleagues, Polanyi was able to see many features of scientific knowing that pointed to the inadequacy of the ideal of detachment in knowledge, and therefore also of the currently fashionable positivistic epistemology that gave support to it. But, if one is to pull people away from an epistemology to which they already subscribe, it is necessary to show them why and how it is inadequate. And one cannot show its inadequacy without becoming thoroughly involved in an inquiry into the problems of epistemology.

Accordingly Polanyi undertook a lengthy and exhaustive study of how we come to perceive and to understand—to "know." The results of this inquiry he published in his major work, *Personal Knowledge,* in 1958.[3] His approach in this work was a fresh one. Having abandoned the notion that knowledge was sheer objectivity, he thought he saw that this false notion of knowledge as simple detachment had, in fact, been nascently present in all Western philosophy, all the way back to Plato. Therefore he felt his own views had to be hammered out on the basis of what he himself could discover, without significant help from the philosophers of the past. His eventual discovery of what he believed to be the true epistemology became in his own eyes a totally new philosophical beginning, a backing off from the current ways of going at the problems of knowledge in order to see them from a truly new perspective. His philosophy owes its freshness, therefore, as well as its initially puzzling and sometimes decidedly negative effect upon many contemporary philosophers, largely to the fact that he did not labor explicitly upon the particular problems of knowledge with which most Anglo-American philosophers have been concerned, nor upon those that classic philosophers have worked with either. He tended to outflank these problems and to raise somewhat different ones upon grounds on which many contemporary philosophers have difficulty finding their footing.

Polanyi was not even aware, at the time that he was working out his own views for *Personal Knowledge,* that some of the continental phenomenologists were bringing forth considerations similar in many respects to his. He discovered Merleau-Ponty later and realized that an affinity existed, and yet he correctly rejected the notion that their views were identical.[4] His position, therefore, turned out to be a fresh one even when compared with the current phenomenologists. It lacked the peculiar style and the framework of assumptions within which they work. And so also it incorporated certain features altogether lacking in them.

The basic term in his new epistemology was "tacit knowing." It made its appearance in his writings for the first time in *Personal Knowledge,* sharing the stage there with "commitment." It tended to take over, in his writings after that, more and more of the functions performed earlier by "commitment." His later book, *The Tacit Dimension,* brought his views on the tacit component in knowing to a climax of clarification, and in its Preface he indicated his own awareness of his movement from "commitment" to "tacit knowing" since the publication of *Personal Knowledge.*[5]

I do not intend, however, to trace the growth and development of this transition. Rather I will confine my attention to the nature and use of Polanyi's "tacit dimension in knowing" as he finally developed it; since this concept turned out to be the basis for the new epistemology for which he had been searching.

His notion of tacit knowing was based on the views originally brought forward by the Gestalt psychologists. It was perhaps natural for Polanyi to turn to a position that in effect attempted to derive parts from wholes, since his chosen opponents, the positivistic epistemologists, had for a long time been assiduously attempting the exact opposite, the derivation of wholes from parts, in very explicit ways. But in any event he was impressed by the experimental evidence the Gestaltists had amassed in their attempts to show that we see objects by supplying forms or patterns in terms of which the various bits and pieces in our perceptual field tend to fall into meaningful place. It seemed clear from some of their experiments that we do not perceive objects by inferring them from their given parts, nor by a process of induction from experience, inasmuch as we frequently see objects as complete even when some parts actually are not present! That is, we seem in perception to be completing a pattern even if this means supplying the missing parts, and without noticing that we do so. For it sometimes requires a special effort for us to notice perceptually that some of the essential parts are indeed missing, even after the fact of their absence has been established in our minds beyond our doubt.

Polanyi thought the Gestalt psychologists had made a good beginning,[6] but that unfortunately they began looking for mechanical explanations of these forms which involved supposing the equilibration of forces in our nervous systems, and so they failed to exploit the important psychological and philosophical possibilities of the central notion about which their discoveries revolved, viz., the idea that in perception we perform an *action*: we create a tacit integration of sensations and feelings into a perceived object that then gives meaning to these sensations and feelings which they had not previously possessed. This notion, Polanyi saw, provided a means of escape between the horns of what he took to be the modern epistemological dilemma.

One horn, Polanyi held, was "phenomenalism." This view, he said, is inadequate. Since it regards sense data as our ultimate information about the outside world and requires of us an inference from these bare data to objects to which these data refer, in order that we shall have knowledge of these objects, it "gives rise to the insoluble problem of the manner in which such inferences can be carried out."[7] Polanyi seemed to be referring here to the problem bequeathed to philosophy by David Hume, which indeed has never been solved without the addition, as in the case of Kant, of apodictic, a priori synthetic principles. But these principles, since they were not supposed to be given as sense data in experience, were suspect in their very a priori character, because of the general empirical and/or phenomenological stance of contemporary thought and feeling. The only other apparent alternative, namely, that inferences from sense data to objects might exist, but be hard to trace because they are unconscious, was suggested as long ago as 1867 by Helmholz, Polanyi pointed out; but he held that this theory did not save the sense-data view, since it has been called into serious question by the observation that optical illusions are not destroyed when their falsity is clearly demonstrated.[8]

Present-day linquistic analysis has, he said, tried to dispose of this problem by affirming that what we actually perceive are objects, not sense data. According to Ryle, sense impressions cannot be observed. Ryle's view claims we are aware of sense data only as qualities of the objects we perceive, said Polanyi. In other words, it claims that what is given us in the most immediate, concrete experience are objects. Polanyi thought that this view fails to account for such facts as are demonstrated, for instance, by experiments with apes brought up in the dark. These apes are observed to need considerable time to learn to see objects. Observations of the eye movements of babies also seem to bear out the same point. Both at first seem to see only sense data, patches of light and color, just as adults do also when they are faced with a puzzling sight. People find a sight puzzling, said Polanyi, when they can at first see only meaningless fragments "and have to make an intelligent effort in order to see the objects of which these are the qualities."[9]

Thus both views of perception that have been advanced by philosophers in modern times seem to be inadequate. Further evidence that the process is neither one of formal inference nor one in which full-blown objects impress themselves directly upon us is provided, Polanyi thought, by Heinrich Kottenhoff's interesting experiment with inverting spectacles. It was found to be possible for a subject who was disoriented, because he was wearing spectacles that inverted his visual field, to find his way about again after a while. But such an ability could be acquired only after days of groping about and it seemed not to be in the least facilitated by verbal instructions informing the subject that "up" was henceforth to be taken as "down" and "right" as "left." After he had achieved success in learning to get about again with no difficulty, the subject, upon reflection, had to admit that the images he saw were still "upside down," but he had reconnected them to other sensory clues, to touch, sound, and weight, in such a coherent manner that he had ceased to notice that the images were still actually inverted. In fact, the very question of "upside down" was difficult for him to answer, presumably since he found that he had even reintegrated his language into the new situation. He had established, Polanyi claimed, a new way of seeing things rightly, and so he found that he once again saw his objects in orderly relation to all of his sense data.[10] Seeing objects would therefore appear from the foregoing experiment to be the result of learning a skill, of learning how to attain a meaningful (but nonexplicit) integration of sensory clues through a sustained and conscious effect aimed at accomplishing this, and therefore to be neither a matter of formal inference from sense data nor one of a direct and immediate perception of objects.

Further evidence that perception is a meaningful but nonexplicit integration of many clues seems to come, Polanyi said, from the common reflection upon what happens when I move my hand before my eyes. So far as immediate givens are concerned, I should, at best, only see my hand constantly changing its color, its size, and its shape, at worst I should see only constantly changing patches of color. But instead it appears that I informally "take into account a host of rapidly changing clues, some in the field of vision, some in my eye muscles and some deeper still in my body, as in the labyrinth of the inner ear," and so what I really perceive turns out to be a coherence among these thousand varied and changing clues in the form of a single unchanging object moving about, and therefore tacitly understood, in my perception, as being seen from continually different angles and distances and under variable illuminations.[11] But it is apparent that this coherence could have been accomplished only tacitly, since I could not have been explicitly aware at the moment of some of the clues that apparently have entered into my coherent perception, those provided by my eye muscles, labyrinth organ, etc.

Two points should be evident here: One is, of course, that I do not need to be consciously aware of all the clues I integrate into a perception. But it is also apparent that there must exist a perceptual mechanism enabling me to pick out "objects" from my visual field and to retain them as integrated wholes even when their sense qualities change. I perceive them to be entities in motion retaining their integrity as objects, instead of perceiving them to be changing their character as objects. Given such a mechanism to start with, I could then learn the skill of using it in a more and more adequate way as time went on, as seems to be the case with infants and with apes originally brought up in darkness.

With respect to the first point, Polanyi held that it is not really new, inasmuch as physiologists, he says, have "long ago established that the way we see an object is determined by our awareness of certain efforts inside our body, efforts that we cannot feel in themselves. We are aware of these things going on inside our body in terms of the position, size, shape, and motion of an object to which we are attending."[12] And this theory is specifically confirmed, he held, by the experiments conducted by Hefferline and his collaborators in which it was found that spontaneous muscular twitches that are not felt by the subject (but are observable to the experimenter by an amplification of their action-current) can be made to function in terms of a purpose by the subject. The experimenter caused an unpleasant noise to cease whenever one of the minute unconscious twitches occurred. The subjects responded by increasing the frequency of these twitches, and thus silencing most of the noise. "Tacit knowing," Polanyi summed up, "is seen to operate here on an internal action that we are quite incapable of controlling or even feeling in itself. We become aware of our operation of it only in the silencing of a noise."

He suggested that this experimental situation is "closely analogous to the process by which we become aware of subliminal processes inside our body in the perception of objects outside." He held that these experiments allow us therefore to extend the scope of tacit knowing to include also neural traces in the cortex of our nervous system, which we have experimental evidence for holding do exist, but which we can never experience in a focal way. In this way we can account for the fact that the inference we make from sense data to an object appears to be so impossible for us to reduce to perfectly explicit terms.[13]

Polanyi attempted to explicate the mechanism mentioned in the second point, required by our ability to perceive objects that maintain their own integrity in the shifting welter of sights and sounds in our perceptual field. Polanyi called our attention to a case in which we become the victim of a certain kind of illusion in which we see an object that fails to maintain its integrity; we see an object we know to be moving, but which we perceive to be changing its character instead of moving. Polanyi pointed out that I can experience a known object so violating its own integrity when I watch my own moving finger through a pin hole. If I move my finger back and forth while looking at it through a pin hole, I see it swelling as it approaches my eye. Even though I would have to say I know it is moving and not swelling, I perceive it not to be moving but to be swelling. It has lost some of its perceptual constancy as a stable object and so I call this experience an optical illusion. I actually see what I have good grounds for knowing is not there. But why am I the victim of such an optical illusion? Polanyi inferred that, since the peripheral field of my vision has been cut off by the restriction of the pin hole, it must be that some sensory clues peripherally available to my eye are essential to my capacity to perceive an object as moving, even when I must admit that I am hardly aware of their presence at all, much less of their integration into my perception. The finger seen through the pin hole, therefore, lacks the visual confirmation of itself as a constant object, moving among its unmoving surroundings, that it had under ordinary circumstances of my observation of it. Having lost its perceptual constancy, Polanyi observed, it has also, in fact, lost some of its perceptual reality for me.[14]

Therefore it seemed to Polanyi, on the basis of this experience, that there must be certain sensory clues essential to what I am seeing, of which I am not focally aware. But it now becomes clear that these nonfocal clues must be of two kinds: (1) There must be, as we have noted before, those clues we have called subliminal: those events in my body, such as eye-muscle movements, movements inside my labyrinth organ, and neural traces in my cortex that I cannot ever directly perceive as part of my visual field when they are functioning in an act of perception. But (2) there must also be some clues that I do see, but only from the corner of my eye. These he called "marginal clues." These I could observe directly if I chose, but it is obvious I do not attend to them directly when I am viewing an object focally. I merely attend *from* them *to* a focal object. Thus my awareness of both kinds of these clues must only be subsidiary to my focal awareness of an object. Two generic kinds of awareness, the subsidiary and the focal, were therefore understood by Polanyi to be fundamental to the apprehension of coherence in perceptual objects. But there are two kinds of the subsidiary, the subliminal and the marginal.[15]

Polanyi went on to show that the marginal can also be broken down into two kinds. Besides what we see "at the corner of our eye," there is another type of clue that also functions marginally in perception. What we see in a marginal way is also influenced by what we have become used to seeing in the past. Polanyi referred for evidence for this to Ames' experiment with a skewed room. Two people are placed opposite each other in two corners of a skewed room: a grown man and a young boy. The boy looks taller than the man to an observer at the other end of the room. This is due to the fact that the room is skewed so that the ceiling is lower at the corner where the boy is standing than it is in the opposite corner where the man is standing. The boy's head is therefore closer to the ceiling. But also the part of the wall opposite the viewer near the boy's corner is closer to the viewer than is the part near the man's corner, by just the proper amount to make the room appear to be a normal, right-angled parallelepiped from the particular position at which the viewer is placed, if he also is required to use only one eye to view the scene. The angles subtended by the skewed room, in other words, are the same as those of a normal room, when viewed with one eye from this particular position.[16]

It would seem therefore that the viewer could either see the boy to be taller than the man, or perceive the room to be skewed. In fact it turns out that the viewer, in spite of the cognitive absurdity involved, perceives the boy to be taller than the man. In fact, a viewer would have to look at the room from a different angle, or tap the walls with a long stick, or take some other action, to be able to "see" the room as irregularly shaped, even though he knows, of course, that young boys are not taller than grown men. There must be some power, Polanyi observed, operating in the situation to induce us to perceive what we do in such a case. It seemed to Polanyi that this power must lie in the area that functions as a background, since the illusion depends upon perceiving the room as a "normal" room. And the room, in this situation, must function as a background; for, Polanyi reminded us, something in our visual field will function as a background when it extends indeterminantly around the central object of our attention. Thus the background area, that which is "seen from the corner of our eyes, or" he added, "remembered at the back of our minds," appears to affect compellingly the way we see the object upon which we are focusing. Its force, however, is so unobstrusively exercised that we seem not even to be aware of the background except through the appearance of the object to which we are attending.[17] An observer, if asked, would have to say he was aware of the room, of course, but it is clear that this awareness is really absorbed by him into the appearance of the objects in it. His awareness of it is only subsidiary, tacit. He takes the room for granted. But why does he take a "normal" room for granted?

Polanyi explained that we irresistibly see the room as having a normal shape, because of another act of tacit knowing (which we shall discuss in more detail later) involving a subsidiary awareness at the back of our mind of a great many "normal" rooms that we have seen in the past. So not only what is at the corner of our eyes, but also what is at the back of our mind functions as a background in perception. The "weight of these memories at the back of our mind," he said, functions as a marginal clue, as part of a background upon which we see the objects, but the nature of which really enters only into the objects' appearance, and is not itself seen separately. What we perceive becomes, therefore, not only a function of simple automatic visual mechanisms, but also a function of what we could say we *know*—what has sunk into our minds as a result of past integrations and the general forms and principles taken by us from them.[18] Previous integrations of clues—previously achieved meanings—slip into the backs of our minds and function there as part of the subsidiary clues forming the background for new integrations of clues with objects.[19] The integrations of clues that have in the past enabled us to see rooms again and again as right-angled parallelepipeds has established a "normal room" background in our minds which functions in a subsidiary way in our perceptions of things in rooms and so contributes to the illusion in Ames' experiment. As evidence for his interpretation, Polanyi pointed to the fact that primitive people who have seen fewer "normal" rooms are less susceptible to this kind of illusion.[20]

But why should this background be so influential in the objects we perceive, instead of the objects of our focal attention being seen merely against the background? Polanyi provided an explanation which reveals more fully the underlying visual mechanism at work. Polanyi pointed out that we see a cow strolling in a field rather than the reverse, a field flowing past a cow. He held that this is because the whole landscape, as far as the eye can reach, includes an infinite range of particulars to which we are paying no special attention. It is, therefore, perceived by us to be at absolute rest. He seemed to mean that, since the landscape fills up the field of our vision, it strikes us perceptually (not necessarily also conceptually) as unlimited in its extent, i.e., as infinite. And, of course, since what fills up our field of vision (the infinite) cannot be seen to be moving against a further background, it has to appear to us to be at absolute rest. Consequently what is perceived by us to be moving relative to it is perceived by us as that which is "really" moving. So in the example of the strolling cow, since the field consists of a totality of unheeded particulars that extends to the edges of our field of vision, it is perceived to be at rest, and the cow is perceived to be moving.[21]

Polanyi seems to imply that the part of our field of vision that does come to serve as a perceptual background for us is not determined conceptually, but rather through the mere mechanics of vision. However, we have also just seen in the skewed-room experiment that what we "know" on the basis of past experience—what general conceptual notions we have formed—can also enter into the determination of the background of our perceptual field. Nevertheless it is our nondeliberative visual mechanisms that Polanyi found are primary in the determination of our perceptual background. If this were not the case, optical illusions would not exist, nor indeed persist, even after our recognition of them as illusions. He demonstrated this by pointing to a rather commonly experienced optical illusion in which an object we see and "know" to be stationary is nonetheless perceived by us to be in motion.

His example is a bridge upon which we may be standing. We "know" it to be stationary relative to the water, by any definition of "knowledge." Yet, if the river is broad and fills up our entire field of vision, the bridge will be perceived to be moving when we look down at where the bridge meets the water. However, the moment we shift our eyes a bit and include the banks of the river in our field of vision, it is the water that will instantly be perceived to be moving, instead of the bridge. This is due, Polanyi held, to the fact that the countryside now fills out the edges of our field of vision instead of the water, and, since the bridge stands as a part of this field (i.e., as a part of the background), it will now be perceived to be stationary, as backgrounds always are. The spot upon which we have continued to focus our eyes will now show us that the water is moving, not the bridge. Thus the spot upon which we are focusing will actually be perceived differently, depending upon what else is seen marginally as filling out the edges of our field of vision and so as serving as a background.[22]

Polanyi thus appeared to be holding that the conceptions and general notions we have formed on the basis of past experience enter only tacitly and as further specifications of what already has become our perceptual background by the operation of our visual mechanisms. The Humeian notion that our past experiences automatically condition us to feel certain expectations for the future must therefore be in error from Polanyi's point of view. From what Polanyi said, it would seem he meant that our cognitive expectations, or what Dewey called our "funded experience," are not effective in determining the background in perception when our visual mechanisms provide us with a background that contradicts this funded experience, our "knowledge."

As for our tendency to integrate some of our sensory field into stable objects in the first place—objects that retain their integrity while moving against a stationary background—Polanyi rejected references to "equili-brations" in our nervous systems, or to any other sort of automatic nervous mechanisms. He held rather that this tendency to integrate some of our sensory field into stable objects comes from our "craving to find strands of permanence in the tumult of changing appearances," which, he says, "is the supreme organon for bringing our experiences under intellectual control."[23] We should note here (while postponing a fuller discussion until later) that, for Polanyi, an intention to bring "our experiences under intellectual control" begins to operate already in basic perception, so that even the basic mechanisms of visual perception were held by him to be teleologically oriented toward the attainment of an intended intellectual coherence. Physiological mechanisms themselves were therefore thought by him to be structured to function toward the goal of attaining meaning, although functioning only mechanically to-ward such a goal, not deliberatively. (Ergo: they sometimes present us with illusions, i.e., are in error.)

Yet, in spite of the mechanical operation of basic perceptual mechanisms, Polanyi held that our perceptions are not heteronomously caused. Rather, he maintained, "we are performing one single mental act in jointly seeing an object against its background." Such a mental act has a focus in terms of which the background functions in a subsidiary way, and so "we are aware of the background [only] in terms of the object's appearance—e.g., of its being in motion."[24] He held that both focal awareness and subsidiary or "from-awareness" exist functionally related in a single, purposive act of mental awareness. But since we cannot discover in our consciousness all the subsidiary clues that we integrate into a perceived object (we admittedly are unable to infer the object explicitly from all our consciously known sense data), Polanyi's contention that a perception is a single mental act must rest upon his reiterated supposition that some physiological events in our body that we can never take note of focally by means of introspection are nevertheless elements actually used by us in a subsidiary way in structuring an integrated object of focal perception—and are not simply causes of such integrations. In other words, he held that "from-awareness" may function at all levels of consciousness from the subliminal to the fully conscious—that some "functions inside our body at levels completely inaccessible to experience by the subject" are elements of which we take account in the total economy of our awareness.[25] We truly do, therefore, "know more than we can tell."[26]

The foregoing is a very important point for Polanyi. For if the factors in perception that lie entirely below the level of any possible focal awareness are not factors of which we are at least subsidiarily aware, then perception is not a single, purposive act—it is at bottom merely a caused event—and what we call "knowledge," being rooted in our perceptions, is then not a result of our purposeful efforts. But if knowledge is not a result of our purposeful efforts, then of course it could not have the quality of being either right or wrong, except by some standards external to it. It must intend to be right, in order ever to be mistaken. If perception and knowledge were not intentional acts, then truth could not be understood to be an ideal toward which we really aspire. And the social consequences of our firmly held belief that it is an illusory aspiration must then be such that, having lost our respect for the ideal of "truth" as a truly operative intention in persons, we have lost our basis for a respect for each other's opinions.[27] "Truth" must then become only a word we apply to whatever it is we are caused or conditioned to think, and so there would be no reason for our not attempting to cause or condition other persons to think whatever we would wish them to think—whether this be the desirability of egalitarian institutions, of elitest institutions, of the dictatorship of the proletariat, of the rule of the Master Race, or of almost anything—except, possibly, of free institutions. It would be dangerous and silly for us to attempt to condition others to think the latter were desirable unless we wished to lose our power to condition others. For truly free institutions are inevitably a means to whatever ends the participants may freely choose, and there is no guarantee that the ends that others may freely choose will agree with ours.[28]

The long-range implications of this epistemological point for Polanyi's ultimate philosophic concerns should become quite evident here. But we shall have to leave to a later chapter the job of doing them full justice. We must confine ourselves for now (as Polanyi did) to establishing on strictly epistemological grounds the contention that all the factors entering into our perceptions function as subsidiary clues to integrations that we *make* (not as causes of what we find to be given us in perception), even when these factors are entirely subliminal. We must confine ourselves in this way, because an epistemology must not be urged simply on the grounds that "good" moral consequences may follow from it. It should be supported because it seems to make better *epistemological* sense than its alternatives. If it cannot be supposed to do this, it cannot, in the end, as Polanyi seemed to be aware, really serve other longer-run aims.[29]

So we must especially point out that the epistemological issue under consideration is important also to Polanyi's shorter range objective of establishing the unavoidability of the tacit dimension in all instances of perceptual knowing. For if it is true that some clues that enter into the intentional construction of our perceptions are not only unnoticed by us as functioning in our perception, *but cannot ever be noticed,* then we must suppose that we "know," rather than merely suffer from conditioning, but further that we always "know more than we can tell" and that all our knowledge is therefore always permeated by a "tacit dimension"—with all the consequences for a theory of knowledge that this point entails. Polanyi therefore thought it was necessary to present further direct evidence for this point from the results of controlled experiments establishing the existence of what psychologists have called "subception."

Let us turn, in the next chapter, to what he regarded as such direct evidence for this point, as well as to some further consequences of it for our theories of knowledge.

# CHAPTER FIVE

# Indwelling

$L$azarus and McCleary, Polanyi recounted, presented a person with nonsense syllables, consistently administering an electric shock after the presentation of some of them. Presently the person showed symptoms of anticipating the shock at the sight of these "shock syllables." On questioning, however, it was found that he could not tell what made him expect the shock. This knowledge that the subject acquired, said Polanyi, is "similar to that which we have when we know a person by signs which we cannot tell." He held that there is a distinct advantage in establishing this point experimentally. He said that

> the experimental arrangement wards off the suspicion of self-contradiction, which is not easy to dispel when anyone speaks of things he knows and cannot tell. This is prevented here by the division of roles between the subject and the observer. The experimenter observes that another person has a certain knowledge he cannot tell, and so no one speaks of a knowledge he himself has and cannot tell.[1]

Polanyi did not entertain the possibility that the above results could be explained as an instance of Pavlovian conditioned stimulus. He had rejected the interpretation that Pavlov put upon the famous experiments in which he induced salivation in dogs by the ringing of a bell. Pavlov rang a bell just before food was given to the dogs again and again until the dogs began to salivate at the ringing of the bell. This he interpreted as replacing an unconditioned stimulus to the response of salivation, namely, food, with a conditional stimulus, the ringing of a bell. Pavlov's interpretation would, Polanyi pointed out, if taken strictly, identify eating with the expectation of being fed, because both can be shown to induce a certain behavior, viz., the secretion of saliva.[2] Pavlov's interpretation certainly did involve identifying two different events, food and the ringing of the bell, since it consists in explaining learned behavior as a simple replacing of one, unconditioned, stimulus or response with another, conditioned, one. Polanyi said that, if this were all there were to it, Pavlov should have expected, say, a red light announcing the imminence of an electric shock in a trained dog to act upon the dog like the shock itself. But, Polanyi pointed out, this is not quite true to what happens. "The dog does not jump and snap at the bell as if it were food, nor does the red light cause the kind of muscular contraction which results from an electric shock." The dog really acts toward the bell or the light as a *sign* of something else. In fact the "'conditioned response' of the dog differs quite generally from his original 'unconditioned response.'" said Polanyi, "in the same way in which the anticipation of an event differs from the effect of the event itself." This criticism of the conditioned reflex theory is well known, Polanyi affirmed, referring to D.O. Hebb's *The Organization of Behavior,* published in 1949, and it "entitles us to say, in contrast to Pavlov's description of the process, that in sign-learning the animal is taught to expect an event by recognizing a sign foretelling the event."[3] In other words, we must say that the dog's learning is mediated by his cognitive capacities. He is not responding merely as a programmed machine in which a number of different stimuli can be programmed to elicit identical responses.

Polanyi pointed out that signs operate in our awareness differently from what they signify. Signs and what they signify are not two equally significant (or insignificant) "items" that happen to get mechanically associated together so that they induce identical reactions. Signs, even in "lower" animals, function always as signs of something else, something more immediately significant to the animal than the sign itself. They function therefore subsidiarily as a medium or tool to the knowledge of something else in which there is an interest taken, and this is true whether what is known as a sign is known in a conscious and thus tellable fashion, or not. He holds, therefore, that various "automatic" or "mechanical" learning theories, which attempt to ignore such a "knowing" function, or to reduce it to something else, are inadequate. They miss the point. Signs function as clues and are known in a subsidiary way as bearing upon a meaningful integration of them forming that which is known in a focal way. That upon which they focus does not reciprocally bear upon them. The name of a building bears upon the building; the building does not bear upon its name.[4]

Gestalt psychology was, therefore, a distinct improvement upon the various behavioristic and mechanical approaches to perception and to learning, Polanyi held. And we owe to such psychologists much of the evidence that supports the notion that perception is a comprehension of clues in terms of a whole. Unfortunately Gestalt theory also eventually fell into the same trap from which it at first offered an escape. Polanyi pointed out that, as the Gestalt psychologists held, much of perception operates automatically. That, for example, much of what we see we do so because of the way in which what extends to the corner of the eye simply serves as the background of the objects we perceive, independently of any intellectual or conceptual views we may have or any efforts made by us—except, presumably, for our efforts to find "objects" at all. For instance, the bridge discussed above is seen as moving through the water of a river so broad that we do not see its banks from the corners of our eyes. But Gestalt psychologists, he held, have been influenced by the objectivistic and mechanical prejudices of our age, and so have tended to work mainly with examples of this automatic type of perception. Optical illusions were therefore classed by them with true perceptions, and both came to be described and explained as a form of automatic "equilibration of simultaneous stimuli to a comprehensive whole. . . . Such an interpretation," said Polanyi, "leaves no place for any intentional effort which prompts our perception to explore and assess in the quest of knowledge the clues offered to our senses." Following such a view we are led to neglect the reasons for recognizing people as "persons who use their senses as centers of intelligent judgment."[5] He seemed to be implying that we tend instead, under the influence of various mechanical theories of knowledge, to regard people as only complex bundles of stimuli and responses—or of automatically attained equilibrations—and therefore as entities whose thinking, being only conditioned responses or equilibrations anyhow, can and should be conditioned or equilibrated "properly," i.e., brain-washed.[6]

But aside from these morally deficient consequences of mechanical theories of perception (to which we have already alluded), Polanyi thought such theories are also deficient, as we have seen, simply because they are not equal to explaining perception. Part of the background operative in perception is due to something other than simple physiologically built-in mechanisms. Some of it is provided by what we think we know of the world, and so is entangled with our intelligent and critical intentions. Besides, perception is part of the cognitive recognition of signs as having meanings when bearing upon something else. And neither of these activities, he thought, can operate wholly automatically.

Polanyi interpreted the work of Lazarus and McCleary on subception as constituting experimental confirmation of his contention that perception, although an intentional act, is one in which we make a tacit use of clues of which we are aware only in a subsidiary fashion. He spun out of their experiment a complex of relations between terms involved in tacit knowing. These were exemplified in the experiment by (1) the shock syllables and (2) the shock. And he thought these terms are related in four different ways: functionally, phenomenally, semantically, and ontologically.[7]

In the experiment referred to, the shock syllables evoked the expectation of a shock. But they remained known only tacitly. Apparently this was because the subject was riveting his attention upon the shock. Therefore his knowledge of the shock was specifiable, in contrast to his knowledge of the shock-producing particulars (the syllables). Since he relied on these syllables for attending to something else, viz., the shock, he did not know them focally in themselves and so he could not specify them.[8]

This knowing of the first term (the shock syllables) only by relying on awareness of it for attending to the second (the shock) is the functional way in which the two terms involved in tacit knowing are related to each other. Functionally they are in a nonreciprocal "from–to" relation. Borrowing the language of anatomy, Polanyi said in *The Tacit Dimension* that we can call the first term "proximal" and the second "distal".[9] It is the proximal of which we have what he called subsidiary awareness—or "from-awareness"—and the distal of which we have what he called "focal awareness."[10] It is always the proximal term, therefore, which we may know but be unable to "tell."[11]

A simple example of how this relation operates in perception is provided, Polanyi held, by the way we know an individual human face. We rely on its particular features quite obviously in attending to the characteristic appearance of the face. We are attending, however, not *to* the particular features, but *from* these features *to* the face. It is the face we say we know, and the features we are often unable to specify fully; sometimes we might be hard put to specify any of them, even though we know the person very well and could without the slightest hesitancy identify his face anywhere.[12]

The perception of a stereo image through a stereoscope was another example frequently used by Polanyi to illustrate his meaning. "We are aware of the two stereo pictures in some peculiar non-focal way," he said. "We seem to look through these two pictures, or past them, while we look straight at their joint image. We are indeed aware of them only as guides to the image on which we focus our attention." They are subsidiary or proximal to the distal or focal image seen with depth.[13] The two different images that we integrate are different in such unobtrusive ways that when we compare them focally we can hardly see what the differences are. "Even if we used powerful methods for measuring them," he points out, "we would find them difficult to itemize." Yet our subsidiary awareness picks them up and embodies them in the focus of our attention with no difficulty whatever.[14]

These two terms, then, are *functionally* related by our attending from the first to the second. In phenomenal terms, or in terms of appearance, what is phenomenally given becomes different for us when we learn to anticipate a shock at the sight of certain syllables. The expectation of a shock, which was only vague and general before, becomes sharply fluctuating, Polanyi observed, and so we must say we become aware of the shock syllables in the apprehension of the shock that they evoke in us. Thus they appear to us only in these fluctuating apprehensions. We are aware of them only in terms of that on which we are focusing our attention, the probability of an electric shock. Our phenomenal awareness of the subsidiary or proximal terms, when they are subliminal, resides entirely in the appearance of the focal or distal term to which we are attending. It is not that they have no appearance or that we are not at all aware of them, but our awareness of them and their appearance comes from the other thing—that shock—to which we are attending when these subliminal elements are present. In the case of a face, we are aware of its features within the overall facial appearance, the physiognomy, to which we are attending. A nose, lifted out of the face in which it appears, will often not even look the same to us as it does when seen in the face of which it is a part. This is the phenomenal side of the functional relation described above, the phenomenal mode of their existence.[15]

These two together, Polanyi said, the functional and the phenomenal, give rise to a semantic, or meaning, relation in that the syllables or features are grasped or understood (as we have noted before) as signifying the shock or the face. They are signs of the distal. Thus it is the distal, or focal, shock or face that constitutes the meaning of the syllables or features, the meaning of the signs. Without their bearing upon the distal they would be meaningless. "It is," Polanyi said, "in terms of their meaning that they [the proximal signs] enter into the appearance of that *to* which we are attending *from* them."[16] For example: The only meaning this nose has is that it is George's nose, but it has this meaning only as it enters into the appearance of George's face. In a representative painting, Polanyi said, brush strokes are meaningless, except as they enter into the appearance of the painting. They are meaningful not when viewed in themselves focally, but only when used subsidiarily to see the painting. This is to say they are meaningful when the painting is seen through them. It is the painting that is their meaning.[17]

The foregoing exposition seems to show that meaning is always attained when a from–to function exists in our awareness. Thus perception, in terms of this epistemological position, is always meaningful. And "meaning," for Polanyi, seemed to signify "signification." This has both the sense that what has meaning, the proximal particulars, are always operating as clues or signs pointing to something else in an act of integration (an act of achieving meaning), and also the sense that what are integrated are always certain particulars that make some intelligible sense when integrated into a comprehensible form or pattern, and so are also significant in the sense of being important to an intelligence.

Meaning, in these senses therefore, is something that must be grasped or seen or created by a mind. It is not a mere equilibration of forces that happens to occur in a non-mind—say, in a computer. For Polanyi's "meaning" was not devoid of intention—the intention to find or achieve a meaning, i.e., the intention to find or achieve a comprehensive and intelligible integration. And a mechanism that operates only as an equilibration of forces must perforce be blind to any intention or purpose or aim of its own. Its "aims" can only be those built into it as operative principles by its designers, not imaginatively held in mind by itself. If the totality of its operative principles are not adequate to the aims of its designers, it cannot be corrected by means of its own actions, and its parts must be reorganized by its makers—unless it has been successfully (in terms of the aims of its makers) organized to reorganize its own parts. Only then are the totality of its operative principles adequate—but still only to the aims of its makers, not to its own.[18] In contrast, a mind, imaginatively holding in mind an aim or purpose of its own, is capable of reorganizing its own parts to accomplish this aim, if such reorganization is needed, and, in the meantime, of recognizing itself as being in error.[19] Therefore the "meaning" of something, as Polanyi used the term, cannot truly be turned into other terms and "said" or "told" explicitly, precisely because it is only a tacit integration of a mind attempting to realize an intention of its own, not any sort of detached, objective "thing" existing independently of a purpose held in some mind. Thus a meaning can only be pointed to by a mind as something existing in a mind. In fact, the meaning of the term "meaning," as Polanyi used it, can only be pointed to by a mind as something existing in a mind, as the attempt to explicate its meaning above surely shows. "Meaning" is, therefore, really a triadic term in that, in addition to the functionally different proximal and distal factors, there must also always be a person, a user, an intender involved.[20]

This implication of tacit knowing has great consequences, as Polanyi claimed. This is so not only for the nature and status of the various knowledge enterprises of man, but also for the nature and status of man's grasp of himself and of others, and of his grasp of his and their place in a universe and in a society of persons. Which is to say, of course, that it has great consequences for the development of a comprehensive philosophical position. Most of the rest of this book will consist of an attempt to spell out all these consequences.

But before we close this chapter and get on with that task we must touch upon the fourth relation, the ontological, since this belongs also to a discussion of perception, even though it constitutes a bridge from perception to a real world to which both perception and conception must be said to relate or to aspire. And so its full significance must also await the discussions incorporated in later chapters.

Polanyi held that from the foregoing three aspects of tacit knowing—the functional, the phenomenal, and the semantic—a fourth may be deduced, one which tells us what tacit knowing is a knowledge of.

This he called the ontological aspect.

> Since tacit knowing establishes a meaningful relation between two terms, we may identify it with the *understanding* of the comprehensive entity which these two terms jointly constitute. Thus the proximal term represents the *particulars* of this entity, and we can say, accordingly, that we comprehend the entity by relying on our awareness of its particulars for attending to their joint meaning.[21]

He maintained, as we have seen, that the two terms involved in an example of tacit knowing—say, the features and the face—are both necessary to each other in an act of knowing. From this it follows that they must, in an act of knowing, form together an entity which comprehends them both. This comprehensive entity must be the being (at least in the phenomenological sense) with which we have to deal in becoming aware of the functional, the phenomenal, and the semantic relations in which the two terms stand to each other. The two terms together constitute this entity. This must be true whether this entity finally turns out to be regarded as a creation of our own minds—following Kant or some of the contemporary existentialists—or a reality existing in itself with which our minds may come into contact.

Reflection upon these functional, phenomenal, and semantic relations has thus revealed that a face does not exist without its features and that its features are meaningless without their bearing upon a face, although neither can be reduced to the other. We deduce, therefore, that they are each part of an entity comprehending them both. It then seems to follow that such an entity has being for us through an act of tacit knowing (it is what the act in its own meaning claims to be *of*) whether we are mistaken or not in our belief that this entity is real.

So it appears that, for Polanyi, what we perceive is perceived as a "something-that-is-there,"[22] whether the perceptual experience be an illusion, a hallucination, a dream, or a perception proper. The phenomenological difference between the first three and the fourth consists only in that, in the cases we call "perception," it is believed by us that the something the perception seems to be of is really a something-or-other in itself, i.e., it is "real." Which is to say—as Polanyi tells us he means to say when he uses the term "real"—that it is an entity that can be expected to exhibit itself in an indeterminate range of future manifestations, and so may be expected to continue to affect our perceptions and actions in the future in those ways in which it has done so already, as well as in unpredictable ways that will reveal further aspects of itself.[23]

Such is not the case with what we come to call illusions, hallucinations, or dreams. But, of course, we do not come to understand our sense experiences to be illusions, etc., until we come to doubt them to be experiences of something real, i.e., genuine perceptions. Polanyi would therefore hold that *all* cases of immediately experienced, sensible experience always involve, in themselves, projections into an object, whether we shall continue to believe all of them to be genuine perceptions or not.

But Polanyi admitted that such a position seems to be controversial. He said that "modern philosophers have argued that perception does not involve projection, since we are not previously aware of the internal processes which we are supposed to have projected into the qualities of things perceived."[24] But, he held, it is evident from the facts involved in our use of tools and probes that in these cases we do transpose away from us the meanings we achieve by them. The feeling of any tool in the hand, say a cane by which a blind man is finding his way about, is transposed by him from his hand that is in contact with the cane out to what the tip of the cane is in contact with. The feeling of pressure on his hand is transposed into the meanings he is focally attending to at the tip of the cane.[25] It is true, Polanyi admitted, that the feelings transposed by perception, unlike those transposed by the use of tools, are hardly noticeable in themselves previous to their transposition, or, in some cases, not noticeable at all. Yet, in view of the experiments showing the existence of subliminal subception, it seems we must say that subliminal feelings do in fact enter into focally perceived objects as surely as other nonsubliminal feelings do. And so if the latter can be understood for good reason to be transposed, so can the former.

Consequently Polanyi held that the argument against projection that hinges upon the fact that we do not previously sense the internal processes is irrelevant to the question of whether or not we do project them away from us and into things "outside." He thought, therefore, there can hardly be any doubt that projection does in fact take place in perception, and thus also that perception entails an ontological relation to a comprehensive entity believed, in acts of perception, to be really in being.

Even subsidiary particulars can, in some cases, be projected from us when we focus our attention upon them. In fact, the features of a face, its particulars, seem, even when functioning as particulars, to be already projected away from us, since they appear, in perception itself, to lie away from us in that face of which they are a part.[26] But we cannot, of course, project away from us in the same manner those irrevocably subliminal subsidiary particulars that lie in unconscious processes deep within our bodies. That is to say, we cannot make focal perceptions of them as they function as subliminal subsidiary particulars. These processes can become perceptual "objects," of course; but only for observers in physiological inquiries. However, they are then observable only in a form in which they cannot function at all as particulars through which their observers can have a perception.

Were we to observe these subliminal particulars as physiological events in, say, the body of a person seeing a cat, said Polanyi, we would not see the cat that their operation as subliminal clues is enabling this person to see. This is, in fact, true even were we somehow to observe focally these subliminal events as physiological events going on in ourselves! We could only see a cat *through* them, through using them subliminally as subsidiary clues in a personal act of perception, i.e., an act of integration that we ourselves perform. From these events we cannot logically or theoretically deduce externally an actual perception of a cat. We must, said Polanyi, "dwell in them" in order to see a cat.[27] But, of course, to see a cat we must "dwell in" all the other nonsubliminal clues involved also. When we are looking at these other clues focally and not dwelling in them, we find that they too lose their function as clues to the perception of a cat.

And this loss is identical with the loss of their meaning. For meaning, said Polanyi, is always lost, sometimes for good, when in order to inspect them focally, attempts are made to withdraw ourselves from those feelings or perceptions, those particulars, within which one is dwelling in an act of knowing—that is, to make them into explicit, external "objects." Brush strokes lose their meaning when studied focally, words do also when looked at or listened to too long in terms of their mere sound or appearance, and so also do features of a face when gazed at steadily in isolation from each other.[28] This loss of meaning occurs because we have left off dwelling in them in order to look at them.

The full significance of Polanyi's epistemological position is not seen, therefore, until it is realized that the joint meaning of those particulars in which an entity is rooted existentially is not perceived by looking at them but rather by dwelling in them,[29] as a blind man dwells in— extends his body into—his cane, in such a way that what he seems to feel in a focal way (the *meaning*) is what is at the *tip* of his cane, not in its handle. The feeling of his hand on the handle has become as subsidiary to him as are the feelings inside his body when he is focusing through them on something else. He has thus extended himself into his cane. He dwells in it as he does in his body. Thus Polanyi was saying that all our knowledge involving our use of tools or probes or instruments of any kind involves our very person, in the sense that we can only achieve it by dwelling in and not on the particulars that make up the entity we are knowing. This point, were we once fully to grasp and internalize it, i.e., to dwell in *it,* would cure us, Polanyi believed, once and for all of our obsession with detached objectivity as the goal of knowledge. We would then suppose we knew only what we were *not* detached from, i.e., what we became aware of only through our actual dwelling in its particulars.[30]

So we must see more fully what this "indwelling" meant for Polanyi, and why he thought we ought to accept it across the board as a necessity in any act of knowing. That is, we must see whether or not Polanyi can induce us to dwell in the notion of indwelling, which is not unrelated to whether or not he can make us see that this notion of "dwelling in" can deal adequately also with other problems of knowledge in addition to perception, including those relating to cognition in general and, more specifically, to science.

# CHAPTER SIX

# Generalization

$A$t this point it should be fairly clear what Michael Polanyi meant by saying that we must dwell in the particular clues, both sensible and subliminal, that go to make up an object of perception. We surely could be said to dwell in the particulars when we determine the shape and position of objects by means of probes and when we see a picture with depth by looking "through" two other single-plane pictures in a stereoscope. And it might also seem to make sense to say that it is a "dwelling in" that spells the difference between the sort of awareness of the particulars one has when he integrates them into his perception of a cat and the sort of awareness he has of these same particulars when he only observes them as events in his own body, or in the body of someone else who is viewing a cat. That is, when he does not dwell in these particulars himself, but makes them the objects of his focal observation. In this latter case, it seems clear, he will not see a cat, but rather will see only these physiological or neurological events.

Perhaps, therefore, Polanyi's view that there can be no entirely objective knowledge might be generally accepted at this point, if it were thought that he only meant to claim that, as all our knowledge is based on perception and as perception can never be wholly detached and objective, so neither can our knowledge. Our knowledge must always involve a perceiver who dwells in the particulars involved and so who personally (and therefore tacitly) integrates them into an object. No explicit and entirely objective demonstration of the perceived object from its sensibly given parts can be provided.

Yet it might be thought that this view of perception, even if acceptable, only tells us something of how the raw materials used by our cognitive processes get in to us, so to speak. Such a view might indeed force us back into a kind of Kantian notion that the world we know must be strictly a phenomenal world (even if a very significantly different phenomenal world from Kant's). Yet objective knowledge (objective within this sort of box) might still be thought of as possible, as it was for Kant. Science, it might be thought, could still proceed by making conceptually objective classifications and correlations among and between our perceptual objects, using the purely logical concepts available to everyone, and so ending up with a kind of intersubjective cognitive objectivity.

Such a view, however, would fail to take into account Polanyi's observation that our perceptions are not given purely by perceptual mechanisms totally uninfluenced by our conceptual activities. The skewed room experiment seemed to show that something like an induction from past experiences forced itself into the character of what it was that we perceived. What is perceptually given, therefore, is not constructed entirely by our basic perceptual mechanisms. It is partly a result of conceptual interpretations, of which, however, we are aware only in a subsidiary way, not focally. And since there is, therefore, no pure perception, there can also be no purely objective induction, because induction, if it can provide us with purely objective results (even within phenomenal limits) must rest upon perceptions that are not themselves influenced by such inductive operations. And since perceptions are so influenced, we have to say that perceptions and inductive conceptions reciprocally influence each other, and the final position reached in this reciprocity can have only a valid *personal* character, not an intersubjectively (or objectively) "correct" one. Perceptions, as many philosophers of science are now saying, are *all* "theory-laden."

So far, in the above remarks, we have been tacitly assuming that the processes of generalization, including classification and induction, are themselves explicitly operating processes, needing only pure and unbiased perceptions in order to operate purely objectively. But, even assuming that these processes themselves were purely objective operations, we have just seen there would be difficulties in supposing we could ever reach what could be called strictly objective knowledge. Yet Polanyi's inquiries into our cognitive processes showed that these processes even in themselves can only operate by making use of a tacit dimension, so that they also depend upon personal indwelling and are thus not wholly explicit or objective operations.

His inquiries into these matters were tied in with his whole critique of positivistic views of science. He held that the "original intention of logical positivism was to establish all knowledge in terms of explicit relations between sensory data,"[1] and to maintain that "the logical foundation of empirical knowledge must be capable of definition by explicit rules."[2] A scientist, understood in terms of these intentions "from the outside," as Polanyi said, might "appear as a mere truth-finding machine."[3] In fact, "by setting up some formal model in terms of probability or constant conjunction," a scientist could "have a machine speak for him, impersonally."[4]

It should appear possible therefore, in terms of such a view of science, to construct a scientific-inquiry machine from which, if one fed it sufficient perceptual data, one could extract objective inductions and acceptable theories. Polanyi, of course, rejected such a notion. He pointed out that assumptions guiding scientific discoveries are, in the minds of their discoverers, "fundamental guesses . . . concerning the nature of things,"[5] not mere summarizations of objective correlations between bits of phenomena. "Scientific propositions," he said, "do not refer definitely to any observable facts." They "are like statements about the presence of a burglar next door—describing something real which may manifest itself in many indefinite ways. . . . There exist therefore no explicit rules by which a scientific proposition can be obtained from observational data. . . . The part of observation is to supply clues for the apprehension of reality."[6] Even if we had such a truth-finding machine as described above, he pointed out, we would still have to accredit the machine personally, that is, acknowledge it to be trustworthy. Its results could not be accepted otherwise. And if we did accredit the machine, he held, it would be because we believed it to be advantageous in terms of some policy or other, such as "simplicity, economy, practicality, fruitfulness, etc.," the values of which we also acknowledged either explicitly or implicitly. And these advantages would be "expected to accrue only because we hold certain beliefs about the nature of things which make this expectation reasonable."[7] In other words, we would be unable to avoid incorporating personal elements into the use of such a machine, even if we had one.

Polanyi endeavored to support these views through a number of critical examinations of particular problems entailed in the activity of scientific inquiry. He considered that the problem was set by the necessity which scientists are under to classify the kinds of entities (or "phenomena") with which they deal. He pointed out that students who are learning a science are unable to learn to make identifications according to kind simply by reference to explicit marks as signs of a particular kind or species. They must learn from a master who shows them cases of a certain type in connection with cases of related types until they acquire a tacit ability to identify them correctly. This ability remains tacit, because it cannot "be told," as Polanyi said, in so many explicit terms.[8]

For instance, medical students, he said, learn to identify different kinds of disorders through having had cases of them identified by their teachers and pointed out to them. Biologists also learn to identify species in this fundamentally tacit manner.[9] These operations of science thus have to be understood basically as skills, he held, not fundamentally different from that of the tightwire performer, the bicycle rider, or the swimmer. The best textbooks and manuals that can be written to give instructions concerning these skills, by breaking them down into their most complete and explicit particulars, cannot instruct a learner sufficiently. There are always unspecifiable clues which he finally picks up and dwells in when he succeeds in staying upright on a bicycle, afloat in the water, or in balance on a tightwire.

Polanyi said:

I . . . regard the unspecifiable parts of knowledge as the residue left unsaid by a defective articulation. Such defectiveness is common and often glaring. I may ride a bicycle and say nothing, or pick out my macintosh among twenty others and say nothing. Though I cannot say clearly how I ride a bicycle and how I recognize my macintosh (for I don't know it clearly), yet this will not prevent me from saying that I know how to ride a bicycle and how to recognize my macintosh. For I know that I know perfectly well how to do such things, though I know the particulars of what I know only in an instrumental manner and am focally quite ignorant of them; so that I may say that I know these matters even though I cannot tell clearly, or hardly at all, what it is that I know.[10]

But the same sort of thing is true, Polanyi held, of the skilled scientist in his capacity of identifying correctly the kinds of material his science deals with.

Polanyi told us:

> Subsidiary or instrumental knowledge . . . is not known in itself but is known in terms of something focally known, to the quality of which it contributes; and to this extent it is unspecifiable. Analysis may bring subsidiary knowledge into focus and formulate it as a maxim or as a feature in physiognomy, but such specification is in general not exhaustive. Although the expert diagnostician, taxonomist and cotton-classer can indicate their clues and formulate their maxims, they know many more things than they can tell, knowing them only in practice, as instrumental particulars, and not explicitly, as objects. The knowledge of such particulars is therefore ineffable, and the pondering of a judgment in terms of such particulars is an ineffable process of thought. This applies equally to connoisseurship as the art of knowing and to skills as the art of doing, wherefore both can be taught only by aid of practical example and never solely by precept.[11]

Polanyi held that such "ineffable" processes of thought are operative in science whenever a scientist structures a whole from parts. In dissection, for instance, he held we can only structure a whole from topographical parts in a nonexplicit, imaginative way. "Dissection," he pointed out, "which lays bare a region and its organs by removing the parts overlaying it," demonstrates no more than one aspect of that region. The "imagination," he said, must "reconstruct from such experience the three-dimensional picture of the exposed area as it existed in the unopened body, and to explore mentally its connections with adjoining unexposed areas around and below it."[12]

An experienced surgeon, therefore, Polanyi said, possesses an "ineffable [a nonexplicit or tacit] knowledge" of that region upon which he operates. Suppose, Polanyi said, we have unlimited time and patience and we cut a body into a thousand thin slices and depict each cross section in detail, and suppose a student should, "by a superhuman feat of cramming . . . memorize precisely the picture of all the thousand cross sections. He would know a set of data which fully determines the spatial arrangement of the organs of the body; yet he would not know that spatial arrangement itself," just as one who knew the longitudes and latitudes of all the towns in England would know what would determine the proper positions of these towns on a map of England, but he would not know or have that map. Nor would he have the information which such a map would tell him at a glance, but which he probably never could derive from positional data, e.g., various possible itineraries among these towns. He would have to construct such a map by exercising his imagination upon his positional data, and then study that. So a medical student, having constructed imaginatively the topography of the body, would be able to infer more about that body than could the hypothetical student crammed with all the explicit bits of data.[13]

Polanyi claimed that such "ineffable" knowledge operates in quite the same sort of way in taxonomy. He held that

> The basic performance of the taxonomist is actually practised every day without any scientific aid, whenever we identify a cat, a primrose or a man. Even animals have this capacity. . . .
>
> Common Law makes the crime of murder, and punishment for murder, dependent on the human shape of the individual whose death has been caused. It demands that through all its variations—caused by differences of age and race, by malformations and mutilations, or by ravaging disease—we should always identify the presence of the human shape. Nor does this demand seem excessive, since no case is known in which an accused has pleaded failure to recognize the human shape of an individual he had killed.
>
> Yet it would seem impossible to devise a definition which would unambiguously specify the range over which human shape may, and beyond which it may not, vary; and it is certain that those who recognize this shape are not in possession of any such explicit definition. Instead they have exercised their art of knowing by forming a conception of the human shape. They have trusted themselves to identify noticeably different instances of what—in spite of these differences—they judge to be the same features, and to discriminate in other cases between things which, in spite of some similarities, they judge to be instances of different features. Sustained by the belief that a human type exists, they have continued to build up their conception of it by noticing human beings as instances of this type. In doing this they have practised the kind of power used for generating a focal awareness of a comprehensive entity from a subsidiary awareness of its parts.[14]

Identification of particular instances of kinds apparently does, therefore, always entail a tacit dimension consisting of clues that we are aware
of only in the appearance of the object of our focal awareness: in this case,
the individual instance as a certain kind of thing. We really do not know
explicitly what all these subsidiary clues are and so we cannot tell them.
This is because we are dwelling *in* them rather than looking *at* them. But,
of course, there is another problem involved in our identification of
members of species or of kinds; this is the very concept of the class itself,
a problem to which Polanyi alluded toward the end of the passage quoted
above.

Polanyi pointed to Plato as the first to raise this problem. Plato
asked: How can things that differ in every particular nevertheless be
properly understood to be the same?[15] Somehow they share a joint
meaning. Yet it is hard to put our finger on just what this is. Polanyi did
not think that Plato's solution, supposing a world of real Ideas that these
instances imitate and that we remember dimly from a former life, was
very helpful in solving this problem.[16] But neither did Polanyi believe
that the attempts of many thinkers since Plato (including most of his own
contemporaries) were very adequate either. He claimed that we cannot
find one identical particular that is shared by every one of the acknowledged instances of a thing, to which we can merely point as objectively
the sine qua non for explicitly identifying any further instances of that
specific thing, and then hold that the exhibition of this particular is the
full meaning of that kind or species.

Polanyi said:

> Once a species is established it is usually defined by the presence of
> certain distinctive key features. But these key features themselves
> are variable in shape, and hence reference to them represents once
> more a claim to the identification of a typical shape in its variable
> instances. This was made clear at the Fifth International Botanical
> Congress, held in Cambridge in 1930, partly for the purpose of
> finding a definition for a species. The features of plants are charac-
> terized by different authors as "ovate, oval, patent, hirsute, cili-
> ate, . . ." but these authors may have quite different attributes in
> mind, said A. J. Wilmott. "The lanceolate of Linnaeus (he con-
> tinued) is very different from that of Lindley. . . . No two of my
> colleagues draw the same form of lanceolate."[17]

Polanyi held, in effect, that attempting to fasten upon some common feature as an explicit criterion for a species only duplicates the

problem, since this feature, itself, then becomes the joint meaning of a class of its own instances, all of which will themselves differ from each other in particulars, but all of which will nevertheless be "seen" somehow to be variables of this feature by everyone who possesses the skill to make such decisions. "The knowledge of key features is invaluable as a maxim for the identification of specimens," Polanyi admits, "but like all maxims it is useful only to those who possess the art of applying it."[18]

To try to avoid this impasse by supposing that the joint meaning of the instances of a class consists in a general conception, under which they all are subsumed, runs into the age-old difficulty of fixing specifically in mind just what this general conception is. Polanyi said that the problem involved in focussing upon such a general empirical conception seems to center "in the curiously *insubstantial character* of the joint meaning ascribed to a group of objects by a general term. Compared with optical illusions or stereoscopic images, general conceptions are abstract, featureless."[19] Universal man is neither tall nor short, fat nor thin, black nor white, etc., etc. Yet "man" is somehow all these things. "Man" is all that men ever have been or will be, and yet we cannot, for precisely this reason, quite bring this "man" into clear focus.[20] "The focus," he said, "in terms of which we are aware of members of a class appears vague and almost empty."[21]

Polanyi thought that this difficulty led to theories about universals that have attempted to reduce them to mere conventions, fictions, or words. The zeal for a strictly explicit knowledge pursued by twentieth-century positivists has induced them, he claimed, to want "to eliminate any reference to a tacit structure of meaning, which is necessarily mental" and therefore far from explicit. He said that Charles Morris' attempts "to identify the meaning of language in operational terms" and "Skinner's behaviorist representation of language" led up to "Quine's associationist definition of meaning."[22] Modern linguistics, Polanyi held, turned its "attention to the sound of language as best suited to an exact, objective investigation, . . . going beyond this only in the study of formal relations underlying the grammatical structure of language. The fact that language is nothing unless it has *conscious* meaning was set aside as a temporary difficulty for modern, strictly empirical linguistics." Attempts were made instead to identify meaning with certain explicit operations.[23]

Polanyi maintained that there is, however, no need to be afraid of the mental meaning of a universal. If we think of it as that which is supplied by a tacit integration of all the known instances of a class, treating these instances as subsidiary clues in which we dwell to see their joint meaning, we should not find the mental meaning of a universal much more mysterious than we find our perception of objects to be.[24] Moreover we need not be thrown into the sloughs of subjectivism or of conventionism. The joint meaning of a class that we mentally see, said Polanyi, "is something real" if it is "capable of yet manifesting itself indefinitely in the future."[25]

Such a joint meaning has, he maintained,

an [sic] heuristic power that is usually two-fold. (1) A universal concept usually anticipates the occurrence of further instances of itself in the future, and if the concept is true, it will validly subsume these future instances in spite of the fact that they will unpredictably differ in every particular from all the instances subsumed in the past. (2) A true universal concept, designating a natural class, for example a species of animals, anticipates that the members of the class will yet be found to share an indefinite range of uncovenanted properties; i.e., that the class will be found to have a yet unrevealed range of intension.[26]

It was just such a true and natural system of classification, Polanyi said, that Linnaeus sought in order to replace his own very useful but artificial system (a classification of plants according to the number and arrangement of stamens and carpels). He thought, said Polanyi, that a "Natural Classification" would be "the Alpha and Omega of Systematic Botany." Linnaeus held that artificial systems only served to distinguish one plant from another, but that "natural systems serve to teach the nature of plants."[27]

The efforts to develop such natural classifications was resumed a half century after Linnaeus, Polanyi informed us, by A. P. de Candolle for plants and by Lamarck and Cuvier for animals. Subsequent work, he pointed out, "has enormously expanded, but not changed fundamentally, the principles of natural classifications." In fact, Polanyi said, Darwin's *Origin of Species* revealed that this system had an even deeper meaning than its authors had ever clearly envisaged. The hierarchy of plants and animals was reinterpreted as branches of a family tree, the successive stages of which could be verified by paleontology.[28]

Present-day scientific taxonomy continues to order species in this manner and is able to fit in new species when they are discovered. The number now so catalogued makes it, in Polanyi's words, a "grandiose achievement,"[29] and "illustrates the most striking powers of tacit knowing." We are able to "focus our attention on the joint meaning of particulars, even when the focus upon which we are attending has no tangible center."[30] Thus, through tacit knowing, we are able to know realities that are other than tangible objects. For surely the classes developed by the biologists, although not tangible objects, are as real as rocks, inasmuch as they have manifested themselves in their own future and have proven able to surprise us with even deeper meanings as time has passed.[31]

Thus according to Polanyi, the conception of a real class is built up from our integration of tacitly known instances of this class, and it continues to be built up and modified, he told us, by our continually noticing such instances. The "standards of normality"—the foci of each class of things, the concepts of which the class is composed—"are somewhat modified," he held, "every time a specimen is appraised . . . to make them approximate more closely to what is normal for the species. These standards are themselves subject to appraisal by the biologist. He will regard some species as well-defined, others as uncertain or altogether spurious."[32] And we must note, Polanyi added, that the process he uses is

> not a statistical observation. Statistics can refer only to measurable parameters varying within a given population. Taxonomy judges non-measurable combinations of qualities within a population selected by the taxonomist himself with a view to the presence of these qualities. Nor is it even true that what is widespread is considered normal. Perfectly normal—as distinct from malformed or mutilated—specimens of a species may be the rarest.[33]

Here we see that identification of members of a species and knowledge of the meaning of this species were understood by Polanyi to be tacit acts reciprocally affecting each other as experience unfolds. When they are successful in delineating a natural species, they continue to reinforce and to inform each other in the form they have achieved. But even then neither of them can be reduced to explicit marks, maxims, or rules in order to continue thereafter to operate automatically without benefit of anyone's personal appraisal. Maxims and rules, he reminded us, elevate our insight into a skill but "would instantly condemn themselves to absurdity if they tried to replace the golfer's skill or the poet's art. Maxims cannot be understood, still less applied by anyone not already possessing a good practical knowledge of the art. . . . [They] can function only . . within a framework of personal judgment."[34]

Consequently the identification of each instance as one of a type is understood by Polanyi to be an act of tacit knowing. In this identification all the clues provided by the particulars of that instance, when dwelt in by a person, become integrated by him into a focal meaning into which all the instances he knows of become integrated, when dwelt in by him as subsidiary clues to the formation of a focal class concept. No finite number of the particulars, viewed focally with an eye toward matching them up can serve in the place of such a both conscious and subliminal act integrating them all.

Besides, even when a "natural" class has been achieved, further experience with acknowledged instances may, as Polanyi says, reveal deeper joint meanings than we had hitherto suspected. In fact, revealing deeper meanings is precisely what we expect real things to do. And this capacity of a scientific object to reveal deeper meanings is the reason why Polanyi held that an operational concept of science, in which the meaning of one's terms are supposed to consist only in their implications, their truths lying only in some formal manner of testing these, is unequal to what science really aspires to, namely, a grasp of realities that are always expected to contain more than the logical implications we can milk from any possible explicitly formalized concepts of them. For, said Polanyi, since "the truth of a proposition lies in its bearing on reality," its implications are indeterminate and cannot be spelled out. Such is the nature of what we mean by the "real." It is what may manifest itself in yet indeterminate ways. And so what our concept bears upon—what our concept really means—is indeterminate, and thus richer than any formal structure we could give to our concept of it at any one time. In other words, the meaning of our concept is that upon which it bears, which is always expected to be something other and more than our concept.[35]

Yet, Polanyi told us, in spite of these remarkable feats of tacit knowing that have enabled us to comprehend immense numbers of natural classes of plants and animals, classical taxonomy has almost ceased to count as a science. The explanation of such denigration lies, he thought, in "a change in the valuation of knowledge . . . a growing reluctance to credit ourselves with the capacity for personal knowing and a corresponding unwillingness to recognize the reality of the unspecifiable entities" established by such knowing.[36]

"Taxonomy," he said, "is based on connois[s]eurship." He quoted

C. F. A. Pantin's description of how a new species of worm is discovered:

> by a peculiar feeling of discomfort that something is not quite right, followed by a sudden detection of the error and simultaneous realization that it is highly significant—"It is a *Rhynchodemus* all right, but it is *not bilineatus*—it is an entirely new species!"

Pantin, said Polanyi, considered this intuitive mode of identification, which he called "aesthetic recognition" in contrast to a more systematic sort based on key features, to be the predominant mode in field work.[37]

Yet the exercise of such skills today is not highly regarded in scientific opinion. Both the knowledge and the subject matter established by such skills are disparaged by being regarded as the results of "merely subjective imaginings." Polanyi recalled that, "When the members of the Fifth International Botanical Congress declared that 'the concept of most species must rest on the judgement and experience of the individual taxonomist,' they invited criticism along these lines. S. C. Harland, for instance, said that he recalled how in Shaw's *Fanny's First Play* the dramatic critic replied, in answer to a question about whether or not the play was good, 'that if the play was by a good author, then it was a good play.' 'The situation would appear to be somewhat similar,' writes Harland, 'in regard to what constitutes a species'."[38]

Polanyi said the answer to this criticism lies behind the Shavian joke. "Just as plays written by good authors are, as a rule (though, of course, not always) good plays, so species described by good systematists are as a rule good species . . . good playwrights and good systematists alike enjoy considerable authority." The rules by which they both work and by which their work is judged are extremely delicate and altogether unspecifiable. You can repudiate the authority of such persons, said Polanyi, only if you refuse to accept any such unspecifiable knowledge. But you then wipe out the very conception of a good playwright or a good systematist—and also renounce the very possibility of knowing a good play or a good species.[39]

Of course, Polanyi continued, "distaste for the inexactitude of systematic morphology," expressed by people like Professor Harland, does not extend to "denying the existence of different animals and plants of typical shapes and structures." Rather, such biologists "only wish to recast the concept of species in the more impersonal terms of genetics."

The "geno-species" which they would prefer to accept "would be formed by a world population of an organism, where there is—or is at least believed to be—a potentiality for an exchange of chromosomal material throughout the entire population."[40]

Polanyi pointed out, however, that the genetic investigation of a population would presuppose its morphological distinctness. It is difficult enough, he held, and often quite impracticable, to observe the outcome of interbreeding within a given population selected by morphological distinctness. But to undertake such genetic experiments irrespective of morphological differences (such as attempting to interbreed flies and elephants), "with the intention of establishing from these alone the boundaries of specificity, would be absurd." No one even contemplates this.[41]

And so, Polanyi said, "It all comes down to this. If you want to bring order into the multitudes of animals and plants on earth, you must first of all look at them." To apply any test for identifying and discriminating the many thousands of millions of insects swarming over the earth without paying attention to their characteristic shapes and markings would obviously be impossible. "Projects for the application of . . . more objective, taxonomic tests, have all set themselves their tasks *within* the existing morphological system." They merely want "to understand it better by bringing to bear upon it the methods of other branches of biology . . . of anatomy, physiology, histology, ecology, phyto- and zoo-geography, etc." They do not really try, he said, to supplant "Natural History in favour of a system based on objective tests. Yet the deprecation of the original conception of Natural History as a contemplative, rather than an analytical, achievement persists throughout modern biology."[42]

Polanyi added, however, that "the joy of seeing animals and plants and of entering into their forms of existence, by carefully studying their shapes and behaviour," is certainly not extinct among naturalists of our time.

He quoted K. Z. Lorenz:

I confidently assert (he writes) that no man, even if he were endowed with a superhuman patience, could physically bring himself to stare at fishes, birds or mammals, as persistently as is necessary in order to take stock of the behaviour patterns of a species, unless his eyes were bound to the object of his observation in that spellbound gaze which is not motivated by any conscious effort to gain knowledge, but by that mysterious charm that the beauty of living creatures works on some of us![43]

Biology, said Polanyi, derives its value ultimately from the intrinsic interest in living things generally shared by humans. "Experimental studies made on animals and plants remain meaningless except through their bearing on animals and plants as known to us by ordinary experience and through Natural History"—in other words, as given to us through our tacit ability to recognize specific shapes, patterns, and types in and among the particular differences of individuals and to dwell in these shapes and behaviors as subsidiary clues to a focal knowledge of this kind of being, this species.[44]

Polanyi admitted, of course, that the scientific study of a subject matter may justifiably destroy the interest we originally had in it, if it proves that the matter is in fact illusory. Astronomy, growing out of astrology, eventually proved astrology to be illusory. Chemistry, growing out of alchemy, eventually proved alchemy to be illusory. "If experimental biology could," he said, also "discredit the existence of animals and plants . . . prove that their alleged typical shapes and their systematic classifications are illusory—in the sense in which the shapes of constellations are illusory—then experimental biology might indeed supersede Natural History and be studied for its own sake, without bearing on Natural History," as astronomy and chemistry are now studied for their own sakes and not for their bearing upon astrology or alchemy. He thought this would be foolish, but consistent. But this is not actually done, he said.

> Instead, we meet with the typical device of modern intellectual prevarication, first systematized by Kant in his regulative principles. Knowledge that we hold to be true and also vital to us, is made light of, because we cannot account for its acceptance in terms of a critical philosophy. We then feel entitled to continue using that knowledge, even while flattering our sense of intellectual superiority by disparaging it. And we actually go on, firmly relying on this despised knowledge to guide and lend meaning to our more exact inquiries, while pretending that these alone come up to our standards of scientific stringency.[45]

Such a denial of contemplative value in science would, he said, if consistently carried out, cut biology off from the intellectual passions from which it takes its origin—our intrinsic interest in living things—and biology could not then stop short of denying scientific reality altogether "to the beings in which life manifests itself." He thought biology may, of course, continue to flourish vigorously, as have other branches of science, in spite of such nonsensical notions, "by wisely disregarding its own professed philosophy." But that it will continue to disregard its own professed philosophy cannot, he held, be altogether relied upon.[46]

The explicit operationalism that seemed then to Polanyi to be currently most acceptable to scientists as a philosophy of science, at least on paper, unfortunately often sets as its goal just such a reductionism as Polanyi called absurd. Such reductionism has by no means since died out. Scientists who follow out such a program are restive with the classifications of experiential phenomena, those making up what Polanyi calls "Natural History." They wish to regard such classifications as, at best, only illusory first steps on the way to truly positive knowledge; that is, knowledge derived from or through the use of instruments that respond to motion and energy changes. This sort of knowledge derived from such instruments seems obviously objective and impersonal to them. Instruments simply read what they do read. Personal appraisal—connoisseurship—is thought to have nothing to do with it. Biology would thus not be a real science to them until it had been totally reduced to the quantitative changes that physics and chemistry so instrumentalized can give us, and until it has stopped regarding frogs and oak trees as primary entities whose shapes and ways are something more than the ephemeral results of various physical and chemical equilibrations.

It was quite obvious to Polanyi, having himself been a research physical chemist for many years, that a very great amount of modern science does proceed by and through its instruments, and that such instruments must always yield quantitative results, not qualitative ones. Yet he pointed out that this sort of instrumentalized, quantitative knowledge also depends throughout upon tacit coefficients. It, too, is the product of unspecifiable skills and is not the purely detached and objective "information" that it is usually assumed to be. He called our attention to the fact that students of science must learn how to use these scientific instruments. Even reading them "correctly" is a skill that requires much practice under a master and, when learned, cannot simply be told to others. In this sense the use of such purely quantitative scientific instruments is also a skill—in some respects, perhaps, even a connoisseurship. [47]

But, in addition to the fact that instruments do not read themselves but can only be read—by connoisseurs—it appears that the "exact" and quantitative results achieved by the reading of such instruments are meaningful only in terms of the particular theories and general notions about the nature of things that function as subsidiary clues dwelt in by the minds of those scientists who make use of these results. Exact, quantitative, even machine-recorded observations, without mentalistic interpretations, would not, in Polanyi's view, operate either to substantiate or to refute any given hypothesis—much less to generate one. He reminded us of what Werner Heisenberg says he once told Einstein. He informed Einstein that in shaping his quantum theory, "he [Heisenberg] proposed to go back from Nils Bohr's theory to quantities that could really be observed." Einstein, Heisenberg relates, rejoined that "the truth lay the other way round. He said: 'Whether you can observe a thing or not depends on the theory which you use. It is the theory which decides what can be observed.' "[48]

Max Planck also, Polanyi said, rejected the claim that one can deal with the merely observable "on the grounds that science is a theory bearing on observations, but never including observations." Planck declared, said Polanyi, "there exists absolutely no physical magnitude which can be measured in itself."[49]

Polanyi provided many examples in his works of how accepted theories affect the interpretations of observations, and indeed affect their very acceptance or rejection as observations. He recounted in one of his examples how the famous experiment of Michelson and Morley, which demonstrated the absence of ether drift and eventually formed the main experimental support for Einstein's relativity theories, was considered a failure by Michelson himself. It was also regarded, Polanyi claimed, as a "real disappointment" by Kelvin and Rayleigh "and Sir Oliver Lodge even said [it] might have to be explained away." The observed results of this experiment were distrusted, Polanyi held, because the ether theory was so firmly supported by the current interpretation of physics. Twenty-five years later, Polanyi recalled, D. C. Miller repeated the experiment with improved instruments and showed the *presence* of an ether drift. But these results were now in their turn rejected, because relativity theory had by this time overthrown the ether theory![50]

From considerations such as these Polanyi early concluded that the positivistic interpretation of science was a disastrous mistake. He clearly saw that there do not exist either the "pure" observations that such an interpretation would require, nor do there exist any strict rules "for discovering things that hang together in nature, nor even for telling whether we should accept or reject an apparent coherence as a fact." Science simply does not present us with any such rules. Rather, he maintained, it shows itself to be grounded throughout on acts of personal judgment. Scientific knowing is, he said, "a kind of integration of parts to whole . . . the outcome of deliberate integration revealing a hitherto hidden real entity."[51]

> To sum up: Science is the result of an integration, similar to that of common perception. It establishes hitherto unknown coherences in nature. Our recognition of these coherences is largely based, as perception is, on clues of which we are not focally aware and which are indeed often unidentifiable. Current conceptions of science about the nature of things always affect our recognition of coherence in nature. From the sighting of a problem to the ultimate decision of rejecting still conceivable doubts, factors of plausibility are ever in our minds. This is what is meant by saying that, strictly speaking, all natural science is an expression of personal judgment.[52]

Thus science, too, even in its toughest, most instrumental form, was a "dwelling in" for Polanyi. He held that, in addition to the clues, conscious and subliminal, in which we dwell in a subsidiary fashion in making our perceptions, we also dwell in our theories, and in the other notions about how things are which lie at the back of our minds, as we construct our hypotheses, arrange our experiments, make our observations, and render our judgments about what all these things "prove."[53] All empirical science is thus, he claimed, inexact. None of it is purely objective or detached. It is necessarily shot through and through with personal commitments and personal judgments in which the participants must dwell, and in which anyone who is to understand a theory or a scientific fact or a proposition about nature must also dwell.

It would seem clear, therefore, that Polanyi held that men can make sense of the operations of scientific instruments, both in their design and in their use, only when they are dwelling in these instruments (as, once again, a blind man dwells in his cane) and thus using them as extensions of themselves toward the objects of their attention in nature. But it would also seem clear that the sophisticated character of these instruments must mean that men can only dwell in them by dwelling in the theories and general notions that make sense of the use and even of the design of these instruments. Observation of the heavens by means of astronomical instruments, for instance, surely tells little or nothing to the unskilled and astronomically ignorant layman who might attempt to look through or at such instruments. And this would be true even had he happened to have read about the way these instruments are used and about the theories lying behind their use. For if this were all he knew of these instruments, he would still lack the skill to use them that comes only with practice, that is, the part of the knowledge of their use which is tacit and unspecifiable. And he would also, at best, know only the explicitly conceptual aspects, that is, the most obvious applications, of the theories that inform the use of these instruments. He would remain unaware of the myriads of tacit elements[54] that lie at the back of the mind of the "acculturated" astronomer when he brings these theories to bear in a subsidiary way upon the focal realities on which the community of astronomers intend their science to bear.

Thus Polanyi made a thorough examination of our most trusted mode for establishing a cognitive beachhead among the welter of our perceptions, viz., the "scientific" mode, and showed that it makes use of the same kind of integrative action that perceptions do, namely, a dwelling in an unspecifiable conglomeration of subsidiary clues that we bring to bear upon the object of our focal attention.

In his words:

I am interpreting the formation of class concepts (along with the discovery of natural laws) as based ultimately on a process of tacit knowing, the operations of which I have exemplified in the learning of skills, the recognition of physiognomies, the mastery of tests, the use of tools, the uttering of speech, and the act of visual perception. The powers of integration which achieve these acts have the same structure throughout.[55]

We have in this chapter followed his demonstration of this point with regard specifically to the scientific identification of individuals as members of species and classes and with regard to some of the problems involved in scientific induction. But, since the problems of induction and identification of kinds are also the two cornerstones of any theory of empirical cognition in general, i.e., of any theory of cognition that roots conceptual constructions in perceptions, we have also been observing how Polanyi moved his new epistemology of perception into problems of conceptual cognition, as such, even as he laid his foundation for a restructured philosophy of science.

Let us in the next two chapters see how Polanyi used these foundations to build a full philosophy of science restructured in terms of his prescriptive needs.

# CHAPTER SEVEN

# Discovery

The major element in Michael Polanyi's prescription for the ills of the modern mind was a revised philosophy of science. He thought a false idea of science has left us with a skepticism about the nature of man and his works. We must, therefore, revise the one to restore the other.[1]

In the last chapter we have seen how Polanyi connected certain crucial aspects of scientific knowing—scientific induction and concepts of classes—to his epistemology of tacit knowing, accounting for them as complex focal integrations of dwelt-in subsidiary clues. These tacit integrations, he held, are not in a general sense different from those making up perceptions and skilled performances. In fact, what the scientist achieves, according to Polanyi, is a very sophisticated kind of perception that makes use of—dwells in—many uncommonly held subsidiary clues. These are based on the currently fashionable general views of the nature of things accepted either explicitly or implicitly by that community of inquirers to which the particular scientist belongs, as well as his own specific theories, special instruments, and tacit skills.[2] Of all of which laymen may be quite innocent.

Polanyi's dynamic view of science is a far cry from formal theories about inductive logic and about the logical structure of science or of scientific method that have had a long development, from Bacon and Hume through Mill to the logically obsessed philosophers of science in our own twentieth century. Polanyi by-passed past efforts at accounting for induction in a formal or explicit manner, as well as the more involved and intricate endeavors to reduce the method of science to a logic of explicit or formal verification, or, in the last stages of Popperian despair, to a formal logic of falsification. These proliferating problems, of course, could not arise in Polanyi's position, and so he did not deal with them in his writings—which is one reason contemporary philosophers of science have largely ignored him. Anyhow, according to Polanyi, these later efforts tended to leave completely to one side the proper problem of scientific induction, namely, a philosophical account of the origin of those hypotheses that such a formal logic of verification—or of falsification—was supposed to bring to an objective and explicit test. This proper problem, the origin of hypotheses, tended to be relegated by these later efforts to psychological or sociological or historical *causes* and hence not to be regarded as part of the formal structure of science. But Polanyi thought that it was rather such a rational or logical account of the origin of hypotheses which was the crucial problem. For, as he said, hypotheses (particularly those created by good scientists) proved to be on the right track far too often to be the results of mere chance trial and error or of nonheuristically oriented, nonrational psychological or sociological factors.[3]

An analysis of the process of discovery thus for Polanyi became the core of a proper philosophy of science. He believed that discovery was what scientists had always sought. Copernicus, Polanyi reminded us, was not trying to find a logically simpler way of describing the phenomena presented by the heavens. His theory was not, in fact, any more successful in describing this phenomenon than Ptolemy's, and not really simpler. For a whole century after his death no differences in predictability could be found between these two theories. Copernicus understood that his discovery amounted to a new and truer vision of *reality*. He and his followers continually rejected the notion that their theories were only new mathematical devices for computing the apparent positions of the heavenly bodies. They understood their theories to be describing real positions of real bodies.[4] Kepler, Galileo, Dalton, Newton, the whole line of eminent scientists down to our own Bohr, Planck, Heisenberg, and Einstein, were all endeavoring, Polanyi claimed, to discover various aspects of reality, not simply more elegant logical correlations of phenomenal data.[5]

It is therefore the heuristic processes of science that must form the basis for a real philosophy of science, Polanyi held. Not only must the question of verification or falsification of hypotheses be dealt with, but also, and more especially, the origin of hypotheses. Michael Polanyi was emphasizing the problem of discovery as the crucial problem in the philosophy of science, and seeking to account for it as part of the method of science, long before people like Kuhn and Hanson began to call into question the strict formalization of "the scientific method."

As early as 1946, in his first edition of *Science, Faith and Society,* Polanyi focused upon the scientific discovery of hidden realities as the main problem in understanding science. He sought to discern the informal method for uncovering these realities, exhibiting little or no interest in rules for verification and refutation, as he said, not because such rules do not exist, but because "there are none which can be relied on in the last resort."[6]

In his *Logic of Liberty,* published in 1951 but consisting of articles published during the 1940s, the picture that we get of the conduct of science focuses our attention upon discovery as the center and core of science. In fact, since this is so and there are no explicit rules for making a discovery and since no discoveries can be made "without creative passion," the individual scientist cannot be directed in his work by other authorities. Science must be free from external direction. It must be self-governing.[7]

The same notion of the importance and nonformal nature of discovery in science runs through other early articles of his concerning science published from 1947 to 1957. By 1958 Polanyi had completed and published *Personal Knowledge,* rejecting comprehensively and completely the formalization of scientific knowing.

His later articles pertaining to science[8] and his book, *The Tacit Dimension,* show how the whole range of scientific activities becomes coherent in the light of his notion of tacit knowing, thereby integrating his philosophy of science into a general epistemology that accounts for science as an intelligible extension of the informal logic that structures perception and cognition in general. In this way of proceeding the informal aspects of science do not become sources of sticky problems crying for resolution but parts of the very essence of scientific achievements.[9]

To begin at the beginning, the primary requisite of a good scientist, Polanyi said, is his capacity to discover good problems—good problems that are not, of course, beyond his resources to solve.[10]

Now, a good problem is one that will lead to great and original discoveries. But there seems to be a paradox involved in the very notion of a "good problem," a paradox that Polanyi told us Plato first pointed out in the *Meno*. To search for the solution to a problem, Plato told us there, would seem to be absurd, since, if you know what you are looking for, then there is no problem. If you do not know what you are looking for, then you cannot expect to find anything. Polanyi maintained this was a genuine paradox, because "to see a problem is to see something that is hidden. It is to have an intimation of the coherence of hitherto not comprehended particulars." Yet in spite of the apparent contradiction involved in claiming to be able to see a problem, pointed out by Plato long ago, Polanyi noted that people have continued for two thousand years to see and to solve many problems. What the *Meno* really shows, therefore, said Polanyi, is not that knowing a problem is impossible (as indeed Plato also thought it did not show) but "that if all knowledge is explicit, i.e., capable of being clearly stated, then we cannot know a problem or look for its solution."[11] Since we apparently do know good problems that can be solved, knowing a problem must be, he held, a kind of tacit knowledge, like the knowledge we have of a face or a class, a knowledge of which we cannot give a fully explicit account, but which nonetheless does exist. He thought this, and not a realm of real ideas, was the true solution of the paradox.

Polanyi thought the intimations we have of a problem are akin to the intimations we have of the fruitfulness of any discovery that we come to accept as the solution to a problem. Somehow we are able to appreciate the wealth of its yet undiscovered consequences. We cannot know these explicitly, of course, for no one does as yet; but we have an anticipatory grasp of them. He thought that this kind of "foreknowledge" must have been what the Copernicans had when "before Newton proved the point" they passionately affirmed that their heliocentric theory was really true. But, Polanyi reasoned, since it is the wealth of these indeterminate future possibilities (because the "real" always possesses such a wealth of future possibilities) that would admittedly be a sign of the truth of a scientific theory,[12] and since we have no explicit knowledge of such still unknown things, we can therefore have no explicit justification for a scientific truth. Our certification of its truth—its "verification"—must always be a commitment which is itself due to an act of tacit knowing, i.e., to a projected vision achieved by dwelling in subsidiary clues (some of them explicitly unknown or even unknow*able* to us). Moreover, this projected vision, like that involved in perceiving a face or a class concept, is understood by us to be a projection to a reality, a reality that we know only through our indwelling of its parts, and that we therefore cannot tell wholly or explicitly how we know. In our pursuit of this discovery, Polanyi said, "we are guided by sensing the presence of a hidden reality toward which our clues are pointing; and the discovery which terminates and satisfies this pursuit is still sustained by the same vision."[13]

Therefore Polanyi maintained that "all knowledge is of the same kind as the knowledge of a problem" and we "must conclude that the paradigmatic case of scientific knowledge, in which all the faculties that are necessary for finding and holding scientific knowledge are fully developed, is *the knowledge of an approaching discovery.*"[14]

Our vision claims to have made contact with reality. This claim is the same as our belief in it. Thus, although our vision is personal, i.e., it involves deep conviction and the very personality of the person who holds it, and although it is also, as a rule, solitary, it is not self-indulgent. The discoverer is imbued with a sense of responsibility for the pursuit of a hidden *truth*. His knowing exercises a personal judgment in relating evidence to an external reality, and thus is undertaken with what Polanyi called a "universal intent."[15]

Polanyi was careful to point out that he meant to say not that our vision is always of a universal truth, but rather that it always has universal intent. Since, if we believe the vision, we believe that it has made contact with reality, we believe that anyone else equipped as we are, and looking where and as we look, ought also to see what we see. This does not mean that everyone else always will do so: our vision may indeed be wrong. But yet it is not certified as right even if everyone else does see what we see; nor is it certified as wrong if no one else is able to see what we see. It is right only if it does make contact with reality, and wrong only if it does not. But there are no irrefutable, explicit signs that say objectively that it has or that it has not made contact with reality. Our conviction that it has done so is always a fiduciary conviction, as are also the convictions of other people seeking to evaluate our vision.[16]

But, as he said, our conviction, if it is honest, is never willful nor self-indulgent, because it is held responsibly with reference to our intention of relating ourselves to a reality, a reality that others also may relate themselves to. In other words, all our honest convictions possess a genuinely universal intent and thus are knowledge, for what we hold with universal intent to be true, we hold to be knowledge.

Knowledge is therefore always personal knowledge. And this "personal knowledge" bridges the gap, Polanyi held, between subjectivity and objectivity. There is no purely objective knowledge, because nothing can be called knowledge that is not personally accredited as knowledge. Facts do not force themselves upon us. What we call "facts" always involve our judgment (with some degree of risk) that something *is* a fact. What is acknowledged as a fact is, of course, something in which we must believe. But it is so acknowledged because we first do, in fact, believe it.[17] Polanyi claimed that St. Augustine was right, therefore, to say that he believes in order that he may know. Polanyi held, however, that this is true for all sorts of knowledge—the scientific included—not just for religious knowledge.[18]

In a different way, subjective knowledge would also be a contradiction in terms. The purely subjective has reference only to the person involved. It lacks universal intent and is known to do so.[19] If I say I am in love with a certain woman, or that I like garlic, I am not stating a fact about the qualities of these entities that are public realities that anyone else ought to be able to see, if only he looks at them with my equipment; since he cannot have such equipment. The equipment he would need would be the exact identical person that I am.

Personal knowledge thus destroys the abstract dichotomy of the subjective–objective. It combines these opposed polarities and is thus the only kind of knowledge existentially possible.[20] Polanyi's book, *Personal Knowledge,* redrew in a wealth of detail the whole *speculum mentis* in terms of this principle.

Since Polanyi admitted that any particular anticipation of discovery, like discovery itself, may turn out to be a delusion,[21] he was not claiming that there is some mystical connection with reality established by an act of faith, such that every act of faith, every belief or commitment, must be true. Or that what we believe is true always is true, simply because we believe it, as if "true" and "believe to be true" were identical terms. Whether or not reality has some power of drawing our minds to it is a question Polanyi entertained but upon which he made no firm decision.[22] Rather, he concentrated on attempting to show how these visions of problems, of discoveries, of classes, of performances, etc., result from our very natural capacity for imagination and intuition, operating in the context of subsidiary and focal awareness. "The surmises of a working scientist are," he said, *"born of the imagination seeking discovery."*[23]

As to the source of energy for our potential imaginative powers, Polanyi told us that the creative thrust of the imagination is fed from various sources. He mentioned the beauty of the anticipated discovery and the excitement of its solitary achievement. He even mentioned ambition for professional success. These motivating forces do not appear to be very occult or mysterious. [24]

Release of these forces is also partially dependent, in his view, on a fairly mundane economic decision. "When the imagination goes into action to start a scientific inquiry," he explained, "it not only becomes more intense, but also more concrete, more specific. Although the target toward which it thrusts is yet empty, it is seen to lie in a definite direction." Consequently, when the problem is adopted, its pursuit must rely on resources felt to be available in a particular direction. These will include such ordinary considerations as the amount of labor and money needed. "No problem may be undertaken unless we feel that its possible solution would be worth the probable expense." These perceptive anticipations of feasibility are neither the result of strict rules nor of chance, he held, nor are they guaranteed by any wealth of learning. Yet no scientist can survive unless his anticipations of feasibility are sufficiently adequate to meet with reasonable success. [25]

A scientist needs exceptional gifts, it is true, in order to succeed. But still these gifts are of the same kind as those that underlie even the mere use of speech. They are actually, he held, those at work in every deliberate action. They are not magical. "They are intrinsic to the dynamics of all from–to knowledge down to the simplest acts of tacit knowing." [26]

Polanyi told us how he thought the imagination works. He said it thrusts forward at each stage of an inquiry, guided by a sense of potential resources. It "batters" its path by mobilizing these resources, consolidating them occasionally in specific surmises. These surmises then tentatively fill up the hitherto empty form of the problem. Thus, these surmises are heuristic probings and should not be viewed as well-defined hypotheses that the scientist will proceed to test methodically in a neutral or even a critical spirit. He believes in them and they absorb his energies. But they are not formal proposals for a solution. They are hunches that often only narrow down the originally wide program of inquiry. They may be exciting and turn out to be crucial; but they are more indeterminate by far than the final discovery turns out to be. Their indeterminacy ranges somewhere between the width of the original problem and the narrowness of its eventual solution. [27]

Theories of scientific "method" that ignore this whole fluid mechanism of tacit knowing, Polanyi said, deny the existence of the passionate personal commitments to one's own surmises that characterize the working scientist. The efforts that lead to his surmises commit every fiber of his being. His surmises embody all his hopes. It is thus a caricature to regard the tentativeness of his early steps as evidence that he is uncommitted. Every step he takes is actually definitive, Polanyi maintained, in the vital sense that it definitely disposes of the time, effort, and material resources used in making the step. These investments inexorably add up to the scientist's whole professional life—and to his ultimate success or failure. He does not therefore cheerfully try this and then that, calmly changing his course at each failure, as though he were engaged in a parlor game merely for passing the time.[28]

Thus in Polanyi's view a scientist is always committed to his own vision of reality. It is no less than himself that he places on the line when he works in certain directions rather than in others. He therefore always tries to prove his theories—never to *dis*prove them. He is not even neutral with respect to his own efforts. Yet he is and must be responsible to the truth. If he is a good scientist, it is because, first of all, his visions of reality are often enough sufficiently true to lead to critical problems and fruitful discoveries, not because he sets out to destroy his own hypotheses or to operate according to some formally "correct" set of rules for scientific inquiry. Polanyi held that because these visions are imaginative creations,[29] tacitly achieved and not specifiable in wholly explicit terms, there is no specific method or recipe for making good discoveries—or good scientists—that is, there are not such and so many explicit steps or rules to follow. Rather, a good scientist must be a genius.

But a genius, like a problem, is also a paradox. Genius, said Polanyi, is understood to involve inspiration, something like the gift of an idea that seems to visit a genius, to come to him—almost always as a surprise. Yet we also understand creative pursuits to be extremely strenuous, to involve hard work and infinite pains. Is there, he asked, a particular sort of hard work that will induce an inspiration to visit us? How can we, who produce an inspiration, be surprised by it? How can we not know from what corner it may come, when we are trying so hard to conjure it up?[30]

"The solution," he held, "can be found on a biological level, if we identify inspiration with 'spontaneous integration' and look out for the effort that induces such integration." He pointed out that when I move my arm to reach for an object, my intention sets in motion a complex integration of my muscles, an integration that carries out my purpose. Since my intention is about something that does not yet exist, it is a project I can conceive of only by my imagination. So it would seem that it is imagination that induces a muscular integration to implement a project that, in my imagination, I form an intent to accomplish. I cannot find an act of will that stands in my mind prior to every deliberate or voluntary motion I make. [31]

We can call spontaneous this integration of muscles and nerves, Polanyi said, since we have no direct control over it. We can induce this integration, or cause it to happen, by an effort of our imagination. But we cannot perform it in the sense of deliberately controlling the integration of each clue. One cannot hit a golf ball by focusing upon all the proprioceptive elements in the swing, relating them specifically and deliberately in a correct way to each other in a deliberate performance. [32] These reflections suggest, Polanyi thought, that "inspiration is evoked by the labours of the thrusting imagination and that it is this kind of imaginative labour that evokes the new ideas by which scientific discoveries are made." [33]

But there would seem to be two elements operating here, one deliberate and one spontaneous. Polanyi carefully sorted them out. He found Henri Poincaré's ideas, expressed in his *Science et Méthode* (1908), very suggestive. In the first stage, Poincaré claimed we rack our brains by successive sallies of the imagination. In the second, sometimes occurring hours after we have ceased our effort, the idea we have been looking for makes its spontaneous appearance. Poincaré told us that this spontaneous process is the integration of some of the material mobilized by thrusts of the imagination. [34]

Polanyi held that it seems plausible therefore to assume that two faculties of the mind are at work jointly from the beginning to the end of an approaching discovery. One is the deliberately active powers of the imagination, and the other a spontaneous process of integration which we may call "intuition." He thought it is this intuition that senses the presence of hidden resources for solving a problem and launches the imagination in its pursuit. Intuition also forms our surmises and eventually selects from the material mobilized by the imagination the relevant pieces of evidence and then integrates them into solutions. [35]

The powers of such a dynamic intuition, Polanyi thought, are the feelings of a "deepening coherence" we have all along the way to a discovery. He held the mechanism of this power can be illuminated by an analogy. In physics we speak of potential energy that is released when a weight slides down a slope. Our search for deeper coherence is guided likewise by a potentiality: "We feel the slope toward a deeper insight as we feel the direction in which a heavy weight is pulled along a steep incline."[36] In this way, he thought, the paradox of the *Meno* is solved. We can pursue scientific discovery without knowing explicitly what we are looking for, because the gradient of deepening coherence tells us where to start and which way to turn, "and eventually we come to where we may stop and claim a discovery."[37] So Polanyi claimed it is intuition that tells us what to look for along the way. But he cautioned us he did not mean by "intuition" a supreme immediate knowledge à la Leibniz or Spinoza or Husserl. Rather, he said, it is a skill for guessing with a reasonable chance of guessing right, a skill guided by an innate sensibility to coherence, which can even be improved by schooling.

But to know in this intuitive, tacit, and unspecifiable way, what to look for does not give us the power to find it. The power to find it lies, he claimed, in our imagination, that is, in our power to form "all thoughts of things that are not present, or not yet present—or perhaps never to be present." He said that the dual structure of deliberate movement, first described by William James as the conscious intention of a movement in the imagination over which we have control, and its muscular performance over which we do not, is analogous to the dual structure of discovery described above, and that it corresponds to the two kinds of awareness present in perception. We may form, in focal awareness, an image of, say, lifting our arm, and find that this image is then implemented by an integration of subsidiary muscular particulars required to lift our arm.[38] Should our focal resolve meet with difficulties in performance, our imagination sallies forth to close that gap between intention and performance. We may say then, paradoxically, that we learn to ride a bicycle by falling off it, even as we "learn" a discovery by finding a problem we do not know how to solve.

Our imagination may strive for years to reduce such gaps between our intentions and our performances. It will be persistent, deliberate, and transitive. But always, he wrote,

> directed on ourselves: *it attempts to make us produce ideas*. We may say then that we are racking our brain, or ransacking our brain; that we are cudgeling or cracking it, or beating our brain to get it to work.

And the action induced in us by this ransacking is felt as something that is happening to us. We say that we tumble to an idea; or that it crosses our mind; or that it comes into our head; or that it strikes us, or dawns on us, or just presents itself to us. We are actually surprised and exclaim "Aha."[39]

So discovery is made

in two moves: one deliberate, the other spontaneous—the spontaneous move being evoked in ourselves by the action of our deliberate effort. The deliberate is the focal act of the imagination, while the spontaneous response to it, which brings discovery, belongs to the same class as the spontaneous coordination of muscles responding to our intention to lift our arm, or the spontaneous coordination of visual clues in response to our looking at something. This spontaneous act of discovery deserves to be recognized pre-eminently as the creative intuition.[40]

Our creative imagination is thus, said Polanyi, "imbued" with our creative intuition. Imagination stimulates and releases the powers of intuition by imposing upon intuition a feasible task. Still, imagination is guided by our intuition in its intimation of the feasibility of a problem and in its engagement in pursuit. So imagination sets actively before us the focal point to be aimed at, but it is intuition that supplies our imagination with the organization of subsidiary clues to accomplish its focal goal, as well as the initial assessments of the feasibility of this goal. Intuition thus guides our imagination. "Sallies of the imagination that have no such guidance are," he said, "idle fancies."[41]

It is finally also intuition, Polanyi believed, that recognizes our ultimate results to be valid. But then our imagination immediately starts to work again, pointing to the inexhaustible future manifestations of these results.[42] It thus starts another cycle of problems and discoveries. One of the implications of this position is that it is not the shortcomings or limitations of a discovery that inspire further inquiry for Polanyi so much as it is the inexhaustible imaginative extensions of it that induce us to move forward into further inquiries. These further inquiries may indeed result in scientific revolutions—changes in our visions of reality so great that everything may seem to be turned upside down. Yet Polanyi did not think that scientific revolutions usually occur, as Kuhn seems to think, by scientists' deliberately adopting startlingly different standards or principles of being or reality—startlingly different "paradigms," in Kuhn's terminology. They quite often occur, Polanyi held, because some scientist believes an already accepted theory more concretely and literally than anyone else has. He thus enlarges an existing intellectual track in a bold and revolutionary manner. Polanyi cited von Laue's discovery of the diffraction of x-rays by crystals, and Einstein's 1905 theory of Brownian motion.[43]

Polanyi explained how changes in the fundamental paradigms of science take place without the necessity of supposing that we must choose deliberately to change them. He pointed out that, because our intuition operates on a subsidiary level, neither the clues it uses nor the principles by which it integrates them are fully identifiable. It is therefore difficult to tell what the clues were that convinced Copernicus of the reality of his system. But the discovery of relativity is

> just as full of unreconciled thoughts. Einstein tells in his autobiography that it was the example of the two great fundamental impossibilities underlying thermodynamics that suggested to him the absolute impossibility of observing absolute motion. But today we can see no connection at all between thermodynamics and relativity. Einstein acknowledged his debt to Mach and it is generally thought, therefore, that he confirmed Mach's thesis that the Newtonian doctrine of absolute rest is meaningless; but what Einstein actually proved was, on the contrary, that Newton's doctrine, far from being meaningless, was false. Again, Einstein's redefinition of simultaneity originated modern operationalism; but he himself sharply opposed the way Mach would replace the conception of atoms by their directly observable manifestations.[44]

The subsidiary presence of the principles entailed in a discovery show us how change in our standards (in our paradigms) occur. In solving a problem our intuition may respond to our efforts with a solution entailing new standards of coherence, new values. In affirming the solution we may find we have also affirmed the new standards as binding upon us. The new values have entered subsidiarily, embodied in a creative action. After this subsidiary entry, these new standards can come to be spelled out and professed in explicit terms. This may make them seem to have been chosen by us. But actually they never were, as such. They were only covertly adopted. Concrete commitments we make to our perceived coherences do bear witness to values—sometimes new values—but the grounds for these values were hidden in the subsidiary clues when these were integrated through our creative action into our perceived coherences. This, Polanyi held, is the way "new values are introduced, whether in science, or in the arts, or in human relations."[45]

So much for Polanyi's views about how scientific discoveries are made, which he thought to be by far the most important and fundamental problem in the philosophy of science. But we must investigate more particularly what he had to say about why and how discoveries become accepted. How he understood the role that "verification" and "falsification" play in their acceptance is important, since these two concepts have figured so prominently in contemporary views about the logic of science.

# CHAPTER EIGHT

# Verification

Michael Polanyi did not think that solutions are accepted as true because they fit certain standards or principles. Why then, we must ask, are they accepted? His answer was a complex one. In general, he held, scientific value is made up of three coefficients: (1) accuracy, (2) systemic importance, (3) the intrinsic interest of the subject matter. What a paper in physics lacks in subject-matter interest it makes up for by its accuracy and the width of its theoretical scope. Conversely, what a paper in biology lacks in accuracy and width of scope it makes up for in subject-matter interest. Living beings are intrinsically more interesting subjects than are pieces of inanimate matter.[1] Thus Polanyi thought discoveries are valued as scientific, because they do seem to scientists to possess one or more of these three qualities to a considerable degree, although the proportions of each factor possessed might shift remarkably from discovery to discovery, and more generally from science to science. He thought the predictive capacity of a discovery is not of decisive importance. Some theories, he points out, are adopted and valued highly that predict nothing. He mentioned as examples Kepler's laws, the Darwinian theory, and all theories involving probability statements, such as quantum mechanics. No individual event can be predicted, of course, if one can only state the probability of its occurrence.[2]

But why or how does any given discovery come to be regarded as a bona fide discovery? Polanyi thought that the assessed value of any given discovery as scientific (in the terms discussed above) also enters into the judgment that it is a true discovery. But, in addition to accuracy, theoretical scope, and intrinsic interest, a discovery must also consist of a plausible answer to a problem, and an original one. "Originality" does not only mean that no one else has discovered this aspect of reality (originality in this sense is taken for granted as essential), but rather it means what Polanyi called its unexpectedness, most particularly its daring and its ingenuity.[3]

It should be quite clear upon reflection that none of the above criteria of scientific merit are specific or explicit criteria. Each of them would require a personal judgment, an assessment by persons who know something of the science concerned. And especially must this be true concerning "plausibility."

What is plausible, both with respect to problems and solutions, is simply what is considered sound in the light of current scientific knowledge. There are no eternal standards. We have noted above Polanyi's reference to the Michelson–Morley experiments and to those later ones of D. C. Miller, in which scientific opinion found their opposite results implausible, even though nothing explicit could be found wrong with the conduct of these inquiries. Polanyi has many such examples scattered throughout his writings. Such cases are commonplace. Polanyi, however, contrary to most people who refer to such cases, did not regard them either as anomalies or as human lapses from the ideal openness that has again and again been said to characterize science and the scientists.

As we have seen, he held that not only are scientists not completely open in a dispassionate and neutral sense, but science could never proceed with its business if they were. He believed therefore that basic commitments to the general shape of things in nature and to the general ways in which nature operates is essential to the existence of a community of cooperating scientists able to get on with their job of inquiry. What it is that has resulted from an experiment cannot even be conceived or known without some sort of machinery of interpretation.[4] Moreover this machinery cannot be spelled out explicitly. For the machinery is not itself focused upon. It is used, dwelt in, in a subsidiary fashion in the effort to focus on results—on problems and discoveries. This is also the reason why the machinery does not exist simply in one person's mind. It is shared by a community of scientists. They pick it up tacitly from their mentors and from each other as they learn to be scientists, and they apply it tacitly in a nonfocal way, and gradually change it in the same way.[5]

The freedom that each scientist possesses to form his own visions of problems and of possible solutions—to be original—can only exist, Polanyi held, within a structure of tacit agreement prevailing at any one time concerning standards, mainly the tacitly held ground rules and limits of plausibility.[6] Philosophers early noted that science proceeded by and through communication among scientists, that it was a cooperative endeavor. But there could not be communication, unless the basic language the scientists spoke was the same. This language consists of the paradigms believed—mostly tacitly, but nonetheless firmly—by almost all the existing members of that particular society of inquirers everywhere in the world.[7]

These basic paradigms, or "premises," as Polanyi usually called them, are always changing. We have just seen something of how he thought they do change. But, as he showed us, they do not usually change by our deliberate choice of new premises, through some sort of deliberate change in our metaphysical doctrines. Rather, the new paradigm is at length seen to be involved in what scientific consensus has come to regard as acceptable solutions to real problems. And such new types of solutions become acceptable, Polanyi told us, because the gradient of deepening coherence enables us to see somewhat beyond where we are, to transcend somewhat our present limitations. We see that something makes sense before we can make out just why it does. As Polanyi has noted, we have not yet been able to see just why Einstein's relativity concepts could have made the sense to him that they did before he had worked them out in as explicit a form as they admit of—nor, apparently, was he any better able to render explicit just why it seemed so plausible to him from the start that the motion of a source of light and the motion of the light itself could not modify each other.

The situation in which each scientist is held to standards of plausibility by the whole community of scientists of which he is a member, as we have seen, is the only situation that makes such a cooperative inquiry possible. But, of course, this situation also limits what can develop at any one time. So Polanyi fully faced the fact that, although one can find innumerable examples in which a science has been benefited by having been protected from the works of cranks and charlatans through its own system of self-government and its commitments to its established visions of reality,[8] one can also find examples in which a truth was suppressed by means of these very commitments.[9] But Polanyi accepted these limitations as the price one must pay to have any science at all.

His refusal to condemn such closed-mindedness among scientists is not due to his never having experienced its effects personally, however. One of his own early discoveries, the potential theory of adsorption, remained unacceptable to his colleagues for twenty years—during which time he could not even teach his own theory to his own students. (They could not have passed their exams in Chemistry!) No one disputed his laboratory methods or his skill. His fellow chemists simply said the matter could not be the way it was. Something was wrong with his results. The general notion prevalent then of the pervasive function of electrical forces in the architecture of matter ruled out for them the possibility of his theory's being true. Now that these notions no longer hold sway, his theory has been accepted. He himself during these years continued to find that the matter was more coherently viewed according to his own theory than in any other way, and so he continued to believe his own theory to be true. Nevertheless he fully accepted, not only the right but the obligation of his colleagues to exercise their personal judgments affirming their own collective ultimate commitments.[10] For, as he says:

Science can never be more than an affirmation of certain things we believe in. These beliefs must be adopted responsibly, with due consideration of the evidence and with a view to universal validity. But eventually they are ultimate commitments, issued under the seal of our personal judgment. At some point we shall find ourselves with no other answer to queries than to say "because I believe so." Only a person can believe something, and only I myself can hold my own beliefs. For the holding of these I must bear the ultimate responsibility; it is futile, and I think also ignoble, to hunt for systems and machines which will take that burden from me. And we, as a community, must also face the fact that there is no system of necessary rules which will relieve us from the responsibility of holding the constitutive beliefs of our group or of teaching them to the next generation and defending their continued profession against those who would suppress them.[11]

In view of the particular position that Polanyi adopted, it is probably not surprising that, in spelling out his philosophy of science, he hardly mentioned such concerns as the logical relations of hypotheses to theories and the logical relations of hypotheses and theories to methods of measurement, computation, algebraic formulization, and instrumentation. He said very little also about the logical structure of verification or falsification. He passed rather cavalierly over all such topics, in spite of their popularity in current literature about the philosophy of science. He admitted, of course, that all these things are essential. Measurements and explicit symbols are ways in which we try to express what we mean to our colleagues. And we also hope to show others by our experiments that our visions are true. He even admitted that the abstract logical format of *modus tollens* fits (abstractly) the method of experimental inquiry (i.e., a hypothetical proposition is false, if the antecedent is true and the consequent is false) and that this means that only one contradictory instance is sufficient to refute a theory, while no number of instances consistent with it can verify it.

But all these, he insisted, like all other efforts to "tell" things—to make things explicit in logical discourse and in mathematics—are essentially meaningless without their tacit dimensions. For instance, whether any particular concrete instance is contradictory to a theory, or is to be thought of as due merely to an error, or even more blatantly, is to be accepted as an anomaly, requires a personal judgment. No event, until it has been given a meaning by a mind, is the contradictory of anything. Polanyi, therefore, thought it is only by virtue of the tacit elements lying behind our explicit machinery of interpretation, and giving it meaning, that the visions of reality actually become communicated between scientists as they see and unfold them to each other.[12]

It is true there are, he said, fairly well accepted rules of experimental verification:

(1) reproducibility of results.
(2) agreement between determinations made by different and independent sources.
(3) fulfillment of predictions.[13]

Yet he held that many examples may be found in which these three rules have all been fulfilled and yet what they thus seem to confirm has later turned out to be false. Striking agreement with these rules may later be revealed to have been due to mere coincidence. Apparent agreement with these rules thus always nevertheless leaves some doubt, and the scientist must judge whether or not he believes such doubt to be unreasonable. And he cannot determine his judgment by recurrence to further explicit rules for applying these rules. As Kant also saw, Polanyi noted, we cannot have rules to apply rules to apply rules ad infinitum. At some point an informal judgment becomes necessary.[14]

So it is also, Polanyi claimed, with accepted rules of refutation. Science, it is correctly said, must submit at any moment to the adverse verdict of observational evidence. (That is, *modus tollens* appropriately expresses its logical structure.) But, Polanyi reminded us, science submits to contradictory evidence "not blindly." Both the periodic system of the elements and the quantum theory of light have been upheld in spite of contradicting evidence. There is "always the possibility that a deviation may not affect the essential correctness of a proposition." Both these cases show that any exception to a rule may conceivably involve not its refutation, but its elucidation, and hence a confirmation of its deeper meaning. As he said, contradictions to theories may often be explained away as due to experimental error, or simply accepted and endured as an unaccountable anomaly.[15]

There is always a residue of personal judgment left in the application of the rules of verification and refutation. Personal judgment must always decide what weight to attach to any particular set of evidence.[16] And so "the final sanction of a discovery," said Polanyi, "lies in the sight of a coherence which our intuition detects and accepts as real; but . . . there are no universal standards for assessing such coherence."[17]

In the end, therefore, it is neither explicit theories nor predictability nor even manipulability that Polanyi thought we seek in science. It is explanation. And Polanyi maintained that "explanation" means "understanding." No explanation explains to us anything that was puzzling if it leaves us not understanding it, i.e., still puzzled. For understanding is the achievement of a plausible coherent pattern that satisfies our former puzzlement. Therefore explanation cannot mean merely a knowledge of certain explicit logical relations nor "subsuming a natural law within a more general law of which it is a special case." These specificities he thought would limit what is essentially a broad field of inquiry to the analysis of only fragments of it. These specificities might all contribute to an explanation, to our understanding of something that has puzzled us. But they are not by themselves identical with explanation or understanding.[18]

He referred for support of these views to Michael Scriven's criticism of such analyses of explanation:

Michael Scriven (1962) has criticized this analysis of explanation, and has suggested that concepts condemned by many logicians "as psychological not logical"—for example, understanding, belief, judgment—might have to be returned to circulation. My account of relief from puzzlement by the spreading of coherence extends Scriven's criticism. To define the explanation of an event as its subsumption under a general law leaves unexplained its capacity to relieve puzzlement and isolates it from numerous other, more fundamental, acts which have this capacity. Explanation must be understood as a particular form of insight.[19]

Polanyi hazarded that this move by Scriven might prove to be a turning point:

Eighty years have passed since Ernst Mach rejected the popular image of science as the true explanation of nature. About twenty years have passed since positivism reached the peak of its aspirations. Much of what has happened since then in philosophy has been aimed at remedying the inadequacies of the positivist programme. The line of revisionism started by Waisman in 1945 by introducing the principle of "open texture," has led Scriven to recognise understanding itself—chief expression of the metaphysical claims of science—as part of the pursuit of science. And now I am asking that we put understanding back to the very position it held, practically unchallenged, before the positivist attack, eighty years ago.

This programme must include an extension of logic into questions hitherto excluded as belonging to psychology or physiology. My analysis of tacit knowing and of the relation between levels of existence have formed examples of such an extension of logic.[20]

Polanyi therefore understood that what he was presenting in his work on the philosophy of science was not at all a proposal to include various psychological, sociological, and historical "causal" factors into an explanation of science, but rather to show what the *logic* of discovery really is. Its logic proves to be an informal one, he thought, a logic showing how a focal integration is formed by dwelling in subsidiary clues, which cannot therefore consist of formal rules. He believed we must call it a logic rather than a psychology, since the integration we form may be right or wrong in terms of our efforts to reach realities, to fulfill a universal intent. For he held that "Any relation which can be said to be right or wrong and any process that can lead to valid results, or fail to do so, forms in this sense a subject for logical analysis."[21]

And, he proceeded,

> I call "logic" the rules for reaching valid conclusions from premises assumed to be true. Currently logic seems to be defined instead as the rules for reaching strict conclusions from strict premises. I think we should reject this definition. No strict rules can exist for establishing empirical knowledge.[22]

But even formal logic, Polanyi held, must lean upon "unformalized supplements, to which the operator of the system accedes":

> Symbols must be identifiable and their meaning known, axioms must be understood to assert something, proofs must be acknowledged to demonstrate something, and this identifying, knowing, understanding, acknowledging are unformalized operations on which the working of a formal system depends. We may call them the *semantic functions* of the formal system. These are performed by a person with the aid of the formal system, when the person relies on its use.[23]

So all logical systems, in the end, must contain informal elements. Tacit dimensions must always exist along with any formal machinery to give meaning and application to it. Thus they ultimately provide genuine explanations establishing logical coherences in what is seen perceptually or conceptually.

To the objection that our system of naturalistic science is proven (or at least rendered plausible) by the objective fact that it works—as against magical systems which do not—Polanyi told us that the work of Evans-Pritchard with the Zande shows us that their beliefs become just as stable as our scientific beliefs. Their belief system does this by denying to any rival system the grounds on which it could take root. Experiences that support such a system are adduced one by one. A new principle (say, of natural causation) could be established only by a whole series of relevant instances. But this new principle cannot get established, if each instance that might possibly refute the old system is explained by some part of the old system as not a refuting instance. These saving parts in the old system may be added as the need arises, if the old system is such that "epicyclical" growth is possible, as it was in the Ptolemaic system. As a matter of fact, any conceptual system that can be said to be complete will possess ways of integrating into itself any experience that may come along, and will thus be seen to work by those who accept it. Such devices as naming as "anomalies" any exceptions to our theories, or dismissing them as due to possible experimental errors, are some of the features that enable our own scientific beliefs to possess the great stability they do have and to continue to be thought to work.[24]

Yet Polanyi clearly indicated his own acceptance of scientific beliefs as true and his rejection of magical beliefs as false. In one sense he admitted he can find no ultimate arguments to prove that scientific beliefs are more correct. Two alternative systems such as these cannot really be argued, he believed, because they share no fundamental principles between them, and discursive argument can only take place when commitment is shared to some common principle to which disputants can appeal. Nevertheless, Polanyi recognized that people committed to fundamentally different views might attempt to convert each other. The only tactic each disputant can adopt in the face of such fundamental opposition is to try to show the richer perspectives that his own view offers, in contrast to the general poverty of the other view, trusting that when one's opponent has caught a glimpse of these vistas "he cannot fail to sense a new mental satisfaction."[25]

As for Polanyi himself, he seemed to think that

> the naturalistic view opens such a noble vista of the natural order of things which are inaccessible to the magical view, and establishes so much more decent and responsible relationships between human beings that we must not hesitate to accept it as the truer of the two.[26]

Still, no arguments that can be adduced for the naturalistic view can actually "compel assent."[27] Even with respect to our own commitment to the naturalistic explanations of science, as opposed to the magical or to the theological, we are left with no guarantee of their truth. We can therefore ground ourselves upon nothing but our own fiduciary beliefs, resting upon our capacities to see coherences, that is, to produce coherences from the clues we dwell in, by means of the use of our intuition and imagination. And, of course, we do not stand in better condition with respect to our philosophic positions. Nor did Polanyi claim to be in any better position for proving the views he was propounding about the unprovability of our fundamental beliefs. As he said:

Only this manner of adopting the fiduciary mode is consonant with itself: the decision to do so must be admitted to be itself in the nature of a fiduciary act. Indeed, the same must apply to the whole of this enquiry and to all conceivable conclusions to be derived from it. While I shall continue to argue a series of points and adduce evidence for my proposed conclusions, I shall always wish it to be understood that in the last resort my statements affirm my personal beliefs, arrived at by the considerations given in the text in conjunction with other not specifiable motives of my own. Nothing that I shall say should claim the kind of objectivity to which in my belief no reasoning should ever aspire; namely that it proceeds by a strict process, the acceptance of which by the expositor, and his recommendations of which for acceptance by others, include no passionate impulse of his own. [28]

Polanyi compiled a list of five indeterminacies to which he believed all our knowledge is subject and which must prevent our ever reaching complete objectivity and detachment, even in our best scientific endeavors. However, we must remember that Polanyi thought these indeterminacies were not simple shortcomings of the human animal, due to aberrations introduced by its ineradicable animality which throw the human animal off course in his quest for pure knowledge. He thought these indeterminacies are necessarily part and parcel of what knowledge is, i.e., they are essential parts of the logical structure of knowledge. Thus they necessitate that an ideal of pure objectivity not only is in full perfection unattainable, as are all ideals, but that such an ideal itself, *as an ideal,* is false, just as the notion that an ideal painting would be one uncontaminated by a style or a mode or a fashion in painting (or even perhaps by canvases, brushes, pigments, or even painters) would be a false notion of the ideal in painting.

Let us close this chapter by listing these five indeterminacies, since they sum up admirably the principal message of our last three chapters.

(1) "Affirmations of reality in nature always have a widely indeterminate content." The real we intend to affirm is always richer in its capacities to manifest itself in the future than we have grasped it to be in our explicit thought about it. Moreover, there is more involved in our present thought about it than we can ever realize at the moment. The most obvious application of our theory is what we could call its explicit content. But the appearance of the reality it bears upon, which we can derive from an intelligent application of our imagination on the concept,

goes far beyond its immediate and obvious applications, just as a map made from specified locations will go far beyond the data used to construct it, and will show us that everything that is really in our thought about a reality was not determinately specified in our attempted explicit statement of it.[29]

(2) The rules for deciding whether a discernable pattern in nature is due to chance or to reality can never be rendered determinate. The decision is made by an act of personal judgment. Such decisions are always like those of jurors called upon to decide whether the pattern of evidence pointing to the guilt of the accused is a real pattern, due to his actual guilt, or is only an apparent one due to chance—like the constellations of stars. What rules could possibly decide, for example, whether the fact that the gestation periods (in days) of a number of animals are multiples of the number $\pi$ is merely a chance coincidence or results from a genuine coherence in nature? Scientists have decided in favor of the former. They have rejected such a coherence, because they feel there cannot be any connections of this sort in nature. Pythagorean visions are now out of fashion. But they did not rule it out by reference to any hard and fast rules.[30]

(3) The grounds of the from–to knowledge involved in all knowing may often be unspecifiable. We may not know on what grounds we hold our knowledge to be true. Skillful performances of all sorts show this to be true. We cannot tell specifically exactly all that we do in order to play a piece on the piano, walk a tightwire, ride a bicycle, or even form a series of sentences into meaningful discourse. We also cannot say precisely how we combine the two pictures we are looking at in a stereoscope into the one we see. We could never specify all the grounds of these performances. But, since we have seen that all forms of knowledge are also performances—from ordinary perception to the discovery of quantum mechanics—we obviously know that of what we know to be true some of the grounds are indeterminate.[31]

(4) Since something serving as a subsidiary when we are focusing upon an object will lose this function when we endeavor to focus upon it instead (and will become a different kind of thing for us), the subsidiary elements we use in seeing any given coherence must remain indeterminate for us, whether or not we ever could bring them into focus. This is not an existential necessity due to the difficulty in tracing the subsidiaries, but a logical necessity, an absolute principle without which we are unable to focus our perception or knowledge upon anything. To focus

upon the motions of our fingers destroys our capacity to play the piano or to type. To focus upon a word destroys the meaning the word has when used subsidiarily in a context. To focus separately upon the two pictures used in a stereoscope destroys the joint appearance they have when we are simply looking through them at their focal integration into one image with depth. To focus upon the subsidiaries in a scientific integration makes us lose sight of the vision formed by their integration.[32]

(5) A fifth indeterminacy is entailed by "the existential choices involved in modifying the grounds of scientific judgment." We have noted that we internalize that which we make function subsidiarily. We pour our body into it.

> We may say that our own existence, which we experience, and the world that we observe are interwoven here. Bodily being, by participating subsidiarily in one's perceptions and actions, becomes a being in the world, while external observations and projects subsidiarily involving one's own bodily feelings become, up to a point, a self-transformation, an existential choice. And this involves our cultural framework. Every time we rely on our traditional grounds in forming a judgment, we somewhat modify their meaning, and on these lines a creative act can renew our grounds extensively.

The way we may modify the meaning of the grounds upon which we form a judgment is, therefore, an indeterminacy, since we do not know, as we form these judgments, just how we are modifying these grounds.[33]

But this is an existential modification. That is, we are modifying ourselves as we modify these grounds, for we dwell in, and therefore incorporate into our own existence, the subsidiaries we use in forming our judgments. The sense should now be very clear to us by which the modification that Polanyi was seeking to accomplish in our philosophy of science incorporates a modification of ourselves, and can therefore function as the "medicine" that he prescribes for the illness of the modern mind. We are what we dwell in, he held, in order to make our judgments.

The false notion that science is truly knowledge because it is detached and objective implies that it (and knowledge itself) is the antithesis of personal involvement. But this notion is not merely a false view of what science and knowledge really are. It also becomes part of what we really are, since it becomes a subsidiary clue in which we dwell and in this way creates the gnawing belief at the back of our minds that the mechanical and naturalistic premises that lie at the basis of scientific explanations somehow also lie at the basis of any real truth about ourselves and about our moral, ethical, aesthetic, and religious achievements. For the understanding of these humanistic achievements entails our understanding of coherences that involve us personally to a quite obvious degree. But the notion that real knowledge is purely objective has led us to think that, in order to achieve knowledge, we must avoid such personal involvement. Therefore the truth about these humanistic achievements must seem to us to be only what we can know about them impersonally, which means that our knowledge of these humanistic coherences, since they do involve us personally, becomes denigrated to the "merely subjective," i.e., to subjectively personal feelings lacking universal application or relevance.

An ethical obligation, for example, gets placed on the same level as a hankering for dill pickles. Logically it becomes a matter of subjective personal taste whether suffocating one's grandmother for the contents of her purse is right or wrong. But, of course, since there is no disputing taste, one's own personal decision about such a question is thought not to involve universal intent. Then about such tastes what we can know impersonally[34] is presumably only: (1) that different tastes exist in one person as compared to another at any one time, and (2) something about their material and naturalistic causes.

We must end up therefore relegating not merely the existence but the very meanings of these humanistic achievements to levels of reality more primary than themselves, because these levels are presumably known more objectively (i.e., more impersonally). This relegation may not at all be a deliberate, conscious judgment. It may never act as more than a clue of which we have only a subsidiary awareness, but which may function to evoke our tacit (and perhaps even our ambivalent) acceptance of reductionist explanations of all humane achievements, explanations that explicitly reduce these achievements to the status of mere effects of more materialist, natural causes. But such acceptance of reductionary explanations tacitly weakens our notion of these humanistic products as "achievements." For some degree of skepticism is raised in our minds about their having really resulted from somebody's successful effort to live up to those values and standards that are supposed to be involved. We may tend, that is, to become cynical about human motives, regularly reducing any apparently generous, ideal, or noble actions to more "natural" motives, that is, explaining them away. To the extent that we do so, we probably would then come to adopt, either explicitly or tacitly, the notion that men's psyches are wholly determined by their atoms, their genes, and their social environments.

We could hardly then avoid at least a suspicion that nature and society together form an immense Skinner Box, and our choices may from this seem to us to be reduced either to passive acquiescence in a system operated through a conglomeration of anarchic individual choices (which we would now, however, tend to regard as not really choices, but only events determined by circumstances in the situation of each person), or a full surrender of what we may suspect is the myth of individual choice to the beckoning of a Utopian order of conditioning (to be established by some school of social engineers)—a position that should, if we ever achieve it, have got us at last well "beyond freedom and dignity."

But surely such a Hobson's choice must eventually prove to be of no real significance to us. And, if so, then the only meaningful choice left open to us might seem to consist either of a life of pure self-centeredness, circling about self-aggrandizement and self-enjoyment, avoiding every sacrifice possible, or else a life embodying an eternal, angry attitude of revolt.[35] But both these life styles, of course, are simply different reactions to the dim awareness that all the moral, aesthetic, and religious meanings we should like to give ourselves to are hovering precariously over an abyss of meaninglessness, of blind atomic interactions to which we have the sneaking but compelling feeling these "values" are really reducible. And so even these two competing impoverished "meanings" (i.e., self-enjoyment and revolt) must also seem, at last, to be of no real significance. They too must begin to look like mere whistling past the graveyard.

Something of this sort, going on at the back of our minds, seemed to Polanyi to be the cause of the hollowness and emptiness, the anomy of the modern mind, the sickness that he believed stems ultimately from our faulty views of science and of knowledge. As we shall see, Polanyi believed that his new epistemology and philosophy of science are able to leave open for us certain other intellectually and conceptually respectable alternatives to those poor choices which we have been exploring above. Should we become converted to his new epistemology, i.e., should we make use of his prescription, he felt we would be ready to try the further treatment that he advised: the development of new, more open ways of understanding living substances, persons, and their various humanistic achievements. He thought the new understandings we would achieve of these things would free us to follow deepening coherences of whatever sort we may find to wherever they may lead.

It is to these matters we turn our attention next in Part Three.

# PART III

*Treatment*

# CHAPTER NINE

# Ontological Hierarchies

Michael Polanyi prescribed a new epistemology and a new philosophy of science as specifics for the ills of the modern mind, supposing as he did that our troubles lie in these regions. He believed that our current assumptions that true knowledge must be something detached and utterly objective, and that only the methods of science fulfill these demands, are related to our loss of confidence in the ideals and moral values that are so essential to the continuance of the tasks that go to make up a free society—including the pursuit of scientific knowledge itself.

The consequences of these assumptions are, he showed, disastrous for us. However, he urged us to settle for a reform of these views of ours not simply because of these horrendous consequences, but because they are not, in fact, the truth about how we achieve our knowledge and about how our sciences actually do proceed to discover and to verify their theories about the nature of things.

Actually, so far as the pursuit of science itself was concerned, it did not matter, he thought, whether or not we held these erroneous views of knowledge and science. We would continue to pursue the natural sciences as we must, regardless of what myths about these matters we say we believe and what we tell each other we are doing. His prescription was not, he believed, required by the scientists per se, not even by the biologists, as we shall see. However, it was required he held, by any of us, scientist or not, when we attempt to elevate our views of knowledge and science into a world view. World views are imaginative projections. They are not products themselves of scientific investigations. How we understand what we are doing in science, and in the pursuit of knowledge generally, becomes important when we assess both our position in the world as human beings and the status of our evaluative judgments.[1]

Polanyi therefore attempted to show us what the consequences of his prescription are when we apply his new and more correct understanding of epistemology and of the philosophy of science to our views of life, of human beings, and of their activities, as contrasted with our older and faulty grasp of what is going on in science and in the acquisition of knowledge. I label this aspect of his work his "treatment," since it attempts to effect a change in these views of ours, a change which not only moves us to what he believed was a healthier state, but also, he thought, to a truer one.

He began his efforts by attempting to help us reform our notions about the nature and status of living things. The reduction of living things to physics and chemistry, which most biologists appear to be striving for, and which most intelligent opinion today seems to take for granted as entirely possible, either results in or flows from the metaphysical notion that such a reduction is descriptive of the true status of living things. Polanyi regarded this notion as dangerous, since it can serve as a logical basis for our current lack of respect for life and for human beings. But he also believed that it was quite fallacious. Watson and Crick, he said, seemed to think that their momentous discovery of DNA all but completed the reduction of living things to physical and chemical processes and that this opinion seemed to be widely held by others. Polanyi maintained, however, that their discovery did nothing of the sort. He pointed out that there are many problems still remaining in the complete reduction of living things to the processes of physics and chemistry.

There is first the problem, he pointed out, of how the inanimate realm ever produced a sample of DNA compound. Calculations estimating the probability that such a synthesis would take place accidentally have shown the chances to be so small, he held, as to make the event appear virtually impossible. Secondly, it is necessary for a DNA molecule to produce a cellular milieu at each stage of embryonic development which will guide it to produce further cellular milieus which in turn will function properly in guiding the DNA molecule to the next stage necessary for successful embryological development. Assuming that DNA acts only in a chemical way, the chemical compounds with which it will react chemically in a way conducive to the full development of the embryo must be present at each stage. But they must come into existence only at the end of each preceding stage. Timing is therefore most important. But no theory yet exists, he claimed, that explains how this can be done in a strictly chemical way. The development of such a theory becomes doubly difficult, Polanyi held, because, as Driesch showed with his sea-urchin embryos, there exists some resilience in the development of tissues. Some tissues can be "pressed" into undergoing changes they do not normally undergo when it happens that some part of the embryo has been prevented from developing in its usual way.

The third problem is that the quantitative increase in DNA chains from those of bacteria to man—from twenty million alternatives to about twelve billion—has, at present, no chemical explanation.

Summing up, Polanyi maintained that the discovery of DNA has not reduced living things to physical and chemical reactions, because (1) we have no chemical or physical explanation for a fundamental fact of the system of living things, the growth of DNA chains; (2) we have no chemical explanation for the historical origin of DNA; and (3) we have no chemical explanation for the capacity of DNA to produce media that apparently anticipate the future development of the embryo.[2]

Polanyi, however, was not content merely to show that, so far, we have not succeeded in reducing living things to physical and chemical reactions, and thus that the claims that the discovery of DNA has done so are groundless. He maintained that it will not be possible for us ever to reduce living things to the processes of physics and chemistry.

He pointed out that the progress we have made in our discovery of physical and chemical operations involved in living things has been made under the assumption that organisms are mechanisms. The implication that has been drawn from this has been that, since organisms are mechanisms and mechanisms work according to the laws of physics and chemistry, organisms must work in accordance with the laws of physics and chemistry. Polanyi thought that not only has this been a very fruitful assumption to make in terms of biological research, but also that it is true. The only difficulty has come from a misconception that has been formed on its basis. The assumption seems to have been made that because mechanisms (and so also organisms) work in accordance with physical and chemical laws, they are wholly explicable as the resultants of the operation of these laws. Polanyi showed that this is not true of mechanisms, and therefore also not true of organisms insofar as they are mechanisms.[3]

He showed us that there are, of necessity, two different kinds of principles involved in the concept of a mechanism. One kind is, of course, the physical and chemical reactions that occur necessarily, given certain physical and chemical conditions. These make a mechanism "work." Unless such principles were operative and unless we could rely on them, no mechanism could work—i.e., there could be no such thing as a mechanism.

But, Polanyi held, there is another kind of principle essential to a mechanism. Polanyi called this kind of principle that which set boundary conditions—limits—within which the other principles operate. These boundary-condition principles determine the structure of the machine, the peculiar organization of its physical and chemical parts. This organization of its parts is not a result of the operation of physical and chemical laws. We know, for instance, that the machines we make are not the random results of physical and chemical equilibrations, but rather of our efforts guided by our knowledge and imagination directed toward something that such a machine can be expected to achieve.[4]

Polanyi attempted to dispose of claims made by dedicated reductionists that, although organisms may seem, like machines, to have this dual control, they have not, of course, been made by man (as machines have been) and they therefore simply have, somehow, resulted entirely from the equilibrations of physical and chemical forces, even though we do not know yet how they could have done so. He maintained (1) that such contentions are gratuitous in that they are making use of blank checks to draw on hoped-for deposits that reductionistic biologists may make in the future. But (2) they are also not in line with the way any biologists really work. Biologists do treat living things as mechanisms with boundary conditions. They regard organs as having functions relative to the whole. They do distinguish organisms from inanimate, open systems, such as flames and thunderstorms. Polanyi held that this distinction is rooted in at least a tacit recognition of the notion of achievement attributed to a center in living organisms in contrast with, for instance, thunderstorms. This necessary connection of the notion of achievement with that of organisms has therefore made the science of pathology essential in biology, whereas it is not even thought of in meteorology. Organisms may succeed or fail in numberless ways, and if we do not know the causes of their failures—their diseases or malfunctioning—we do not know all there is to know about them.[5]

"Achievement" is therefore an essential concept involved in the biologist's understanding of living things. "By contrast," Polanyi reminded us, "hydrochloric acid can never fail to dissolve zinc. Nor can it dissolve platinum by mistake. Only living things can make mistakes." He therefore held that biologists not only are never really reductionistic, but that they cannot be, in the face of the demands of the subject matter with which they are dealing.[6]

Thirdly, he argued from the function of DNA as a code that the attempt to consider DNA as having been only chemically structured is not intelligible. The carrier of a message, he reminded us, must be chemically and physically neutral to the messages it is to carry. To the extent that impressions appear upon a page or a tape through equilibrations of natural forces they do not constitute a message. They tend to interfere with messages. They are blurs or noises. The appearance of impressions that are to serve as coded messages must not occur as simple resultants of a chemical affinity between the paper and ink blobs of certain shapes and sizes. If they did, they would not constitute a message. They would constitute specks and blemishes on the tabula rasa we require as the background upon which we wish to transcribe a message. If there are good physical reasons, he said, why rocks tumbling down a hillside would come to rest in the shape of English letters spelling out English names, then rocks could never serve to spell out the name of a town on an embankment.[7]

Thus if the items in a DNA chain were arranged the way they are because of chemical necessities, they could not serve as messages. But we find, Polanyi said, that the position which each item has in the chain is not due to one necessary equilibration of chemical forces, and therefore that it *can* function as part of a message. Each item of a DNA series consists of one of four alternative organic bases (actually, he said, two positions of two different compound organic bases). Polanyi noted that DNA is not a medium suited ideally for a message, since its four organic bases do not have perfectly equal chemical probability of forming any particular item in the series, i.e., there is some redundancy, but the redundancy is not enough to prevent DNA from functioning as a code.[8]

The point made here, Polanyi said, holds regardless of whether or not this structure has come about through chance. Whatever its origin, it can function as a code only if its order is not due to the forces of potential energy, i.e., if its specific order is not chemically necessary. What Polanyi seems to mean here is that, if the order of the items in a DNA molecule were chemically necessary, there would be only one sort of DNA molecule and so only one "message" in existence—which would be the same as saying there would be none, that DNA is unfitted to carry messages, because the order of its items could not be varied. Under these conditions it would only be capable of entering dynamically into relations with other molecules, as all other molecules are, not at all capable of entering into linguistic, i.e., communicative relations, with them. But since its order is not due to chemical affinity, DNA is able to serve as a code.[9]

Modern theory, Polanyi pointed out, wishing to confine itself to physical and chemical forces and modes of operation, is thus left with nothing but chance as the originator of the particular structures of DNA molecules (chemical affinity having been ruled out). The difficulty with this situation is that the probability that these molecules might have acquired their meaningful structures by mere chance is even much less, he claimed, than the probability that piles of rocks rolling down hillsides should have come to rest in ways that are meaningful in terms of the English names of the towns where they are located.[10]

The plain case is, however it may have come about, that DNA and every organism structured by it are meaningful organizations of essentially meaningless matter. Organisms, he explained, are meaningful both in terms of their structures and in terms of the meanings they are able to achieve, as against the structures and behavior of inorganic molecules and bodies. He maintained that this is a fact. Moreover, he said, if we cast an eye at evolutionary history, we cannot avoid noticing that the overall general direction in which evolutionary development has proceeded is that of attaining ever greater meaningfulness—again in terms of both structure and capacity for the attainment of meaning. There is a striking panorama of progress from one-celled plants, capable of little more than sustaining themselves and reproducing their kind, through minute animals, capable of sensitivity as individuals to their surroundings and of learning some sustaining habits, to more and more complex (and meaningful) animals, to mammals, and finally to man, whose capacity for achieving meanings seems still to stretch limitlessly before us. There would therefore seem to be, Polanyi said, a gradient of meaning involved in evolutionary development, inasmuch as purely chance mutations and natural selection would not appear to be able to account for the direction that evolution has obviously taken.[11]

Polanyi held that eyebrows should not be raised at the admission of such a gradient into biology, since we do in fact make use of the notion of directional gradients in other sciences, such as physics. Our physics is structured by the notion that forces draw matter toward more stable configurations of forces. A close analogy can be drawn between how such a gradient operates in quantum mechanics and how a gradient of meaning could be supposed to operate both in embryological development and in the evolutionary development of species; as we saw in our last chapter he held that such an analogy exists between quantum mechanics and the advancement of scientific thought through discovery.

Quantum mechanics, he reminded us, assumes (1) a field of forces, or energy, operating with certain probabilities toward stabler sets of potentialities. It also assumes (2) that these potentialities are not always being actualized, because the forces involved may be friction-locked. Quantum mechanics in addition assumes (3) that catalysts or accidental releasers of these friction-locked potential forces may appear, allowing these forces to become actualized. An explosion (one way to actualize friction-locked potential forces), he pointed out, may be triggered by a number of releasing events, including the spontaneous disintegration of an atom. Such a spontaneous event may be treated by scientists as an uncaused event, since, although it is controlled by probable tendencies, it is never necessitated by these tendencies. Both these probable tendencies and the directional gradient minimizing potential energy, said Polanyi, may evoke the ensuing event, but not cause it, i.e., not necessitate it.[12]

Polanyi held that, in an analogous fashion, the growth of an embryo may be evoked (and so controlled, but not caused) by a gradient of potential shapes in a field of shapes. He mentioned experimental work done by the biologists H. Spemann, Paul Weiss, and C. H. Waddington which tended to show that embryological development is controlled by fields of potential shapes. Polanyi held that embryological development and also evolutionary development can be understood (1) to be evoked by the accessibility of higher levels of stable meaning analogous to the more stable potentialities of forces in quantum mechanics. He went on to say that (2) the attainment of these potentially greater meanings may be blocked by the locked-in code of a given DNA molecule, analogous to the friction-locked forces that cannot actualize their potentialities in quantum mechanics. (3) The tension generated by such blockage may be released into further development by accident (such as a mutation-causing event in evolutionary development) or by the operation of releasers or inhibitors (in embryological development) or through the occurrence of first (uncaused) cause—spontaneities analogous to the disintegration of an atom. All these biological releasers are analogous to the catalysts or accidental releasers in quantum mechanics. We could then call what results a creative development (or an emergent) because it can be said to be evoked by and so controlled by, but never fully determined by its potentialities and its releasing agent. These developments may either succeed or fail to achieve a greater or more stable meaning. This dimension of success or failure added to inanimate matter is therefore understandable in these terms as an emergent feature belonging as a boundary condition to a biological level of being that has emerged out of a strictly physical level.[13]

As we have noted before in passing, Polanyi also showed us that this model of quantum mechanics can be used in understanding discovery in human thought. To see a problem and to undertake its solution is to see a range of potentialities for meaning that appear to be accessible. Heuristic tension in a mind, then, might seem to be generated much as kinetic energy in physics is generated by the accessibility of more stable configurations. The tension in a mind seems to be deliberate, however, by contrast to that in a physical system. A mind strives to comprehend that which it believes to be comprehendible, but which it does not yet comprehend. Its choices are therefore hazardous, they may succeed or fail, but are not "determined." Nevertheless the choices are not made at random. They are controlled (as well as evoked) by the pursuit of intentions. These choices resemble quantum mechanical events in that they are guided by a field that nevertheless leaves them indeterminate. They are therefore also "uncaused" in that there is nothing in the range of our knowledge that determines or necessitates them to become what they do become.

Holding these views, Polanyi could not help but find that looking for the conditioning circumstances, the "causes," that account behavioristically for human thoughts or decisions is wholly inappropriate, just as inappropriate as it would be to look for such necessitating "causes" in quantum mechanics. Thus, discoveries, for Polanyi, do not differ in overall form from inanimate events, but only in point by point content.

The field that evokes or controls or guides discoveries is not a field of more stable configurations or forces, but a problem. And discoveries do not occur spontaneously, but are due to an effort to actualize certain hidden potentialities; the uncaused action that releases them is not a physical event but an imaginative thrust.[14]

Polanyi maintained that these reflections show that it is possible to view embryological and evolutionary development, as well as developments in thought, in terms that render them analogous to the strictly physical level of being, but not, however, as reducible to this physical level. Such a view, he held, is also superior to present biological views. It succeeds in accounting for the rise of living organisms exactly where present views fail: (1) How boundary conditions acquire other principles of behavior in addition to those of the material they bound becomes explicable, that is, through a creative reorganization of an existing organism's DNA chain in response to a gradient of deepening meaning. (2) We are no longer faced with the hopeless task of attempting to explain sentience by concepts taken from the insentient. Sentience can now be understood to be a structural feature of higher boundary principles of organization and operation, rooted in and dependent for their existence upon a lower, insentient level, but added to those principles which structure the lower, insentient level. This understanding would further open the door to the notion that being exists in hierarchical levels, rather than simply in the one-dimensional plane which, according to Polanyi, most modern biologists still follow Laplace in assuming.[15]

Polanyi pointed out that although the Laplacian ideal of universal knowledge would have to be transposed into quantum-mechanical terms today, this is immaterial. The notion that a full and complete science of the atoms plus a map of the topography of the universe of these atoms would enable us to know (with or without ranges of probability) any past or future state of affairs in the world would remain the same. It is this notion that dwells, Polanyi said, at the heart of the fallacies flowing from science today.

But the real fault of such a grandiose world view, he informed us, is that it would, even if achieved, tell us absolutely nothing that we should be interested in. Let our question be about primroses or frogs. A total world topography would tell us nothing about them, for we need to have grasped first the identity and physiognomy of primroses or frogs before we could identify any particular concatenation of atoms as theirs. We therefore cannot rely only upon the principles of their atoms, but also upon the principles of their boundary conditions to be able, to say when primroses will bloom or frogs croak. Unless we know the confining boundary conditions for their atoms, we will not know what their atoms will do. We won't even know what atoms are theirs. But, if we know their boundary conditions (from our studies directly of primroses and frogs, as such, not from physics), we then should know what primroses and frogs will do, quite often regardless of whether or not we know what their atoms are doing![16]

Polanyi further reminded us that, as a matter of fact, certain parts of the science of physics itself would be unknowable, if we possessed only Laplacian "universal" knowledge. The laws of gases, derivable as they are from correlations of the temperatures and pressures of gases, would have been unknown to us, since there is no specific temperature of a given body of gas, and no specific pressure either, unless the atoms of the gas exhibit randomness. From a random organization of atoms we can read nothing; it is only from their random concatenation that we can read a temperature and a pressure and thus the correlation of these that are the laws of gases.[17]

Polanyi demonstrated in many ways his case for the existence of an hierarchical organization of being which he held ensued from pyramiding sets of boundary conditions. Language, he held, is a hierarchical organization. One cannot deduce a set of words simply from the sounds humans make. Words are constituted by boundary conditions or principles that harness or organize sounds. So the words of a language place limits to sounds. Yet words require sounds in order to exist, even though the principles involved in sounds are not rich enough to give us words, as the principles of a propositional calculus are not rich enough to give us an arithmetic. Grammatical principles in turn then set boundaries for words and enable us to make sentences. A style of language places boundaries on sentences and so on until one has a whole speech bounded by the ultimate principles of an intended communication. He pointed out that games are also so structured. The rules of chess make strategies possible, but do not establish or "cause" any strategies. Strategies will have principles of their own which will give boundary and structure to moves thus selected from all those moves made possible (but not made actual) by the rules. Machines, as we have seen, consist of higher and lower levels and are therefore also examples of hierarchical organization—as are living creatures.[18]

In fact, he held that everything we perceive or know *must* exhibit a hierarchy of being or principles, because of the very way in which we know. The ontological entities of which we become aware are comprehensive entities, including both those elements of which we are focally aware and those of which we are only subsidiarily aware. These are, respectively, the whole and the parts of the thing perceived or known. When we see a face we are focally aware of the face as a whole, the form or gestalt of the face which enables us to identify it again anywhere. But the face ontologically, as a being, has parts. These we are only subsidiarily aware of when we are focusing, through them, upon the face.[19] We can, of course, focus our attention upon some of these parts, say, the nose or the lips. But then we lose sight of the face and instead it is these parts that become focal wholes, with parts of them perceived in a subsidary way. We cannot make any feature serve in a subsidiary way and in a focal way at the same time. If we focus upon it, we cannot focus through it. We can, said Polanyi, either look at our spectacles or through them. We cannot do both at once.[20]

Polanyi thus believed that our experience and observation show us that everything we perceive has parts upon which the whole is dependent for its existence, but it also is a whole the character of which is not derivable or deducible from its parts. It arises only from, or more correctly out of, an integration of its parts—accomplished in space and time for the thing, and in the mind for the knowledge of it. Since these parts and wholes can form an ascending or descending series, an ontological hierarchy is generated from them.[21]

Thus we see that the notion of ontological hierarchies as structuring everything is not only an empirical fact of perception for Polanyi, which he believed can be continually established by further and further inquiry, but it is necessarily entailed by his epistemology. It is not an extra principle added gratuitously in order to reach certain desired conclusions regarding living things or human beings.

At the peak of this ontological hierarchy, for Polanyi, stands man, not because of certain religious or anthropological myths, or wishful thinking on Polanyi's part, but because in order to understand man's activities one must resort to boundary principles that organize bodies of lower-level principles and matters. Not only must man have sentience in order to do what he does, but he must bound this sentience with individuality, as all animals do. But we see that this individuality is bounded in turn by social principles, since man is a gregarious animal. In addition, this sociability of his is given a further, higher boundary of language. His language is still further bounded by the various systems of language-action which he develops: science, law, poetry, etc. All of these pyramiding levels of being enable him to succeed or fail in enterprises far beyond the capacity of his fellow animals, although some of his failures in these enterprises are like theirs in that they are merely due to errors or mistakes. But resting on top of all these levels of meaning is the further capacity of man to do evil, that is, not only to make mistakes, but to violate obligations entailed in these various language-action levels in which he dwells, as well as those unique obligations of an even higher boundary condition, that of morality. These levels and the kind of successes or failures they entail are completely beyond those of other animals. Man thus is at the top, because he is the only creature known to us able to act at the level of good or evil. And this sort of activity is structured by boundary principles that transcend all the capacities that other animals also possess in varying degrees, even though this higher activity depends upon all those lower capacities for its existence, in true hierarchical fashion.[22]

# CHAPTER TEN

# Personal Participation

With the advent of man, Michael Polanyi said, a whole new world of meanings burst into view. This is the world created by man, that which Polanyi, with Teilhard de Chardin, called "the noosphere." It might seem obvious that man could know these realities only through his participation in them and indeed, as Polanyi reminded us, such thinkers as Dilthey long ago maintained that the stuff of the humanities can only be known by such personal participation. However, as Polanyi noted, these thinkers seem to have implied that the knowledge we achieve in the sciences is not achieved through personal participation, but rather as spectators, using the ideal of detached objectivity. Polanyi, however, tried hard to show us that personal participation is involved in all knowing, which is, moreover, always a sort of doing or creating. Knowing of any sort, he maintained, is the creation of a meaningful integration of subsidiary clues, dwelt in as a projection toward the achievement of a focally known whole—even in the cases of perceptual objects and of the sciences.[1]

For Polanyi, therefore, the meaningful integrations achieved by man in the noosphere form a continuum with those achieved in perception and knowledge, in the sense that they are all examples of the tacit triad: (1) a mind (2) dwelling in subsidiary clues and (3) creating a meaningful integration of these clues into a focally known whole.[2] Perception does this, ordinary knowing does this, scientific knowing does this, poetry does this, religion does this. These various kinds of integrations are all the same also in making use of the creative imagination[3] and in that there is no way to establish their truth or their reality in a thoroughly detached, impersonal, objective way—even though they are all created with universal intent, not as subjective entities whose status is understood to be merely "true for me."[4]

But Polanyi, of course, never lost sight of the fact that there are differences between the integrations and realities forming the noosphere and those existing prior to the noosphere. All of our integrations, he held, are understood by us, when we believe them (or believe in them), to be realities, in the sense in which he used the term "reality," namely, that which we think has an existence not fully determinate in our present grasp of it and which we therefore expect to exhibit itself in the future in yet indeterminate ways. If we believe that a hydrogen atom is real, that is, not exhaustively simply what we have at the moment explicitly said it to be—not a mere conceptual construct—then we do expect that it may display qualities in the future which we cannot predict from our present understanding of it. This is to say that we suppose we may make further discoveries about its nature or behavior, because it will make further manifestations of itself available to us, which it could not do if it were exclusively merely the understanding which we have of it up to now. In other words, we are supposing that the object of our concept is real, that it has some nature of its own into which we may penetrate further.[5] He maintained therefore that Copernicus and the early Copernicans, Galileo, Kepler, et al., did not think their Copernican theory (that the sun was the center of the system of planets) was a mere conceptual device for collating observational facts into a conceptual system, as the later positivists tried to make out that they thought. These Copernicans, Polanyi maintained, believed that their theory referred to the way realities actually were. Polanyi claimed that scientists always think they are referring to the way realities are, regardless of whether they claim to be positivists or not.[6]

In the same way, the political and legal systems that men have created, their economic systems, their languages, Eliot's *Wasteland,* Michelangelo's *Moses,* and Beethoven's Ninth Symphony, are realities. They are thought by us to have structures rich enough to make us suppose that they will exhibit to us a presently indeterminate range of future manifestations. That they are creations of man does not rob them of their reality, if reality is understood as Polanyi understood it. But the origins of these realities are different from the realities that perception and scientific knowing are concerned with. These latter are understood by us to exist, Polanyi said, independently of man's activities. Man's perception and his science thus strive to attain to an adequacy to what is already there. Polanyi held, therefore, that their truth is subject to what we must call a process of verification. The truth of what man has created, on the other hand, must, he said, be subject rather to a criterion of their validity.[7]

We hold the beliefs we do hold about the non-noospheric realities and we create the noospheric realities with universal intent; this is the basis for our claim that they are true—whether subject to verification or to validation.[8] The difference between verification and validity therefore lies, Polanyi held, in another direction than in the presence or absence of our universal intent regarding them.

We have already discussed in Chapter 8 how Polanyi thought that modern science verifies its theories. It is interesting to note that the sciences themselves, in this view of Polanyi's, must be regarded as creations of man and thus as parts of the noosphere. As such, sciences also might be said to be regarded as valid if they are accepted by us. And Polanyi does sometimes speak of our acceptance of them as valid. But because they themselves refer themselves to those realities supposed to exist from origins that are not man-engendered, their validity (that is, our acceptance of them) rests upon whether or not we have, in accordance with the standards of science, sufficiently verified their doctrines. Science is therefore part of the noosphere, for Polanyi, but the realities it attempts to refer to are not. All the rest of the noospheric realities engendered by man have, therefore, a validity differently based from that of science.

Partly because of this circumstance, Polanyi held, science in the modern age has tended, at least tacitly, to claim to have a monopoly upon achieving knowledge of reality. This often unspoken claim has led to our tendency to assign an honorific status to tangible realities, since science appears to us to deal with these, and to regard all other sorts of possible entities or meanings (those created in the noosphere) to be merely epiphenomenal or illusory. Polanyi made the startling counterclaim that as a matter of fact a stone is, if anything, less real than a mind or a problem, because we expect a far narrower range of indeterminacies in the future from a stone than we do from a mind. He therefore did not think that the works of minds lacked reality because they were intangible.[9]

These views about the realities of our integrations follow, of course, from Polanyi's epistemological contention that each thing we know is a comprehensive entity composed (1) of parts known only in a subsidiary way and (2) of the integrated whole that we make (with universal intent) from these parts and which we know only focally. This notion of comprehensive entities is, as we have earlier noted, the ontological aspect of his subsidiary–focal doctrine. If this is true, it then follows that the whole of reality must be structured hierarchically (as we have seen in our last chapter), and there is no reason to think that a higher sphere of being which emerges from an immediately lower sphere, and which encompasses it with boundary conditions and principles not reducible to the lower sphere, is not also a sphere of reality.

As we have seen, a frog is a reality, surely. It is a peculiar structure of physical and chemical parts which has an individual center of action and a definite set of characteristics which its parts do *not* have. The anatomy of a frog is extremely complex. Moreover it has an individually centered program of development from fertilized egg to maturity which exhibits the operation of many principles not operative in the atoms and molecules of which it is composed, and which therefore cannot be deduced from them. Like a propositional calculus not rich enough in principle to deduce an arithmetic from it, physical and chemical laws are not rich enough to deduce or explain a frog's behavior. The behavior of a frog reaches levels undreamed of by its atoms. It is a different (and higher) order of being.

Looking across the field of living things, we see these principles operating in the hierarchy of biotic levels. The vegetative boundary system leaves open the possibilities of movement by muscular action, but is not rich enough in principles to establish it. In turn, the principles of muscular action leave open the possibility of innate patterns of behavior, but do not establish any. These innate patterns then leave open the possibility of their being modified by intelligence, but do not necessitate it. Intelligence, once established, then opens wide-ranging possibilities for the exercise of still higher principles—such as the moral— but does not simply as intelligence necessitate these.[10] Yet organisms structured by any of these levels must surely be said to exist.

Thus what first comes into existence when a nervous system is bounded and structured with a center, such as exists in man, i.e., a mind, should certainly be said to be also an existing reality. And what comes into existence at this point when we add man's capacity to imitate sounds and to mean something by them (i.e., language) is eventually no less than the whole noosphere, the "firmament of obligations," as Polanyi called it. Man creates it, but he is under obligation to it as he lives and becomes the kind of creature he actually is. For at some point it was man's mind that created (tacitly at first) the principles of truth and beauty and morality as principles that should guide his behavior. Why should we not suppose that these, too, are new spheres of being and that these too should be considered realities among all the others that have been pyramided on top of each other in the long history of the world. Once brought into being they have a structure and thrust of their own, and we find ourselves subject to their intrinsic standards, just as we are in mathematics, for instance.

Polanyi seemed to think that the function of these realities is to create obligations binding upon us and thus to direct our lives. He believed that we in the modern world have adopted, because of the advent of modern science, a strange view of the universe and of our position in it that leads us to doubt the validity of these obligatory realities created by man and to attempt to undercut them by reducing them to complex effects produced by the lower level of drives for power and profit upon which they rest existentially.[11]

Marxism was for him the most powerful modern movement of thought that has made such an attempt. If all the "ideological superstructure" of man is ultimately derived only from the economic interests of the dominant class, then truth and beauty and moral principles are nothing in themselves and ought not lay claim to our allegiance or our respect. But Polanyi thought that the thrust of most of the other modern systems of thought also takes this direction. It seemed to be his hope that his new insight into epistemology, and into an ontology correlated with it, would lay the foundations for a rebirth of faith in the reality of these "spiritual entities," as he sometimes called them, and therefore in the integrations created in science, poetry, art, religion, and morality.[12]

Indeed, he maintained that all of these levels of reality should be included in the science of biology, since biology is the study of life, and life, in man, has taken this shape. He said as we proceed to survey the ascending stages of life, our subject matter will tend to include more and more of the very faculties on which we rely for understanding it. We realize then that what we observe about the capacities of living beings must be consonant with our reliance on the same kind of capacities for observing it. Biology is life reflecting on itself, and the findings of biology must prove consistent with the claims made by biology for its own findings.

And as we shall find ourselves accrediting living beings with a wide range of faculties, similar to those which we have claimed for ourselves in the foregoing enquiry into the nature and justification of knowledge, we shall see that biology is an expansion of the theory of knowledge into a theory of all kinds of biotic achievements, among which the acquisition of knowledge is one. These will all be comprised by a generalized conception of commitment. The critique of biology will then turn out to be an analysis of the biologist's commitment, by which he accredits the realities on which living beings rely in the stratagem of living. And while these realities will fall into line with the realities to which our knowledge of inanimate things commits us, another line of generalization, ascending from the I–It to the I–Thou and beyond it to the study of human greatness, will transform the biologist's relation to his subject matter to that between man and the abiding firmament which he is committed to serve.[13].

Polanyi appeared to be saying here not only that biology must, in the end, encompass all the activities of men, but also that the biologist must tend, at the upper reaches of his inquiry, to merge with his subject matter, since his very work as a biologist must be part of his study. Therefore so must everything leading up to it, as well as all that which goes beyond it. It should be clear at this point that knowledge, in this expanded version of biology, must be achieved through participation in that of which we have knowledge.

But biology today, of course, is not expanding its range in this fashion. It is rather more intent on reducing itself to physics and chemistry. And modern physics seems mainly to be mathematical. Even should these reductions prove to be possible, we still would not, according to Polanyi, have escaped all personal participation in the structuring of our knowledge. Polanyi made a case for our personal participation even in the formal sciences of mathematics and of symbolic logic. The sciences of modern symbolic logic, mathematics, and mathematical physics are often regarded, he said, as models par excellence of detached objectivity, impervious to personal participation. However, he held that it is "nonsensical to aim at the total elimination of our personal participation in such formal sciences." "The legitimate purpose of formalization," he acknowledged, "lies in the reduction of the tacit coefficient to more limited and obvious informal operations" but not, he added, to its "total elimination."[14]

He pointed out that the operations of digital computers as machines of logical inference coincide with the operations of symbolic logic. The procedures involved in the construction and use of such computers are identical with those used in a logical deductive system. "(1) The procedure designates undefined terms; (2) it specifies unproved asserted formulae (axioms): and (3) it prescribes the handling of such formulae for the purpose of writing down new formulae (proofs)." This procedure might appear to eliminate personal participation, substituting formal elements for "merely psychological" elements—those that Polanyi called "tacit."

> However [he said], this attempt to eliminate the personal participation of the logician must leave at each of these points an irreducible residue of mental operations, on which the operations of the formalized system itself will continue to rely. (1) The acceptance of a mark on paper as a symbol implies that (a) we believe that we can identify the mark in various instances of it and (b) that we know its proper symbolic use. In both these beliefs we may be mistaken, and they constitute therefore commitments of our own. (2) In agreeing to regard an aggregate of symbols as a formula, we accept it as something that can be asserted. This implies that we believe that such an aggregate says something about something. We expect to recognize things which satisfy a formula, as distinct from other things which fail to do so. Since the process by which our axioms will be satisfied is necessarily left unformalized [recall that we cannot have rules for the application of rules ad infinitum] our countenancing of this process constitutes an act of commitment on our part. (3) The handling of symbols according to mechanical rules cannot be said to be a proof, unless it carries the conviction that whatever satisfied the axioms from which the operation starts will also satisfy the theorems arrived at. No handling of symbols to which we refuse to award the success of having convinced us that an implication has been demonstrated can be said to be a proof. And again,

this award is an unformalized process which constitutes a commitment.

Thus, at a number of points, a formal system of symbols and operations can be said to function as a deductive system only by virtue of unformalized supplements, to which the operator of the system accedes: symbols must be identifiable and their meaning known, axioms must be understood to assert something, proofs must be acknowledged to demonstrate something, and this identifying, knowing, understanding, acknowledging, are unformalized operations on which the working of a formal system depends.[15]

Logical operations, Polanyi reminded us, are symbolic. Logical symbols may represent states of affairs. Indeed, they must be tacitly held to do so or logic can have no application. But the manipulations of these symbols are not symbolic of states of affairs, but rather only of the transformation of one conception of a state of affairs into another conception of a state of affairs implied by the first. "They evoke," Polanyi said, "the conceptual transformation which they symbolize in the same way as a descriptive term like 'cat' evokes the conception for which it stands." In other words, we dwell in logical manipulations, projecting a conceptual transformation of ourselves as we dwell in a word, projecting ourselves through it to the concept for which it stands. "The tacit component of a formalized process of reasoning is [thus] broadly analogous to that of a denotation. It conveys both our understanding of the formal manipulations and our acceptance of them as right."[16] Such understanding and such acceptance is not a function either of a computer or of a set of logical deductions. Understandings and acceptances are tacit, personal participations of a mind in these processes. Without such participation no meanings can be generated by such procedures.

A logical "proof" does not constitute a real proof with no quotation marks around it without an acceptance of it, as such, by someone; and one cannot be convinced of a proof, unless he grasps the logical sequence from which it has resulted as a purposeful procedure that makes sense.[17] Grasping such a logical sequence is grasping a whole, a gestalt, of which the parts are seen in a subsidiary way rather than in a focal way. They are meaningful parts of the proof only in the whole of which they are parts. One must sometimes go over and over a formally correct "proof" before one sees it as a whole and so believes that it does in fact prove an inference.

What Polanyi said about logical deduction he also applied to mathematics, of course. However, he had some things to say about mathematics in addition to these. First of all, he said, it is clear there are no rules for solving problems. There can only be vague maxims. Solving a mathematical problem is a heuristic act that leaps across a logical gap.[18] Solving a problem is like recalling a forgotten name, in that we direct our attention to the known data that bear on the problem, but only in a subsidiary way, not focally. We use or dwell in these data subsidiarily as clues to the unknown, as pointers to it and parts of it. Progress is made, of course, only if our casting about for a solution is guided by a reliable sense of growing proximity to the solution. This tacit ability to anticipate a hidden potentiality is essential, Polanyi thought, both first to see a problem and then to set out to solve it.[19] As we saw, he generalized this recognition as the basis of all discovery.

What we do, of course, in mathematics is to sense a hidden inference from given premises and then invent a transformation of the premises which increases the accessibility of the hidden inference. The mathematician works his way toward discovery by shifting his confidence from intuition to computation and back again. This procedure, in fact, Polanyi generalized, represents the whole range of operations by which articulation disciplines and expands the reasoning powers of man.[20]

There is also, Polanyi pointed out, a special participatory, tacit coefficient operative in mathematical induction. Mathematical induction starts by proving a series of theorems which apply to successive whole numbers, each theorem being derived from the previous one. But then it concludes that the theorem is generally true for all numbers. To draw such an inference, Polanyi said, a mind must look back upon a series of demonstrations to see and generalize the principle of its past operations.[21] It cannot deduce this principle formally from the instances. Polanyi maintained that such induction is analogous to the Gödelian process of innovation. The Gödelian sentence arises from a reflection upon what has been said. The process of deductive inference produces a situation which irresistibly suggests (to a mind reflecting upon the matter, not to an inference machine) an assertion not formally implied in its premises. We match the Gödelian sentence with the facts to which it refers, namely to its own undecidability within the system when it asserts that the axioms of the system cannot be proved to be consistent. We then assert it as an added axiom, independent of the axioms from which it was indeed constructed, but from which it could not be decided or asserted as a proven logical inference. Polanyi held that such innovation in mathematics and logic shows the operation of tacit thought in the crossing of logical gaps,[22] and thus in the expansion and further development of logical and mathematical systems.

But perhaps Polanyi's crowning assertion against objectivism—against rejecting the process of personal participation—in our interpretation of mathematics was his rejection of the notion that our acceptance of mathematics rests on the grounds that it supposedly possesses "freedom from self-contradiction," i.e., the notion that mathematics has to be accepted because it is a set of tautologies.

> To this, [he said] it must be objected in the first place that it is false. Tautologies are necessarily true, but mathematics is not. We cannot tell whether the axioms of arithmetic are consistent; and if they are not, any particular theorem of arithmetic may be false. Therefore these theorems are not tautologies. They are and must always remain tentative, while a tautology is an incontrovertible truism.[23]

Why then is mathematics accepted? He held that mathematics is accepted because it is intellectually interesting and beautiful. It satisfies our intellectual passions. It is, he asserted, only this informal and personal appreciation of mathematical value that can distinguish what is mathematics from a welter of formally similar, yet altogether trivial statements and operations. This informal appreciation of mathematics is "the inarticulate coefficient by which we understand and assent to mathematics." This governs our choice of axioms and our recognition that some theorems derivable from them are mathematically significant while an infinite number of others are simply trivia.[24]

Polanyi pointed out that the situation was essentially the same in mathematical physics as in mathematics. Intellectual beauty is recognized as a token of a hidden reality. This tacit coefficient gives direction to the research and scope of modern physics and is basically the way our personal participation enters into the knowledge that we acquire in physics.[25] The present purely mathematical framework of physics, he held, is part of the personal subsidiary elements tacitly shared by modern-day physicists. Mathematical frameworks were not satisfying to previous generations of physicists who rather dwelt in a framework of mechanical models.[26] So even mathematical physics is a product of personal participation.

Thus, even were the proposed reduction of living things to physics and chemistry carried out successfully, we might note that it would not, for Polanyi, succeed in eliminating personal participation from biology. As we have seen, Polanyi presented us with many other good reasons why biology must be unsuccessful in its efforts to reduce itself to physics and chemistry. In addition, if man's whole behavior ought to be included in the study of biology, he held there were even more momentous reasons why biology should refrain from attempting such a reductionism. For strictly construed, such a reductionist view must hold that Beethoven's Ninth Symphony and Shakespeare's *Hamlet* are only the observed results of equilibrations of physical forces in and among the real subatomic particles at these particular space–time locations in the universe where we would have observed Ludwig van Beethoven and William Shakespeare composing these works. A full causal explanation would of course have to involve the whole prior history of the universe à la Laplace.

But actually, of course, nobody thinks of trying to give subatomic explanations of man's artistic achievements, if for no other reason than that of their obvious practical impossibility. And certainly the behaviorist Skinner stops far short of doing so. Nevertheless attempted explanations of man's behavior (and there can be, in this view of things, no logical reason why this should not include the composition of symphonies and the writing of plays) do exist that follow such models. Polanyi held that neurology is based on the assumption that the nervous system functions automatically according to the laws of physics and chemistry to determine all the operations we normally attribute to the individual mind. He maintained that psychology shows a parallel tendency toward reducing its subject matter to explicit relationships between measurable variables, relationships which could always in theory be represented by performances of a mechanical artifact.[27] He believed that these reductionisms currently in vogue in biology, neurology, and psychological behaviorism are all logically related to the basic assumption of a one-level universe of atoms, which alone possesses true "reality"—everything else that we see or say we know being only necessary results of their interaction and thus reducible to them, even though no effort is made to run their account down to the level of the microparticles.

Polanyi pointed out to us that our understanding of a hungry animal choosing food, or alert, listening, watching, and reacting to what it notices, is an act of personal knowing similar to the animal's own personal act which our knowing appraises. It is therefore achieved not by detached observation but by participation in what we observe—by our dwelling in it. Our knowledge of such an active, perceptive animal, he said, would altogether dissolve if we entirely replaced it by our focal knowledge of its several manifestations. We can only be aware of what the animal is doing and knowing by being aware of these several manifestations subsidiarily in a from–to relation to our focal awareness of the animal as an active, intending individual. Our attempts to specify and list the observable particulars can do no more than highlight some features, because of the complexity and variability of the comprehensive act. And anyhow the meaning of these highlighted features will have to continue to depend on an unspecifiable background known to us in a participatory way through our indwelling of the act as a whole. We can understand the meaning of the animal's actions by reading the particulars of its action, not by observing these particulars in the way we do the inanimate processes.[28] Polanyi wrote:

> Behaviorists teach that in observing an animal we must refrain above all from trying to imagine what we would do if placed in the animal's position. I suggest, on the contrary, that nothing at all could be known about an animal that would be of the slightest interest to physiology, and still less to psychology, except by following the opposite maxim of identifying ourselves with the centre of action in the animal and criticizing its performance by standards set up for it by ourselves.[29]

Whatever plausibility behaviorism may exhibit is due, Polanyi claimed, to a process he called "pseudosubstitution"—"a gesture of intellectual self-destruction kept in safe bounds by its inconsistence" in borrowing the qualities of the very powers it sets out to eliminate. The behaviorist, for example, describes learning in objectivist terms, such as "stimulus," "control," "response;" but these can be shown to apply to the process of learning only because their meanings are understood through tacitly smuggling into them their bearing on the mental events involved in learning, which are all along kept covertly in mind. He referred to Noam Chomsky's review of B. F. Skinner's book, *Verbal Behavior*, in which Chomsky made the same point about Skinner's work. Chomsky, said Polanyi, presented many illustrations of such behavioristic paraphrasing and held that you either use the stated objective terms literally—whereupon what is said is obviously false and absurd—or you use them as substitutes for the terms they are supposed to eliminate. But then you would not have said anything else than what you would have said with terms referring to the mental states that the behaviorists have tried to avoid.[30]

Polanyi's point seems to have been that no particular behavior stands out of the welter of motions an animal exhibits as something worth investigating unless such actions have first acquired a meaning (i.e., are recognized to belong to a focal whole) in mentalistic terms through our participatory dwelling in them, and thus through our reading a meaning into them. Whatever objectivist terms we invent to call these sets of actions in place of the ordinary mentalistic terms which are to be discarded, the mentalistic meanings remain tacitly in mind, giving meaning to the patterns of behavior and thus to the objectivist terms we have given them.

Polanyi found that there are three logical levels that philosophers of science distinguish, based upon their distinction between our knowledge of things and our reflection upon our knowledge of things. First, there are the objects of a science; second, the science itself; and third, meta-science, the logic and epistemology of that science. The science of inanimate objects is thus only two-storied, because it consists only of the objects of the science (level one) and the science of them (level two).[31] Some parts of biology are also two-leveled, Polanyi held: those parts that observe an individual body simply existing by itself. But biology becomes three-storied when it observes an individual doing or knowing something. This is because, he maintained, when an animal is doing or knowing something, the commitment it makes in such an action may be true or false, since the animal may be right or wrong in its action or knowledge. The biologist's understanding of this commitment must therefore entail a theory of rightness or knowledge; such a theory is thus analogous to the third level, that of logic and epistemology.[32]

Among living things, Polanyi pointed out, there are three general kinds of commitment. One is primordial, a vegetative commitment by a center of being, growth, and function. It is not therefore in any sense deliberate. Another kind is primitive, that of the active-perceptive state, which is in a sense deliberate, since the animal takes action in reference to its needs; yet it is not a responsible commitment in the sense that those of a consciously deliberating person are. The third type is such a responsible commitment. Biology, being about living things, is therefore at its own level (that of the science itself) inclusive of all three of these levels. It "is a responsible commitment which appraises other commitments."[33]

In its narrower sense, Polanyi said, biology is a responsible commitment that appraises primordial and primitive commitments. As such it is even at this level three-storied, since it must deal with criteria for success or failure of these lower organisms and of their actions. It is also participatory in a fuller sense than are our sciences of the inanimate world. We cannot understand what goes on in these organic commitments without using the organism's actions as clues to their meaning (i.e., without dwelling in them as the organism does with reference to its needs and wants), as well as clues to the organism's proper development. By dwelling in their behavior and so understanding what orients its particulars, we observe, for instance, that animals are puzzled, that they try ways of solving their problems, that they are seeking food or a mate, that they fear—even, in higher animals, that they dream. We would be hard put to sort out their behavior into significant patterns, even for the purpose of behavioristic correlation, if we could not use our capacity for indwelling. Polanyi held that, however much some biologists may attempt to conceal even from themselves that they are resorting to such indwelling, it is clear that they do make use of their capacity to do this.[34]

When it comes to the appraisal of the third type of commitment, the responsible, the kind of participation it requires forces biology into a radically different situation. Here biology's appraisal of responsible commitments must include the appraisal of its own as well, and its observations, Polanyi claimed, must extend beyond biology in the narrower sense "into a domain that may be called 'ultra biology'." Our knowledge of the living being is thus elevated "into a *critical meeting* of it."[35]

We thus rise stage by stage, he said, from morphology to animal psychology, and our convivial participation in the living organism becomes increasingly richer, more intimate, and less unequal. When we arrive at the study of human thought, our participation becomes at last mutual. "A conscious, responsible person—the biologist—is now appraising the achievements of another person of the same rank, whose thoughts can claim respect on the same grounds as his own." Their mutual reference to the same grounds of thought expands itself into a common acknowledgment of a knowledge superior to their own: the superior knowledge of their culture, mediated by the great men who are founders and exemplifiers of that culture.[36]

Polanyi wrote:

> The feelings by which we appreciate the achievements of beings lower than ourselves, involve an extension of ourselves by which we participate in their achievements. But though the naturalist is inspired by the love of nature, and all biology derives its interest ultimately from the fascination exercised on us by living beings, even the most passionate animal lover receives no instruction from his pet. Only as the biologist's participation rises to the level of human companionship, does it become distinctly self-modifying and thus eventually loses altogether its observational character, to become a condition of pure indwelling.[37]

When we surrender our person to the standards of another person's superior knowledge for the sake of becoming more satisfying to ourselves in the light of these standards, the three-level structure of biology gives way once more, Polanyi said, to a two-level structure but not to the same two-level structure it had before. At this point the two levels consist of (1) a man—at the lower level—centering on (2) things higher than himself. Biology at this point coincides with our commitment to the intellectual standards of our culture, the firmament of obligations under which we dwell and to which we have obligations. We cannot look upon these commitments in a noncommital, detached, wholly observational way without destroying them. Here "scientific observation" must coincide with participation, or there is literally nothing to observe. "You cannot," he said, "express your commitment non-committally."[38]

> If he turns back and examines what he respects in a detached manner . . . he dissolves their power over himself and his own powers gained through obeying them. . . . Then law is no more than what the courts will decide, art but an emollient of nerves, morality but a convention, tradition but an inertia, God but a psychological necessity. Then man dominates a world in which he himself does not exist.

When he has lost his obligations, Polanyi said, he has lost his voice and hope, and been left behind, meaningless to himself.[39]

Polanyi therefore thought that only the acceptance of an ontological hierarchy, in which we believe each level has a reality of its own, with emergent structural principles unique to itself, can free us to take the meaningful integrations created in the noosphere seriously as comprehensive entities existing in their own right as precisely what their meanings say they are. Doing so would also, he thought, open to us a belief in the reality of the obligations entailed in the various structures of the noosphere and lead us to see both the paucity and the dangers of psychological behaviorism. Were we to adopt the hierarchical view of the world he was arguing for, he thought that we might be able once again to believe in the traditional values that nihilism and its resulting moral inversions have destroyed, without fear that we were losing our intellectual integrity.

We must note here, however, that Polanyi thought that these beliefs in values and obligations were actually free commitments—that their truth cannot be objectively demonstrated in any way. His "treatment" (his suggested reformation in the ontological views we dwell in in our life-sciences), were we to accept it, would therefore only remove certain contemporary obstacles to our making commitments to noospheric values. It would not and could not cause us to make such commitments, either in the physical sense of bringing them about in our minds necessarily (that is, causing them) or in the rational sense of showing us that we must logically make such commitments (that is, showing us sufficient reasons for them). His approach would only tell us that the idea of a multi-level universe makes at least as much sense as, if indeed not more than, does the idea of a single-level universe, and that, should we find integrations made from these noospheric values meaningful, there can be no ontological or metaphysical reasons for us not to accept them as valid integrations.

This position is somewhat like that of William James in his "Will to Believe," in which he held that we will be unable to exercise our will to believe (in this case, in religion) if the view of the world involved in it is not a viable alternative for us. Polanyi could be said to have been attempting to create for us the viability of such an alternative view of the world.

Polanyi was always very clear about the fact that all views, including this one, if held, must be held in the absence of demonstrable proof, and recognized as due to the basic beliefs and commitments in which we are dwelling. He thought that conversion from one world view or one philosophic position to another was possible, but not because of conclusive arguments for the new and against the old. Conversion, he thought, as we have seen, occurs when a person sees that a new world view would seem to open many more possibilities for a richer field of meaning than the one he previously held. But even conversion to this position, Polanyi held, is subject to the very same limitation which it points to. He took Gödel's theorems very seriously. No conceptual system can ever demonstrate within its system its own consistency. Belief in it is always based on personal, tacit grounds, extraneous to the system, when we rely upon it to get us to what we believe to be the truth about anything.

Because participation at the highest level required for an understanding of men's works and ways is virtually the same as what is required of a person in the performance or appreciation of these works and ways, it becomes necessary for an inquirer to understand what goes on in the actual performance of these works. His participation is therefore not with a part of his being—with the various clues he dwells in personally in making his integrations—but, as we shall soon see, with the whole of his person in an actual performance. He must, as Polanyi said, be "carried away" by a poem, a painting, or a religion—even in order merely to understand it as the comprehensive entity it is. The degree of his participation is therefore much higher at the third logical level than at the other levels. But Polanyi also came to hold in his last lectures and in *Meaning*, his last book, that the very kind of participation is different.

There are hints of this sort of participation in his earlier works. In *Personal Knowledge* he held, for instance, that what a religious person understands as a miracle can never be given a natural explanation. It must always be a supernatural event. If it can be explained naturally, it is no longer to be regarded as a miracle. A person's participation in his religion is such as to enable him to bring together events occurring in nature with a Cause that is not in nature; it seems clear that this participation is not of the same order as that which the person uses in his perception of natural objects and the knowledge he achieves of natural events either in or out of the sciences. It is achieved through his tacit dwelling in religious rites, ceremonies, worship, prayer, and doctrines.[40]

Later, as we shall see in a subsequent chapter, he abandoned the use of the word "supernatural" for that of "transnatural," which he then made use of to speak of integrations made not only in religion but in the arts as well, and he coupled this terminology with a notion of personal participation that differed not only in degree but also in kind from the sort of personal participation essential for perception and for knowledge.

# CHAPTER ELEVEN

# The Arts

Michael Polanyi moved into his discussion of our unique mode of participation in the arts by pointing out the differences between the function of signs and that of symbols. He held that the most elementary use of language is to serve as indicators in the designation of things, i.e., as signs. He held that the connection between a word and that of which it is a sign is not, as has been commonly supposed, that of simple association. A word, he said, bears on that of which it is the sign and which is its meaning.

As Polanyi described it:

On entering Trafalgar Square in London, you can see the National Gallery and the Nelson Column. Once you have looked at them in turn, each might recall the other in an equal manner. But suppose you become aware of the tourist guide pointing at the Nelson Column; you notice the Column and the guide's finger in two different ways. The Column is interesting in itself, but the guide's finger is interesting only in its capacity for directing attention to something other than itself. If the guide then tells his audience the name of the Column, its members are not interested in the sound he utters but in this sound's capacity to direct their attention to something other than itself, i.e., the Column. They may remember both the Column and its name, but the Column will be remembered for its own sake, while its name will be remembered only because of its meaning, which is the Column. The word in use has in fact no interest in itself, as an object; in this it is very different from the object it names, which is interesting in itself as an object.

This refutes the theory of verbal meaning as an equal association of word and object and confirms instead our view that such meaning consists in a from–to relation.[1]

Words used in this denotative sense are indicators, pointing something out and therefore being used by us in a subsidiary way, as other such indicators, such as maps and road signs and formulas, pointing us to something of some interest. As such they are not themselves objects of interest. As subsidiaries bear, then, upon their focal meaning, they are not equal partners, and we are not as interested in them as in what they bear upon.[2]

The class of tacit-knowing operations that are involved in instances of indication—of sign behavior—are these in which the sign is of no intrinsic interest as compared with that of which it is the sign. Polanyi schematized this as:[3]

$$-\text{ii} \qquad +\text{ii}$$
$$S \rightarrow F$$

Polanyi said:

It is the object of focal attention that possesses the intrinsic interest (+ ii). It is what is at the end of the cane that engages the blind man's interest, not the feelings in the palm of his hand. It is the meaning of a communication in words that engages our attention and interest, not the words as such. In fact, an accomplished linguist may not even be able to say later in what language a particularly interesting communication came to him![4]

Polanyi called these kinds of integrations of subsidiary clues "self-centered integrations." They are self-centered, "because they are made *from* the self as a center (which includes all the subsidiary clues in which we dwell) *to* the object of our focal attention."[5] He provided us with an exemplary list of them.

Sensory clues fused to perception
Two retinal images fused to three-dimensional sight

Two stereo pictures fused to three-dimensional sight
Deliberate motions fused to intended performance
Actions taken in causing something to happen
Establishment of part–whole relations
Structure of a complex entity, e.g., a physiology
Series of integrations forming a stratification
Use of clues to establish reality of a discovery
A simulation identified with a simulated object
Recognition of a member of a class
Use of a name to designate an object[6]

Polanyi contrasted these meanings to a group of meanings or integrations in which subsidiary clues do *not* function as mere indicators. The location of our intrinsic interest is shifted in these from the focal object to the subsidiary clues, resulting, said Polanyi, in our being "*carried away*" by the meanings in this group. He explained why and how this second group "carry us away," in a manner in which none of the integrations listed above do, by first showing what is involved in symbolization.[7]

Polanyi wrote:

> A name becomes attached to its object to some extent and comes to form part of it. There is a similar link between a nation and its solemnly unfolded flag: the nation's existence, our diffuse and boundless memories of it and of our life in it, become embodied in the flag—become part of it. The structure of meaning found in medals, tombstones, and other things of this kind is quite the same. Such intrinsically uninteresting objects of our focal attention do not *indicate* something, as other intrinsically uninteresting things do, for example sounds used subsidiarily as words for denoting an interesting object. Flags and tombstones *denote* a country or a great man but they do not bear upon them as words bear upon their objects; they rather *stand for* such interesting objects, which is to say they *symbolize* them.[8]

Because of this, Polanyi held, the focal object in symbolization is not of intrinsic interest to us as is the focal object in indication. The focal object in symbolization is only of interest to us

> because of its symbolic connection with the subsidiary clues through which it became a focal object. What bears upon the flag, as a word

bears upon its meaning, is the integration of our whole existence as lived in our country.[9]

The flag means what it does, as a flag, because we have put our whole existence into it. We have surrendered ourselves to it. Our personal participation is thus not merely the self-*centered* one seen in the meanings discussed up to this point. It is rather, Polanyi said, a self-*giving* sort of personal participation. We are "carried away" by it because we have surrendered ourselves into it. The flag reflects back upon its subsidiaries and fuses our diffuse memories. Our perception of the focal object, the flag, carries us back toward those diffuse memories of our lives in our country that bore upon the focal object to begin with (as subsidiary clues such as words do). We might say it has provided us with a perceptual embodiment of our diffuse memories. We now, as somewhat integrated selves, are thus picked up into the meaning of the symbol, as a symbol. It is not the mere piece of cloth that it would be were it only a matter of our perception of it. Tombstones and medals, Polanyi said, may also be understood in this same manner.[10]

This continual reciprocating activity involved in our experience of symbols makes it impossible for us to say either that we generate this activity through the symbol or that the symbol generates it in us. Both must be the case, and so our "perception" (if that is the right word) of a symbol is possible only through our imagination. There is no merely linear direction, as there is in indication, in which a word or formula bears upon the object of our awareness, but not the object upon the word. In the case of a symbol each side bears upon the other.

Unlike the indication-type of integration that Polanyi diagrammed by a straight-line, one-directional arrow from S to E, he maintained that for diagramming symbolization integration we must make the arrow loop in order to take account of this complex, mutual interaction of both S (the subsidiary clues) and F (the focal object).[11]

The integration of      +ii      −ii

our existence:          S⟲►F

This schematization shows the reversal of the location of our intrinsic interest. In symbolization, our intrinsic interest (the ± ii) lies in the subsidiary clues rather than in the focal object of the indication process.

Polanyi moved from this discussion to the difficult problem of metaphor. He held that the power of metaphors to move us deeply had never been adequately explained. It must lie, he held, in the capacity readers have to connect the diverse matters in a metaphor into a whole. Polanyi thought that the manner in which he held that we integrate clues into a focal whole—ranging from ordinary perception to generalization and including all our use and understanding of language—provided the basis for our understanding of what goes on in a metaphor.[12]

A metaphor, he held, is composed of disparate parts. One thing is said to be another thing, which is never said in any naturalistic understanding of them. He gave a number of examples, but concentrated particularly upon one in order to show what he thought is involved in metaphors. He quoted from Shakespeare's *Richard II*:[13]

> Not all the waters of the rough rude sea
> Can wash the balm from off an anointed king.

He pointed out that in prose these words would simply assert that the balm used in anointing a king sticks so firmly that not all the waters of the sea can wash it off, implying that an anointed king cannot be deprived of his office, because he cannot be deprived of his balm and that it is his anointment with this balm that makes him a king. Understood naturalistically, this claim is, of course, absurd. As Polanyi put it:

> It does indeed affirm such a claim in the literal meaning of the words used, but it means something more than this literal meaning. The semantic mechanism by which a clear and forceful metaphorical meaning is established is the same as that by which a flag is made to symbolize a country—with the difference that the flag (as a piece of cloth) is meaningless in itself, while the verbal projection of the seas trying in vain to wash the balm from a king, though fanciful, is far from meaningless. In fact it presents a tremendous spectacle to our imagination.[14]

There is also a symbol used in this metaphor, but unlike the flag as symbol, it has a significance of its own. The "tremendous spectacle" indicated by the words—that of all the seas trying in vain to wash the balm off an anointed king—is itself meaningful, even if fanciful. And it is akin to the notion of the inability of mere power to deprive a king of his legitimate authority. So, Polanyi held, a metaphor results "when a symbol embodying a significant matter *has a significance of its own* and this is akin to the matter it embodies."[15]

The tenor bears on the vehicle, but, as in the case of a symbol, the vehicle (the focal object) returns back to the tenor (the subsidiary element) and enhances its meaning, so that the tenor, in addition to bearing on, also becomes embodied in the vehicle.[16]

The subsidiary element, the tenor, the eternal authority of a king, through the work of our imagination, bears upon the vehicle, the focal object in this metaphor, the vain work of all the seas upon the balm. The one bears upon the other because the spectacle in the metaphor provides an imagined embodiment for the subsidiary idea of the king's permanent authority. But the vehicle, the focal object, the spectacle of the seas, also reflects back on the tenor, the notion of the king's inviolable authority, and enhances its meaning. That is, the spectacle makes the king's authority more vivid and alive to our imagination.

Polanyi diagrammed it thus:[17]

$$t \text{ [tenor]} \qquad v \text{ [vehicle]}$$
$$+ii \qquad\qquad +ii$$
$$S \longleftarrow \circ \longrightarrow F$$

As for our rapture in the metaphor, Polanyi believed this arises when we add a level to this work of the imagination by involving ourselves in it:

As in the symbol, so in the metaphor: the subsidiary clues—consisting of all those inchoate experiences in our own lives that are related to the two parts of a metaphor—are integrated into the focal object (a metaphor). The result is that a metaphor, like a symbol, carries us away, embodies us in itself, and moves us deeply as we surrender ourselves to it.

The metaphor from *Richard II*, the story of the sea and the balm, which in a literal sense is preposterous, is suffused with the feelings—with the king's angry pride and defiance—and so becomes enlarged into a powerful and moving image, embodying our own diffuse experiences and thus giving us an object in which to see them as integrated.[18]

The full diagrammatic representation of this was provided by Polanyi:[19]

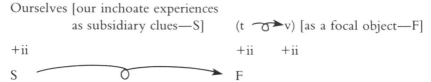

Ourselves [our inchoate experiences
          as subsidiary clues—S]      (t     v) [as a focal object—F]

+ii                                    +ii      +ii

S                        O                    F

The metaphor, the imaginative integration of both its parts (the tenor
and the vehicle), functions now as a whole, as the focal object (F), while
the inchoate experiences in our lives, which it integrates through its
reflexive bearing upon them, serve as the subsidiary elements (S).[20] Each
of these is of intrinsic interest to us, and each bears upon the other for its
meaning, as the tenor and the vehicle do in the metaphor.

The analysis of a metaphor is thus very complex (it is like a wheel
within a wheel) and the integrations in it are all made by our imaginative
feelings. They cannot be given explicit statement. Metaphors, like jokes,
Polanyi told us, lose their effectiveness if they are explained in detail. In
such explanations we switch our focal attention from our focal meaning
(the imaginatively perceived meaning of the metaphor) to those subsidiary clues of which it is the meaning, and so the function of its subsidiaries
(which is to bear upon their meaning) cannot be performed, since we
have ceased using them as subsidiaries, that is, we have stopped dwelling
in them, by focusing our attention upon them. Just as Polanyi has told us
before that a word, focused upon itself as an object, loses its meaning
(i.e., that we can only use it meaningfully as a subsidiary bearing upon its
object, that is, upon its meaning) so the subsidiaries, our inchoate experiences, if focused upon, lose the meaning they acquired through being
embodied as subsidiaries in the metaphor, the object of our focal attention. Metaphors therefore assist our selves to become more integrated
wholes—more meaningful selves—through our surrendering ourselves
to being carried away by our participation in metaphors. Metaphors,
through our participation in them, literally establish meaning in our
lives—a meaning that could never be established through perception or
scientific knowing, and certainly never rendered explicit and "told" in
any prosaic fashion. The tenor and the vehicle, joined in our minds
imaginatively as they are, are naturalistically incompatible. They can
only be joined by our imagination when suffused with feeling in a
moving metaphor.[21]

Representative poetry, like metaphors, Polanyi held, is composed of
two incompatible parts. One is what he called the story it tells us—a

story that can be stated in prose. The other part is what he called its frame. This frame is composed of the formal features of the poem: "its rhythm, its rhymes, its sounds, its grammatical construction, and the peculiar connotations of the words used." Again, we can examine all these parts separately; but such explication, he held, "dims and may even efface the meaning of the poem."[22]

He held that, after such analysis, the meaning of the poem may be brought back to us with even a deeper understanding, if we once more simply dwell in these parts, as subsidiaries, and turn our focal attention away from them to the poem as the whole that is the meaning of their parts. But through its explicit analysis the poem may have irrevocably lost some of its freshness. He held we cannot substitute a set of explicit relations between the parts—a focal knowledge of the frame and the story—for the meaning that is only achieved through our dwelling in the parts (the frame and the story) as subsidiaries to the meaning of the poem.[23]

The existence of a frame, Polanyi said, also serves to detach the poem as a distinctive artifact from our ordinary run of life. A poem is not, therefore, a communication of facts. It is something heard only by the imagination. The prose content of a poem, its story, often sounds shabby, said Polanyi; but the integration of the story with its frame performed by our imagination can be beautiful and moving.[24]

Polanyi called our special attention, in connection with the representative arts, to the fact that all these self-giving integrations involve our capacity to integrate incompatibles. We can integrate clues in perception and in scientific knowing that, before we integrated them, seemed incompatible to us. But the difference is that we finally do see them in a naturalistic frame that enables us to see them at last as naturally compatible. Each advance in science from Copernicus to Einstein and Planck has required us to change our perspectives on the universe in order to see its integrations as "natural." But we have been able to do this, and, once we have, then our contemplation of phenomena in these terms has not required a further act of the imagination.

In the arts he maintained, however, that such acts of the imagination are always required every time we contemplate any of their artifacts. For the clues they require us to integrate can never be seen by us to be naturally integratible. Such integrations, said Polanyi, are thus *trans-natural*.

Polanyi pointed this out vividly in his remarks about the incompatibility of the frame and the story in a play.

> In witnessing a murder on the stage, we are aware of the setting and the antecedents of the stage murder, which are incompatible with the murder's being genuine; yet—just as in the case of the metaphor—we do not reject these contradictory affirmations, which would make the stage murder a nonsensical deception, but call upon our imaginative powers to integrate incompatible matters into a joint meaning. The joint meaning has, in a play, the peculiar quality of a dramatic event visible only to the imagination, just as the meaning of a metaphor, produced by integration of its two incompatible constituents, is known to us only in our imagination.[25]

"Stage plays," he reminded us, "have a remarkable range of subsidiaries. The playwright, the director, the actors, the designers, the whole theater and the mechanisms of stage properties . . . ."[26] We do not respond to a stage murder as if it were real, nor do we have to engage in a "willing suspension of unbelief" (to use an unhappy phrase of Coleridge) in order not to do so. The whole frame of the performance sets the play apart for us, detaches it from the ordinary run of life. But we are integrating features that are not naturally compatible. The spectacle of the stage murder, which carries us away and moves us deeply, is not compatible with the obvious staging of it as a play. Yet Polanyi held that, as in the case of symbols, metaphors, and poetry, it is the act of the imagination bringing these two incompatibles together and, in the process, reaching back into our own inchoate experiences and feelings for the clues that makes the whole integration of the play (frame and story) meaningful and powerfully moving for us. It is all this that makes what goes on on the stage more moving and meaningful than such actual events in our ordinary lives could be.

Again, as in the presence of great poetry, we ourselves become more meaningful to ourselves in the presence of great plays. And the same is true of representative art for Polanyi. Again there is a frame and a story. The story is what the painting represents. Its frame is the canvas and paints, the brush strokes, and the combination of shapes and colors. Polanyi showed us how these are strikingly incompatible in the case of the apparent visual depth, which is part of the story in a painting, and the flatness of the canvas upon which it is portrayed.[27]

This demonstration of his also enabled him to point out that it has never really been the function of art to imitate the objects that it portrays in its "stories." Art, even obviously representative art, has not been interested in creating the illusion that the objects it represents are real, that is, are really there. He showed us that painting fails as art when it tries to achieve such truly imitative effects. He pointed to the trompe l'oeil effects of such paintings as that on the ceiling of the Church of Saint Ignatius in Rome. When one stands in the center of the nave and looks up, one sees the pillars of the dome continue on up into Heaven. The effect of the painting is an illusion of the pillars really continuing up beyond the real pillars. Yet if one moves from the center, the illusion is destroyed, because one sees the painted pillars as merely painted, due to the fact that they are now distorted. By contrast he pointed out that in a painting that we take to be a work of art and not an illusion of reality, what we see on the flat canvas is never distorted even when we view it from an angle. This cannot be due merely to the fact that the painting is on a flat surface while the paintings of the St. Ignatius pillars are on a spherical surface, because if we take a photograph of a painting from an angle, we find that the images in the painting are in optical fact distorted when seen from an angle. We see a painting through our imagination and thus as a work of the artist's and of our imagination, because we grasp its frame in a subsidiary fashion (as a camera cannot do—it must "see" everything focally) and so we see the work from all angles just as we would from a position directly in front of it. It is an artifact for us, framed by its own subsidiaries of which we are always aware in a subsidiary manner and thus detached from our ordinary life. What presents us with an illusion cannot be so detached from our ordinary life, since we do not, tacitly, frame it, as we do a work of art.[28]

Polanyi went on to point out that if we make the canvas, the brush strokes, the texture of the paint, and so forth, into focal objects, we lose our grasp of the meaning of the painting. For we do not then see the story. The story can only be seen by our dwelling in the elements of the frame in such a way as to integrate them into the whole that is the painting.[29]

What might seem to be a difficulty for Polanyi, namely, nonrepresentative painting (since it lacks a "story"), was actually turned by him to his advantage. He held that when first the poets, such as Baudelaire, in the mid-nineteenth century began to write poems whose story content was inchoate, and then when later artists began to paint such paintings, and later still when the Theater of the Absurd began to create such dramas, people had to recognize (in order to see anything in them) that all of these kinds of art were nothing but works of the imagination from start to finish, from their inception and creation by the artists to their readers' or viewers' appreciative grasp of them. The incompatibles that the imagination had to integrate into a meaning were now not simply a frame and a story, but the very words, lines, and forms, episodes and speeches presented. These were, in any naturalistic frame, incompatible. Men who tried to find something in these artifacts were, of course, thrown entirely upon their imaginations in ways that could not be hidden from them by the age-old supposition that a work of art was a mimesis and should be judged by how real it made its story seem to us.[30]

Of course, even in these forms of art which Polanyi called "visionary," there is a frame that detaches them from our ordinary life, but part of that frame is precisely what is said or put on the canvas in shapes and figures. For these also served to detach the work from our ordinary life just as any remaining formal elements did. Watches do not run down over the edge of tables in our ordinary experiences.[31]

For Polanyi it is also this movement toward visionary art of various kinds that helps us see how the problem of the validity of art can be understood. Works of the arts cannot, we can surely see by now, be verified for Polanyi. If we can consider them true and real in any sense, it is not because they truly portray anything that exists—the world, ourselves, our lives. In a very real sense they can be said rather to create a world, a self, and a life for us—or rather perhaps induce us through the work of our imagination to create these things. Their validity therefore rests for him precisely in their power to do this and to continue to do this for us. Polanyi could not, therefore, provide us with explicit criteria of any sort for assessing the validity of any work of art. He could only tell us that it is valid, if it does move us deeply, carries us away, induces us to create a work of our imagination in its presence which involves our surrender of ourselves to it, and results in the further integration of our inchoate experiences into a meaningful whole, a life, a self.[32]

Where then, we may ask, is the universal intent he spoke of? It lies in the fact that what we have been induced by the work to integrate is something which we believe it can also lead others to integrate, if they view it from the perspective and with the equipment we have. The work, to be valid, must not merely move us because we happen to be the idiosyncratic person we are, for then we should not suppose that others also ought to be so moved and thus that it is a good work of art. It is not for us a mere personal icon or love object, much less something that satisfies our own personal desires and gives us pleasure. It "bears witness" beyond our own personal satisfaction with it "to the presence of an inexhaustible fund of meaning in it which future centuries may yet elicit." It is thus for us a work of art with "universal validity."[33] Perhaps it is because of this feature that he believed we should have great respect for the tastes of the band of artists themselves who create the works, and should rather blame ourselves than them if we are not moved by the works that moved them.[34]

There are three more realities of the noosphere that are formed by a transnatural integration of incompatibles and that belong in the group of self-giving integrations, according to Polanyi. These are rites, myths, and religions; they were, for Polanyi, involved in each other. Let us therefore discuss them together in the next chapter.

# CHAPTER TWELVE

# Religion

T aking off once more from his inter-
pretation of what constitutes a symbol, Michael Polanyi interpreted rites
and ceremonies by noting first that actions as well as objects, may be
symbolic. An action itself may be without intrinsic interest, but may
acquire such interest by serving as an embodiment for some other action
which is considered of essential importance.[1]

A symbolic action will also become metaphorical, he held, when the
symbolic action bears some resemblance to the action it embodies. The
Christian rite of baptism is an instance of this. The pouring-on of water
resembles the ordinary utilitarian action of washing, and so the rite
becomes symbolic of the cleansing of our sins.[2]

As in the case with poetry and other works of art, rites and solemnities—ceremonies—"break into the course of our current occupations
and set free the imagination from the cares of the day." In painting and
drama, as we have seen, it was the basic techniques and instrumental
material, said Polanyi, that detached them from the course of our normal
experience. In poetry, it was the special poetic devices used in the text.
In all these cases, Polanyi summarized, the power to arouse our imaginations and isolate our minds from day-to-day affairs lay in their artificiality. They are not natural occurrences or ordinary phenomena.

They strike us as artifacts. The same, he held, is true of rites and ceremonies. Their artificial character is emphasized by their breaking directly into our daily lives through decreeing a pause in our ordinary activities in order that we may perform them.[3]

Polanyi in quoting Helmut Kuhn wrote:

"What we celebrate in a feast and consecrate in it can be of many different kinds, but it is basically always the same: it is the content of truth in our existence or in the existence of a society." And he discerns profundities even in the light-hearted celebration of an ordinary birthday: "When we celebrate and solemnize the passage of our life, we confirm thereby the whole natural order, of which human life with its cycle of birth and death forms part." Subjects that lie deepest in our existence are most fitly recalled in traditionally recurrent forms, since an "established" way of doing so expresses our affiliation to a comprehensive and lasting framework much better than a form we simply improvise for the occasion.[4]

Polanyi said that works of art

by their detachment . . . stand outside time and hence speak to us of one single moment. Centuries may pass over a work of art; but if it be still recognized, it will still speak of the same moment. Our feasts, ceremonials, and solemnities are also withdrawn from the day and from our passing lives. Although they do speak often of the past, they are nevertheless themselves outside time in what they seek to convey. They are timeless moments, whether what they celebrate is personal or historic.[5]

Polanyi maintained that we have a special difficulty in truly dwelling in formal rituals and customs, which of course we must do, if they are to be meaningful to us. Our modern temper, he held, balks at things that are as essentially unoriginal as traditional rites and ceremonies. We think they are only shallow pretenses because they cannot, being simply decreed by tradition, be expressive of genuine feelings. He claimed this attitude misses their point. It is the very artificiality of traditional forms that makes it possible for them to act as a framework detaching the important events in our lives (birth, marriage, death, etc.), which they embody, from our ordinary run of life and so giving them a forceful and lasting quality.[6]

Destroying formal occasions "in the name of authenticity has the effect," he said

> of diffusing our existence into scattered details, deprived of memorable meaning. Only through our surrender to such occasions do we find ourselves affiliated to a comprehensive, lasting framework which gives meaning to our life and death and to the myriads of separate events in between. Otherwise we do not see the universality that we share with others. Occasions, such as our birth and death, and those of others whose lives we share, can be seen as essential to a lasting whole of things when marked by appropriate ceremonies or rites.[7]

However, the basis for our meaningful participation in rites and ceremonies lies, he held, in myths that in some sense we believe to be true. Here also, Polanyi held, the modern mind meets with great difficulties. We do have our myths; but the trouble is that our reductionist, scientistic myths tend to destroy for us the meaning of all rites and ceremonies.

Myths, Polanyi noted, are structured throughout by symbolic actions that are metaphors and that make up a large part of rites and ceremonies. Polanyi relied to a considerable extent for his views about myths upon the work of Mircea Eliade and to some extent that of Ernst Cassier. His analysis concentrated mainly upon archaic creation myths in order to show the structure of myth and how myths are related to rites.

Creation myths, Polanyi echoed Eliade, narrate a sacred history to us. They relate events that take place in primordial time, the fabled time of the "beginnings." This is the sacred time of the nontemporal instant—the "Great Time," as Eliade called it. It is thus not the profane time of our everyday existence, the continuous and irreversible time we know in our ordinary existence. It is the "once-upon-a-time" of "in the beginning." It tells us of the origin of the world, of plants, animals, and men—and of the characteristics of man. It tells how they become mortal, sexed, organized into societies, compelled to work, etc. But it tells all this as having its origin in events in the Great Time.[8]

In rites and ceremonies one recites and performs the origin myth and through these actions of his becomes steeped in the sacred atmosphere in which the miraculous events took place. The recitation and performance reconstitutes that fabulous time, and so becomes, as it were, contemporary with its events. The sacred thus progressively permeates the ordinarily temporal sphere and invests the moments of a person's life with great meaning, a meaning derived from the time of the Great Time.[9] Polanyi declared,

> The recital of a myth is an experience that is detached from the day-to-day concerns of the reciting person in the same way as the frame aspect of a work of art detaches us from the concerns of the day. It raises us to a timeless moment. What happens when we accept a myth is what happens when we listen to great poetry or a great play or view a great painting: we are overcome by it and carried away into its own sphere, away from the sphere in which we lived a moment ago and to which we shall presently return. It is the kind of detachment that we experience by observing a festive occasion or a day of mourning. The detachment associated with rituals prescribed by archaic myths is clearly akin to religious devotion.[10]

> Our personal involvement in the world is *with some parts of the world*, while the conception of creation encompasses the *whole* world—the world that lies beyond or under or through all its parts. The one is concerned with things as parts, while the other ignores these matters and has the totality of all conceivable experiences as its object. Creation is the event by which all conceivable things are believed to have come into existence; and the creator, or creators, are supernatural in the sense that they transcend all particular matters. In this sense, therefore, myths of creation are untranslatable into terms that apply to things within the world. Archaic myths and the invocations of archaic myths are therefore of an intrinsically detached nature. They are wholly other than actual human experience.[11]

So Polanyi maintained that myths also can affect us only if they can detach us from our ordinary world of experience. But this they can do, he held, because the events described or portrayed are wholly other than actual human experience. To believe the myth and to live it through its rites is thus to carry us away to a transnatural integration, such as exists also in art and poetry, in which incompatibles (which remain incompatibles) are combined into a meaningful integration by a feat of our imagination.[12]

But religious integrations such as the myth of creation, Polanyi held, are different from the transnatural achievements of poetry and art.

These religious conceptions speak of the entire universe and of our destiny within such boundless perspectives. They are therefore, he held, mystical and sacred. A myth, he stated, speaks of events as recollected, not merely represented. The myth is assumed to be true, therefore, and not merely a poetic representation of things. The rapture it engenders is greater than that engendered by art. But in what sense could we suppose myths to be true? Polanyi pointed to the magic and superstition connected in archaic thought to myths, and indicated that we must separate the truth of myths from such beliefs, if we are to think of myths as true, for our naturalism involved in our acceptance of modern science will not permit us to accept magic and superstition.

We are driven by archaic myths to intuit a mystical union of all and the loss of a clear conception of separable parts. Polanyi referred to the *via negativa* of Christian mysticism, as in the union of incompatibles entailed in Nicholas of Cusa's *coincidentia oppositorum*. This is a radical anti-intellectualism which is not entirely acceptable, since, as Polanyi reminded us, "St. Augustine said enviously that it was free to the simple-minded but closed to the learned." Polanyi seemed to be indicating that our acknowledgement of the truth of myth must rest on more intellectual grounds. [13]

In attempting to ask how we might accept truth in myths, Polanyi explored the possibility that the archaic mind that generated these myths along with vast numbers of clear absurdities may have operated differently from our modern mind. He rejected this proposition, largely because he thought that it is quite possible to explain how the absurdities of archaic thought could have arisen without such an assumption. We may suppose, Polanyi held, that the absurdities of archaic thought were due simply to an excessive use of the same integrative powers applied, perhaps more wisely, by modern thought. [14]

Whether integration results in establishing perceptual or cognitive facts or in producing works of the imagination, Polanyi reminded us, the process is essentially informal. Proof of this, of course, lies in the fact that there are qualities present in the integration that are not present in the subsidiaries used in composing it, whereas in a formal process nothing is present in the result that was not present in the premises, i.e., that was not an implication of them. Hence, Polanyi argues, there can be no strict, formal, rules for accepting or rejecting the validity of an integration.

The fact that integration is always a choice is sometimes hidden, because we are so used to deciding that a particular set of clues means one particular thing—say, an elephant. But Polanyi used as an example the controversy about Velikovsky's views (in *Worlds in Collision*) to show that some integrative inferences appear plainly acceptable to some and just as plainly absurd to others. The differences lie in different assessments of plausibility; but plausibility cannot be formally demonstrated, Polanyi held, and thus the controversy about Velikovsky's theories has continued for many years. The differences between modern and archaic thought are of the same sort.

Archaic people's observations of causality were based upon the same kinds of inference that we use today: a temporal sequence of events or a recurrent contiguity of facts. *Post hoc ergo propter hoc* and *juxta hoc ergo propter hoc* are principles used by both modern man and his archaic ancestors. They are indeed, as Hume showed, the proper guides for empirical thinking. Modern man differs from archaic man only in his judging whether certain kinds of observed spatial or temporal contiguities should be regarded as coincidental or as causal.[15]

We use a view of the general nature of things (derived mostly from our sciences) in applying the principles of causation, in order to judge whether contiguities are coincidental or causal, which differs from our ancestors' view of the general nature of things. Even so, Polanyi reminded us, fear of magical causes persists even in intellectual circles today. The Athenaeum Club in London, Polanyi said, has no bedroom numbered 13. Christian services use the invocation of mythic origins to invoke the divine presence—and precatory prayers continue to be uttered.[16]

There are some principles involved in magical relations that we do not use today, however. The principle of the alter ego and (what it is really a part of) that of *pars pro toto* were used by the archaic mind to identify a part with the whole to which it belongs. A man's name, his image, shadow, painting, wax model, etc. were supposed to give their possessor power over the person to which they belong. Polanyi held, however, that all these bear upon the man as subsidiaries to the focal whole that he is, as all subsidiary from–to relations bear upon all meaningful integrations. The archaic mind seemed to be more sharply impressed than we are by the sensory quality of meaningful relations, and its imagination greatly exaggerated (in our judgment) the interactions of subsidiaries and their focus, especially when the object is a human person. Polanyi pointed out that we do not find the names of inanimate things, such as bows, arrows, rivers, parts of broken inanimate objects, in this magical way identical with their wholes. Polanyi thought that the

far greater indeterminate manifestations of human minds as compared
with the manifestations of other things may well lend to a person a
mysterious quality that stimulates the imagination to make such dynamic
connections between a person and what bears on that person.[17]

For Polanyi,

> It is most interesting to note at this point that the modern mind errs
> in the opposite direction. Its conception of meaning *fails* to note the
> deep-set qualities of from–to relations and seeks to reduce the hu-
> man mind to a predictable system of responses.[18]

Totemism is another instance in which the archaic mind differs from
the modern. When a member of a primitive tribe identifies himself with
an animal we may well explain this by the principle of participation
which we have noted, Polanyi said, as operative in all of our integrations.
We dwell in the clues that we integrate, or we extend ourselves into them
when they are outside our body, as in tools. We treat them as part of our
bodies. We have seen that such participation is accentuated in the case of
our knowledge of living things—more and more so in the case of human
beings and of animals having a structure similar to our own. We dwell in
and relive thereby the very motions by which these animals carry out
their actions. This is a sharing of lives and is not due to a deliberate effort
on our part. Dead bodies and their abuse affects us deeply even when we
wish it not to. When much of life consisted in hunting or being hunted,
it is understandable, Polanyi believed, that men's imaginative participation in the life of animals might go well beyond the participation we
actually require to know them, and so become totemistic. After all,
Polanyi pointed out, we ourselves readily identify two objects that we
can readily distinguish from each other. We do this when we identify
two animals as the same species. The Bororos who identify themselves
with one sort of red parrot may do so in the same manner by regarding
themselves and these red parrots as belonging to the same class. They do
not, he noted, ever mistake a tribesman for a parrot or vice versa.[19]

Besides, he reminded us,

> Many scientists and philosophers have, for centuries now, asserted
> that all human beings, including themselves, are automatically func-
> tioning machines. Some modern thinkers have made this even more
> telling by arguing that machines possess consciousness and can have
> every kind of human feeling. To many of us this identification

seems absurd. To them, on the contrary, the view that men have minds which control their actions is the absurd view.[20]

It simply must seem plausible to the Bororos to identify themselves with red parrots, as it seems plausible to many modern men to identify themselves with machines. But, he reminded us, plausibility cannot be demonstrated. It is an informal inference, not a formal one.

In summation, Polanyi said,

> In certain respects the archaic view of things is of course different from what is loosely known as the modern scientific view; but while the range of difference may be wider, the difference itself is perhaps not deeper than the differences in views about the plausibility of coherences held by various groups of people in a modern Western university.

> In evaluating the differences between the archaic and the modern approaches, we have to maintain that the archaic mind is better in many ways. It is right in experiencing names as part of a named person and an image as part of its subject; for a name is not a name, nor an image an image, except as a subsidiary to the focal center on which it bears. And such is the nature of all meaningful relations. Admittedly, the archaic mind tends to exaggerate this coherence to the point of absurdity, but it is closer to the truth than the modern view, which has no place for the quality and depth of these coherences nor, therefore, for the full extent of the subsidiaries that are necessary to their composition. This difference becomes essential in the observation of those comprehensive entities that can be observed only by indwelling. The archaic mind recognizes indwelling as the proper means of understanding living things. Modern biology and psychology abhor this approach to life and mind. The import of their teaching tends rather to be that we are all machines and, in the last analysis, mere atomic topographies. These ideas of Galileo, Gassendi, and John Locke, coupled by Humean associationism, have paved the way to the achievements of modern science, but at the same time have deprived everything that is of primary interest in the world of any grounds of meaning for us.[21]

Polanyi therefore assessed the question of the truth in myths along these lines. He reminded us that all empirical knowledge is rooted in subsidiaries that are to some extent unspecifiable. A corollary to this, he said, is that the range of verbal statements is unlimited. Poetic meaning can richly clarify our own experiences and express them effectively. Looking at the myths of archaic people in this light, we see that they are as clearly works of the imagination as are works of art. And, like works of art, their truth can consist only in their power to evoke an experience in us which we hold to be genuine. Polanyi reminded us that

> Eliade says that the myth of creation makes us aware of a deeper reality that we inevitably lose sight of in our personal pursuits. It sets us free from a "false identification of Reality with what each of us *appears to be or to possess* . . . . The myth continually re-actualises the Great Time, and in so doing raises the listener to a superhuman and suprahistorical plane; which, among other things, enables him to approach a Reality that is inaccessible at the level of profane, individual existence."[22]

Polanyi held that the myth of creation opens to its followers a view of the universe that makes them feel at home in it. Looked at from the perspective of this myth every major event of a man's life evokes for him his descent from his cosmic origin. Every major enterprise he undertakes is undertaken as a rehearsal of the mythical act that first performed such an enterprise. The myth teaches us knowledge of perfection in nature and in virtue. It links those who thus possess this knowledge to an endless company of fathers. On sacred occasions mythical knowledge provides experience of thoughts beyond the range of men's individual lives.[23]

> These results of accepting the myths of creation produce in us experiences that we can believe to be largely genuine and therefore largely true. A belief in the gradual emergence of man from an inanimate universe reveals to us that the dead matter of our origins was fraught with meaning far beyond all that we are presently able to see in it. To set aside an achievement as full of meaning as this— as if an emergence of this sort could happen any day by mere accident—is to block the normal sources of inquisitive thought.

> Man's origin is a mystery which the myth of creation expresses in its own way. And the image of man's destiny, as derived from his mythical origins, is much nearer to our own experience of our own lives, to our experience of human greatness, to our perception of the course of our history since history began, and to our experience of the shattering forces of our utopias than is the image of the barren

atomic topography to which the ideal of detached observations seeks to reduce these matters.

There is, therefore, an important truth in the archaic myth of creation that is missing from the present ideal of scientific knowledge, and in this sense we can agree with Eliade when he speaks of the creation myth as being true.[24]

Let us now turn to Polanyi's understanding of religion and the nature of our acceptance of it. Religion, for Polanyi, is also a work of the imagination. It is a sprawling work, since it incorporates myths, rites, and ceremonies, such as we have been discussing, and also doctrines and worship. As a transnatural integration, it is, for Polanyi, an integration of incompatibles. Moreover, it is detached from our ordinary life by a "frame"—as are works of art. In rites, as we have seen, it is myth that gives them an import. It is not only what is said in the myth that detaches it from the practical affairs of our lives, but, according to Polanyi, it is even more the rites and ceremonies, recreating its expressed actions which detaches the myth from our ordinary lives. As a matter of fact, each serves as the frame for the other's story. An action in ordinary time and space—a ceremony—is framed by one outside ordinary time and space. But such an extraordinary action—the myth—is also framed by an ordinary action, the ceremony. They are incompatible with each other; but they are joined together into a meaningful integration by our imagination. The same is true of worship. The infinite God can hardly be glorified by the praise of finite humanoids. The story—God's praise and glory—is not compatible with the frame we give it—our formal or informal worship. Prayers of thanks and precatory prayers also bristle with incongruities. Yet all these parts of worship, when we dwell in them, enable us to see God. Through our imaginative efforts to integrate rites, myths, and acts of worship, i.e., when we dwell in them as subsidiaries, we see God as the focal object of our attention, as that which gives meaning to all these dwelt-in clues.[25]

Just as in art, Polanyi saw that the transnatural integration of incompatibles which results in God also serves to integrate the inchoate, incompatible aspects of our own lives. Only, it is our *total* life that becomes at last integrated in the presence of God, "all the false starts and stops in our lives, the blind alleys, the unfinished things, the loose ends, the incompatible hopes and fears, pains and pleasures, loves and hates, anguishes and elations, the memories, the half-memories, the forgotten moments that meant so much to us at the time, the disjointed dailiness of our lives—in a word, all of our inchoate memories and experiences"— the faith and hope that we will be given the power by the grace of God to do what we know we must do, but which we know we are not able to do.[26]

> Our myths tell us of the Fall and how and why we are excluded from the Paradise we long for as our natural state. But they also tell us of the Redemption and of the power and grace of God that is to be dispensed to us as needed.[27]

Polanyi addressed himself to the problem of what stands in the way of our acceptance of religious integration. Sacred myths, he told us, give embodiment to the rituals in a religion. But, of course, the myths contain a story and thus have a representational content—as a work of representational art has. Just as the representational content of a work of art—say, a play—must seem plausible to us, so the representational content of religious myth must seem plausible to us, if we are to accept it.[28]

But what sort of plausibility must sacred myths have in order to gain our acceptance? Polanyi reminded us that their plausibility cannot lie in our regarding their accounts of events as factually true in the way in which day-to-day events have a plausibility. Their events have not occurred in secular time. Their very detachment rests upon these events as having occurred, not in ordinary, but in "Great Time." So the plausibility of the story in these myths must be of another order from that of the story in representational art.[29]

Visionary art shows us, however, that even when the story content of a work of art has no plausibility, it is still possible for our imagination to integrate these incompatible elements into a meaning that cannot be expressed in any set of coherent, explicit statements. But something seems to be different in religion, since not all those who can find meaning in the visionary arts can find it in religion. Why are the myths and rites of religion less easily integrated than visionary works of art?

> The reason [wrote Polanyi] lies in the fact that even when all the representational details in the myths are clearly and frankly regarded as impossible (as the "contents" of visionary art are), the *import* of

these details must still be thought to be *plausible*. For, unlike the contents of a work of visionary art, the contents of a religion will have as their import the story of a fundamentally *meaningful* world, whereas the import of a work of visionary art is rather that the world is a meaningless heap of inchoate things. Therefore, if we can regard religious myth as plausible, the sort of world that religious myth represents—a meaningful world—must be thought by us to be plausible. We must be able to say: if not this story exactly, then *something like this* story is how all things are put together. In other words, it must be plausible to us to suppose that the universe is, in the end, meaningful.[30]

Men are therefore not likely, said Polanyi, to find meaning in religion until the views they have of the universe are such that they can once more seriously entertain these meanings as representations of the way things could indeed be.[31]

As we have seen, Polanyi claimed that there is no scientific reason why we cannot believe the religious hypothesis that the world is meaningful. He has shown us that a supposition that a meaning gradient exists not only runs into no evidence contrary to it, but is a help in explaining certain features of embryological and evolutionary development, as well as how we make discoveries in science. In other words, he thought his work showed us that the "story" content of religious myths, viz., that the world is meaningful, can have plausibility for us.[32]

This is, of course, not yet to accept religion. For it must be a particular religion that speaks to us. It "must discover and uphold" its own satisfaction in itself for us. No merely pragmatic or "ulterior advantage can make us believe in God."[33] But should a religion speak to us, we need not find an obstacle to its message in a supposedly scientific view of the world which holds that the world is a meaningless conglomeration of atoms, or that only the tangible can be real.

Thus Polanyi believed he showed us how to apply his prescribed new epistemology and philosophy of science to the job of restoring the possibility of our belief in those intangible, transnatural comprehensive entities that enable us to acquire more integrated and meaningful selves.

How he thought this would finally save us from the disorders of the modern mind we will explore in the next chapter.

# CHAPTER THIRTEEN

# The Free Society

Although Michael Polanyi made many tangential references to art and religion throughout his life, he did not deal with them until late in his life in the detail we have outlined in the preceding chapters.[1] These detailed views were first put forward by him in the form of a lecture series at the University of Texas and at the University of Chicago in 1969. They were developed further by him in another lecture series the following year given at the University of Chicago and in a further and last one in 1971 at the University of Texas.

The lectures on metaphor, poetry, art, myth, and religion given during those years appeared in published form (with my help) in 1975, just before his death.[2]

They form, as I have said, part of his treatment for our ills. They showed us, in his view, how we might understand these human achievements as the ways in which we could, in an unabashed way, restore to man a belief in the meaningfulness and significance of human life and its achievements which he thought our mania for detached objectivity and its concomitant scientism had robbed from us.

Armed with such an understanding of what has been achieved by these works of the imagination, we could allow ourselves to be carried away by them and to dwell in their rich meanings without suffering from the fear that we were degenerating from rational objectivity into various forms of utter subjectivism. Rather, we could understand that our participation in them elevated us into spheres of being which were higher than those of our biological or even our psychological life—higher even than those generated by our obligations to truth and justice.

Here he offered us theories about the status of these works of the imagination which did not reduce them to such interests or urges and instincts as our scientistic approaches to them did. Most of all they would not be understood to be "ideological superstructures" derivative from, and ultimately reducible to, economic class interests. They rather contained (as he had already maintained in *Personal Knowledge*) standards and principles of their own in accord with which their validity could be judged, just as he held that mathematics did. Meanings established in these works of the imagination were therefore as real as those established in mathematics. Universal intent could thus be seen to be involved in these meanings as well as in those of science, perception, and knowledge generally. We thus deal with realities in these areas in the same generic sense as we do in science. That is, they all meet the criterion of our regarding as a reality whatever we feel would exhibit itself in unexpected ways in the future—that which has principles inherent in its own level of being which we never have more than an inkling of at any one moment in our lives. They are never mere subjective constructs. They are also legitimate subjects of personal knowledge.[3]

In one sense, therefore, this final work of his constituted the peak of his achievement, in the sense of the end at which all his efforts had been aiming. And yet, as Aristotle once observed, when there are things to be done, the most important thing is not simply to know them, but to do them. Art and religion and mathematics are to be *done*—both in the sense of our endless working at their construction and in the sense of our endless appreciation of them through the constant activity of our imagination in dwelling in them toward a grasping of their meanings—which also becomes, in the cases of art and religion, the very meaning of ourselves, the structuring of our lives as meaningful.

Long before he had worked out just how he thought all these human activities fit into his conception of the subsidiary–focal structure of our awareness, Polanyi had been concerned about securing the conditions essential for these activities. In the *Logic of Liberty*, he generalized from the structure of the community (or "republic") of science to the various other kinds of articulated human endeavors, such as those of the arts, religion, and law. He indicated that these were all also polycentric problems that required, as did science, that participants enjoy the freedom to make individual and personal contributions. This freedom, if it were not to dissipate itself in chaotic and unproductive efforts, had to exist within a context of a dedication to the abstract ideal ends appropriate to these activities. In more existential terms, this freedom required a dedication to the more concrete, particular aims actually held in common by these participants, which formed them into their several different communities.[4]

Such necessary freedom required a particular sort of society and government in order for it to exist. Polanyi therefore made a broad distinction between a free society and a totalitarian one on the basis of whether or not the activities of the participants in such communities as these—and the activities of the communities themselves—were directed by public authorities. If government interfered with their spontaneous activities to direct their activities into what it supposed were the most socially useful ones, it would inevitably destroy them and with them the dedication to their ideal ends. The society, of course, would then cease to be free.[5]

Respect for these spiritual ends (such ideals as truth, beauty, and justice) thus required public respect for the self-government of these various communities of dedicated researchers, artists, legal practitioners, and worshippers, whether or not their efforts, principles, standards, and commitments could be seen by anyone else to be furthering what might be conceived to be the public interest. Chiefest of sinners against this requirement, for Polanyi, as we have seen, were of course the Marxists and their right-wing counterparts, the Fascists. For these people did not even pay lip service to the spiritual concepts of truth, beauty, and justice, and thus saw not the slightest reason to turn over the definitions and accomplishments of art, science, law, and religion to self-defining communities of devotees of such fictions as truth, beauty, and justice.

But utilitarian thought, even in the sophisticated guise of pragmatism, was also a threat, because such thought more subtly undermined the freedoms of these various communities by trying to justify them solely on the grounds of their supposed tendency to contribute ultimately to the public welfare. That utilitarian and pragmatic arguments were thus denigrating and endangering these essential freedoms was less obvious and, since these views were not explicitly aimed at destroying ultimate allegiance to such ideal ends, they generally only weakened these "public liberties" (as Polanyi called them—"public" because public goods and activities were managed within such liberties). Such utilitarian positions therefore provided rationalizations for the continuance of these liberties. They proposed that such liberties could be deduced as generally important and desirable from the principle of the greatest happiness for the greatest number—or from some necessities encountered in seeking adequate solutions to social problems. Such deductions were not actually or strictly logically valid, Polanyi believed: but not too much harm resulted from these charades as long as people continued to believe that these theories really did entail such implications. However, as we have seen, Polanyi thought it was not a good idea to stake our commitments to these ideals upon such shaky grounds.[6]

He held that these ideals actually could not rest on cognitively logical grounds. They simply were ultimate commitments that we either did or did not make. Ethical theory, therefore, held no interest for Polanyi and he said very little about it.

Moral principles he certainly did talk about, however; they consisted of personally recognized obligations to respect truth, beauty, and justice as continually defined and redefined by scientists and other scholars, and by artists, poets, novelists, and jurists. These personal obligations he thought of as simple, ultimate commitments that were his because he had absorbed them from a social culture that was committed to them. They were thus simply part of what he referred to as his "calling." They could not be demonstrated as eternal truths involved in the nature of things. Other people, he thought, were in a like situation.[7] This fact, he maintained, made the existence and further development of a free society very precarious. The most we could do was to admit that we were, indeed, committed to these ideals—if we were—and to understand intelligently what this meant in order that they might be further developed and protected by those who were their acknowledged custodians.

It therefore became of utmost importance to Polanyi that we should not embrace an epistemology or an ontology which called the truth of these ideals into critical question; he thought the history of modern man amply demonstrated that acceptance of such an epistemology must be the first step in our loss of commitment to these ideals in view of the fact that they did not rest on objectively or logically conclusive grounds, yet continued belief on the parts of citizens generally in the ultimate reality of these ideals was the only basis for the existence of a free society. A free government, i.e., one in which all the citizens are free to take an active part in choosing public officials and policies, was, for Polanyi, an extension of the notion of the Republic of Science. Thus there must also be a context uncritically accepted in which this freedom could be exercised, in keeping with the logic of liberty consisting of certain ultimate convictions or ideals held in common by the citizens. These must be, as we have said, commitments to truth, beauty, justice, and other traditional ideals, such as mercy and fraternity. Without these, Polanyi held, no free community is possible. So a free society is made up of people who are committed to these ideals.[8]

As a result, since such common commitments either do or do not exist at a particular time and place, a free society either will or will not exist at that time and place. If they do, it will, if they do not, it will not. If they do, but they are destroyed, it will also be destroyed. Thus a free society, if it ever exists, is necessarily adrift. We cannot tell where it will go or what it will become. No one is in a position to control it. But this, he maintained, is simply what it means to have a free society. It is not planned, it cannot be planned. Planning a free society is a contradiction in terms.[9]

This brings us back to Polanyi's early and persistent rejection of Marxism and of socialism in general. Let us recapitulate the gist of this rejection from Chapters 1 and 2.

That Marx wished to plan a whole society is not as evident from his writings as that he wished to plan a whole economy. Polanyi held that the planning of a whole economy seemed to Marx, Engels, and at least all their early followers, down to Lenin and even to many socialists in our day, to be the only real alternative to the market and profit mechanisms used by private capitalism to manage the economy.

Marx, of course, tried to refrain from simple moral condemnations of capitalism and even from pragmatic concerns about the difficulties into which it got. He did not in general argue for communism as a cure for either the moral evils or economic deficiencies of capitalism. But this seems strange to many modern socialists and communists and their sympathizers, because, as we have seen that Polanyi made quite clear, the moral passions of men for a good, indeed a perfect society have been in fact (although not in Marx's theory) the underlying motivating force for the widespread acceptance of Marxism, and perhaps they still are. In contrast to the picture of an operational socialism, a going capitalism, operating as it does on the profit motive, seemed synonymous to many with greed, with cold disregard for the economic underdog, with exploitation, and, in short, with self-interest running wild. The picture of a projected communist society, by contrast, could not help but exert a strong appeal to people's underlying moral passions for benevolence, equality, compassion, altruism, peace among men, and mutual helpfulness (i.e., for cooperation rather than competition)—or, briefly, for the morally perfect society.

Marxism, however, came in the guise of a scientific prediction of capitalism's evolving into socialism, not by means of moral persuasion but simply through the real impersonal historical inner economic contradictions of capitalism and by the impetus provided by the class interests of the massive and inevitably growing proletariat. Polanyi thought this gave embodiment to these moral passions which they otherwise obviously lacked, both in the existing capitalist society and in the intellectual framework of the amoral scientism that most educated people firmly believed in, on the Continent at least. Therefore the proponents of Marxism thought the ruthlessness supposedly required by the movement needed no moral apology—first of all, of course, because anyhow no moral principles could be defended intellectually. At the same time, however, the end result gave secret satisfaction to people's hidden or repressed moral passions. Thus was born, as we have seen, the strange frame of mind that Polanyi named "moral inversion."

Polanyi, as we have seen, tried to analyze the growth and development of this frame of mind to account for the impact that Marxism had upon the people of his day—and that it still does, for that matter. Yet he did not attack the movement toward economic planning only through such historical theorizing. He very early was involved in action against the threat he saw to a free society from a planned economy.

Let us ask just what he thought this threat was in order to see why the action he took made sense to him. First of all, the philosophic position embodied in the then popular movement toward a planned economy, and which would come into power with it, was itself a threat to intellectual freedom. For this position was the historical and materialist determinism that formed the intellectual backbone of Marxism. As we have seen, it claimed that all the "ideological superstructure" in society—ethics, political theories and institutions, legal systems, philosophies, arts, sciences, and religions—had come into being to bolster and support the owners of the most important resources required by the mode of production of the day (which in our day is, of course, capital).

Whether men knew it or not, the Marxists held, all of this superstructure was formed to aid those owners in the retention of those resources and their dominant political power in the society. All of these "superstructures," Marx held, were ideological systems with principles and structures of their own; but they were not the guardians of the "true" and "real" values and ideals that they seemed to be to those who worked within them. They served rather a function related to the class interests of the owners of vital resources, in our day the capitalists. These ideological structures and their principles had no legitimacy beyond this function and therefore could claim no right to freedom and self-determination for their adherents in the face of the revolutionary class interests of the proletariat, those interests in fact historically destined to prevail. Therefore, these ideologies and their adherents could, and must, be dealt with ruthlessly in support of proletarian class interests.

Thus, regardless of what one thought of the desirability or non-desirability of social economic planning, the Marxist movement had to be opposed, Polanyi held, if we were committed to the ideals that the various intellectual communities of people espoused. Truth, for instance, for them could not be "party truth," and we must oppose any efforts to make it so.

Polanyi very early not only wrote much about the danger from these ideas for a free society, but also lent his support to various societies and conferences of scholars where efforts to plan science were exposed as deathtraps for science and where counterefforts to bolster scientists' commitments to free inquiry, unhampered by governmental ends ulterior to truth, were encouraged. These efforts were in opposition to the planning of science, regardless of whether the proponents of planning were Marxist or not, since the planning of science of any sort subordinated the particular spiritual ends espoused by science to management in the interest of a supposed social good.[10]

The strong movement in England to plan science gradually subsided. Whether, or to what extent, this may have been due to the efforts of Polanyi and others who shared his view is, of course, difficult to say. Government influences upon the direction whether positive or negative in which science and other intellectual efforts are to go has, of course, not disappeared there or elsewhere. It is present throughout the world. It comes and goes in strength and in different disciplines. Polanyi thus regarded it as an ever-present danger in all contemporary societies.

Even supposing that a planned economy could be espoused without also espousing Marxist materialist determinism, Polanyi still found the notion threatening. Assuming that a government controlling all capital funds were to confine its planning only to industry and were simply to make funds available for research to academic institutions and to organizations of scholars to use as they saw fit with no strings of any sort attached, with no effort to plan research (for the possibility of which there is some evidence in Europe), nevertheless such planning confined strictly to economic activities, Polanyi held, would be disastrous for our industrial economies.

Polanyi eventually became an economist at one stage in his career largely through his investigation of this question. He determined that an industrial economy cannot be planned. He wrote a number of articles showing the impossibility of doing this. An industrial economy can be physically carried on only from many centers producing many different things. How many items of any product should be produced, and through the use of what resources, cannot be solved by establishing what Polanyi called a corporate order of commands from the top. The span of units that can be effectively controlled by central direction is not of sufficient width. Adjustments must be continually made at every point, and these cannot wait for the necessarily myriad levels of request and command to travel upwards and back down. Each center must be free to make these adjustments in terms of the situation prevailing there and then. In other words, the problem of managing an industrial economy is a polycentric one that can only be solved by calculations made from many centers.

Besides, it is only through such polycentric activity that the productive factors can be given a value relative to each other. Production factors must be priced as well as the finished product, in order to know what resources are most valuable or economical to use. But if items are priced without the particular participants estimating what these items seem to be worth in the prevailing situation, they can only be arbitrarily priced, and allocations will have to be out of step with what people involved in production or consumption will think they are worth. This will result, Polanyi held, in scarcities, surpluses, and black markets, and also in inflation. The adjustment of supplies to effective demand can only be made if one allows the price to fluctuate in a free market—free in the sense that all parties may bid what each thinks the item is worth to him, or simply buy or refrain from buying at that price, perhaps making or using some other product or resource, or none at all, in place of what one has been making or using.

Thus Polanyi argued that the economic system in an industrial society is a polycentric one at its very root and can only operate through the spontaneous interaction of free economic centers. Whether capital is privately or publicly owned, he held, can make no difference.[11]

Since a planned economy cannot function, the question may be asked, how then can it be a dangerous threat? Polanyi maintained that the effort to put it into effect could cause such severe problems for an industrial society that production could be seriously hampered, if not destroyed, and widespread suffering could result from these dislocations and curtailments of productive capacity. He held that this was exactly what happened in the Soviet Union when Lenin at first tried to do without markets, money, and pricing. At last, Polanyi said, even Lenin despaired of it (as Trotsky put it, it would take a Universal Mind to do the job) and he reintroduced money and market pricing.[12] Polanyi claimed that, although markets are regularly interfered with in the Soviet Union, market pricing is still the basic mechanism they have had to use to operate their economy.[13]

What was still missing, however, in the Soviet Union was the acceptance of the idea of profits, and thus the success or failure of any productive enterprise lacked any standard by which to measure it. The Soviet Union, he held, operated like one vast holding company. There was thus no capital market for the redistribution of investments. Capital was distributed by a government department without reference to the solvency of enterprises. Since profits were not sought nor taken into account there was no test of managerial success. The famous Five-Year Plans were in fact, he held, more summary predictions than plans.[14]

Polanyi thus tried to show, from economic considerations alone, that a planned economy is an absurdity. In connection with this he noted a strange anomaly. Capitalist economists have tended to assume that central planning is possible and to point to its dangers to other freedoms in arguing against it. Socialists have tended, however, to say less and less about central planning, having learned from experience its severe limits.[15]

In addition to these abstract negative criticisms we have been outlining, Polanyi also took a much more positive step toward combating the spread of Marxism and its accompanying efforts to plan societies. In order to do so, he tried to determine what, in fact, constituted the real criticisms of capitalism and how they might be met.

Complaints about the moral shortcomings of capitalism do indeed have some real substance, he held. He maintained, however, that it is possible to show the public generally how a capitalist economy works and what the legitimate roles of money, markets, pricing, and even profits are. To this end, back in the 1930s, he produced diagrammatic and animated films in order to show how money circulates in a free market, and why and how it works to get things that the public wants produced and how it gets them into the hands of consumers.[16]

In explaining why he thought such films could provide the explanations he thought the public needed, Polanyi noted that there were three main sets of symbols: verbal, mathematical, and visual. Of these, the visual are the most useful.

> Words are powerless to convey a description of complex things which are far out of sight; mathematics are too intricate to become popular. Give a man a full description of England not illustrated by maps and ask him to plan an itinerary from Manchester to London. The man is a genius if he succeeds in a year. Present him with a list of numbers stating the latitudes and longitudes of all the places in England and if he knows geometry he will work out the route in a month. But give a child of ten a map of England and he will read to you directly all the alternative routes.[17]

He held that to communicate how our economic system works we have to invent another sort of map. The symbols we use must be graphic or visual. But a map is a static affair and the economic system is essentially dynamic. We must see what happens under changing conditions, so the map has to become a diagrammatic picture in motion—a film. But he saw it must also contain animated cartoon characters in order to communicate visually just what does happen in our system and how the parts operate the whole.[18]

Polanyi maintained that he had had very good success in communicating the working of the system to general audiences. Such popular education, he held, would go a great way toward enabling people to feel at home in the system ruled by Adam Smith's "invisible hand." This sort of popular education was not, however, all that needed to be done.

The greatest difficulty with the capitalist system, Polanyi asserted, has been its recurrent business crises, its trade cycles, and the consequent periodic deflation and unemployment. This difficulty rests, he held, upon a real deficiency in the system. The salutary automatic adjustments made by "the invisible hand" in the economy, due to the operation of supply and demand in a free market, do not extend to the problem of the supply of money. Just when business becomes bad and more money is needed, credit tends to shrink in supply under free market conditions, adding further to the deflation. Contrariwise, when times are good and prices begin to rise, credit ought to shrink in order to stabilize the situation, but instead it tends to expand in a free market, adding further to the inflation.[19]

The discovery by Keynes that the supply of money held the key to trade cycles made it possible, at long last, to do something about them. Polanyi advocated (in his reply to a memorandum circulated by Cabinet officers Jewkes and Robbins in 1941) that the Keynesian theories about the supply of money should be used in order to secure full employment through deficit government spending, i.e., the government's deliberately pumping new money into the economy during each recession and then pumping it out later during the subsequent boom. He claimed this reply of his made him a pioneer in the advocacy of deficit spending as a remedy for unemployment.[20] Here, and later at considerable length, Polanyi argued that governments could iron out the trade cycle problems by their own monetary policies and thus cure the one real economic deficiency endemic to a free market economy.[21]

These Keynesian ideas have since become generally used by modern governments and have indeed taken the edge off the recurring cycles of deflation and unemployment to which the free market system is subject. Currently, however, they have come under more and more criticism as being the suspected cause of our persistent inflation. Polanyi, of course was aware of the danger of inflation, however, he thought the extent of the danger was exaggerated because of "historical recollections." "In the past," he said, "the issue of new money has invariably been used by Governments in urgent need of money who were unable or unwilling to raise it by taxation." These were mostly weak or reckless governments who wanted to escape public control or found themselves not strong enough to collect taxes. He thought fears of such an occurrence were not relevant, since the issuing of new money would be, in such a policy as he was advocating, strictly controlled for the purpose of "maintaining the stability of monetary circulation."[22] He admitted that expansion of currency was a movement towards inflation. But full employment cannot be attained, he held, without full circulation of money, and so, if we want full employment, we will have to "approach the proximity of inflation." Any ensuing "waves of excessive monetary expansion" can "be checked by increases in taxation."[23]

Since the ideal behind the policy is to stabilize monetary circulation, it must also include bringing down overexpansion of the supply, as well as preventing overcontraction. It must be professional economists who tell us when to do which, and so the operation of this policy, Polanyi maintained, "will inevitably involve a considerable amount of responsibility for the expert economist in government employment." Their functions, he held, must become wider and more independent, although these executive functions of theirs must also be kept "within reasonable constitutional limits."[24]

In order that this be accomplished, the public must be informed and consulted, he maintained. If it is uninformed, it will be misdirected and will put the wrong kind of pressure upon its political representatives in government.[25] One real danger, Polanyi saw, was that people might generally acquire too great an interest in economic security. He held that a free market cannot be operated without some risks, both to employers and to employees. If economic security is the overriding concern among people, then the only way to truly avoid all risks of business failure and of unemployment would be to provide continually "rising tides of monetary circulation." The "permanent state of inflation" which these "rising tides" would cause would, he thought, bring on an "external scramble for goods and labour and . . . ceaseless wrestling with regulations which try to keep the scramble within bounds." And these results, he maintained, would "render life intolerable."[26]

So one of the things a public must be informed about is the reasons why a certain measure of insecurity must be accepted in an industrial economy. There must be some losers. "There must be a certain amount of business failures: of capitalists going bankrupt and of workers and employees becoming unemployed." It must be understood that businessmen have to take risks and workers face the possibility of losing their jobs. An industrial economy cannot be operated by people who will not take such risks.[27]

The only alternatives to this kind of risk taking (beyond the unsatisfactory conditions of permanent inflation outlined above) are the primitive economies of self-sustaining farmers and the medieval economy where each person has his assured niche to which by birth he belongs for life. No industrial economy can be managed in these ways, because it cannot remain stationary: it requires constant mutual readjustments of its parts—and we now have so many people that they cannot survive without an industrial economy.[28]

But what level of insecurity should be accepted? How much residual unemployment should be tolerated? If true full employment were the only goal, the expert economist ought to be able to tell us, within an increasingly narrow range of accuracy, just how much money the government should be required to pump into the economy, and when, as well as when the reverse should occur, when money should be siphoned out by increased taxation. Polanyi seemed to be of the opinion that such a single-minded effort to maintain full employment might result in a state of rather permanent inflation. Besides, he held, it would result in a "universal 'seller's market' both in labor and in goods." Workers would become excessively ready to abandon their jobs to better their situation and businessmen would cease trying to give their customers even a minimum of service.[29] There is then a point at which the government will have to restrict the spending of money in order to control the evils of overemployment. This restriction must bring on some uncertainty and insecurity, and so Polanyi held: "*At the point where these restrictions become intolerable, the practical limit of circulation and of employment is attained.*"[30]

This point, in a democracy, Polanyi maintained, is determined necessarily by the pressure of public opinion acting upon the government. Thus it is imperative that public opinion be well informed. Polanyi wrote:

> The annual parliamentary decision to fix the level of the national money income should express the popular balance between the desire for fuller employment and the reluctance to accept further restrictions on contractual freedom. This alternative must be so presented to the public that it should be in a position to judge intelligently and to make its influence effective in a reasonable fashion. It must be brought home to the voters what they may expect from a reduction and what from an expansion of circulation, so that they may acquire a sufficient appreciation of the issue and exercise wisely the kind of general control which constitutes their proper democratic function.[31]

Polanyi believed it was possible to inform public opinion concerning these matters. Popular education in economics was absolutely essen-

tial, he asserted, and, on the basis of his own experience with nearly a
hundred audiences of his films, he held that it was indeed possible.[32]
Polanyi, as we have seen, thought that visual symbols are more easy to
understand than verbal or mathematical ones. Verbal accounts of economic matters cannot show economic fallacies as clearly as can visual
presentations. Economic fallacies, he maintained, exist because they are
rooted in a "sectional account of economic life." The immediate consequences of an economic measure are more obvious at the point it first
takes effect, as in the help provided for a home industry by cutting
imports. "Its effects on economic life *as a whole* are not traceable to the
ordinary mind." A verbal account of its effects must trace separately or
successively the various channels that stretch out to the whole in order to
see how they would affect the whole. You do not see, he said, the effect
of throwing a stone into a small pond through tracing the separate paths
of the droplets of water displaced by the stone. But if you observe the
pond as a whole when the stone is thrown, you may immediately see that
the result has been a rise in the level of the pond, as if you had poured
more water in it.[33]

A diagrammatic picture may be crude or wrong, he said, but it
cannot be illogical. You may, in discussing in words a complex matter
that is out of your sight, contradict yourself without noticing it. He held
that, for example, if two chess players who are not experts at playing the
game blindfolded play a game by indicating their steps in chess language
only, after a few moves they will be putting figures into places already
filled, thus contradicting themselves. With a chessboard these inconsistencies cannot occur, because they cannot be carried out physically, and
thus not visually; the same is true in a diagram. Therefore economic
fallacies will easily become evident even to ordinary people when you
make them visual with mobile diagrammatic symbols. Alternative
economic policies and their consequences can thus be readily seen even
by novices in economic theory.[34]

Polanyi thus held that an economic system dependent upon markets, pricing, and profits, as supplemented by intelligent control of the
quantity of money needed to maintain the levels of money circulation
and of employment which are seen to be desirable in terms of their
consequences, was truly logical and essential to the management of the
kind of industrial economy on which we are all now dependent. Furthermore such a system was one which could be managed democratically
by an informed public opinion. He held, however, that we are placed

under a stringent obligation to take effective action in so informing this public opinion.[35] Such informative action is thus a part of Polanyi's proposed treatment.

So much for the difficulties inherent in the system itself. Polanyi thought they could be remedied. But what of the moral dissatisfactions modern man seems to find in the system? What of the views that it develops greed, asocial or even antisocial self-interest, and a callous disregard for those individuals who are losers in the competitive battle for economic goods?

The moral problem, Polanyi maintained, really lies in the disparity existing between the personal view and the social aspect of economic activity:

> The production of commodities for the market, the acquisition of money, is turned by the proverbial invisible hand into the service of the community. But the hand is invisible. The activity of the individual is starkly acquisitive. He does not even feel that what he does is useful to anybody. Nor does he know where the border lies between acquisitiveness which is social in effect and acquisitiveness which is antisocial. He is frustrated of his social meaning, he is left perplexed as to the extent of his social duties.[36]

Polanyi wrote:

> So long as the working of the economic system and the supreme hand directing it remain invisible, even the most useful form of self-seeking will be performed in a callous, narrow-minded spirit, and such a spirit will permeate the whole community, breaking it up into groups of rival interests ready to use all their economic and political powers to fight against the others.[37]

> No wonder that men revolt against the domination of such an undiscriminating acquisitive spirit. In reaction against it they demand to realize fully their civic responsibilities and to act with a direct view to the social purpose.[38]

Modern man, he claimed, is frustrated by perplexities of this sort that the economic system forces him to face—much as Pavlov's dogs were made neurotic when the differences between the symbols in terms of which they had been conditioned to salivate and not to salivate were decreased to a point beyond their capacity to discriminate. It was not for lack of food, but for the uncertanties in being fed, that these dogs broke down. Thus, Polanyi observed, the "Rumanian peasant submits to fate when his crops are ruined by hail but revolts when he is ruined because for reasons far beyond his scope the price of wheat has fallen on the world market. Men who held out patiently through the war will rise up against an inexplicable state of unemployment, which by comparison with war is a mild inconvenience."[39]

One of our problems, said Polanyi, is that the discovery that the market price of labor, capital, and commodities was the only way to provide a just reward to each of these factors was made by people who were utilitarians, and the defense of such a system, Polanyi wrote, has so far been largely in the hands of utilitarian thinkers. Polanyi held, however, that utilitarian philosophy, later called economic liberalism, failed to see that the just reward of the factors of production did not necessarily lead to a just reward of the people disposing of these factors— and it developed no theories about how this latter just reward should be assessed. These utilitarian liberals generally seemed to suppose that the idea of a free market could be applied properly to all human relation-ships. Therefore, they opposed all legislation regulating labor conditions and objected to all services made available free to individuals by the community—even sometimes to free education. As we have seen, their economic theories also gave no reasonable account of the trade cycle, and so their theories left the unemployed in a depression without any conso-lation. Such economic liberals often even objected to any action to help the unemployed.

But the general weakness of the utilitarian defense of the free mar-ket, Polanyi held, is this:

that its philosophy makes self-seeking the supreme principle in economic life and assumes that people are happy if their blind acquisitiveness is transformed into a maximum efficiency. In fact, blind acquisitiveness is repugnant to the social instincts of man. If he cooperates with a community he wants to be conscious of a common purpose. Accordingly, he revolts against the idea that the community should refuse responsibility for giving its citizens op-portunity to work and live an educated healthy life.[40]

This revolt, in our century, has taken the forms of Communism and Fascism. Communism, as it first arose, attacked all these weaknesses of utilitarianism outlined above, Polanyi pointed out. "It demanded that exploitation, marketing, the trade cycle should be wiped out and the acquisition system replaced by a community consciously working for its common needs."[41] Polanyi maintained that this powerful appeal was disastrous, because of two fundamental errors. The first was, as we have seen, the supposition that an industrial system could be run without the guidance of competitive prices, wages, and profits. The second error was even worse, he held. This was the theory of class war. Because it lumped all the managerial and technical staff, the civil services, and the learned professions in the class of the nonowners, together with the workers, and then classed all the peasants, tradesmen, and craftsmen with the rich capitalist owners, the Marxian division of classes between owners and nonowners actually acted to provide the rich with more powerful allies than they had ever had. The masses of the lower middle class, seeing their ways of making their livelihood threatened by the Communist movement, had to join the rich against the workers, where-as the better off employees and professional men did not actually, as the theory held they would, merge into the proletariat, but kept up their previous association with the rich. This theory actually put the workers into a disastrously weak position and succeeded in solidifying those who opposed them into the counterrevolutionary movement called Fascism.[42]

Polanyi thought that the kind of education in economics that he had begun would enable us to combat these fundamental errors. The touch-stone for greater power and income must be seen by the ordinary man to lie in the operation of a completely impartial principle that is of such a nature that it can subsist under the rule of impartial law. Such an impartial principle, he said, can only be the principle of free competition. But, this principle must accept two exceptions to its operation, he insisted. One is that, "Where it is technically impossible to destroy monopoly or to enforce competition without reducing productivity, it removes the industry concerned from the field of private enterprise either by ownership or control." And the other is that "It provides crutches, from the general social fund, for individuals (*but not industries*) who are too weak to stand up to competition."[43]

Although a large part of the moral problem, he supposed, was our inability to see how our own self-centered efforts and our own pressing for our own economic betterment and profit could, through the opera-tion of the free economic system, fulfill social goals and give us the satisfaction of feeling ourselves to be part of the team, nevertheless moral difficulties with the system also arose quite naturally in men's minds from another source. These arose because of grossly unequal distribution of the economic goods, where this unequal distribution could be seen to occur from monopoly privilege or from individual incapacity to compete on equal terms for these goods. Governments thus needed to act to relieve both these deficiencies. Polanyi maintained that, contrary to the usual stance taken by those who see the absolute necessity of the market's managing our industrial economies, such a free system could still exist under an umbrella of a considerable amount of so-called "free" social services. These, of course, would never be costless; but their costs could be widely distributed without harm to the market economy.[44]

He declared that the adherents of laissez-faire erred in assuming that only one optimum economic system was possible. Polanyi held that since

> there exists an indefinite range of relative optima towards which a market economy can tend . . . it is the task of social legislation to discover and implement improvements of the institutional frame-work, for the purpose of deliberately modifying the system of spontaneous order established by the market,

which would then establish a different economic optimum.[45]

It is true that there would be some limits to the amount of such "free" social services. No one, of course, could know just where those limits were. Beyond these limits the operation of the market would become seriously hampered and the growth of capital investment would become insufficient. Polanyi did not see serious problems, if the State distributed such things as education, health care, and other "social amenities" to all on an equal basis.[46]

He also advocated control of water and air pollution and of the destruction of our natural environment. All of these would simply add across the board to the general cost of production and would not injure any particular firm or industry. Something for nothing did not exist, but such ends as these could never be adequately handled by the market; we would, of course, lose our measure of exactly how much these things were costing us and thus of whether they were worth it to us in terms of other goods. There can exist, he said, no market for the exchange of odious sights, sounds, and smells, so we cannot tell through market pricing, and thus not at all, whether the costs of their eradication are worth it to us economically. We shall simply have to make the collective judgment that we either do want them eradicated or do not, and that we do want every person to have certain goods, or we do not.[47] We will of course have to pay for whatever we decide; but we will never know just how much any particular decision has cost us.

Much of the undesirable effects of a free market economy therefore can be eliminated, Polanyi claimed, without destroying the polycentric system we inescapably need. Much—but not all the effects. Polanyi remained convinced that we must give up moral perfectionism. To acknowledge that you need engines to pull trains, he said, is also to accept that their efficiency is limited, they are noisy, and they sometimes run over people. To deal rationally with any problems caused by engines, one has to stop hankering after trains without engines. The same, he held, is true of the commercial organization of production and distribution. Our "train" cannot run without it, imperfect as it will always be.[48]

As he saw it, our moral systems exist as higher spheres of our being, resting upon lower systems of profit, power, and parochialism, much as the mind rests upon the brain. He provided us with a very simple particular illustration of these two levels of morality. A judge, he said, might be motivated by a number of private motives for becoming a judge—ambition for status, for power, for respect, for money, or whatever. But he cannot actually be a judge, i.e., play the moral role that defines what a judge is supposed to do as a judge unless he follows certain "standard motives:" to find the relevant laws and the relevant facts and to make a decision based upon these laws and facts which either follows the precedents or creates a new precedent on grounds that his colleagues can find reasonable, or which he supposes they ought to find reasonable.[49]

Such lower self-interested motives as the judge's private motives for wanting to be a judge are what makes possible our higher moral operations, Polanyi claimed; but it is clear that these lower interests must inevitably also sometimes limit the higher moral operations from fully satisfying their own emergent principles of action. So we can say that our capacity for intelligent self-interested activity makes possible the emergence of our moral ideals and principles. However, these latter can never be deduced from the former, just as he held that an arithmetic cannot be deduced from a calculus. (We have here another instance of the necessities involved in a hierarchical organization.) So moral principles can also never be reduced to these self-interested principles, as if such a reduction would constitute adequate understanding or explanation of them. We must hold our moral principles as the unique form of being they are and submit to them as obligations, or else we must find that in fact we do not hold them at all, i.e., we are not dwelling in the moral sphere of the noosphere.[50]

We see therefore that, for Polanyi, social systems cannot be morally perfected in accordance with any conceivable moral principles, and the free society cannot be so perfected either. We must accept an irreducible modicum of moral imperfections in all our social relations. This does not mean, he thought, that we cannot gradually improve our societies. It does mean, however, that we cannot find a panacea for all our woes; so we must refrain from radical action aimed at the full and immediate establishment of justice and brotherhood in all their purity. We must acknowledge that we can reduce unjust privileges only by graded stages, and never completely. He maintained that to try to demolish them all overnight would create greater injustices in their place. He warned that "an absolute moral renewal of society can be attempted only by an absolute power which must inevitably destroy the moral life of man."[51]

The import of all this for Polanyi was that we must acknowledge that a liberal, free society is of necessity also profoundly conservative. Insistence upon a right to the independence of thought involved in the growth of science, art, and morality is subscribing to a kind of orthodoxy, which, though it specifies no fixed articles of faith, is regarded by its adherents as virtually sacrosanct. It is not a society open to the denial of that upon which it rests. We must, he added ruefully, also acknowledge that this orthodoxy is backed by the coercive power of the state and financed by the beneficiaries of office and property. Thus, he claimed, we are left with the moral necessity of "an allegiance to a manifestly imperfect society, based on the acknowledgment that our duty lies in the service of ideals which we cannot possibly achieve."[52]

As in art and religion, so also in moral integration a union of incompatibles seems to be involved. Polanyi, however, was wary of maintaining that it is these very incompatibilities in our moral duties that "carries us away" morally, as he did hold such incompatible elements do in the arts and religion. The acceptance of unrighteousness in our moral interests seemed rather to be a hard necessity, which a true view of our situation forces upon us, much like the limitations imposed on our intellectual attainments by our need of a physiological brain in order to think at all. He had hinted in his last lectures that morality was indeed a union of incompatibles; but when I asked him if he meant that morality, like art and religion, moved us deeply *because* it was a union of these incompatibles, he replied that he did not think so.

How and why, then, did he think that moral obligations can move us so deeply even as we recognize that they can never be fulfilled? Perhaps a clue to how he thought they do so can be found in his remark that men, unlike other living organisms, seem to need "a purpose that bears on eternity. Truth does that; our ideals do it."[53] Truth bears on eternity, he said. Perhaps this is because the truth is eternal. But truth, for him, is also something we are eternally seeking. There are no objective signs that we have found it. We have to make a judgment, he held, that what we have come to is the truth. We hold that it is the best we can do with our universal intent. But *is* it? There is no way by which a detached objectivity can certify that it is. We must accept the responsibility for being right—or wrong. As Polanyi maintained,

> the emergent noosphere is wholly determined as that which we believe to be true and right . . . . It comprises everything in which we may be totally mistaken.[54]

Following his position concerning truth and his coupling of "truth" with "ideals" as instances of purposes with a bearing on eternity, we may suppose that we can say the same things about ideals that he said about truth. About all of them we may be totally mistaken. Yet they bear upon eternity and satisfy our deepest longings for eternal purposes. And this would be enough, he added, "if we could ever be satisfied with our manifold moral shortcomings and with a society which has such shortcomings fatally involved in its workings." He suggested that probably only a religious solution may exist for this final dissatisfaction, and that such a resolution might become more feasible for modern man than it now is "once religious faith is released from pressure by an absurd vision of the universe."[55]

In view of this remark it might seem that religion is finally the peak of man's life for Polanyi and the final resolution of human problems, and that this final chapter of our exposition of his thought is somewhat of an anticlimax. In one sense religion was the high point for him, inasmuch as religion expresses the fullest achievable integration of man's life with his world. Yet it would not be correct to say that Polanyi's proposed treatment of the ills of the modern mind consisted in simply urging it to lose itself in the contemplation of the Divine (even though in doing so it is, in one sense, wholly finding itself). Polanyi was, as has probably been noticed, an incurable moralist. We have moral duties, he insisted. He did not think that religion was the source of all our moral duties nor of all the other duties entailed by the noospheric firmament of obligations which we have set over ourselves. Neither did he think that moral imperatives depend upon the power of God. Religion, for Polanyi, seemed to have been connected with morality primarily in making us better able to live with our necessarily limited moral achievements. Those of us, for instance, who discover how to dwell in that fullest integration of the most incompatible of incompatibles, the Kingdom of Heaven, may indeed have found the only way in which our transcendent hunger and thirst after righteousness can ever be fulfilled. This achievement might indeed help to pull us away from the social poison of moral perfectionism.[56] However, Polanyi seemed always to be sure that religious faith was not all that was needed to remedy the troubles of the modern mind—if indeed it was needed at all for that purpose.

He wrote:

> In an answer to the question: "Would you agree that a religious attitude is the only antidote to the predominantly scientific attitude?["] I would answer: no, I wouldn't agree. I shall tell you why not. Take such beliefs as we have to hold in order to preserve a free society which believes in justice and in which there is sufficient confidence among citizens that they can look towards a peaceful solution of problems that might arise among them. I do not think that beliefs of this kind—which ultimately all lie outside of religious faith—are likely to be restored if we concentrate in the first place on the question whether or not we can believe in religion.[57]

To sum up then, the truly ultimate aim of Polanyi's efforts was to try to reinforce our traditional beliefs in truth, justice, mercy, and fellowship, all of which are required as the grounds for the continued existence of a free society. For this reason he found we needed to develop an epistemology adequate to humane thought and to use it in the reformation of those views of man which will lend an ontological basis for his grasp of his own dignity and high calling in the universe. This reformation, he held, would include the abandonment of reductionistic views in psychology, sociology, and biology in favor of an ontology of achievement in evolution and in the life of man through the truth and dignity of the transnatural integrations possible for man in all the arts and in religion, as well as of those meanings we achieve in morality and in the sciences. All of this would also entail our active espousal of the free development of the several enclaves of men and women centering around the polycentric tasks in science, law, the arts, and religion, all of which morally require freedom for the pursuit of their spiritual ends and ideals, those "bearing on eternity." Thus, Polanyi maintained it was not merely a lack of religion that ailed modern man. It was the lack of all these understandings which we have just summed up; for this lack devitalized and dehumanized him—indeed, it made religion itself impossible for him.

The vital importance of our espousal of a free economy, centering around open markets, supply-and-demand pricing, and profits, but also an understanding of its deficiencies and of how to remedy them he held, was not at all based on the notion that any of these economic matters entailed transcendentally spiritual or ideal ends, intrinsically valuable in themselves. Economic freedom was not an end in itself worthy of being served; it could hardly be said to be a purpose bearing upon eternity.[58] However, the maintenance of a free economy, with private property, open markets, profits, et al, was important partly because an industrial society could not be managed without it, but also because without it some version of a planned society was bound to emerge which would denigrate intrinsically valuable goals and their concomitant activities to the status of mere means to other utilitarian ends. For the same reasons, therefore, the deficiencies of a market economy had to be faced and solved—the trade cycle and those morally shocking results of equating the just price of factors in the market with the just share for the people disposing of these factors. To meddle with market pricing in an industrial society would destroy productive capacities. But to allow people to become without mercy the victims of market pricing (to say nothing of monopolies and oligopolies) would in the end destroy the free society by causing people to turn, in moral and physical despair, to some form of totalitarianism and thus to eliminate the pursuit of all those purposes which in fact do "bear on eternity."

Michael Polanyi thus often sounded like a table-thumping evangelist—and always like a moralist—to the consternation and embarrassment of many contemporary philosophers and thinkers. He was incessantly urging a call to action on the part of people in the free world (1) to reach an understanding of the grounds upon which their world stood and to remain committed to these as unimpeachable principles, and (2) to support the cause of freedom for the sake of the spiritual entities of truth, justice, and beauty.

# PART IV

*Evaluation*

# CHAPTER FOURTEEN

# Rationale for an Evaluation

In this last part of the book I will attempt an evaluation of Michael Polanyi's work. I say "attempt" because it would be presumptuous for me to claim to have accomplished an adequate evaluation of such a comprehensive innovator as Michael Polanyi. His total work presents a serious challenge to various contemporary concepts and attitudes, and calls for responses from many quarters, if we are to see its true value. It is my hope that what I shall say here will call forth such response.

Let me begin by noting that an attempt to treat a disorder is to be evaluated finally, as an acid test, by the resulting condition of the patient. It is no doubt for this reason that Polanyi himself considered, toward the end of his life, that his work had been a failure. After all, his final purpose had been to restore the modern mind to a healthy confidence in its own powers to achieve meaningful organization of its thought, aspirations, and manner of living. He felt that the various segments of the Western intellectual and cultural world had not, in general, been persuaded by his efforts. To be sure, he had, he knew, won a number of converts in a great many different fields of human endeavor; but by and large on the whole the modern mind seemed to him to be no better off than when he had found it. He had, for instance, expected to cause some stir at Oxford. But years after he had come there as a Research Fellow at Merton College he still found himself and his ideas virtually ignored. He actually had a greater following in the United States. But he certainly had not changed the main flow of ideas there, either.

Those of us who thought that the full impact of his work lay still in the future were unable to console Polanyi. There was no "bird in the hand." This was not, I believe, personal disappointment at not having been acknowledged as the savior of Western Civilization. Like any practicing physician dedicated to healing rather than to science in some abstract sense, he could not help but feel that the operation could not be a success, if the patient was still in danger of dying. That one may have learned from performing such an operation how better to perform them and that this knowledge in the long run might turn out to be extremely beneficial, may have seemed to him to be a rather far-fetched rationalization of a manifest failure.

It is also possible, of course, that the medicine prescribed by Polanyi may simply be very slow in taking effect and that it may take a generation or two to do so. There is some evidence that this may be what is happening. Many people in various fields, whose ideas seem to be moving in the direction in which Polanyi tried to point us, but who never mention Polanyi in their writings, will admit under questioning that they know Polanyi has done something very similar to what they are attempting. Could their acquaintance with Polanyi's thinking have had no effect upon their own thought? This seems most unlikely.

Such long-range effects as these, however, can flow only from those parts of a system of thought which seem to be sound to the persons so affected. Let us therefore shift our evaluation from a consideration of the success or failure of Polanyi's work with reference to his own overriding intention to an evaluation of the soundness of some of his most important doctrines and theories. If they are sound, surely they stand a good chance of some day being accepted. And if they are capable of working changes in mental attitudes and aspirations, as he thought they were, they may yet succeed in rescuing the modern mind from its self-abasement. On the other hand, if they are not sound there will be no hope of their effecting a cure.

Let us turn first to what we have called in the first part of this book Polanyi's "diagnosis." In a nutshell what Polanyi claimed is this: the modern mind is suffering from two diseases. These consist of two false ideals: that of detached objectivity or explicitness as the ideal of knowledge and that of perfectionism as the ideal in moral and social concerns. Together these two ideals—actually incompatible—have worked themselves out historically into what he called "moral inversion." These two ideals have had their origins respectively (1) in the denial of the role of traditional authority by the progenitors of the modern scientific movement, and so in the denial of the essential role of belief or faith in acquiring knowledge; and (2) in the legacy left us by Christianity, the hunger after righteousness, full and complete.

The historical details of just how he thought these two ideals worked themselves into our contemporary frame of mind, which included the development of sense-empiricism into reductionism, positivism, skepticism, nihilism, the secularization of Christian religious ideas by Marxism, and finally ruthless totalitarianism, with its accompanying moral inversion, are all outlined in Part One. The ultimate abandonment of belief in our traditional moral principles and ideals left "homeless" the passion for righteousness, engendered by generations of Christianity, he maintained; but abandonment of belief did not eliminate this passion. It found a subconscious place in the hard-boiled realism of the Marxists, the supposedly realistic manner in which the ultimate fulfillment of righteousness in the classless society would develop from the ruthless and unrestrained conflicts of class interests (an idea, he claimed, that was then redefined and totally brutalized by Fascism as the concept of a conflict, not between classes, but between the have and have-not nations).

One offshoot of these modes of thought was the destruction of the basis for freedom in the sciences themselves, since positivism left the sciences with nothing but purely arbitrary bases, rather than commitments to reason and truth. Why these bases should not then be supplied by the needs and wants of the planners of societies, since these bases were anyhow arbitrary, turned out to be unanswerable by those many scientists who had themselves come to subscribe to no other philosophy of science but positivism. They had no grounds for arguing for their right to be free to choose their own bases, since they had stopped asserting that science was committed to an ideal that generated binding obligations, viz., truth.

If not even science could lay such a claim to freedom, it was clear to minds that were devoted to explicit and detached objectivity that ethics and politics, art and religion could not do so either. In the Anglo-American sphere the process did not proceed to its logical conclusion, as it did on the Continent, because, Polanyi held, religion in Anglo-American circles was enlisted rather illogically on the side of social "progress," rather than against it, and thus did not become so completely discredited. In addition, dodges such as utilitarianism and pragmatism were invented in England and in America which made it look as if ethics and politics could also objectively or "scientifically" be taken into account. This made it possible for democratic political institutions to develop which avoided totalitarianism even after it became clear that neither ethics nor religion really had objective grounds upon which to rest. Freedom was thus in fact also left without adequate philosophic grounds in Anglo-American circles—which has left it an endangered species there too, even if it has not, as yet, been exterminated.

What shall we say to all this? Polanyi's view of the historical causes of our present frame of mind is a massive and complicated one. Like any comprehensive view of historical causes, it can be criticized at many points by historical scholars. What can be demanded of any historical view is not proof beyond any conceivable doubt, i.e., not absolute proof, but rather that it can be understood as a plausible account. It is difficult, however, to say whether it is plausible or not, for, as I believe Polanyi correctly pointed out, what is plausible cannot be given explicit criteria (i.e., there is no objectively detached way to establish plausibility). It is irreducibly a personal judgment resting on tacit clues. Historians will have to say from their own shared feelings of plausibility whether or not Polanyi's interpretation of our history is generally acceptable to their scholarly community. Educated people in general, who are the people addressed by Polanyi in his work, will have to use their own tacit, personal standards of historical plausibility to judge this. Polanyi cited much evidence for his historical interpretations. He also referred to many other thinkers who agreed with various parts of his comprehensive interpretation, notably those relating to "moral inversion."[1]

As for myself, all I can say is that, all things considered, his views on these matters seem plausible to me; I should think they would to others as well. Surely we can see that such ideas that he says are in the minds of modern men and women clearly are or have been in our minds, and they do seem to be related, logically and historically, to the ideas to which he claims they are related.

The only serious threat to his position that I can see is the very one he is combatting, that is, the materialistic interpretation of history and of thought which maintains that men's ideas are the resultants of their various physical situations and of causes external to what goes on in their minds. Such a view is not beyond any *conceivable* doubt; it may be true. However, a view such as this denies any reasoned view of any claim to truth. If any particular reasoned view were true, it could only be so coincidentally and therefore could never be reasonably judged to be true.

But it must be admitted that the preceding sentence could itself lay no claim to being true, if it were true that all our ideas are determined by external conditions: it too would have been caused by some other factors operating on one's mind. Indeed, the reasoned view itself that all reasoned views are merely resultants of conditions—that they could not even possibly be some sort of insight into real conditions—must, logically, entail that it also is only such a resultant and so not necessarily true. Probably the first one to point out this conundrum was Plato. This argument does not, as Plato also understood, refute a causally deterministic view of thinking beyond any conceivable doubt. However, it does refute it, I would affirm, beyond any *reasonable* doubt, for such a view could provide ground only for our not resorting to reasoning at all. If therefore we are to any degree committed to thinking about things, we must assume that our thoughts are at least some part of the irreducible causes of our behavior.

It seems to me that people have been coming more and more to the view that it is not so much what happens to people that determines their behavior, but how they interpret what happens to them. The phenomenologists and existentialists have clearly made much of this point. And strict behaviorism is no longer the only order of the day in psychology. Even such an adamant behaviorist as B. F. Skinner, who holds that human beings originate nothing, that everything is a function solely of the environment (including, of course, a person's genetic endowment)— even Skinner, in *Beyond Freedom and Dignity*, finds that the biggest danger to the development of his science is the idea of the "autonomous man." The whole work seems to be devoted to the effort to rid us of this idea, which would seem to mean that even he thinks an idea (the idea of the autonomous man) infects our behavior in an intolerable way and renders our efforts to change it by operant conditioning almost impossible. So let us set it down that, in the main, Polanyi's account of our difficulties ought to be regarded as a possible and even a plausible one.

Now let us turn to what I have called his "prescription" for the ills of the modern mind. The key point in this, as Marjorie Grene (whose views I will discuss later) has made very clear, is Polanyi's important distinction between the subsidiary and the focal as inescapably present in any perception or understanding. This is the key point, because, if his contention is true, then our recognition of this distinction will undoubtedly put a different cast upon our views of what is going on in perception, science, art, religion, and political and moral philosophy. Personal participation in all of these will be understood to be absolutely essential. Furthermore, the ideals of explicit analysis and detached objectivity will be seen to be false ideals that will not only mislead us, but also destroy our confidence in the work of our minds, and even, at last, in our fundamental humanity. Conversely, our recognition that such personal participation is essential will open for us ever-expanding vistas in the attainment of meaning and thus of respect for man and for his capacities.

The myriad of details involved in Polanyi's spelling out this new view of epistemology can result in interminable disputes among scholars. But I believe that most of these disputes about the details, insofar as they are about the central features of this view and not about its less essential aspects, proceed from a denial of his key contention that subsidiary–focal operations are inherently involved in any interpretation, recognition, or meaning with which we come up.

Strangely enough, the most serious criticism of this position comes from someone who is very friendly to Polanyi and his views. It comes from Rom Harré, who maintains that Polanyi is correct in his basic contention insofar as perception is concerned, but incorrect with regard to conceptual knowledge. Since this is a serious and well thought-out criticism, we must deal with it at greater length in a chapter of its own.

Those ideas of Polanyi which I have outlined as "treatment" open up a whole series of problems. They range over the fields of psychology, biology, art, religion, and social philosophy, and might be thought not to be reducible to a basic point. I believe that it is possible to find such a key point, however, and that this key is Polanyi's contention that there exists an ontological hierarchy. All those ideas of his presented in the third part of this book are in very complex ways related to the ontological hierarchy, and no critic has put his finger precisely upon this fact. We will therefore find instead that Polanyi's views in this respect have been most seriously questioned by Grene, one of his foremost supporters, and, I think, quite inadvertently, by another proponent of his view, Thomas Torrance. It will be necessary, therefore, to devote chapters to their criticisms.

I will thereafter close this book with a few modest criticisms of my own concerning certain features of Polanyi's thought, and with my own overall assessment of the value of his work.

## CHAPTER FIFTEEN

# Can "From–To" Awareness Be Ubiquitous?

Michael Polanyi's positions on perception, cognition, scientific discovery, and scientific justification introduce a myriad of problems and topics for debate about which contemporary philosophers might argue without end. Still, his views on these and related matters form a syndrome resting upon the concept of tacit knowledge—of the necessity of a from–to, subsidiary–focal structure for all knowledge. Therefore, although disputes may arise about any particular feature of Polanyi's analysis, the whole of it will fall if his view of tacit knowing is unsound. Bits and pieces of his views might, of course, turn out to be salvageable upon other grounds, but the main thrust of his intentions would be lost.

As I have noted in the previous chapter the strongest criticism of his view of tacit knowing is that of Harré. Harré points out that Polanyi uses the "proximal–distal" (subsidiary–focal, "from–to") idea in "three sorts of cases:" (1) perception, (2) the meaning of a sentence or a work of art, and (3) theory in the act of understanding. All of these Polanyi regards as tacitly learned skills involving from–to relations. This breadth of application raises problems, according to Harré. These arise from the fact that there are in these three sorts of cases distinctly different kinds of entities between which he claims the from–to relation stands.[1]

In perception the relation stands wholly between items belonging to perceptual or experiential fields—or in the "real world," as Harré calls it.[2] In the second case, of meaning, it holds between "items of the first category to something propositional."[3] He seems to mean that written or spoken words or paintings are perceptual items in the "real world," and that we go from them not to other perceptual or "real" items, such as from the particular features of a face to the face as a whole, as in perception, but to what is "propositional." I feel constrained to note in passing that it is not clear to me that Polanyi ever held that the meaning of a word is a proposition, much less the meaning of a work of art. Possibly Harré simply thinks that it is, regardless of what Polanyi thought, and, of course, he may be right. But let us not try to settle these issues at this point, but rather acknowledge that there is indeed something different in the distal or focal elements in the two cases. If "proposition" can be understood to be something like a concept, as opposed to a perception, then there is a difference in what the "froms" lead us "to" in the two cases.

In the third case, says Harré, moving from theories to understandings, we are involved wholly with the "propositional" in both terms.[4] Again, let us understand that theories and understandings are both conceptual as contrasted with perceptual, and that "propositional" may be meant to express the distinction.

Now it is clear from what we have explored of Polanyi's thought in the second as well as in the third part of the book, that this is indeed just what Polanyi does—and indeed wholly intends to do, as far as I can see. What is wrong with this?

Harré holds that if both extremes, perception and theory, are taken as examples of a more general structure of knowing, then "revealing the tacit" in the first case is a "different exploratory process" from "revealing" it in the other.[5] Again let me note in passing that although Polanyi was indeed anxious to reveal to us *that* there were tacit elements which we used in a subsidiary way in all our perception and thought, it is not at all clear that he wished to develop some way of "revealing" these in the sense of making them all perfectly explicit. Indeed this seems to be what he was *not* trying to do, since he thought it was logically impossible—we would always have to know more than we could ever tell, in that we would always have to dwell in something else in a subsidiary way whenever we made anything explicit or focal.

It does appear that Harré seems to think of "revealing" as making the tacit explicit, since he says that the task of revealing the "sensory elements of empirical experience . . . might of course be a task which a Polanyian psychologist might undertake."[6] He also tells us that after much discussion with Polanyi it appeared to him that Polanyi

> was prepared to take the view that the kind of analytical schema which the Oxbridge realists . . . have been promoting, of the analogical inter-relation between the components of theoretical knowledge, was a device by which tacit knowledge could be systematically explored, though not exhausted.[7]

Polanyi did, of course, recognize that many of the subsidiary elements involved in any instance of tacit knowing could be discovered, and so could become objects of our focal attention—although not while we were using them in a subsidiary way. In the first place, if Polanyi had felt himself to be totally unable to bring any of them to our focal attention, he would not have been able to present to us any evidence that there was indeed a tacit dimension to our knowing. He also held that our knowledge is increased and expanded by a continual journey back and forth between analysis and synthesis. Sometimes analysis may destroy meaning, he maintained, but when we can again synthesize the parts into the whole, we know more fully after analysis than we did before and may achieve more control in this way.[8] Therefore, any sort of analysis which helped to render more of the subsidiary components focally known, without disintegrating our central focal meaning beyond repair, was not only acceptable to Polanyi, but highly desirable. He could hardly have been the first-rate chemist that he was without holding such a view. But it would be difficult to maintain that his overriding purpose in developing his theory of the subsidiary–focal distinction was that of rendering the tacit explicit. Harré's final phrase in the quotation about, "though not exhausted," is a most important qualification that Polanyi would always have added.

As Harré looks at the problem, it would be one thing—an exercise in psychology—to reveal the tacit components of our perceptions, but a wholly different thing to engage in an epistemological inquiry that might reveal for us "the theoretical or *cognitive* conditions of experience." This latter, Harré continues, might well consist of a "contribution to the understanding of the Kantian schematisms by which the categories inform experience. The 'from–to' theory might be a gloss on the Kantian theory of the schematism."[9] Harré's point seems to be that, because these two different sorts of inquiries would be methodologically poles apart, Polanyi's "from–to' notion could not provide one single method for revealing or explicating both of these different kinds of tacit components, and these two sorts of cases therefore could hardly be simply two examples of the same epistemological form.

There is another possibility, however, says Harré. One could take "the perceptual case as merely a model for tacit knowing." It would consist only of a way to "get a grip on the 'from–to' relationship," so that we could then apply the model to "the propositional sort of case." This latter application would then leave us free to treat the propositional sort of case in a perhaps wholly different way.[10]

He admits, however, that he does not think Polanyi intended the perceptual case to be merely a model for the cognitive case.[11]. It appears to me that he is right in this. Polanyi did mean, as I read him, for us to take both cases as a subsidiary dwelling-in *to* a focal meaning or comprehensive entity, partially or wholly established by our own imaginative and integrative capacities.

Yet Harré finds insuperable problems in this. He points these up sharply by dealing with involvement of theory in perception. When this occurs we perceive something differently, because of a theory we have somewhere in our mind. He maintains that W. T. Scott's contention that tacit perceptual knowledge and tacit theoretical knowledge are simply combined subsidiarily into a focal object by a mind, raises the question of how these two kinds of knowledge are related. They cannot be related, he holds, in a "from–to" fashion from one to the other, since both elements are subsidiary to the focal object. One of them cannot be both subsidiary and focal at once. But it also cannot be a relation of logical dependence, inasmuch as one of the elements is perceptual and consequently is not "propositional."[12] Nor can the difficulty be resolved by any univocal "from–to" structure, say Harré, since the two types of cases, the perceptual and the theoretical-propositional, are fundamentally different.[13]

To reveal the tacit knowledge involved in perception—"to bring it out"—he holds, requires two steps. The first is "perceptual, psychological, analytical, etc.," in other words, digging it out, apparently. The second step, he says, is "descriptive," and therefore, he holds, what is subsidiary in perception is not properly called "knowledge."[14] He appears to be assuming here that it does not become knowledge until it becomes "propositional," i.e., "described." Harré is therefore rejecting a large portion of Polanyi's *Personal Knowledge,* as well as much of his other work, where Polanyi labors long and hard to convince us that all of our explicit knowledge (our propositional and descriptive knowledge) rests upon various kinds of non-critical, prelinguistic knowledge capacities which we share with the lower animals. Animals, Polanyi contended, clearly do recognize, for instance, kinds of things, even though they lack the language capacities to know these kinds explicitly, i.e., propositionally. Thus "we (as also do other animals) know more than we can tell." Harré seems to be saying "we know only what we *can* tell."

Harré, however, does hold that there is such a thing as tacit knowledge. It is those propositional or theoretic elements which we are disattending from when we are using them (dwelling in them) to attend to something perceptual, or possibly even something theoretical. So he holds Polanyi's "from–to" theory is acceptable, but not as revelatory of the logical structure of tacit knowledge. This logical structure, Harré insists, is analogical. Polanyi's "from–to" theory is thus only a dynamic theory about "how tacit knowledge is revealed, explicated, made explicit." It works something like this:

> I pass from ordinary solid objects to my understanding of fundamental atoms, and the world of solid objects becomes the thing I disattend from in getting a grip on my concept of the underlying atom. That, of course, itself can then become a "from" object, but at another time. I can then disattend from that, from my underlying atomism, to my conception of the molecule and that would then fade into the role of the subsidiary. I think, then, we can defend the application of the Polanyian "from–to" in this dynamic way. That is, if we ask, "How is it that people came to formulate these concepts?", then we can see that the structure of the formulation might very well be on one day "from–to," on another day "to–from," and we set up a series of "from–to" relations through a series of different kinds of objects. But I do not think that this will do for revealing the structure of the tacit knowledge because the moment we reveal the propositional content of tacit knowledge the natural method of explication is our old friend the combination of necessary conditions and analogical relations.[15]

Harré presents us with an example of how he thinks Polanyi's dynamic theory works. Harré explains how Clausius and Maxwell made the laws of gases intelligible. He says they imagined a swarm of molecules conceived as Newtonian objects and they showed that the way these imagined objects behaved was, in a sense, analogous to the way real gases behaved. How did they know how such molecules might behave? Harré says they never tell us; but we know that they and all those who understood what they proposed shared a belief (something propositional) that was essential to their theory, a general atomism: all things consist of little hard particles. This generally shared conception of the world was not related directly to the notion of the molecule, since molecules were not exactly little hard particles. But they were "just *like* little lumps" of such matter. The objects proposed for a scientific theory should be analogous to the primitive objects of which the world is composed. And how did they know what these primitive objects are like? Another analogy—they were like ordinary objects in our own natural world.[16]

Harré claims this is a much simpler explication of the structure of the tacit knowledge underlying Clausius and Maxwell's work than the notion of "from–to." A description of the "from's" and the "to's" seems to him impossible to determine in this case.[17] It appears that Harré thinks we would have to go "from" the perceived objects of our world "to" the primitive theoretical objects that make up the world in our general idea of atomism. But then we have to go from this atomism to our idea of how molecules behave, and then from that conception to our theory of the laws of the gases. Specific concepts or entities are here functioning as both subsidiary and focal at the same time, if this is the logical structure of our tacit knowing! Of course, if these are only the dynamic steps by which people came to formulate their concepts, then the same element could function now as a "to" and later as a "from" without any difficulty.

This seems so simple a point that we must surely ask why Polanyi never saw it, especially since Harré informs us that he had many discussions of this very problem with Polanyi and was unable to determine whether or not "he was satisfied that an analysis of that type of situation can be given in terms of the 'from–to' relation."[18] This statement would seem also to imply, of course, that he also could not determine whether Polanyi was dissatisfied with his "from–to" relation as a satisfactory analysis of a situation.

I also have had many discussions with Polanyi about the possibility of his "from–to" relation being a logical one; it was always clear to me that he was adamant in his insistence that it was a logical relation, not merely a psychological explanation of the dynamics of theory construction. How could he have been so blind to Harré's point?

First of all we should note that there is a distinct difference between what Harré calls "logical" and what Polanyi called "logical." Harré clearly does not accept anything as logical which is not a case of explicit logic, i.e., that proceeds by the formal rules of a symbolic logic in a way that can be duplicated by an "inference machine." Logic is always explicit, or it is not logic. Polanyi, of course, took issue with this basic view, and thought there was a logic of tacit inference. It was not an explicit logic, of course. It was tacit—and it was the way in which a mind dwelled in subsidiary clues to reach correctly a focal meaning across an explicitly logical gap. It is clear, of course, that one does this in perception, which, because the elements are not propositional in their function, Harré does not call logical at all. But Polanyi insisted that we also do this in our discoveries in science, as well as in our justification of these discoveries. We cross an explicitly logical gap.

In spite of the many basic notions of Polanyi which Harré simply brushes aside in his criticism of Polanyi's views on this matter, his criticism strikes at a point at which Polanyi's notions would seem to be most vulnerable. How can one suppose that the use of theories (which surely are propositional) as grounds for other propositional statements is anything but explicitly logical, in terms, as Harré says, at least of "our old friend the combination of necessary conditions and analogical relations"?[19] Isn't it stretching things to try to make the journey from one propositional statement to another into the same thing as our dwelling in the features of a face in a subsidiary way to get from them to a gestalt of the face as a whole? What can be said to this criticism, except to repeat what Polanyi himself has said on many occasions: there are many indeterminacies in our understanding of a proposition, which stand as grounds for our conclusions from it.

Although we can give a logically explicit definition of what we mean by "necessary conditions," we cannot render perfectly explicit our understanding of when it is that these conditions are satisfied. We know, if we are an acculturated and practicing scientist in a particular discipline, when these conditions are satisfied, in our judgment, for our particular science; but we cannot reduce our judgment to a complete, finite set of criteria. We never make our judgments in this explicit manner—not in the dynamics of discovery, not in our justifications and criticisms.

Nonetheless Polanyi always held that we do not make our judgments illogically, nor even alogically, that is, only subjectively. These judgments may or may not be sound, and therefore they may be correctly or incorrectly structured by us.

Polanyi insisted that this means our judgments do have a logic, since the function of logic is to correctly assess what is really implied by something else. We can, in tacit inference, however, only acquire a tacit awareness of the correct rules (much as we do when we correctly ride a bicycle), an awareness which becomes implicitly more right as we become connoisseurs, in contrast to the explicit rules of inference that we arrive at in formal logical inference, which can be turned over to an inference machine. Actually, of course, as Polanyi showed, our proper application of even these hard rules—and thus in a very real sense their true meaning—also rests upon many indeterminant, subsidiary elements in which we simply dwell. In all cases, therefore, we need a mind to synthesize subsidiary elements into a focal entity or meaning, and always across explicitly logical gaps.

That this condition, our need for a mind in making judgments, exists also in our recognition of any analogy should perhaps be even more evident that in our handling of "necessary condition." What is involved in seeing an analogy is not simply noticing that two things are the same, which might be done by an electronic device that scanned each of the two cases point by point. It is determining that two different things have a significant similarity. They are like "in respect to" something. Again, one could program a computing device to find this out, too, but only if one decided in what respect to tell the machine to look for the similarity.

As Harré says, molecules "are not really little lumps of matter. They are just *like* little lumps of matter."[20] But in what respect? How are they "like"? One has to come to this analogy with something in mind. But, as Kuhn said in the "Postscript" to the second edition of his *Structure of Scientific Revolutions*, we cannot determine an exhaustive set of explicit, finite criteria to answer: "With respect to what?"[21] What is to count as analogous is a product of many tacit notions, and even feelings. Ask us if certain things are alike in such and such a particular manner and we can answer "yes" or "no" by reference to the complex of tacitly held notions that we have in mind. But we cannot reduce these notions to a neat set of operational rules in which we can have a confidence that they would never need correction, revision, or addition. In terms of what may they need such changes? Obviously in terms of what we have only tacitly in mind. So it does not appear to me that Harré has refuted, or even shaken, Polanyi's position on the necessity of our knowledge (as well as our perceptions) being rooted in the tacit, as structured by "from–to" relations.

This, of course, does not settle the question of whether or not Polanyi's contention *can* be criticized. It would seem to me that one could show that Polanyi was wrong only if one could point to some knowledge that is wholly explicit. It is not sufficient, however, to show that our knowledge—which, as Harré says, "we all agree is based on a buried foundation, the tacit"[22]—is thereby rendered wholly explicit, if in fact we can unbury the foundation by focussing our attention upon it; for our focal awareness of this foundation may then in its turn, as Polanyi seemed to have insisted, still depend upon our dwelling in some further subsidiary awareness to bring it into explicit focus. Harré's view of Polanyi's work, although he seems to regard it as of real significance, appears to empty it, in fact, of any significance, since he would merely have it inform us that we are not always focally aware of everything upon which our knowledge is based but that we can dig it out and focalize it. People have been thinking this since Plato, at least. But to have seen that some part of any knowledge, perceptual or propositional, which we in fact hold at any particular time, must rest in what we can only in that focal awareness of it be subsidiarily aware of is, as Grene says she now thinks (and that Polanyi first expressed to her when he was writing *Personal Knowledge*) the truly unique and original insight involved in his thought.[23] To be able to refute this contention would be to call very seriously into question almost everything Polanyi has done.

But that all our empirical knowledge does rest upon some grounds known to us only in a subsidiary fashion seems to me to be irrefutable for several reasons. One is derivable from the necessities involved in our use of computers. The truly and wholly explicit is just what comes out of a computer in a physical sense. It seems patently obvious that it is in no way "knowledge" until it is interpreted as such by a mind with reference to some purpose. Neither would what we feed into it be knowledge for the computer. It is so only for us. Therefore we contribute something over and above, and different from, these detached, objective, and explicit physical items. Surely the same thing is true of words. If we found a million pages of what might appear to be a written language, it would be all meaningless to us (even if it included what might seem to be a copious dictionary) if in fact we had no knowledge as to how one could dwell in these words as clues to nonlinguistic meanings, and thus to knowledge.

The same difficulties arise with respect to perception. Almost no one now thinks, as many modern philosophers did until quite recently, that perception is the same as stimuli—or that we perceive stimuli. What we "see" may be triggered by stimuli and stimuli may enter into what we see; but we do many things with the stimuli, including incorporating theory into it. Our observations are, in the current jargon, "theory-laden." This part of Polanyi's views Harré too seems to accept. How we construct our perceptions seems to be a source of interminable squabbles among contemporary philosophers; but that we do construct them seems now fairly generally accepted. And surely everyone knows that we "disattend" from some of our stimuli as we make them into the perceived. What could prevent us from seeing that this circumstance must make all our knowledge personal? For "observation sentences," as Quine argued, must generally be accepted in our day as "the court of appeal for scientific theories." Can we any longer accept his definition of an observation sentence as "one on which all speakers of the language give the same verdict when given the same concurrent stimulation"?[24] We know that not even all scientists do this. So what happens to our "court of appeal"? It must also become personal—or else we must give up observation sentences as the basis for the findings of this court. But where then should we turn? Modern philosophers seem to know of no other more reliable place to go.

It seems to me at this point that if these arguments could be answered in a way that would put the matter beyond reasonable doubt, then Polanyi's basic contention can be refuted, or at least rendered highly suspect. Given the exhaustive ways in which he has argued his case, the burden of proof rests on his opponents, and they have not rallied to the occasion. Merely to ignore his thought is manifestly insufficient at this point, for he has challenged modern thinking. I am waiting to see the reply, as was Polanyi. And he was greatly disappointed to see the meager quality of such criticism as did come his way.

Polanyi's thought, of course, contained more than this basic contention. As we have seen, he managed to meddle in many intellectual affairs besides epistemology and the philosophy of science. Partly he thought that his demonstrated ability to use this "from–to" notion to make sense in many areas of human concern might constitute some evidence for its value. But, as we have seen, he had further aims that concerned healing what he thought ailed the modern mind, and he only stopped trying to further these aims when old age and death silenced him. Having diagnosed our modern ills and proposed treatment for them, he felt he had also to apply it, and so he did. Let us turn now to an evaluation of his applications.

# CHAPTER SIXTEEN

# Is Epistemological Antireductionism Sufficient?

So far, we have found that Michael Polanyi's new direction in epistemology and in the philosophy of science appears to be sound. Whether or not it is also, as he held it to be, the proper prescription for those ills besetting the modern mind can only be determined when we find what use can be made of it in the treatment of these ills, along with what actual or probable results occur from its use. Let us turn therefore to those aspects of Polanyi's philosophy which I have grouped together under the rubric of "Treatment." As might be expected, this aspect of his work led him into a considerable number of topics. A thorough analysis of all the possible criticisms of his positions on these many topics would extend this present work to several volumes, inasmuch as a considerable number of different literatures would have to be canvassed and brought to bear upon his several positions. These would encompass specific areas in biology, psychology, metaphysics, theories of language, of metaphor, of poetry, of art, of myth, of rites, of religion, of economics, of politics, and of ethics and social philosophy.

It is impossible in a volume of this scope to do justice to criticisms of everything in his work related to all these fields. The magnitude of such an endeavor would make anyone despair of having enough lifetimes to complete the job. I have begun to see also that such an attempt might end up disintegrating into a ragbag full of shreds and patches the complex texture he has woven out of these many matters. A general assessment of the value of his efforts might very well be lost in a vast number of specific criticisms of restricted scope and interest.

It is perhaps possible to better assess the value of what he has done in these areas by focusing our attention on certain key features which underlie his efforts. First of all, his particular views in these areas rest upon a general theory of ontology. Secondly they rest in a practical way upon some general methodological principles for getting at what he thinks is true in these areas. And thirdly they rest historically and empirically upon some general assumptions concerning the basic contemporary structures that we have to deal with in our time.

Bearing in mind the various positions we have seen Polanyi espouse in the third part of this book, we should be able to see that none of these views of his become wholly cogent, in the way he has dealt with them, without his contention that our world is hierarchically structured, analogous to his epistemological structure of "from–to."

Marjorie Grene seems to clearly understand this dependence—which appears to be why, although she is enthusiastic about his "from–to" ideas, she is distinctly cool to a good part of those ideas of his which I have discussed under "Treatment." Grene is perhaps Polanyi's strongest and most prestigious philosophical supporter. Her association with him goes all the way back to the years when she worked as his assistant while he was writing his *Personal Knowledge*. Therefore her rejection of his ontological hierarchies has to be taken very seriously.

She argues that Polanyi's "from–to" reformation in philosophy is extremely important and long overdue, and that philosophers have not yet seen that it provides the new direction they need out of the contemporary impasse in epistemology and the philosophy of science. It provides, she believes, an escape from reductionism. Specifically she thinks it makes clear that knowledge of the mind and knowledge of the brain are not identical, nor are the mind and the brain identical, and it explains why this must be so in a way that avoids anything like vitalism, spiritualism, or mysticism—in a word, that avoids a metaphysical dualism of any sort. However, she believes that Polanyi failed to understand fully these admirable consequences of his position, and went on, especially in "The Structure of Consciousness," to defend dualism by "*defending* the mind's separateness from the body." She quotes him as also saying in "Logic and Psychology" that the mind and body are two different things, just as our common sense tells us they are."[1]

These statements are instances of his general position that "being" is organized, as she quotes, into a "stratified universe" of hierarchies in which the higher sort of being emerges from the lower part. She says that her further studies "about evolutionary theory, both its subtleties and its limitations" have made her "sceptical about cosmologies of emergence in any form." She also connects his later work "on art, and especially on metaphor," with his mistaken notion of emergence into higher strata of being.[2] The import of this aspect of his work has been, she maintains, to abandon an essential point that is necessarily "part and parcel of the theory of tacit knowing," namely, "the incarnate nature of mind."[3]

It seems clear from what we have covered of Polanyi's views in this book that he maintained that a lower level makes possible the existence of a higher level and also sets limits to its achievement. But our understanding of the higher level entails our grasping certain principles of operation that are peculiar to that higher level and not therefore reducible to the principles we use in understanding the operation of the lower level in which its existence is embodied. Possibly Grene would subscribe to such a statement as this, as her reasons why reductionism is a futile undertaking.

Just where then do they part company? I think a clue to their differences may be found in Grene's remark: "In fact it occurred to me that much as, by Wittgensteinians, the meaning of a word was alleged to be its use, so for Polanyi (and in fact) the meaning of the brain was the mind, or the meaning of the brain was its use, which is the mind." To be sure, she does caution us that this statement would have to be "refined" so as not to "degenerate into Rylean behaviourism, let alone into come kind of 'central-state materialism.' " However, she maintains, "the concept of from–to knowledge should allow one to work along these lines, and should certainly prevent, not support, a return to the notion of a 'separate' consciousness or thinking thing." She offers a possible explanation of how Polanyi came to be misled about this aspect of his thought, attributing it to the fact that "he was so much concerned to refute the 'denial of consciousness' by behaviourists" that he fell into the error of asserting that the conscious mind was a separate entity, as had Descartes.[4]

It would appear that Grene thinks our recognition of the from–to structure of knowing alone is sufficient to preserve us from reductionism. Since it shows us that reductionism is not possible on epistemological grounds, she thinks there is no reason to try to refute reductionism on ontological grounds as well. Trying also to do the latter endangers the notion that mind must be embodied, and opens the door to dualism, which, she thinks, philosophers today will not accept as a means of avoiding reductionism.

She is certainly correct in holding that Polanyi felt epistemological nonreductionism was not adequate. He castigated Kant for stopping at that point. Kant in his *Critique of Judgment* saw that it was impossible for us to understand "organized beings" (organisms) without using a teleological principle. Kant held, however, that this principle was supplied by our minds only for the purpose of understanding organisms; it was a regulative principle, not a constitutive one. For Kant, organisms, as phenomenal objects, were constituted by the same categories that constituted any other phenomenal objects (inanimate bodies). Polanyi ridiculed any clinging to ontological reductionism in this way yet acknowledging our inability to cognize an organism fully without the use of principles in addition to those we use in cognizing inanimate entities. It appeared to him that there was no good reason to deny to the entity we were cognizing any property or principle of operation that we had to acknowledge as cognitively necessary for our grasping it.

Polanyi freely acknowledged a leap across a logical gap whenever what we cognize in a thing is attributed to our belief in the existence of this cognized feature in the "real" entity. This was one of the indeterminacies that he held was irreducible in our activities of knowing. He agreed that there was no detached, objective way—no explicitly logical way—in which we could bridge the gap. But he thought our failure to acknowledge that we really do think our best knowledge about an entity is in fact true of that entity—our assumption of a skeptical posture that our conception is merely how we are constrained by our mental apparatus to construe that entity—was one of the unreasonable deficiencies of "critical" or "skeptical" philosophy which he thought had fathered so much of our modern malaise of thought. His rejection of this position was the reason why he thought he could describe his own work as "post-critical."

The question, however, is not only what ideas might be advantageous for us to help rid us of our current intellectual obsessions. As we have seen Polanyi also held that the question was what is true, i.e., what is to us defensible as beyond reasonable doubt?

Is it Grene's or Polanyi's position that is more defensible on this score? If it is Grene's—if the ontological leap is unnecessary or unreasonable—then Polanyi's whole grand notion of a "stratified universe," a hierarchy of beings becomes, as she seems to think, extremely dubious. Minds and organisms as beings, as well as all the noological levels of "beings" from art to religion which emerge from our minds and which he calls on us to accept as such become a vast series of mistakes that mar Polanyi's genuine achievements in philosophy. For contemporary thinkers they detract from the attractiveness of his unique epistemological contributions. In other words, Grene appears to think that all these "beings" unnecessarily confuse the issue for comtemporary thinkers.

Let us look at Polanyi's arguments for making the leap from his "from–to" structure of tacit knowing to his ontological hierarchy. We must ask whether, or to what extent, it might be sound. In the first part of *The Tacit Dimension*, Polanyi, as we have seen, distinguishes four aspects of tacit knowing: the functional, the phenomenal, the semantic, and the ontological.[5] The first three of these seem to be those that Grene accepts as sound and extremely useful notions about how we acquire our perceptive and our cognitive knowledge. The focal (or "distal," as Polanyi called it in that work) is the meaning of the subsidiary (or "proximal"). The mind, being the focal or distal is, Grene says, properly understood as the meaning of the brain (the subsidiary or proximal). This is what Polanyi calls the semantic aspect of tacit knowing. The functional and the phenomenal aspects are not so much in question here, so we need not discuss them; both Grene and Polanyi seem to agree in general upon their structure and soundness.

It is perhaps over the fourth aspect that they part company. Polanyi said that we "deduce" the ontological aspect from the other three; but he did not actually give a formal deduction. He merely said: "Since tacit knowing establishes a meaningful relation between two terms, we may identify it with the *understanding* of the comprehensive entity" constituted jointly by these two terms. The "proximal term represents the *particulars* of this entity" and so "we can say . . . that we comprehend the entity by relying on our awareness of its particulars for attending to their joint meaning."[6] We attend, he says, "*from* these internal processes *to* the qualities of things outside." We transpose our bodily experiences into the perception of things outside us and so meaning is transposed "away from us."[7]

Phenomenologically this contention that we transpose meaning away from us seems to be true and, of course, he was able to cite a myriad of examples. If we agree that this is a phenomenological fact, perhaps the only question that can arise is that, although it regularly appears to us that the meanings we achieve in our "from–to" procedures resides in entities outside ourselves, is it necessarily true that they do? Might it not merely seem to us that they do and yet really are only inside us? Kant, of course, took that position, since according to him the only objects we could know were phenomenal objects and in their phenomenal shape only inside us, since the "outer" space they appeared to occupy was itself inside us, i.e., was a form of our perceptive capacities. It must be said, therefore, that Polanyi's contention is certainly subject to a conceivable doubt.

It is not clear, however, that Grene wishes to doubt everything that is open to any conceivable doubt. Indeed, one of the great virtues of Polanyi's basic epistemology for her seems to be that he has shown us that this sort of Cartesian doubt is a fruitless epistemological principle that has wrought havoc upon our efforts to understand what goes on in science and in knowledge generally.[8]

The question must therefore rather be whether or not it is reasonable to assume that there is a marvelous coincidence between the way we know things and the way they are, in and of themselves, in the universe. It could easily be said, of course, that this is not always the case. The parts of the entity that we cognize are not always thought to be identical to the parts that function for us as subsidiary parts of our focal awareness of the entity. A particular cat, for example, as an entity in the world, a whole individual organism, is, we think, composed of many parts: organs, tissues, cells, molecules, atoms, etc. Someone's focal perception of that cat would not necessarily contain all these parts as the subsidiaries of which he is aware. Indeed, we might maintain that the subsidiaries of which we are aware subsidiarily when we perceive that cat are only various sensations and feelings inside us, not the existential parts of the cat.

Let us, to begin with, assume that Polanyi knew this very well, and we can then also assume that actually his contention was simply that, just as there is a stratification of our knowledge of an entity into a whole and its parts structured into the subsidiary and the focal, so there is the same kind of stratification in the entities we understand our knowledge concerns. That is, there is a stratification into parts that play a subsidiary function in establishing the whole of which they are the parts—not that the subsidiary parts in a focal entity are necessarily identical to the subsidiary parts in our focal knowledge of it. Let us assume, in other words, that Polanyi only intended to tell us that there is an analogy between how our knowledge is stratified and how being is stratified.

Polanyi did say flatly in the second part of *The Tacit Dimension*, entitled "Emergence," "It seems plausible to assume *in all . . . instances of tacit knowing the correspondence between the structure of comprehension and the structure of the comprehensive entity which is its object.*"[9] The examples he gave in elucidating this, however, show a fine disregard for whether or not, or to what extent, the subsidiaries in the one are identical with those in the other. In other words it is clear, in the context, that he was speaking of those structures as being the same, not necessarily asserting that their parts are the same. The identities which he found to exist in the structures of both types were very clearly expressed by him in this passage:

> (1) Tacit knowing of a coherent entity relies on our awareness of the particulars of the entity for attending to it; and (2) if we switch our attention to the particulars, this function of the particulars is canceled (sic) and we lose sight of the entity to which we had attended. The ontological counterpart of this would be (1) that the principles controlling a comprehensive entity would be found to rely for their operations on laws governing the particulars of the entity in themselves; and (2) that at the same time the laws governing the particulars in themselves would never account for the organizing principles of a higher entity which they form.[10]

He did not clearly claim here that things appear to us to be as they are simply because of the structure of our tacit knowing, but rather only that things are structured in such a way that there is an analogy between them and our way of knowing. How did he know that this is so? He did not deduce the structure of both from some grand, overarching ontological principle that makes it necessary for all things to be structured this way. He simply here found that many things are in fact so structured. He found it impossible to reduce the operational principles of some wholes in his experience to the principles operative in their parts. I write "some" because he saw that not every whole turns out to have emergent principles and thus to be an emergent being. Mountains do not and so are not, nor is the solar system. There are wholes that seem to be totally explicable as the sum of their parts.

Therefore he did not seem to be contending here that the reason we cannot epistemologically reduce all things to their parts is because the structure of our knowing apparatus makes it necessary for us, when we seek to understand the parts, to use different principles from those we must use to understand the working of the whole. Rather, it seems to be because he saw some wholes do in fact work on different principles from their parts and are therefore double- or multilayered entities. His examples range from machines to chess games to speeches and minds and organisms.

On these grounds it becomes a question of whether such entities he claimed exhibit principles of operation not involved in their parts really do so. Do minds actually have powers that we do not believe their parts have? If so, then minds are composite entities composed of two sets of capacities, one being that of the mind's material parts, organized into a brain, the other and higher one providing the boundary conditions for the use of the lower-level set of principles. To say that "the mind and body are two different things" would then be correct, although not necessarily implying that the mind excludes the body from its being. The mind is something more than the body and so it is possible for a body not to have a mind. Yet it may not be possible at all for a mind not to have a body.

Indeed, this is precisely what Polanyi held. He specifically held that the mind depended upon its embodiment in a body for its existence. In conversations I had with him he explicitly rejected the notion that the mind could continue in existence after the death of the body. So he did not hold to anything like a Cartesian dualism. The mind was nothing and nowhere without the body. Mind was indeed incarnate. To know anything, the mind needed to dwell in the subsidiary clues provided by the body. Yet the mind had operational principles and powers different from the body's and thus was a different thing. I asked him if he then thought that there could be no afterlife without a resurrection of the body and he agreed without hesitation, although he did not seem to believe at all that a truly dead body could ever be restored to life.

The crux of the matter seems to lie, therefore, in whether or not the mind does possess powers that its parts (its body and so its brain) do not possess. It was here that consciousness or sentience became so important to Polanyi. To deny that consciousness existed seemed to him to be phenomenologically absurd. It might be conceivable to doubt that any other organism possessed it; but he could not doubt that he himself possessed it as a quality of his own existence. Actually Polanyi thought it extravagantly unreasonable to doubt that other persons also possessed awareness—or even that at least much, if not all, animal life did too. But he maintained that it was equally extravagant and unreasonable to suppose that inanimate things had the quality of consciousness. In answer to my question about why he did not regard Whitehead's extension of sentience to all of existence to be a possible resolution as to how we could be sentient, he simply replied that it was not necessary to our understanding of anything in the inanimate world to postulate any sort of consciousness as operative there. Therefore, since no one, he maintained, has been able to deduce the peculiar qualities of consciousness from the operation of physical particles, nothing was left but a recognition that sentience was a newly emergent power that arose when basically inanimate matter was organized in certain ways.

But since a lower level merely leaves boundary conditions open by its own operations, no lower level could gain control over its own boundary conditions and so bring a higher level into existence that would control these boundary conditions. The logical structure of a hierarchy therefore implied "that a higher level can come into existence only through a process not manifest in the lower level," which, he said, is what qualifies this as an "emergence."[11] Therefore, ontologically, not merely epistemologically, reductionism was he held impossible where such a hierarchical arrangement seemed to us actually to exist.

In an individual human being, he held, we can see all the levels of evolution.

> The most primitive form of life is represented by the growth of the typical human shape, through the process of morphogenesis studied by embryology. Next we have the vegetative functioning of the organism, studied by physiology; and above it there is sentience, rising to perception and to a centrally controlled motoric activity, both of which still belong to the subject of physiology. We rise beyond this at the level of conscious behavior and intellectual action, studied by ethology and psychology; and uppermost, we meet with man's moral sense, guided by the firmament of his standards.[12]

In addition to conscious behavior, he therefore thought that the mind possessed intellectual powers and, furthermore, moral principles which are not reducible to man's lower levels. Since, as he went on to say, "all these levels are situated above the inanimate levels . . . it follows that none of these biotic operations can be accounted for by the laws of physics and chemistry," even though "they all rely for their operations—directly or indirectly—on the laws of physics and chemistry which govern the inanimate."[13]

Grene thus appears to be wrong in assuming that Polanyi had reintroduced Cartesian dualism into his system. The mind and body *are* different, but there are no unincarnate minds for Polanyi. However, she is correct in her assertion that he definitely held to a "stratified universe." But this would only be an unsound position if one could assert that there are no entities in the world actually possessing powers, principles of operation, qualities, or capacities not possessed by the subsidiary parts of which they are composed. In one sense Grene does seem to accept that there are such entities in existence; but she seems to say that this is so only because epistemologically we are unable to render absolutely explicit how the subsidiary parts bring these qualities or powers into existence. We can only see them doing this by our processes of tacit knowing.

Polanyi said that these beings are real, and Grene sees no necessity for this. But it followed for Polanyi that they are real in terms of his root criterion for reality, namely, that what is real for us is that which we expect to manifest itself in new and indeterminate ways in the future. Since we expect this of minds and of individual organisms, they are as real as cobblestones, said Polanyi—indeed even more real. If we think something has the power to operate, to be and to do, then we think it is real—and this is not simply to think of it, but to think of it as real. Such a "thing" is therefore, he thought, a being on its own. But is it? In his articles on the irreducibility of biology to physics and chemistry, Polanyi maintained, as we have seen, that the notion that DNA functions as a code in the development of organisms means that organisms, like machines, have to be understood as systems involving two kinds of principles: those prevailing between their parts, the laws of physics and chemistry, and those establishing and maintaining boundary conditions for these operations and which thus control their scope and direction. DNA provides the boundary conditions for structuring the parts of an organism to accomplish the functions they do carry out.

Some research on this empirical question seems to corroborate Polanyi's views on the actual existence of powers in living things beyond those possessed separately by their components. H. H. Pattee has made detailed studies of how these two levels interact within the development of a cell; he has concluded that both these two levels do operate in such development and that there is a complementary interaction between what he calls the "linguistic" and the "dynamic" modes of operation in the cell. "Living systems contain their own descriptions."[14] By linguistic he means quite literally something written rather than an analogue of the system, such as an image or model of it. "This implies the existence

of a symbol system, syntactical rules for combining symbols into inter-
pretable statements and a mechanism for effectively writing, reading and
executing such statements."[15]

Complex systems, like living entities, that do not exhibit a tendency
to degenerate or lose their function must have, as he claims systems
theory shows, such a self-describing or self-programming dimension.
This capacity constrains the system beyond the laws operative between
its parts. It must function to harness the forces of natural laws in much
the way Pattee thinks Polanyi argues that it provides the boundaries for
these systems in a reliable and adaptable way.[16]

How the linguistic and dynamic modes interact is the central problem which, he says, has not yet been faced seriously. But he claims it is
"the fundamental fact of life" that living systems must contain their own
descriptions and therefore must have something other than the dynamics
of their own parts to account for their design, repair, adaptation, and
evolutions, as he says Polanyi has shown also to be true for machines.
For machines, this is obviously the languages of the human brain; but for
living things this must be their own languages.[17] It would appear that
they must therefore be composite beings, and that one level, the linguistic, must be higher or more dominant than the other, as Polanyi already
said was necessary.

Grene is right, of course, that one can accept and use Polanyi's
from–to notion of knowledge without extrapolating it to his "stratified
universe"; but there do seem to be many cogent reasons for accepting
this part of his thought as well, if one frees Polanyi's later work from her
mistaken notion that it necessitates a belief in disembodied minds or that
any of the higher levels we can find in the world exist in disembodied
form.

We have shown that it is possible to understand Polanyi's views of
the "ontological aspect" of tacit knowing as simply meaning that the two
levels in the entities we find in our world are only analogues to the two
levels we find in our knowing processes, not that they are composed
necessarily of the same identical subsidiary parts used by our minds in
establishing our focal awareness of them. Now let us return to the sense
in which Polanyi appears to mean that, in fact, they are indeed so
identically composed.

Our perception of, say, a cat makes use of those sense stimuli and
feelings that are dwelt in by us when we see this object. We integrate
them into the focal object that we see, by a tacit process that we cannot

make wholly explicit—certainly not while we are seeing the cat—which, in fact, we can never make wholly explicit at all due to the fact that any of the subsidiary clues we discover and focus upon will always themselves be an integration of other subsidiary clues. As we have seen, this seems to make our tacit subsidiary elements different from those belonging to the actual cat.

However, since we are not only sentient but cognitive and acculturated people, among these clues will also be some concepts, paradigms, or theories that we have internalized and dwell in when we perceive an object. Therefore, the more we think we know about cats, the more of these concepts there are in us which will function for us as subsidiary clues. So if we have contemporary theoretical knowledge about what we think are cats' biological composition, it is possible that all of this knowledge will also function in a subsidiary way in our perception of the cat, and thus that our focal awareness of the cat will also contain as subsidiaries our notions of the tissues, organs, atoms, molecules, etc., that we understand to be parts of the cat. In fact, to Polanyi, a biologist so viewing the cat will have failed to grasp the ontological truth of what he sees if he fails to allow himself to dwell in all these subsidiaries and so fails to find that their meaning is the cat, the whole cat—he will fail to grasp the cat conceptually if he instead focuses explicitly on all these parts of the cat.

In this sense Polanyi seems to mean literally that we deduce the true ontology of the cat from the exigencies of tacit knowing. As we dwell in all these parts to grasp the cat epistemologically, so does the cat in order to exist ontologically, as a cat. It is this participatory indwelling that gets us to the true knowledge of what the cat really is. In this strict sense all of our comprehensive phenomenological entities are also at the same time and in the same way understood by us to be ontologically comprehensive entities composed of two levels: the subsidiary and the focal, the proximal and the distal. And the inevitable projection of the meaningful, or focal, object outward means that real beings, for us, must be conceived of as being structured with at least two levels; thus our whole universe is a stratified one.

Since the parts of any entity achieve their meaning only through their integration by a mind into a focal whole, to seek to reduce our world to its parts in order to understand it is to fail to understand (or even to be aware of) all those entities that only emerge into view when we integrate their parts through tacit knowing. Polanyi's often-repeated ridicule for Laplacean ideas rests upon this implication of tacit knowing. I do not doubt that these contentions of Polanyi's are paradoxically the reason Grene thinks that Polanyi's concepts are simply epistemological and are quite sufficient without making the leap out of them into a "real" world structured by them. She believes it should be sufficient to know that the mind is the meaning of the brain and of all the parts of the body involved in "minding" anything. For her this seems to provide the proper basis for all the methodology we need in order to inquire into and to understand our world. Recognizing the necessity of our using this from—to structure, we will not mistake biology for physics and chemistry, psychology for biology, politics for psychology, nor art for politics by misapplying a methodology that is adequate for dwelling only in the subsidiaries of what we are specifically focusing upon.

Were Polanyi only a phenomenologist perhaps this should be sufficient for him. But Polanyi always insisted that as a scientist he believed in the methods of science and so also in its aim to discover what external reality is. Our beliefs, he always held, could be mistaken. How could they be, if there were no touchstone of reality against which to measure them? Science is not satisfied, he held, only with making up a marvelous conceptual system that is beautifully articulated and that ties together all the phenomenal data we possess. He thought such a limited conception existed nowhere but in the minds of positivistic philosophers. Copernicus, Polanyi insisted in arguing against a positivistic interpretation of his work, believed there was a world really like that expressed by his theories. The planets, which he understood to be real entities in themselves, actually revolved about the sun, which was also thought to be a real entity. Newton believed the force of gravitation actually existed and that there really were atoms whose only inherent power was inertia. He did not think his ideas were only conceptual constructions. Einstein thought the world really was as his theories said it was and that quantum mechanics could not be correct, since it could not also be true of the world. God, he believed, would not roll dice with the universe.

Every scientific achievement, Polanyi held, was fed by a vision of how things are which was seriously held by someone with universal intent and with the understanding that the manifestation of things might prove their visions wrong. As we have seen, this is one of the basic reasons why, although Polanyi held that the subsidiary—focal was applicable everywhere, he also held there was a real distinction between the way it worked in perception and science and the way it worked in art and religion.

His intention to project the comprehensive entities into what exists beyond his own grasp of them is a most important part of his thought, without which all things have only the reality of the meanings or focal integrations we happen to achieve. If these were to be the only realities we admitted, then the separate unique intentions of science, art, and religion could only be confused hopelessly with each other.

The world for Polanyi must be hierarchically organized, because that is what comes out of an epistemology adequate to the way in fact we do know anything, inasmuch as knowing is rooted in a hierarchical "from–to" structure. To deny it is to deny that this epistemology is adequate to determine what is. Certainly Polanyi hoped that his epistemology was adequate.

In the end it would appear that Polanyi's basic contentions in this part of his work can be rejected only on two grounds: one, that there are no entities in the world whose operative principles cannot be reduced to those of their parts, or two, that the ontological projections of an epistemology are mere speculation and may be disregarded, or substituted for by others based on other grounds. Since evidence I have seen does not seem to support the contention that there are no such layered entities in the world, but rather that, in fact, there are, and since I see no sufficient reason why the ontological projections of an epistemology should not be respected as much as the epistemology itself is, I must conclude that I think Polanyi's basic ontological foundations are as sound as his epistemology.

But this does not mean that the logical gap does not exist between our own accepted ontology and the belief that it does in fact accurately state the way things are. There is no way to demonstrate with logical rigor that we must believe that any given ontology is true of the world. There is no objective way to match the two. In fact, there can be no objective way to prove the existence of anything beyond our own awareness—and even this would be a somewhat strange use of the notion of objectivity. We either do or we do not commit ourselves to beliefs in certain existences. And, as Polanyi has shown, there can be no way to state our commitments noncommitally, i.e., in a wholly detached and explicit manner. We would always have to add, to any such attempted statements, that we are, in fact, committed to them!

Therefore Polanyi has not indeed proven that our universe is a stratified one. In fact, it was an integral part of his whole philosophy that nothing of this sort can be proven. Whether or not he has made it seem reasonable is a decision each of us will have to make. I can only say I find his stratified universe reasonable. It is obvious that Grene and perhaps many others do not. I hope I have shown some of the cogent reasons involved in our differing decisions.

# CHAPTER SEVENTEEN

# The Problem of Polanyi's Divarication

Having dealt critically with the first underlying theoretical principle of Michael Polanyi's work in nonscientific areas—his general notion of ontological hierarchies—we come now to a critical consideration of the second basic feature that also underlies them all: the methodological principle that he thought uniquely applicable to these non-scientific areas.

Polanyi made a methodological distinction, as we have seen, between the way in which we make use of the subsidiary–focal (the from–to structure of knowing) in our perception and in our knowledge of nature and the way in which we make use of it in the arts and religion (and possibly in our moral life). He called integrations of the former sort "self-centered" and those of the latter "self-giving." Participation of the self was, as we have seen, involved in both kinds.

But in the self-centered integration we project the focal object of our awareness out and away from us (as from a center) into a reality understood by us as existing independently of us and of our knowledge of it. Such a reality, therefore, can never be incorporated completely into our own being. This reality remains a separate being in itself, whatever it is, and its future manifestations therefore serve as the touchstone or the truth of our ideas of it. Perception and cognition of such a reality

therefore may be in error and thus always require what he called "verification." It is true that there can never be a hard and fast, final, and
wholly detached objective method of verification, i.e., of determining,
without any personal involvement, whether or not our theories and
convictions about these realities truly match the way they really are. But
our universal intent in our grasp of such a reality is fulfilled by our honest
conviction that our ideas of it can be verified by any inquirer who stands
where we stood, because the entity itself is thought by us to be an
independent reality that exerts an acknowledged authority over our ideas
of it—or anyone else's.

In the other sort, the self-giving, we find we are, as he put it,
"carried away" by the object—whether it is a work of art, a symbol, a
rite, or a god. And it is this capacity of the object of our focal attention to
"carry us away," to "move us deeply," which makes our understanding
of it, our meaningful integration of it, into a focal object valid for us. We
validate it on these grounds, rather than verify our views of it as adequate
to describing it as a thing existing in itself independently of us. What is
important to us in, say, the play *Hamlet* or Michelangelo's *Moses* are not
the given characteristics of these entities (the play and the statue) as
existing objects in the world. Although they do exhibit, of course, in
their physical existence as some sort of objects in our perceptible world,
certain perceptible features, the meaning of these features in their impact
upon our feelings, our hopes, our fears, and our personalities or lives
make the mere perception, analysis, or cognition of these physical features seem relatively unimportant in themselves. Polanyi held in the case
of symbols such as a flag or a tombstone, for instance, that the focal
awareness of the object, as a perceptible object, lacks any intrinsic interest for us.

Yet the object as a whole, including its existence as a symbol, is of
great intrinsic interest to us, because the object—not as a cloth or a stone,
but as a symbol—reaches into the innermost recesses of our feeling-life
and acts as an embodiment "out there" of the meaningful unification of
these feelings. As a result, these feeling elements in our being become,
he held, subsidiary elements of the object in its existence as a symbol, and
so make the object what it is at the same time as they make it personally
part of what we ourselves are; thus carrying our personal selves away
into the object in which we find ourselves reflected to ourselves. The
ordinary objects of perception and of our mundane and practical knowledge of "things," however interesting they may be to us, do not ever do

anything like this. In the case of symbols, both the clues and the focal integration, therefore, become in this way intrinsically interesting to us. Polanyi then went on from symbols to add layers of complexity, as we have seen, to this basic way of understanding which, he believed, explains the power of metaphors, poems, plays, paintings, and ultimately of religions, to move us so deeply and to acquire such validity for us. This is so, he maintained, even though, or perhaps precisely because, their "stories," their subsidiary parts that appear to represent entities in the world, are never mistaken by us as presenting reliable, true, and verifiable states of affairs.

Now although not an impossible account of these matters, this view of the differing ways in which we form or integrate meaningful entities in our experience as persons can come under many different kinds of attack, of course. It is not possible in one book to exhaust them all—or perhaps for any one person to do so.

Many of the possible attacks will simply flow from epistemological points of views that are antithetical to Polanyi's. Since it is not his epistemology I wish to evaluate at this point, I will not deal here with these, but rather consider some criticisms of what he does with the arts and religion that have been raised by critics who appear to accept Polanyi's epistemology.

One view is, once again, that of Grene. I do not cite again her dismay at the way in which Polanyi seems to her to pile beings on top of beings in a hierarchical fashion, even into the noological sphere created by man himself. We have already discussed to some extent her objections to this aspect of Polanyi's thinking. I refer rather to another objection that she raises, to the foundation he laid for a "philosophy of art" or aesthetics, an objection to what she believes is a mistake in his own terms, i.e., to a flaw in the capacity of his work to fulfill its own intentions. Another criticism I wish to deal with is not expressed by its author as a criticism. It consists in assuming that Polanyi was doing something that the writer obviously thinks he should have been doing in order to be true to his own intention and to his subject, when in fact Polanyi was not, I believe, doing this. This view is, I think, a misunderstanding of Polanyi; but it may indeed provide some grounds for a criticism of what Polanyi has in fact done.

Grene holds that one of the chief values of Polanyi's from–to epistemology is the way in which it bridges the gap between scientific and humanistic concerns by showing us that all meaning or knowledge requires the subsidiary–focal poles and so requires our personal participation in it. Not only do art and religion require our participation, but science does as well. As a result Polanyi showed us that the invidious distinction that our epoch has made between "science" and every other, nonscientific, activity or discipline has no reasonable foundation. According to Grene, Polanyi showed there are no sound epistemological grounds for making such a distinction, and therefore we can respect all the many kinds of meanings that we are in fact able to achieve. None are wholly objective or wholly subjective; rather, all are "personal."

It seems to Grene that the distinctions Polanyi finally made, in his later views on metaphor and art, between these and ordinary perception and science tended to blunt the edge of his own sword and to reintroduce some sort of distinctions between these two general kinds of articulate human activities. Such distinctions, she seems to fear, might easily become invidious once again, and thus come to work against Polanyi's own intentions. For it seems fairly clear that Polanyi intended to help us reach a way of understanding our knowing activities which would enable us to respect our own deepest commitments and meanings, regardless of whether or not they could be understood to be supported by our modern sciences.

We must therefore ask two questions: (1) Has Polanyi done damage to his own cause by reintroducing the methodological or epistemological distinction between sciences and humanistic endeavors which he had eliminated? (2) Is the distinction he introduced sound, or at least more sound than his failure to introduce it would have been?

In one very real sense the answer to both questions rests upon an answer to the second one, since if it would have been unsound for Polanyi to have failed to make this distinction then failure to make it would have been more damaging to his cause in the long run than has been the apparent fissure that it introduced into the unity of his system. Polanyi, as we have seen, was acutely aware of this very kind of long-run danger to his position, should he be tempted to rest any part of his effort on unsound positions. Did his constant efforts to avoid such dangers founder at last toward the end of his career on the distinction he made between art and science in *Meaning*?

In view of the basic importance of this second question, let us try to answer it and then see what, if any, implications this answer has for the first question. In this chapter we can only make a start on this task. The question, we shall find, will lead us into a somewhat involved inquiry.

To begin with, we will need to explore the views of the eminent theologian Thomas Torrance. We need not deal here with his views in their full complexity. He is an intelligent and well-read thinker, not only in theology, but also in modern physics and the history of science and his work shows the heavy influence of all this knowledge. However, by concentrating on certain very fundamental and important aspects of his views I believe we can grasp their import and begin to answer our second question.

Torrance knows Polanyi's thought very well. He is, in fact, at present the literary executor of Polanyi's estate. I do not know whether his reading of Polanyi's unpublished manuscripts and of his last book, *Meaning*, has changed his views on what he believes Polanyi thought about religion, so I will be taking my cues about what Torrance thinks from his publications prior to Polanyi's death and the publication of Polanyi's last work. These views of Torrance's are very solid and coherent, and represent with respect to the import of Polanyi's ideas a generic position still generally held by many supporters of Polanyi among theologians, such as Richard Gelwick.[1] Therefore I think it justifiable to give them special attention here.

Torrance thinks that science in the Western world has gone through three eras: that of the Greek essentialists, of the recent classical instrumentalists, and of the present, the third era, which science has now entered largly under the influence of Einstein and his immediate predecessors and contemporaries. This present era in science is characterized, Torrance holds, by concepts of a *"multivariable organic order* or *open field-structure,"* and calls into question "the split between structure and substance, form and matter." It provides "evidence for the grounding of scientific knowledge in the objective structures and transformations of the real world," as against the *a priori* structure which was imposed upon our notions of what exists by the old Newtonian concepts of absolute space and time. He holds that "Einstein applied the concept of the metrical field . . . to embrace all phenomena, replacing the old framework of absolute space and time by the space–time continuum as the objective but imperceptible structure for the ordering and understanding of all events." Space–time, in this view, ceased to be (as absolute space and time was thought to be) a continuum devoid of matter and energy which acted upon and gave structure to whatever matter and energy was in it, without itself being acted upon. Space–time became instead a four-dimensional continuum, "with a reciprocal action between it and the constituent matter and energy of the universe, together with an inner connection between mass and energy."[2]

Since this meant that our notion of the universe could now be one of dynamic interrelatedness among all things in it, the old dualism between inquiring subject and its object (and so also between substance and structure) need trouble us no longer. Structured matter is simply what we find it to be *a posteriori*. Our concept of space–time (as opposed to space *and* time) gives us a methodological framework permitting structured matter to exist as it inherently is, unrestricted by the forms of absolute space and time thrust upon it, much as Whitehead, and possibly even Plato long before him, also seemed to think. Form interrelates with matter and matter with form and both of them with space–time in an integrated, conceptually intelligible system.

Of course, as Torrance says, since "light moves with such a high velocity that our senses cannot cope with it in relation to the relatively low velocities of our ordinary experience," we cannot "visualize therefore a non-Euclidean four-dimensional continuum," and so space–time continues to be "refracted through our crude observations in space and time." Space–time, the ultimate field, becomes for us therefore nonobservable and intangible. As a consequence, "separate space and time remain inalienable aspects of the real world as we experience it"; but because of the concept of space–time which we can now put "behind" all our experiences, the function performed by primary qualities of providing an objective continuum in a real space and time is no longer necessary. This function of providing an objective continuum "is now fulfilled by configurations *of space–time* (invariances and symmetries, and relations between vectors, semivectors and tensors) which transcend any [one observer's] coordinate-system and thus retain the same standard value regardless of the 'observer'." We do not have to try to make a fictional or conventional rational synthesis "at the level of our observational experiences under the limits and conditions of low velocities," as we did have to when we were considering space and time to be separate, absolute conditions for the existence of all things. Instead, we develop explanatory correlations "with concepts and relations drawn from a higher level of reality," i.e., from space–time.[3]

Our methods for deriving concepts therefore must now change from abstracting them from our observations, inasmuch as this way of deriving our concepts abstracts their forms from their empirical content (their "matter") and thus distorts our knowledge of the real world. The new method entails the relation between our concepts and our experience no longer being seen as a logical one, "but," says Torrance, "a translogical or an extra-logical" one. With this shift we become unable "to say precisely how concepts are correlated with experience, or to devise a clear-cut systematic method for that derivation." We could only try to do so by devising various artificial abstract systems, as was done by Newtonian physics. He thinks this inability to render all our steps logically explicit becomes more and more "evident the further we penetrate beyond immediate and crude observation into the inherently nonobservable structure of the space–time framework of the universe." Space–time becomes "an *experienced imperceptible*, an intangible magnitude" for us, since we find that it does embrace all our human experiences and "serves to disclose that knowledge at all levels arises on grounds that are not always or completely identifiable."[4]

Relativity theory thus achieves "the closest and most precise correlation of actual empirical content" (what it is we do in fact observe) with "fundamental theoretic constructs." We abandon the supposition of a flat universe of matter in motion in absolute space and time, which not only cannot explain certain field phenomena in physics, but also places an unbridgeable chasm between matter and consciousness, between the brain and the mind. The universe instead becomes for us miltilayered, since we are open to the notion of the existence of other fields composed of lower-level fields. "Space–time" becomes for us therefore not merely an instrumental tool for conceptualizing certain kinds of high velocity phenomena, but the highest-level field, the very structure, as Einstein said it was, of "existence and reality."[5]

So objectivity is now "grounded in the invariant relatedness inherent in the universe, in which form and being, structure and matter, coinhere" in the "synthesis . . . of space–time . . . through the natural correlation of their different levels" of reality.[6] Torrance says we have to somehow "probe into the depth of being in order to grasp it in its own inherent forms and patterns, without being caught in the treachery of abstraction and reduction to what we already claim to know"—the rubrics of our crude observation. We cannot start from discrete particulars and aggregate them into wholes through empirical generalizations. We must, as Torrance says Einstein tells us, "keep attending to all that the field embraces in its profound relationships until the relevant principles have revealed themselves to us." We must acknowledge this "informal and inarticulate operation of the mind" in order to account for how we are able to do this.[7]

Torrance believes that "Polanyi has thrown a great deal of light" upon how this revelation of relevant principle occurs. His "tacit inference" enables us to know more than we can tell which nevertheless "has such a bearing upon the real world that it carries with it an anticipatory awareness of a coherence in nature upon which we may rely as a clue in the development of explicit knowledge." The structure of ordinary perception and of scientific intuition which Polanyi explained to us is, according to Torrance, "after all but another form of learning from nature."[8]

According to Torrance, both Polanyi and Einstein noticed that if "our concepts and their proper interconnections are *intuitively* related to and controlled by nature or the real world," this "implies an astonishing harmony or correlation between its inherent comprehensibility and the structure of our human comprehending." Torrance points out that Einstein called it "a miracle."[9]

This connection between theory and experience is itself something that can only be experienced. But it must occur, Torrance holds, since we can only accept a theory when we do grasp a referential or ontological connection between deductions from the theory and a set of empirical facts. The only thing that can be involved, since no direct comparison between them can exist (they are two different things), is an "*analogical reference . . .* an indirect comparison . . . between 'empirical facts' imported by the theory and an actual set of empirical facts."[10] He seems here to accept Polanyi's notion that the subsidiary clues in which we stand do become integrated into a focal object by the action of our minds in a nondeductive and essentially creative and even intuitive way, and that we cannot render completely explicit all the grounds or clues involved.

Torrance holds, then, that this way of understanding what science is doing fits what contemporary science is in fact doing, for which thinkers such as Einstein, and especially Polanyi, have tried to provide an intelligible basis. It also connects the structure of scientific knowledge to our natural experience and thought, and extends an unbroken bridge between the various sciences, from mathematical, through the biological, to the human sciences. Wider and deeper heterogeneous aspects of reality are thus opened up for scientific investigations which might have been ruled out by earlier conceptions of scientific method: Indeed, writes Torrance, "man, himself, cannot be excluded from the syndrome of action and reaction in nature, either as rational agent investigating the universe or as an essential participant in its rational and objective structure." Thus the deepest nature of the universe, through the interaction between man and the universe, must be seen to assume a form in which this nature can be disclosed and expressed, just as other aspects of reality can be.[11]

As a consequence of all these reflections, Torrance believes that in the ontology and the methods required by the new science, and also in the epistemological and ontological views of Michael Polanyi, he has found a secure foundation for the extension of science into the "science of theology"—into a development of the science of God Himself. All Torrance needs to launch such a science is the presence in our experience of a field to investigate, an aspect of reality, that demands, because of its own nature, such a theological analysis. This he makes bold to say has been provided for us by "the Word of God." In a sense he literally means the Scriptures, the Bible. But it is clear he means something more than the precise words written in the Bible. He means The Word, the message from God conveyed in these words.[12] It seems very clear that he does not mean, however, to say that this message is only what people have taken to be the Word of God. He means a genuine and actual revelation made by God to men. "God," he says, "communicates Himself to us . . . speaking to us in person . . . and sounding His word through (*personare*) to us by chosen instruments." He agrees with Barth that the reality of God "is not simply our self-consciousness and consciousness of the world raised into an objective reality, not merely a reality of God for us, but *God's own inner and proper reality* in which He is independent of us and our knowing, as other aspects of reality are."[13]

Torrance says that this is parallel to what we find in the exact sciences today. We do not any longer give the rationality of nature to nature by supplying it with forms (such as space and time and primary qualities). The "rationality of nature objectively transcends our experience of it and so commands our respect for it that we are ready to *let it speak for itself,* so to say, and to subject our formulations and apprehensions to its criticism and guidance." He holds that this is what Polanyi taught. "According to Polanyi," he says, "it is this vision of a reality beyond sense experience, of a rationality with 'implications that extend indefinitely beyond the experience which they were originally known to control' that science has its deepest sense of objectivity."[14]

His footnote reads:

> Professor Polanyi's words are: 'Man has the power to establish real patterns in nature, the reality of which is manifested by the fact that their future implications extend indefinitely beyond the experience which they were originally known to control.'[15]

Formally, Torrance says, it is the same in theology. The difference is only that in theology "a Word . . . a *Logos*, is "a Word to be heard as Truth to be acknowledged," not merely "a rationality to be apprehended and interpreted . . . Theological thinking is thus more like listening," he says, "than any other knowledge, a listening for and to a rational Word from beyond anything that we can tell to ourselves and distinct from our rational elaborations of it." We therefore have to distinguish between "the given *in its own self-interpretation* from the interpretive processes in which we engage in receiving and understanding it."[16] Torrance makes his meaning even clearer by stating his disagreement with John Baillie's position that the "propositional" element in religion (the working out of the faith in words and concepts) is only a second-order derivation from reflection upon faith. Torrance says that, on the contrary, the propositional element in religion "arises out of the immediate conceptual context of our intuitive knowledge of God." Without a Word from God, Torrance holds, "some articulated communication from Himself," we would be thrown back upon ourselves to prove His existence and put words in His mouth. We would thus clothe Him with our own ideas and make Him into a "dumb idol." We would have no genuine knowledge of God, but "be left alone with our thoughts and self-deceptions."[17]

We are questioned by the Word; it is not, as Torrance claims Tillich holds, that the Word answers our questions. Tillich's "answering theology" is an answer to man, says Torrance, not to God.[18] Thus Torrance holds that "genuine theology is distrustful of all speculative thinking or of all *a priori* thought"; it "keeps its feet on the ground of actuality." It is *a posteriori* thinking, which follows "the given and communicated Word and Act of God as its material for its reflection." It is "*empirical*" because it is thought about from a "real experience of God" and so "determined by God."[19]

We believe God to be reliable and faithful, onmipotent and infinitely good, says Torrance. Yet from the view of logical form there seems to be a problem in "the facts of evil and suffering in the creation." But we find this problem only when we attempt, he says, to construct "omnipotence" logically by carrying the brute force we find in nature "to the $n$th degree, and then setting beside it a notion of 'infinite goodness' derived in a similar way through logical construction and projection out of our common human ideas" of what is satisfying and painless. Omnipotence and infinite goodness "contradict each other in the face of evil and suffering of our world." But, says Torrance, we find God overcoming the merely logical contradicton through "the Cross of Christ" where "He is found at work in the depth of measureless evil and the unappeasable agony of mankind . . . achieving reconciliation and bringing unity through atonement." In this, "faith penetrates deeply into its understanding of the faithfulness of God." In such ways as this Torrance holds that theology reconstructs the notions of God's power and goodness, as he says, "from what *God* has done and does do," instead of from hypothetical possibilities "logically detached from the facts of existence." In this *a posteriori* way theology finds the premises revealed only at the end of our inquiry into what "*God* has done and does do." We do not start from these premises *a priori* and deduce our science logically from them.[20]

We can never understand theological statements, therefore, if we detach them "from their referring function." He also here commends Polanyi for being right in maintaining "that theological statements cannot be understood or treated aright except by those who engage in and dwell in worship ('heuristic vision') and theological inquiry."[21] This tacit knowing and indwelling which Polanyi shows us to be involved in all knowing is also involved here, inasmuch as it is only "through religious experience," Torrance says, "in the context of tradition and the continuity of the life of the Church where learning through others, meditation upon the message of the Holy Scriptures, prayer and worship regularly take place, that these basic convictions and primary concepts take their rise."[22]

Torrance regards all this as God's revelation of Himself to us, given to us freely by His own "supernatural Grace."[23] The inquiry in theological science is therefore for him not the kind of inquiry that takes place in the natural sciences. In "natural science we operate with sequences in which precedence and subsequence belong to the same series on the same level of existence;" but we cannot assume the same sort of connection obtains between these "contingent realities and the Ultimate reality" upon which they depend and which "gives them their meaning." We must therefore know God both "in His utter difference from us," as a nonphenomenal Being, and "where He encounters us within the sphere of our contingent existence." One without the other is inadequate. So theology must "clarify our knowledge of Him both in terms of the creaturely objectivity which His self-revelation to us has assumed in our world of space and time, and in terms of the transcendent objectivity of His own eternal Being." We therefore cannot treat Him as we do those natural objects which we know through experimental investigations and of which our knowledge then functions instrumentally for us to make natural things work as we stipulate. This instrumental mode is "scientifically inappropriate to the living God, for it would not be the Lord God but an idol that could come under our power like that, and it would not be theology but magic that could conjure up and manipulate 'the divine' like that."[24]

Torrance quotes Polanyi on the distinction between the miraculous or supernatural and the natural: "to the extent that any event can be established in terms of natural science, it belongs to the natural order of things. . . . It is illogical to attempt the proof of the supernatural by natural tests, for these can only establish the natural aspects of an event and can never represent it as supernatural." If we can experimentally verify the resuscitation of the dead, both Polanyi and Torrance say that this would disprove the miraculous nature.[25]

It is thus the Incarnation that seems to Torrance to be the central point of reference in the Christian faith to the depth and perspective of our place in the universe. It is in "the *hypostatic union*" of God and Man in Jesus Christ that "the invisible structure of God's interaction with creaturely existence intersects the invisible structure of space–time," and so becomes a unique field of its own for our scientific investigation.[26] He shows how the basic Christian doctrines of creation, redemption, and the Holy Trinity are also essentially involved in this central reference point. He therefore holds that, whereas we use discovery in natural science, we must use revelation in theological science.[27]

It is evident that Torrance has made copious use of Polanyi's ideas, from his notion of the nature and structure of science to the nature and structure of religion and theology, and the similarity of his views to many of those expressed by Polanyi must be by now quite evident. Yet there seems to be no hint in any of Polanyi's works that he thought of theology as a "science." In fact, he seemed to be at some pains to make an important distinction between the two. How does Torrance, in Polanyi's name, manage to obliterate this distinction and in what sense can his views, in fact, be construed as a criticism of Polanyi's work, as I have asserted at the start of my discussion? Let us see in the next chapter how Polanyi's views on religion compare with Torrance's.

# CHAPTER EIGHTEEN

# Polanyi contra Torrance

It is fairly clear that the views on re-ligion that Michael Polanyi expressed in his later years are quite different from those that Torrance develops. To begin with, the necessity of a real revelation by a transcendent being in order to get religion started is nowhere set forth in his final work. It is true that myths seem to him to form a starting point. Yet the myths he chooses to elucidate, following Eliade, are quite obviously not believed by him to be literally true accounts of the intervention in space–time (or even in space *and* time) of a transcendent, real being of some sort. They are primitive myths and not supposed by him, surely, to be believed by any of his audience. The truth of these myths turns out to be simply that they portray the universe as meaningful, and this is true in the sense, not of being verifiable, but of being valid. Validity in these works of the imagination, among which the arts also fall, is their capacity to "move us deeply" or to "carry us away," to incorporate in an imaginative way our hopes and fears and our chaotic experiences into a final or ultimate integraton of meaning. Ver-itably, for Polanyi, it seems that, as Christ said, "the sabbath was made for man and not [as Torrance would seem to have it] man for the sabbath." Torrance, therefore, might wish to reject these later views of Polanyi's as he did the similar views of Tillich.

Both Torrance and Polanyi make a distinction between the kind of realities that natural science deals with and the kind that religion or theology deals with. But their distinctions are quite different ones. Torrance's is between a transcendent reality (a supernatural Being), over and beyond the realm of natural events, and those merely natural entities interacting with each other in space–time. Because this supernatural Being needs to enter into the world of objects, theology also deals with a unique individual person and with unique events in history, whereas science finds unique individuals or events, as such, empty of significance for its goals of more general or universal knowledge.

For Polanyi, on the other hand, reality is defined univocally as that which we expect to show itself in indeterminate ways in the future. Yet according to Polanyi there is one subset of realities which exists independently of our knowledge of them and which science seeks to uncover or disclose, as well as another subset of realities, those of the noosphere, brought into being, in a sense, by our creative efforts through them to achieve meaning in our own lives. These realities are real in that we may expect to see more of what they mean as time goes on—as in great works of art and religion. They are comprehensive entities, whose depths may surprise us. They are also real in being valid. But it would be an illusion to think they existed before we discovered them.

The only shred of reality, in the sense of existence independent of us, that God has in Polanyi's later thinking is the gradient of meaning in biological development that seems to evoke greater meaning in all life and thought. But, in addition to being immanent, not transcendent, the existence of such a gradient of meaning is highly speculative. It is also not identical to the God of any religion. Its inclusion in our science of biology can only serve the purposes of theology by providing us with a way of understanding natural science which would leave the faith of religion (that the world is meaningful) not scientifically absurd. It could not provide scientific support for the factual or independent reality of any supernatural or even transnatural beings.

Since Polanyi's *Meaning* was not available to Torrance when he wrote the works referred to, let us turn to Polanyi's earlier *Personal Knowledge* to see whether or not we find support there for Torrance's extrapolation. This is, in other words, to ask whether or not Polanyi in his last work fundamentally changed his mind about religion.

Religion, Polanyi said in *Personal Knowledge*, stands in a similar relation to both mathematics and art with regard to "external experience." "External experience is indispensible," he wrote "both to mathematics and art, *as their theme*." His point was that these disciplines are related to experience; but that corroboration from external experience is not required in mathematics and art as it is in the natural sciences. To someone, he said, who is "prepared to inhabit their framework," they "convey their own internal thought, and it is for the sake of this internal experience that his mind accepts their framework as its dwelling place." He then added that "religion stands in a similar relation to non-religious experience."[1]

Religion, he held in *Personal Knowledge*, builds up its own universe, using secular experiences as its "raw material." Every great articulate system "is constructed by elaborating and transmitting one particular aspect of anterior experience in terms of its own internal experience." The convert, he said, surrenders "to the religious ecstacy" that the "articulate framework of worship and doctrine" evokes and "accredits thereby its validity." This, he added, is "analogous to the process of validation" in art. It therefore seemed to him to be the "religious ecstacy" evoked by the whole framework of our religion which "validates" our religious thought, rather than our ability to "verify" our thought by reference to some intuitive contact with some reality pre-existing independently of our discovery of it.[2] God "exists," he held, "in the sense that He is to be worshipped and obeyed, but not otherwise; not as a fact—any more than truth, beauty or justice exist as facts. All these, like God, are things which can be appreciated only in serving them."[3]

This language is in sharp contrast to the way in which he had already written in that book about the referent of science. He had said scientific theories claim "to represent empirical reality." Part of the ground for this in a scientific theory is the theory's calling "attention to its own beauty"; it is in this sense indeed "akin to a work of art which calls attention to its own beauty as a token of artistic reality." But it is clear from the context that these are not the same kinds of "reality." One he was careful to call "empirical," the other, "artistic."[4]

He later told us "An empirical statement is true to the extent to which it reveals an aspect of reality . . . hidden to us, and *existing therefore independently of our knowing it*. . . . Assertions of fact necessarily carry *universal intent. Our claim to speak of reality serves thus as the external anchoring of our commitment in making a factual statement*."[5] This latter *function* of "reality" in our assertions, as we have seen he maintained, fits any sort of articulate enterprise. He indicated that all articulate systems—even those that he claimed we could validate rather than verify—"claim the presence of something real and external to the speaker."[6] This keeps them from being merely subjective and imbues them all with universal intent, as we have seen. But there are important differences in the kind of expectations we have that the external real entity will exhibit yet undreamed-of properties, which, as we have seen, is for him what enables us to call it a "reality." "In the natural sciences," he said, "the feeling of making contact with reality is an augury of as yet undreamed-of future *empirical* confirmations of an immanent discovery; in mathematics [and we could add, from what he has said before, also in art and religion] it betokens an indeterminate range of future germinations within mathematics *itself*"[7] and *mutatis mutandis*, within art and religion. The kinds of realities which are disclosed in these different systems of thought are therefore different. He said specifically that in mathematics "disclosure is of a pre-existing possibility for the satisfaction . . . of pre-existing standards of intellectual merit," established within mathematics itself. "All this applies of course," he added, "emphatically to artistic innovations." He said this specifically in contrast to the revelation of "something that already existed," with which we deal in science.[8]

Earlier in the book he had clearly said: "Artistic beauty is a token of artistic reality, in the same sense in which mathematical beauty is a token of mathematical reality. Its appreciation has universal intent, and bears witness beyond that to the presence of an inexhaustible fund of meaning in it which future centuries may yet elicit."[9] "The bearing of natural science on facts of experience," he went on to say, "is much more specific than that of mathematics, religion or the various arts. It is justifiable, therefore, to speak of the verification of science by experience in a sense which would not apply to other articulate systems. The process [in these latter] . . . is a process of *validation*."[10] "Religion . . . with the great intellectual systems," he remarked, "such as mathematics, fiction and the fine arts . . . are validated by becoming happy dwelling places of the human mind," in spite of the fact, he added, that "the force of religious conviction does depend on factual evidence and can be affected by doubt concerning certain facts."[11]

Polanyi's discussion of how religion does "depend on factual evidence" will illuminate the issues I find between Polanyi and Torrance, and will enable us, at last, to come to some critical conclusions about them both.

To begin with, the true "Christian enquiry," Polanyi said, is not really theology, but "worship." However, "religious worship can say," he claimed, "nothing that is true or false." It is rather a "framework expressing its acceptance of itself as a dwelling place of the passionate search for God . . . . Only a Christian," therefore, "who stands in the service of his faith can understand Christian theology and . . . enter into the religious meaning of the Bible."[12]

What, then, is theology for Polanyi, if it is not "Christian enquiry"? "It is," he said, "a theory of religious knowledge and a corresponding ontology of the things thus known. As such, theology reveals, or tries to reveal, the implications of religious worship." It can be "true or false," therefore, "but only as regards its adequacy in formulating and purifying pre-existing religious faith."[13] It will be noted that this is precisely that concept of Baillie which Torrance rejected, as we have seen.

Theology and the Bible, however, said Polanyi, make statements. "Can their statements," he asked, "be said to be true or false?" "The answer," he claimed, "is neither yes nor no."[14] The truth of theology, he quoted Tillich as maintaining, "is to be judged by criteria which lie within the dimension of revelatory knowledge." He said that this was a confirmation of his own conception of "progressive Protestant theology."[15]

This might appear to be a position similar to Torrance's insistence that revelation is required to launch theology and to provide facts for it to explore. Yet Polanyi's answer to his own question about whether or not a theology is true was "neither yes nor no." It was not *both* yes and no. These two statements are not logically equivalent, of course. To say that something is neither true nor false, would have to mean that these two "predicates" cannot be meaningfully assigned to it. If we assume that Polanyi meant that religion, like art and mathematics, cannot meaningfully be said to be true or false, since its statements cannot be understood to describe empirical facts in the universe, then what he said in *Personal Knowledge* would appear to agree very well with his later views— and so also with his distinction between these articulate systems and those of the natural sciences. That distinction provided the basis, as we have seen, for his contention, made already in *Personal Knowledge*, that these nonscientific, articulate systems were subject only to validation, not to verification as was natural science.

We must, however, bring this notion of his meaning into line with his statement quoted above that religious conviction does "depend on factual evidence." "The two kinds of findings, the religious and the natural," he held, "bypass each other." He went on to explain that "the Christian faith does not express the assertion of observable facts and consequently you cannot prove or disprove Christianity by experiments or factual records." He then applied this view to belief in miracles. As Torrance has quoted Polanyi, he maintained that to attempt to acknowledge the existence of miracles on the strength of factual evidence is illogical because, if successful, it could only disprove the miracle. If one could "experimentally verify" the "conversion of water into wine or the resuscitation of the dead," one could only show that the event is a natural one, not a supernatural one. "Observation," he said, "may supply us with rich clues for our belief in God; but any scientifically convincing observation of God would turn religious worship into an idolatrous worship of a mere object, or natural person."[16]

But how then can religious conviction depend at all upon factual evidence? Polanyi did not elaborate upon his statement that it does. It appears that he thought that religion invests certain events with "supernatural significance." However, Polanyi pointed out, whether or not such an event so invested has taken place at all "must be established by factual evidence." If there is no such evidence, it cannot, of course, be invested with "supernatural significance," nor with any other sort of significance, because it never existed. Biblical criticism, therefore, Polanyi held, as Torrance also points out, can shake—or corroborate— "certain facts which form the main themes of Christianity."[17]

Polanyi, however, did not regard the existence of such factual evidence as the sine qua non for our convictions concerning religion: "But evidence that a fact has not occurred may sometimes leave largely unimpaired the religious truth conveyed by a narrative describing its occurrence." His example is the creation narrative in the book of Genesis. This, although he seemed to imply that the evidence against its occurrence is overwhelming, "remains a far more intelligent account of the nature and origin of the universe than the representation of the world as a chance collocation of atoms." The "biblical cosmology" expresses—"however inadequately—the significance of the fact that the world exists and that man has emerged from it, while the scientific picture denies any meaning to the world, and indeed ignores all our most vital experience of this world." He had already indicated in *Personal Knowledge* that his own interpretation of "the scientific study of evolution" can be seen to be a clue to God. Even this perception is not, however, in any sense a "factual" proof of God. The "proof"—the validity of the religious view—rests on its providing a "happy dwelling place" for our human minds.[18]

Polanyi thus found that his views are confirmed by Tillich's, as we have seen. Although Tillich pointed to the importance of revelation and found that it is mediated through historical events, he held it is not exposed to critical analysis by historical research, since it does not imply factual assertion. As Polanyi might say, its findings are established, like those of mathematics and art, by their agreement with criteria within their own dimensions.[19]

Therefore although Torrance leaves us with the impression that his views are consonant with those of Polanyi, it seems clear that they really are not at several important points. It is essential for Torrance that certain historical events shall have occurred lending themselves to reasonable interpretation as supernatural revelations by God to man—specifically the occurrence of the incarnation of God in Jesus Christ. Belief in the truth of such historical events was not essential to religious validity, in Polanyi's view. Not only did he make this clear in both his early and his late writing, but he also declared that Tillich's theology had the closest affinity with his views. And I am told it was Tillich who once said that Christianity would be as true and valid as it now is even if it could be proved that no one had ever been crucified in Judea. Polanyi quoted him with approval when Tillich wrote: "Knowledge of revelation, although it is mediated primarily through historical events, does not imply factual assertion, and is therefore not exposed to critical analysis by historical research. Its truth is to be judged by criteria which lie within the dimension of revelatory knowledge."[20]

In view of everything we have taken into account in this chapter, it appears to me that Torrance is wrong in insinuating into Polanyi's views on religion and theology his own views concerning the necessity of the supernatural origin of religion in historical revelations made by God. I can find no evidence in Polanyi's published work that he held such a view or, indeed, that his position could form a foundation for the development of such a view. In fact, as I have tried to show here, I can find much evidence for the notion that he was in fact in opposition to it.

In addition, there exists an unpublished lecture of Polanyi's in which after stating that by the "transnatural" he did not mean the "supernatural," he made the following remarks:

But here the question arises whether the transnatural powers which carry us away in a religious devotion only bring us to the threshold of religious faith. Must the transnatural be surpassed by the super-natural? . . . I am inclined to doubt it.[21]

In his notes for another talk he wrote:

> The meaning which the Bible has and the ritual of religious ser-vice . . . may be deeply moving to us. It can be so, if we turn to it as to an association of symbols . . . .
>
> This meeting and this argument have made me think of the way I would wish to be buried. . . . "Corruptible puts on incorrupti-ble," "Death, where is they victory?" I now realize how revealing such words are of our destiny even though there is no information given by them. And I can think now of the depth of my whole life being expressed by the words, spoken by the congregation on their knees, "Our Father which art in heaven," and so on, though literally I believe none of the Lord's prayer.[22]

I believe these are fairly clear statements of where he stood on the issue we have been considering.

I recall myself trying upon several occasions—once when he was preparing some of the lectures on which *Meaning* was later based—to convince him that no religion could be founded without its including somewhere in its lore the notion of its own real supernatural origin, and that the supernatural was therefore a necessary feature of any religion that established itself. I never succeeded in getting him to admit this. He really had a difficult time understanding a belief in the factual reality of the supernatural in religion as anything much more than magic or superstition. His own view of the magnificent sweep of religion, in particular the Christian (*sans* supernatural) seemed no doubt to him to belie this necessity. He was enthralled by the imaginative, transnatural union of incompatibles involved in it, and did not seem to find the supernatural elements in this vision to be any more necessary to hold as statements of fact or of reality than he found the story in poems and plays necessary to hold as statements of fact or reality. Thus neither poetry nor religion seemed to him to be important sources for further historical or scientific knowledge of realities preexisting somehow independently of our own existence, nor to rest for their validity upon such knowledge. I believe, therefore, we must say that his understanding of religion was quite different from Torrance's. Torrance's view may thus be seen to embody what is in fact a criticism of Polanyi's.

The only other scholar whom I know to have made this point is Terence Kennedy, who says that "Honesty demands that we acknowledge that Polanyi was not religiously committed nor did he have religious faith as this is understood in Christian theology." Polanyi bent "his whole strength," says Kennedy, "to opening the door to religion and to showing the philosophical legitimacy of religious knowing." For him, Kennedy tells us, religion "is the highest reach of man's mental existence;" but "it has no genuinely objective, historical reference. . . . It is rather an extension of the world of art, and its meaning does not go radically beyond the symbols and myths of ancient cultures."[23]

Kennedy says that a number of people have "treated Polanyi as a man of Christian faith in its full realism in spite of his declared contrary intention." He mentions Gelwick, as well as J. C. Keidann, and R. C. Prust, in this connection.[24] He thinks that Torrance "recognizes how Polanyi's theories are agnostic about the fully ontological powers of religion" and has "made justifiable adjustments to Polanyi's theory of myth and religion." Kennedy seems, therefore, to agree with my view that Torrance and Polanyi differ on religion and, in general, where and how they do. He also seems to approve of Torrance's emendations of Polanyi's views, although he does think Torrance has somewhat "undervalued" the dimensions of myth and religion expressed by Polanyi. Torrance, says Kennedy, has emphasized "the transcendent in preference to the immanent and anthropological" on which Polanyi had concentrated.[25]

Although Kennedy generally thinks very highly of Polanyi's philosophical thought, he is distressed that Polanyi did not show us where his transcendent "values exist independent of our thinking them." Note the general assumption here that to be a reality something must exist independent of our thought—even if what we are talking about are moral values. It is obvious from his text that Kennedy thinks that Polanyi should have grounded his values in the being of a transcendent God. In effect, he thinks that Polanyi should have gone on to finish his thought somewhat in the direction that Torrance took.[26]

But we have seen that the difference of science from the arts and religion which Polanyi emphasized in *Meaning* can also come under possible attack from a different perspective with quite a different end in view. Grene, we have noted, has attacked the distinction from the standpoint of Polanyi's having reintroduced the very kind of distinction which she thinks his earlier work had gone such a long way toward overcoming. She thus finds him having become inconsistent with his earlier work and with what clearly had been his original intentions. But, as we have also seen, she has been greatly concerned as well with his introduction of an ontological hierarchy which threatens to populate the universe with a host of ghostly beings existing independently of their embodiment in "lower" levels of being. However, the distinction which Polanyi made between "transnatural" and "natural" integrations, which is part and parcel of his distinction between the realities dealt with in science and those in the arts and in religion, a distinction she rejects, would seem to be the way in which he kept his views of these kinds of realities from filling the universe—at least, from populating it with those realities that he maintained we call into existence in our noospheric activities. For these latter as he saw them, are clearly tied in their existence to the lower level of humans' mental capacity to generate articulate systems. Polanyi does not provide in any sense for their existence independent of the lower levels—not even, as we have seen, for the ghostly existence of the mind as separable from the body. How else can he prevent what Grene fears without introducing the distinction which he does?

On the other hand, Torrance must surely look askance (as Kennedy thinks he does) at this distinction with its concomitant implication of a difference between the realities dealt with in natural science and those dealt with in religion. He must reject this aspect of Polanyi's thought, because it does *not* populate the universe with ghostly beings existing independently of their embodiment in the articulate lower levels of human existence! It appears to me from conversations with other theologians generally friendly to Polanyi's views that there are many who find the distinction he introduces questionable. Generally speaking, God is thought of as the ultimate reality for theologians, or at least for those who also tend to be religious.

We must therefore, in the face of the discontent we find among many of his followers with the sort of distinction he made between the sciences and the arts and religion, return to the question we proposed in the last chapter: Is this distinction he made truly sound in fact and is it in line with his general aims, even though it causes such discontent? Let us attempt to answer this in the next chapter by dealing with two strong further articulations of this discontent.

# CHAPTER NINETEEN

# Can Dualism Be Avoided?

In the face of dissatisfactions with the distinction Michael Polanyi has made between the realities with which science deals and those with which the arts and especially religion deal, let us ask: If we do not make the distinction Polanyi made between science and the arts and religion, what must be the results?

There are two critical views of this distinction that have come to my attention which are instructive, because they illustrate the two major ways of eliminating the distinction. One way is to maintain that the analysis of knowing which Polanyi gives for science is the only viable one, and—presumably—that he should have carried this sort of analysis over into art and religion. In a sense this view could be said to consist in "scientizing" art and religion. The other way would be to "aestheticize" science—to say that the way Polanyi dealt with art and religion was the way he should have dealt with science.

To take the former criticism first, I refer to Sheldon Richmond, who argues that Polanyi, in the way in which he and I have handled art and religion in *Meaning*, has converted his "theory of tacit knowing into a theory of tacit meaning."[1] Richmond maintains, as we have seen Grene also does but on other grounds, that this conversion is inconsistent with what Polanyi was doing in his earlier work and destroys the possibilities his earlier position held for the unification, as Richmond puts it, of Polanyi's "philosophy of the science-culture . . . and his philosophy of the non-science cultures . . . when they are viewed as providing the defining principles of man at his level in the hierarchical structure of reality."[2]

> Polanyi's philosophy of science, on [the] one hand, views man as a seeker of knowledge through applying or reinterpreting the tacit premises and the impersonal standards of the science-culture. On this view man is a creature who must submit to impersonal and inarticulate standards: standards which he can grasp only when he attempts to live them, and standards for which he accepts responsibility. On the other hand, when viewing man as a creature who attempts to impose meanings on reality, we view man as a creature who does not submit himself to impersonal standards. Rather, on this view, man tries to make sense of reality in the light of standards which make sense for him. . . . The point at issue . . . is whether man tries to find what is there regardless of what makes sense for him.[3]

To view man as a knower or truth-seeker, Richmond holds, is to seek to explain "how man increasingly conforms the subsidiarily known areas of science to the independent structures of reality." To view man, on the other hand, as a sense-maker, is to seek to explain how man uses "the subsidiarily felt areas of art, myth, and religion . . . to conform reality to his standards of meaningfulness, to what makes sense for him."[4] Before this shift in his philosophy, Polanyi had presented us, according to Richmond, with a fairly successful resolution of the central antinomy of modern philosophy: "the antinomy between science as nihilism and science as humanism."[5] Richmond appears to think that with this shift to a theory of tacit meaning, Polanyi began to engage in what might be called wishful thinking.

Richmond believes that the virtue of Polanyi's work was, before *Meaning*, to effectively supplant "rationalism" and "liberalism" with "tacit rationality" and "tacit liberality." He was thus successful in providing from *within* the "science-culture"—without destroying the effort toward rationality in science—a "hierarchy of explanatory principles appropriate for the understanding of the various levels of nature." Such a hierarchy then provided grounds for the reality of "natural norms" or "operational principles" able to define "man as a cultural animal" at the level of his own scientific activity. Such natural norms included those of freedom and truth.[6] As Richmond views the accomplishments of Polanyi's earlier work, nihilism had been thus removed from naturalism, and humanism rendered consistent with naturalism—indeed even shown to be derivative from it.

Richmond admits, however, that without a further analysis of art, myth, and religion there would be a "gap in Polanyi's framework"—that "Polanyi requires a theory of how the principles which define man as a cultural animal apply to non-scientific cultural forms."[7] Exactly how this gap is to be filled without "converting" tacit knowing into tacit meaning is, however, not faced in Richmond's article. The closest he comes to shedding light on how this might be done is in his contention that both myth and religion tend to oppose the current "naturalistic world view of science which denies that anything has intrinsic worth." He argues that this opposition is useful because it is in agreement with "accepting Polanyi's metaphysics into science." That inclusion would provide for "an [sic] hierarchy of scientific operational principles defining the natural norms of various levels of reality."[8]

In other words, Richmond seems to say that myth and religion are valuable when they are shedding light on or reinforcing our grasp of some kind of independent reality. But he seems to imply that the truth of their contributions would anyhow already be known in the true understanding of our "science-culture" supplied by Polanyi's "metaphysics" and by a reformed science incorporating this metaphysics. So it is not clear how these non-scientific cultures, in Richmond's view, can be understood as instances of tacit knowing *sui generis* as distinct from tacit meaning and how art could be thus understood is not even hinted at by Richmond.

It should not be hard to see that the difficulties raised by Richmond stem from his apparent assumption that all intellectual endeavor must be oriented toward establishing views of reality. And by reality he obviously means not those integrations brought into existence by our own efforts to achieve meaning, but realities that already exist independently of our thought, to which we must strive to make our thoughts conform. This sort of reality is indeed, as we have seen, the sort that Polanyi held our natural sciences are oriented toward discovering. How all of the "non" sciences are to be understood as also oriented toward the discovery of realities that exist independent of our thought is not at all clear from what Richmond says.

Thus we see that to reject Polanyi's distinction because of an assumption that nothing can count as real unless it can be thought to be something existing independent of our thought, and that all human articulations must aim at such realities, is to place the arts, myth, and religion in a most awkward position. If these articulations are only to duplicate the findings of science, they would seem to be superfluous. One would have to wonder what they were for. If, however, they are to supplement the sciences, they all become potential competitors of science and then we must ask which of these pursuers of knowledge of that-which-is we are to follow, in case of conflicting findings: If we regard what the sciences tell us as more trustworthy, we end up downgrading the arts and religion; if we regard what the arts and religion tell us as more trustworthy, we end up denigrating the sciences.

It is not hard to see which alternative Richmond would prefer. If he is serious about the need always to submit to "impersonal standards," and if these are always and only provided by the externally existing realities to which scientific inquiry submits itself, as he seems to say, then he must suppose that art, myth, and religion have to submit themselves to what Polanyi called "verification" by empirical reality. In what way Beethoven's Ninth Symphony, Michelangelo's *Moses*, or the doctrine of the Incarnation or Holy Communion could submit to the impersonal standards of empirical reality is hard to imagine. The arts and religion in Richmond's philosophy must surely find their role has become the mere purveyors of scientific "party-truth," so to speak—pressed into the service of giving an emotive push toward a "reformed" scientific view of reality. This, of course, could only pervert and destroy them. To be restrained from establishing meanings for our lives from within their own self-set standards (because we must only deal in "tacit knowing," not in "tacit meaning") must reduce them to mere caricatures of themselves as they are understood by those who are dedicated to their pursuit. Art and religion must become inauthentic when governed by ulterior purposes. The totalitarian regimes of our century have certainly taught us this.

Let us turn now to a view which is essentially the reverse of Richmond's, one which might be said to attempt to reduce Richmond's "science-culture" to his "non-science cultures"—or, at least, to art—rather than vice versa.

Ronald L. Hall holds that the distinction made by Polanyi and myself in *Meaning* between science and art "hides a deep affinity between science and art," namely that science is, like the arts, more aesthetic than it is existential.[9] In his essay Hall says he uses Stephen Crites' distinction between the aesthetic and the existential—meaning by the aesthetic "a purified form as a self-contained possibility, free of temporality," and by the existential something that Hall calls "the historical field of human action *in concreto*."[10] Both of these are integrations in a good Polanyian sense, as Hall says. They each make use of the subsidiary–focal concept of tacit knowing. But the existential makes use of a projection into temporality through action, unlike the aesthetic, which negates temporality by giving it only a form which is temporalized.

He holds that this is just what Polanyi means by the "framing effect" of art. "The existential . . . is transformed into the aesthetic by virtue of a frame which isolates a certain feature of the existential and bodies it forth in abstract ideality."[11] Polanyi, as we have seen, indeed held that a work of art such as a poem or a drama is "detached" from our ordinary life by its "frame." Not only this, but, as Hall goes on to say, the frame also cuts the work off from its author. The work of art has an independent existence and can be appreciated even if we are ignorant of its author. Hall remarks that this view has also been echoed by Louis Mackey and Hannah Arendt.[12]

Hall says that he believes Polanyi's account of art is basically sound and illuminating. But problems arise for Hall when he finds Polanyi, in *Meaning*, contrasting art and science. In Polanyi's earlier works, Hall claims Polanyi held that art and science were grounded in the same structure of inquiry, and the imaginative, creative person was the central feature of this structure. The scientist was not a cool, aloof robot. He was, like the artist, passionately and personally involved in making novel and creative and imaginative integrations. Not only science, but art as well, made claims to universal intent. The grounds of both science and art were neither objective nor subjective, but personal.[13]

Nevertheless, Hall points out, Polanyi in *Meaning* has made some puzzling distinctions. He indicates Polanyi's claim that scientific discoveries are subjected to much more impersonal tests than are works of art, that artistic images cannot be tested by experience in the way in which the contents of science can, that the pursuit of science involves the imagination only minimally in comparison with the pursuit of the arts, and that science asserts facts based on observations, while the arts involve values based on acceptance.[14]

Hall says that we might overlook these apparent drifts back into a sort of positivistic dichotomy of the arts and sciences were it not for the fact that Polanyi clearly declares scientific meaning to be indicative, rather than symbolic or metaphorical as are meanings in the arts. Polanyi is thus placing science in the existential frame rather than the aesthetic, since indicative meaning is the language of the existential, not the aesthetic.[15]

Hall claims that this is a false view of science. For the most part, he says, scientists do not deal with ordinary experiences. They focus on certain aspects of experience and consider these aspects as in abstraction from concrete experience. Furthermore, the relation of the scientist to his work is abstract and detached. The scientist, like the artist, does not reveal himself in and through his work. Thus, Hall maintains, there is a framing effect in both, and so this effect does not serve to distinguish art from science, but rather shows their affinity. They are therefore both aesthetic enterprises, and this, he claims, is "much more in line with Polanyi's original work."[16]

As we have seen in our discussion of Torrance's views, Polanyi made the distinction between science and the arts even more explicitly in *Personal Knowledge* than he did in *Meaning*. Hall's contention that his views in *Meaning* represent a drift back to positivism seems to be without grounds—unless, of course, such a drift to positivism can also be found in *Personal Knowledge*, which, I believe, Hall does not think is so.

Although Hall, in his quite good summary of Polanyi's views on metaphor and art mentions the integration of incompatibles which takes place in metaphor and in art, and the surrender of ourselves in art which carries us away and makes for Polanyi's distinction between "self-giving" and "self-centered" integrations, he takes no account of these features in inveighing against Polanyi's efforts to differentiate art from science. These features are surely not found in science, nor does Hall claim they are. He simply ignores them.

But more important, it seems to me, is the fact that if we think of science as another art form—if we aestheticize it—we must suppose that science, like art, has ascended to a position outside the "historical," day-to-day experiences of man and really has nothing to do with them, which indeed Hall does assert. However, this contention is surely extravagant. Our technologies grow directly, sometimes by imperceptible degrees, from our sciences. What the chemists and the physicists do discover and interrelate into systems are interactions that structure our daily experiences and which we use to understand them more fully and to redirect and control our existential situations. No such technology applicable to our everyday existence arises from art. In view of the current criticisms of the extent to which scientific knowledge has changed the way in which life is lived and, in many cases, has almost irrevocably damaged the environment, it should surely be surprising to many to be told that science ascends out of historical situations and simply enables us to appreciate them in an aloof, aesthetic manner. Possibly ancient science, devoted as it was at the hands of the Greeks to beauty and natural piety, might qualify as in some sense aesthetic. But our science is existential in a deadly way.

Polanyi, of course, having himself been a first-rate physical chemist for many years, knew this fact about modern science quite well. He held that science was a more disciplined and thorough way than common cognition to acquire an understanding of the structures that permeate our historical and existential environment; he reiterated again and again his belief that our sciences deal with the realities that exist independently of our thoughts and endeavors, and give us the most reliable knowledge we could have of those realities. He always maintained that he was committed to science as an orientation toward reality. In fact, he considered the positivist contention, that science only consists of convenient and logically simple ways of correlating sense data and has nothing to do with reality, a colossal error. Far from constituting a "drift back to positivism," Polanyi's views of science as "existential" are necessary in order to avoid just such a drift.

Hall's confusion of science with art and his puzzlement about Polanyi's obvious efforts to distinguish them can be seen to arise from his failure to grasp the distinction Polanyi makes between the kind of realities with which science is concerned and the kind with which art is concerned. This is just the same failure we found to have been at the root of Richmond's difficulties. Since both science and art are involved with the imaginative integration of subsidiary clues into meaningful focal wholes by active persons, according to Polanyi, it might indeed be difficult to distinguish them adequately were it not for the different intentions involved in the making of these integrations. In one case there is the intention to try to get at the "reals" of which the situation is actually composed independent of our thought, and which therefore requires observation and verification of the meaningful integrations we have achieved. The other case is the intention to create these meanings that depend for their validity, not upon verification but upon our acceptance, only accomplished when they do in fact carry us away literally into themselves and integrate our lives along with their own integrations. They are thus also "realities" in that they are truly meaningful in their own terms and by their own standards (i.e., they are not reducible to lower levels of being). Thus, once created, they have a life of their own, the full import of which we are never wholly aware, but are continually discovering, as we also do with the other independent sorts of realities. Thus the effort to avoid the distinction Polanyi made by assimilating science to art ends in distorting the reflexively known character of science, just as the reverse efforts of Richmond to assimilate art, myth, and religion to the sciences resulted in distorting the reflexively known character of these "non-science cultures."

It would also appear from this attempt that the distinction Polanyi made must be made somehow. Since there are many obvious similarities between art and science in the basic epistemological framework that Polanyi used for all articulated systems, he must also distinguish them most basically, as we have seen he did in *Personal Knowledge*. This he does by distinguishing between the realities involved in them according to our efforts to establish these realities, that is, by whether the realities reached are thought by us to exist prior to our efforts or posterior to them.

Perhaps some other single way can be found to conceive of these two "cultures" which will not denigrate or distort the character of any of them nor necessitate distinguishing them from one another. It is difficult to imagine what sort of concept this would be that would still be consistent with Polanyi's basic subsidiary–focal notion of tacit knowing and meaning. (These two, I submit, are really the same thing for Polanyi. "To know," for Polanyi, is to understand, as we have seen; and for him this is, as we have seen, to achieve integrations that are meaningful to the person doing the integrating.)

Just as Hall complained about Polanyi's failure to aestheticize science, so he also went on to complain about the fact that Polanyi did aestheticize religion. Religion basically is existential, Hall thinks, not aesthetic. Polanyi, by using in its analysis the pattern of his fundamentally sound way of dealing with art, has given us a view of religion which is, Hall claims, "at best incomplete and at worst dangerously misleading."[17]

Hall holds that the "medium through which humans encounter themselves, others, and God is the medium of ordinary, everyday, pedestrian language, that is, through the word *in concreto*. The language of such primary religious encounter is not symbolic or metaphorical," as Polanyi held; "rather, it is indicative." However, Hall claims, it does not use the third person indicative, which hides the speaker, as in science but the first person indicative, in which the human and divine appear as concrete "I." "In historical religious encounters," he says, "personal relationships of dialogue and revelation replace the poetic anonymity of the aesthetic encounter." Since Polanyi, according to Hall, has not recognized the historical dimensions in religion, he has poetized religion, made it an abstraction or an aesthetic experience. Transportation out of the existential thus becomes for Polanyi, Hall claims, the true goal of religion.[18] Through it we come to reside in aesthetic rest and repose high above the existential realm of day-to-day life. As we have seen, Polanyi did say that myth and ritual are essential in religion and do take us out of mundane time into the "Great Time" of which Eliade writes.

Hall admits that we may sometimes need this aesthetic rest and that historical myth and ritual may function as aesthetic abstractions in fulfilling this need. All that Hall wants to do, however, he says, is to "deny that these abstractions are the sole, or even the primary, field of religious encounter."[19] He holds that Eliade, upon whom Polanyi seemed to rely for this view, speaks also of a different ontology, which he calls the ontology of "history." In this expression of religion, "myths, rituals, and worship . . . serve to intensify the experience of the existential, the historical, the concrete."[20]

Thus Hall seems to hold that religion, contrary to art and even science does enter into our day-to-day experiences and intensifies them, rather than providing an aesthetic escape from them. For Hall, religion is rooted in the encounters in mundane time of dialogue and revelation— the time of "the word." Hall does not indicate as clearly as Torrance does to what extent the "dialogue" and "revelation" are meant literally; but since he holds that the encounter with God is of the order of encounters with ourselves and with others, it would seem that he may mean something very similar to what Torrance does.

It indeed may be that all going religions are rooted in some sort of supernatural revelatory contact believed to be with God. This either may be a concrete experience of the believing person, such as Moses' experience of God's speaking to him out of the burning bush, or else is believed by others to have taken place concretely in the experience of one's accepted spiritual leader at some time in the past. If this sort of concrete revelation is necessary to religion, then Polanyi's views on religion are indeed inadequate, since it seems very clear from what we have said in relation to Torrance's views, that Polanyi has rejected any such supernatural contact as an essential part of religion.

But is this supernatural aspect of religion truly necessary? Kierkegaard declared that Abraham was the true knight of faith, because he trusted God even in the face of His totally incomprehensible command to him to sacrifice his only son, Isaac. Not only must this have been morally a terribly wrong thing for him to do to his own son, but Abraham was very old, and God had promised to make of him a great nation. Moreover He had promised to do so through this very son, Isaac. No good of any sort could be seen to come of this sacrifice in any conceivable way. Moreover it was, in itself, God's breaking of His own promise! Yet the story does not record that Abraham's faith in God wavered, even for a moment. But could Abraham have had such a faith had he not, in an existential and concrete sense, felt that God was a real Being who really spoke to him? Could he have had such a trust had he thought that God was only a kind of aesthetic union of incompatibles? Even raising the question seems absurd. It must surely seem that perfect faith and trust of the order of Abraham, or of those awaiting execution with their families in the inhuman confines of a concentration camp—or of any soul in a hopeless, helpless, desperate situation from which there is known to be no escape, and no conceivable justification or purpose, either—could hardly exist in the absence of a belief in the real existence or being (in the sense of being independent of our thought) of that in which or in Whom one has such faith. And yet, would not even that faith be a faith in the existence of a union of the most wholly and completely incompatible incompatibles that can possibly be found? How can we understand that our God, a good God, either has or has not forsaken us in such existential situations? It appears that even Job and Jesus could not resolve this. Polanyi may therefore be right that even the supreme object of our religious faith is just such a union of incompatibles as he maintained, and that He (or it) cannot be given an understandable position in whatever realms of logically or rationally coherent beings we may suppose exist.

Yet is God understood by any knight of faith to be without existence or being? I think not, however incongruous such a faith may be.

Upon what then can such a knight ground his understanding? How can we grasp that such an incomprehensible God can exist without a revelation from Him existentially, historically, concretely experienced by someone some time in the past? When we look at the matter in this way, it surely must seem that Torrance, Hall, and possibly many others may indeed be right that such a historical event as this is most essential.

Why then was so perceptive and sensitive a person as Polanyi blind to this aspect? Perhaps it was because he was no such knight of faith. Perhaps he was never truly religious, as Kennedy maintains. Polanyi did speak approvingly of the faith that was St. Paul's—the hope that grace would be given us to do what we found it impossible to do on our own—and he said that even the scientist, each in his own science, always operates with such a faith and hope. Yet Polanyi did, as mentioned earlier, despair toward the end of his life. He did lose hope. Perhaps his faith was always confined to a hope concerning the fortunes of his own activity or of those results that could be experienced in his own time. He did not seem to think that if he had not been successful in moving modern thought, his ideas nevertheless would be effective some day—much less that, even if they were not ever to be successful, it did not matter, all was well; God was in His heaven. Perhaps Polanyi did not believe, as Epictetus said the wise man should, that the gods exist and rule all things well, so that even our failures must be thought by us to be for the best. Perhaps he did not believe this. But we are not justified in selling short anyone's "state of grace."

Let us reflect that there is the possibility of a curious juncture of the existential and the aesthetic at the top. Without the kind of encounter we have been discussing (whether one's own or what one believes is another's) it may be that I have no basis for my faith. My faith cannot perceptually, logically, naturally, or rationally bring together the manifest incompatibles we have seen to be involved in religion, myth, rites, and their concurrent theological concepts. And so the union of them that I form in my notion of God is surely an integration of my imagination much like those I must make in art. But, because of this, I therefore cannot altogether free myself from doubt that there is, in fact, any such union or God, even after the encounter. How do I know it was the voice of God which I, or someone in whom I have faith, has heard? The grace to believe that it was, regardless of doubt, may be the "crown" bequeathed in religious salvation: "Lord, I believe. Help Thou mine unbelief." "My strength is made perfect in weakness." "Blessed are they who have not seen and have yet believed." Maybe these, after all, are the ultimate incompatibles that have to be integrated into a meaning—with or without an encounter.

At any rate, a faith which faces, and encompasses within itself its own doubt, may perhaps be the key to Polanyi's views and the reason the supernatural aspects of religion were of no importance to him. Religious faith would have to overcome the doubt about these supernatural aspects, as well as any other doubts. Perhaps because he looked at things in this way, more than for any other reason, Polanyi found himself feeling more akin to Tillich than to any other theologian.

But let us realize that this faith, even with an existential encounter thrown in, quite coherently could still be described as fully aesthetic. For the effect on us of such a faith is to open up our hands and to place them fully into God's, in such a way that we do not even offer to advise Him how or when to solve our problems. We simply move into a rest far above our day-to-day concerns in a perfect trust in Him. This, in the end, may be the greatest faith of all. For such a faith would have to know that it, itself, cannot be accomplished by its own powers, as St. Augustine maintained. When it exists it is a pure gift of God, as St. Paul and St. Augustine have declared it to be. So that a demand for anything more than this—for a revelation or a sign from Heaven—is a failure to trust completely in God, and an arrogant demand to know God as an idol or talisman may be known. Did Polanyi also hold this to be the ultimate truth about religious faith? Perhaps.

Or perhaps Hall is right and in a very simple-minded way Polanyi stood transfixed before the beauties of the religious integrations and allowed them to carry him away as would a magnificent work of art. This would surely not be the worst way to understand religion. So let us conclude that in one very down-to-earth sense Torrance and Hall are right about religion; but that the possibility exists that in a far more sublime and humbly heroic sense Polanyi may also have been right.

I can go no further than this in an evaluation—or even in an exposition—of Polanyi's views on religion. He seemed never to wish to discuss them to any great extent whenever I raised questions about how he personally felt or thought about religion. Usually he ended up saying he did not know much about it, that he was not a theologian

Must we say then that his distinction between science and art, myth, and religion are sound? It surely fits coherently into his whole position and appears to be adequate to the different phenomenological characteristics of these various human enterprises—with the possible exception of Polanyi's omission of the supernatural element in religion. And yet possibly even that omission can be seen to make sense. Furthermore, it does not yet appear to be possible to construct viable alternatives to this distinction. What other criteria for its soundness are there which should be met—given the basic notion that there are no fully complete and explicit criteria for the truth of anything? As to the question of whether or not this basic notion itself is so, Polanyi was the first to maintain that there can be no explicit criteria available for an answer to this one either. Obviously, if there were, this basic contention that there are none would not be true! Gödel, take note!

We argue as fully as we can for any position we hold; but if these arguments always have a tacit dimension embedded in subsidiary clues in which we simply are dwelling, then we can never fully demonstrate even this. About philosophizing, Polanyi said very little. But one of his remarks is reflexively very wise. He said that "time and again men have become exasperated with the loose ends of current thought and have changed over to another system, heedless of similar deficiencies with that new system"; "every system of thought has of course some loose ends tucked away out of sight, and the system I am trying to build round the conception of personal knowledge will also leave many questions in abeyance." "There is," he said, "no other way in philosophy than this."[21]

Recognizing that there may be some loose ends tucked so well away that they have escaped my analysis, I nevertheless believe Polanyi's distinction is at least as well grounded as any made by any philosopher; I therefore consider it a sound one. As to the first question: Has Polanyi done damage to his own cause by developing this distinction? In the longest run, if the distinction is really sound, he cannot possibly have, of course; it does appear from what we have seen that his position is stronger and more coherent with this distinction that it would be without it. In the short run obviously he has displeased both those who admire the strength and no-nonsense quality of his epistemology and his philosophy of science and those who consider him the savior of religion and theology as ways to establish realities far more real and transcendent than those discovered in the sciences, but just as "scientifically" respectable as these. But if both these kinds of supporters wish to throw away parts of what is essential to a meaningful whole in Polanyi's thought, their continued support might only serve to obfuscate his total message, simplifying it to such an extent that it would never have the effect it could otherwise have upon those who have eyes to see and ears to hear.

With such partially blind friends, Polanyi quite possibly would need no enemies to nullify his efforts. So it may not be that, if such partial supporters of his views turn away from him, his fortune as an influential philosopher will be damaged.

Is this then all that need be said? Are Polanyi's views four-square and impregnable? I do not think that all features of Polanyi's philosophy are impregnable. Some of his "loose ends" are not quite out of sight, and I will be commenting in my last chapter on some difficulties I see. What I have been concerned to do in these past few chapters was to see whether the most fundamental and key positions espoused by Polanyi, upon which rest so much of his thought, were sound. It seems to me that the key positions are his ubiquitous use of the subsidiary–focal structure in epistemology, his contention for ontological hierarchies, and his differentiation of the sciences from the "non"sciences, including the assumption that the realities dealt with in the sciences are understood to exist independent of our thought, whereas those in the arts and religion are creations of our thought without archtypes anywhere, except in the inherent structures of their own enterprises. And my conclusion is that all these are sound beyond reasonable doubt, with the possible exception of his conviction that religion has no need for belief in the real existence of a revelatory Event.

# CHAPTER TWENTY

# And Sub Specie Aeternitatis

As we have noted earlier, Michael Polanyi's goal was to free his contemporaries from certain disabilities with which he saw we were afflicted. His plan for his last project he set in terms of moving man from a loss of meaning to its recovery.[1] He thought this could be accomplished, as we have seen, by exorcizing from our minds the twin devils of the ideal of knowledge as detached objectivity and the ideal of action as moral perfectionism. And this he hoped to do by the development of a new epistemology that would bypass a forced choice between subjectivism and objectivism. Instead it would provide an analysis of both perception and cognition in terms of a combination of subsidiary and focal awareness and, in so doing, incorporate our person into the process, an epistemology which he named appropriately "personal knowledge."

We have investigated what Polanyi found this approach entailed, and we have subjected the most crucial and basic parts of it to some scrutiny. We have, I think, found that he developed a system in these terms which is truly comprehensive and viable. Those of us who have understood and accepted it do indeed no longer suffer from these two demons. We no longer hanker after objective knowledge, or perfectly explicit statements, or proofs beyond conceivable doubt, yet we have not lost our conviction that some of our beliefs are true and that we do, in fact, have real knowledge of some matters. This is a paradox; but it states a truth for us.[2] We see clearly how we may put these two stances together in a satisfactory whole and so how we may get on with our pursuit of actual knowledge and with our open-eyed acceptance of the implications of what we do believe is really true. Our inquiries are no longer hampered by being forced into reductionism because of a flat, one-dimensional view of what is "basically" real. Nor are we driven into skepticism because of a positivist view of knowledge which must eschew any reference to what is "real" in order to retain a certain ersatz logical purity.

We also do not burn with a zeal for moral perfection in our societies, understanding how the moral level emerges from a lower social level of parochialism, profit, and power, and is therefore both made possible and limited by these factors, just as is any other emergent higher level of being. This frees us from seduction by the impossible ideal of a planned economy and from any form of totalitarian control over the various functioning parts of a society which, because of the nature of their tasks, cannot operate except in a polycentric manner through the free interaction of many centers, that is, through the systems of spontaneous order generated by the economic needs of our industrial society, of our passions for truth, for beauty, and for justice, as well as for the attainment of meaningful religious and philosophic integrations of man in his universe.

We therefore are appalled by the fact that Polanyi's work has been so poorly received by the intellectual world. Not only has it not been generally accepted, it has not even been generally heard of, at least not in its totality. This means that even when it has been noted, it has most often received a poor hearing. Such a book as this is, of course, an attempt to remedy this sorry fact.

Can Polanyi's work itself be criticized for its failure to secure an adequate hearing? It seems to me there are several reasons that have made it difficult for his views to achieve the impact which they might, resting upon factors deeply embedded in what Polanyi was saying and in how he was saying it.

Let us look at some of these. One assumption upon which he was working throughout his writings, his lectures, and his organizational efforts is the one made very obvious in this book: that the philosopher's role is basically that of a physician. The job of the philosopher is to be critical of the wrong turns and the wrong principles of thought and action to which he finds his contemporaries are committed and which he believes are destructive, or at least debilitating, for human life and society. The philosopher's further role is to offer suggestions as to how these turns and principles may be reformed.

Looked at historically, this is not an unusual assumption concerning the role of the philosopher. Most of the classic philosophers in Western culture, from Socrates on—or at least from Plato—have quite obviously assumed that such was the philosopher's proper role and have advanced their philosophic views and systems within such a framework. However, this assumption of Polanyi's has been in flat contradiction to the assumptions of most contemporary philosophers, especially in Anglo-American circles. Philosophers, some even impressed by some points Polanyi made, have complained in their reviews that he marred his work by too much sermonizing and moralizing, too much earnest warring against the deadly effects upon our lives and societies of a failure to reform our views.

The analytic philosophers of our century, first in terms of logical positivism and later of ordinary-language analysts, dominant in England and America when Polanyi was writing and lecturing, have had, compared with Polanyi, a very myopic view of what philosophy should be doing. For them, philosophy could not save the world. It had much more modest and specialized goals. Before philosophy could handle any of the larger questions that philosophers had traditionally tackled (if philosophy could ever handle them), it would have to clear up language problems. Therefore it had to first clarify and purify the ways in which we talk about things. Indeed, as many saw the task, this was all it could ever do. As one of these philosophers, G. V. Warnock, once contemptuously expressed to me, Polanyi was not a philosopher at all. He was only a *philosophe*. The general format within which Polanyi expressed his views was anathema to by far the greater part of English and American philosophers of his time. They were unable to take him seriously and his views engendered very little discussion among them.

Those Anglo-American philosophers, I might add, who felt that the analytic philosophers were off on the wrong track were generally philosophers who took the views of the great earlier philosophers in our tradition very seriously. But they were also turned off by Polanyi because of what they took to be his superficial views of the great non-analytic philosophers.

Professor Carl Friedrich wrote one of the most perceptive reviews of Polanyi's *Personal Knowledge*. He even seemed to grasp why it was structured as it was, and he was favorably impressed. But he complained that Polanyi was obviously unaware how much he was in agreement with at least parts of what some of the greatest philosophers had written, for example, Kant and Hegel, and Whitehead in our own century.[3] Polanyi not only seemed to Friedrich to think certain of his ideas had never before been expressed, but he seemed to think these philosophers were among his enemies! He sometimes even poured ridicule upon them. Thus Polanyi's misconceptions about our classic philosophers was also not calculated to induce the nonanalytic philosophers to take his views very seriously. His ignorance was, of course, very understandable. His own field was not philosophy. It was physical chemistry and, later, economics. He was an outsider, coming into philosophy with some very real philosophic problems engendered elsewhere, but without the explicit or tacit knowledge of the field of philosophy which others, who had served their apprenticeship inside the field, had. His relative ignorance of the field was in fact a good example of his own thesis that any field of human knowledge contained much that was tacitly acquired through an acculturation process and which could not be found anywhere in explicit statements. Nevertheless, it was a limitation that also blocked a full and fair consideration of his work in these nonanalytic circles.

On the Continent there were, of course, analysts among the academic philosophers. Those who were not were, however, phenomenologists and/or existentialists or Marxists. Philosophy, for the phenomenologists, too, was not involved in larger questions. It had to get clear how thought was rooted in the more immediate and intuitive human experiences and why our theories about these experiences were all of rather secondary importance. Polanyi seemed to be saying that man's theoretical systems were really of great importance—in fact, that they tended to enter, as subsidiary clues, into the structure of our immediate experiences, our perceptions. Those phenomenologists who also were existentialists were activists; but for them action could not reliably be informed by theoretical views—except the theory that man is totally free in making his constructions. Being bound or obligated in any real sense by theoretical views was hardly an idea with which they could be comfortable. Polanyi's obvious commitment to traditional science was to them, perhaps, the most appalling of all his commitments.

The Marxists were indeed interested in using philosophy (their particular philosophy) to save the world. But their notions of what this entailed were almost in point-by-point opposition to those of Polanyi.

Besides, he had made it clear that Marxism was the most formidable foe of all those things that he found most precious and true. So there could, of course, be no acceptance there.

Most of the support he did obtain came from dissidents from what was going on in other, nonphilosophic enterprises, since his criticisms of reductionism and of the ideal of detached objectivity were evidenced to them in the manifestly wrong ways in which they found their own disciplines operating. Few academic philosophers, however, found Polanyi sufficiently clear or sound to be interesting enough to discuss seriously with each other.

It is true that many new ideas in philosophy in the past have been introduced by outsiders not involved in any of the academic schools of their time. Their views, however, were not immediately accepted by the schools. It took time before such views were incorporated into the work of academic philosophers. Hobbes, Locke, and Hume's ideas, for instance, had to wait for Kant to become accepted. Since then, their philosophies have become part of the pantheon. But they had a hard time with the academic philosophers of their own day.

However sound Polanyi's views might be, and however relevant to the philosophic difficulties of our time, it is not surprising that they seem to have had so little effect upon philosophers in our time. This is so, given their many unacceptable features to comtemporary, card-carrying philosophers of our day, which I have just recounted.

Let us therefore raise the critical question of whether or not philosophers ought to play the role of physicians. Was Polanyi right or wrong in his contention that they should, whether or not it is fashionable to hold this view

If philosophy does not play this role, what results? We should surely be able to see in our day what results. Philosophic tomes and articles today have the general reputation of being esoteric and indeed arid. Even scientists have generally found very little useful or even true—for them in the great field of the philosophy of science. Somehow, what the philosophers of science say about science has tended to be unrecognizable to scientists as related to the science they know. The questions raised and answered in many different ways by different philosophers taking up each other's ideas have often seemed to scientists not even to be relevant questions. Some philosophers are now beginning to deal with some of the philosophic problems really lying at the basis of how science is done, and these (including Polanyi's views) are seen by scientists as relevant. These are larger questions, however, than have generally been raised in at least the first half of our century. If they were pursued and put in the context of a whole philosophy, they would be the large kind of questions with which Polanyi has dealt, along with the classic philosophers. But philosophy, although most recently gradually backing into these larger questions, is still generally not fully involved with them.

In addition, it seems obvious that philosophy must have some support, like any academic pursuit, from the general public. If philosophy seems to be somewhat a private game, pursued by humanistically anemic persons for their own enjoyment, it is doubtful that philosophy will continue to have the support it needs. At best its welfare will become endangered as time goes on. For there is nothing in it even for ordinary educated people in other spheres of cognitive or active endeavor, let alone for the general public. From this pragmatic standpoint, too, it seems that a philosophy studiously avoiding entanglement with the larger issues seems to be jeopardizing its own existence.

But let us take note of something more immediate, essential, and telling. The larger questions, especially those created out of reaction to the short-sighted or debilitating thought and ways of our time, are bound to be raised by some human beings. If philosophy as an academic enterprise does not play this role of critic, other people in other disciplines will do so. This good money will tend gradually to drive the bad out of circulation, the reverse of Gresham's law, and so philosophers who have been bringing or will bring their minds to bear upon these problems will once again become more respected by the educated public; philosophy, in the role of physician, may thus experience a revival.

There is more than a little evidence that this is beginning to occur. A group of philosophers, pursuing, as they call it, the ideal of "pluralism" in philosophy, is organizing to achieve positions of influence in the American Philosophical Association, to supplant the analytic philosophers who have controlled the Association for so long. Among those working at this are many who all along have understood and respected the historically great philosophers and who share with them the belief that philosophy still needs to pursue the larger questions that intelligent human beings must ask and that must turn them into critics of the intellectual and action shibboleths of our time. Their degree of success in these attempts must indicate that many philosophers today are beginning to awaken.

So Polanyi, I believe, was sound in assuming that as a philosopher his role was to be a physician. Yet, not being the fashion of his time, this stance of his would not endear him to his contemporaries in philosophy.

There is also another assumption that seems to be behind what Polanyi was doing. This one may also have contributed to his lack of success in converting his own age to his views. As we read Polanyi's account of how Europe fell under various kinds of totalitarian government, we find him giving an account that almost wholly rests upon his identification of various disastrous ideas engendered in people's thought by certain developments in their philosophic views. He makes a case, as we have seen, for how these views developed and how they led to the popularity of totalitarian movements of the left and the right in Europe to the point where they could assume total control of people's lives, especially in Russia and Germany.

Polanyi saw his problem to be how to explain why intellectuals came to support these movements as strongly as they did—especially when they were, in the process, losing control over their own activities as intellectuals, and so, in a sense, working against what surely should have been their own interests. He did not give us an historical account of other non-ideational factors which were leading nonintellectuals also to support such movements. This omission may be viewed by historians and sociologists as a serious defect in Polanyi's account. But of course we must realize that Polanyi was not trying to write a history of that time. He was simply trying to show how and why Marxism especially held such appeal for intellectuals then, and even after World War II in England, where scientists were still supporting the idea of a socially planned or controlled science.

One of the lessons Polanyi drew from his experience with these times in Europe was how wrong Hume had been in asserting that the errors in religion were calamitous in their effects, but that those in philosophy were merely ludicrous. For Polanyi the philosophic errors of Marx and his followers had caused a calamity to Europe and the world every bit as bad as, if not worse than, any calamities ever caused by errors in religion. Marx, of course, was living proof that ideas do have consequences and therefore that the ideas that intellectuals hold to be true can be very important in determining the sort of society we may usher in.

To Polanyi, therefore, it was business of the first order to straighten out our ideas. So he was led, step by step, into articulating a new

philosophy that would provide a respectable intellectual basis for supporting a free society, rather than a totalitarian one that promised to set
everything right. In this I think he was successful, as I have said, so that I
think it would be difficult for anyone who has understood what he said
to support a planned and controlled society, even as a means to the best
of ends.

But the unspoken premise in his efforts to do this seems to be that
such a set of ideas as he provided, if accepted by the intellectuals, will in
fact be instrumental in the growth and protection of a free society. It
apparently seemed to him that if intellectuals, through their wrong ideas,
could play a major role in ushering in a totalitarian system—and continue to support it—it would apparently seem that they, through right
ideas, could also usher in and support a free society. That they could and
would support a free society, if they shared his ideas, is, I think, very
likely true. However, that they could usher it in in this way, or save it
from internal attack from nonintellectuals, is, I think, *not* necessarily
true. As Eric Hoffer has warned us, one of the diseases of intellectuals is
that we think we are more respected and influential in our societies than
in fact we are. It may be that, in fact, we tend to be swallowed up in "the
general public" and more largely ignored that Polanyi thought. He
envisaged a system of political freedom operating largely the way a free
scientific or academic "republic" does. In such a republic there is indeed
democratic freedom and equality for all to participate. But there are also
respected leaders of opinion, and even authorities of a sort. They are
freely recognized by members of their community as the best in their
respective fields, in terms of the criteria of excellence accepted and
emulated by all members of the scientific community. They are not
authorities merely because they have been successful in attaining an
official position through political maneuvering.

Polanyi was thus led to maintain that, just as is the case in the
republic of science, a free democratic political republic cannot exist
unless there are some basic ideals, principles held in common by all the
members of the political community. These make it possible for there to
be differences of opinion about public policies which are nevertheless
respected by all sides. When any one of them is implemented, it does not
destroy the right of those who hold different views to remain critical and
to continue their efforts to persuade their government to pursue a different policy. Those who hold different views can be tolerated, because
the basic aims to which public policy is directed are not in question, viz.,

maintaining respect for the ideals or "spiritual entities" pursued by various professional communities in the society, and so also respect for their freedom to pursue these. As a result, the freely chosen leaders would simply be those whose devotion to these principles and ideals was most outstanding and wise—along the lines of the way this system works in the republic of science. Their real leaders, in other words, would be their most respected moral leaders. This was the "logic of liberty" Polanyi elucidated so fully in the book of that name and in numerous other places as well.

If a free society really does rest upon the devotion of the general public to such ideals, then unfortunately we cannot show that Polanyi's work did very much to induce devotion to such beliefs in the minds of the public. In the first place, he spoke throughout his career almost exclusively to the intellectuals—not to the man in the street, not to the nonprofessionals, the nonacademics, the noneducated (except perhaps for his early efforts to educate the public in economics). Very few of these ordinary people would ever have been able to understand his sophisticated work. Even college students seem to have considerable difficulties with much of it.

It is possible that Polanyi assumed that it was only the intellectuals who might be tempted, because of their intellectual seduction by the ideal of moral perfectionism, expecially as decked out in "scientific" guise by the Marxists, to flag in their devotion to the ideals essential to the existence of a free society. He may have assumed that the common man was naturally devoted to them (at least in our culture), because common men grew up believing that such ideals were already embodied in the free communities of scientists, artists, jurists, etc., and therefore respected them.

It may be true that most people in Western societies would, if asked, say that they respected the ideals of truth (even, possibly, scientific truth), justice, beauty, mercy, and those associations of people committed to these ideals. I think it is not necessarily true, however, that the untutored common man is, in fact, quite as devoted to them as Polanyi may have supposed. There are contrary principles at work in life. These are often parochial and chauvinistic, sometimes related to economic concerns, religious beliefs, and/or pure self-interest. It is not only large corporations and business interests that regularly act to subvert the ideals of truth and justice. Labor unions, as well as unorganized workers, do so; even professional people, such as teachers (including college professors), physicians, lawyers, dentists, and clergymen, ride rough-shod over these ideals, at times, trying to subvert their government into protecting their particular interests from market conditions and to secure advantages for themselves or their particular group.

This behavior is, of course, an example of lower-level social parochialism, power, and profit which Polanyi admitted form the basis for the higher level of the moral and ethical and which therefore also limit its attainment. But there is often more to it than this. These interested actions are often very real competitors of the higher moral principles for the ordinary citizen's highest devotion and commitment in action. The common man does indeed sometimes feel uneasy when he has flouted truth or justice in the service of these more ignoble ends. But he goes ahead and does it nonetheless—sometimes asserting that he has to. Let us try to see why he may think he has to.

One concrete example of how greater devotion to such less than ideal ends acts to wholly subvert—not merely limit—the ideal end of justice is the ubiquitous activity of plea bargaining in the courts. Everyone will admit that it is justice for a person to receive the penalties fixed for disobeying those laws that he has in fact disobeyed and not to receive the penalties fixed for disobeying those laws which he has not disobeyed. Yet only a few philosophers and a very few legal professionals (and hardly any laymen) actively argue against violating these principles through the practice of plea bargaining—and almost everyone does it. When a plea bargain has been reached, it is because the accused feels that, circumstances being what they are, he has got the best deal he could hope for. The prosecutor, for the same reason, feels the same way and so does the judge, since this frees him from conducting a long time-and-energy-consuming trial. The noninvolved ordinary citizen, when it is explained to him how, in the absence of such nonjuridical disposition of so many cases, he would have to submit to higher taxes in order to pay for the additional courts that the additional trials would necessitate, is also satisfied with the practice of plea bargaining. Since everyone concerned is satisfied, what, people say, can be wrong with the practice? The answer is of course, "nothing," if no one is overly devoted to the ideal of justice.

My purpose with this example is to show how, in fact, the ordinary man does not need to be seduced by a sophisticated intellectual theory supposedly showing a certain ideal to be hollow in order to succumb to acting against this ideal in his own interest. He naturally tends to act against ideals when the institutional system of laws and customs are such as to make his following these ideals too costly for him. In fact, if he looks like a fool when he does follow them.

When a free society in Polanyi's terms does exist, it is apparently therefore not simply because of a widespread devotion to these several ideals. This is not to say, of course, that a free society might not indeed be subverted by subscription even merely on the part of intellectuals to a theoretical or philosophical position emptying these ideals of any "reality"—as by simply reducing them in theory to other more basic interests and motivations, as does Marxism. Polanyi appears indeed to be right in his contention that this can, and has in fact, happened. But a free society surely might exist without a widespread and serious devotion to such ideals. Indeed it is otherwise hard to see how one ever could exist. Kant once said that a proper and adequate government might be designed even by a race of devils, provided only that they were intelligent. This may be an overstatement, yet its truth, so far as it has any, lies in what Kant meant by it—and what the apologists for the United States Constitution, the authors of the *Federalist Papers*, meant. A set of institutions that relies for its operation largely upon the baser interests and desires of mankind, rather than upon their moral ideals, can be a viable one in terms of its probable survival and a rough approximation of justice. For, *if* other conditioning circumstances are favorable, many diverse interests can develop and all can receive something they each want, while none can get strong enough to get everything it wants.

Conceiving what institutions might succeed in the special circumstances of our time in fulfilling the demands for a viable, free, and tolerably just society is the real problem of politics, insofar as it is at all an intellectual problem. Polanyi's analysis unfortunately does very little to induce us to give serious considerations to this tough and unpalatable problem. It induces us rather to give more attention to the attractive but less fruitful task of inspiring a rededication of the whole population to the ideals of truth, justice, mercy, beauty, fellowship, and the like. However important and intrinsically valuable such devotion would be, we can perhaps have a tolerably free and just society only when our circumstances and institutions are properly articulated with each other. Then conscientious dedication to our ideals does not cost us too much individually in other goods to which we are also devoted; but even then we can do it only partially, of course, as Polanyi also knew.

Polanyi's views, I believe, are not fully adequate to what it takes to create and to maintain a free society. Yet I think his notion that a free society rests upon the existence of polycentric orders in many self-regulating enclaves of dedicated persons, and upon a polycentric order achieved in its own political governance, is sound. Such a society is, at least in our time, manifestly important to the activity of truly human beings. Such an insight should be helpful to some degree in supporting a free society, to the extent that such a society depends upon its members' conceptual views, and certainly as a guide to our efforts at designing—or redesigning—our institutions.

However, it seems to me that Polanyi overemphasized the extent to which the workings of a society depend upon concepts in the minds of the bulk of its citizens about how the society ought to function. As we have just noted, he thought a free society depended upon the dedication of people generally in the society to certain ideals or spiritual ends and principles. We have seen that this may indeed be so, but perhaps to a much more limited extent than he thought—that, in fact, certain complexes of political institutions, in connection with certain historical circumstances, might be more essential to the existence of a free society than widespread devotion to these ideals. Nevertheless, widespread skepticism about the ultimate value of these ideals must surely be as disastrous as he thought it would be.

Similarly, he thought, as we have seen in Chapter 13, that the general public could be educated to make reasonable choices with regard to economic policy. There has been some effort by a few economists to educate the general public in economic matters, without notable success; in fairness it must be said that these efforts have never been as extensive or intensive as Polanyi advised. One reason why these efforts have been inadequate may be that it is apparently hard to interest any great number of people in the study of economics, no matter how it is presented. The "dismal science" seems to remain dismal to most people. Besides, contemporary economics seems even less than slightly interested in political economy, having given it up for an esoteric econometrics, bound to be useless in the task of educating the public in sound economic policy.

We have also found, in our application of the Keynesian principles to economic policy, that it is not difficult to get the creation of new money in the face of recessions, but apparently that it becomes extremely difficult politically to get it back out, even when those who think this necessary make every effort to explain to the public why inflation cannot be halted without such curtailing of the money supply. It is not that the public does not want inflation contained; it does. But no one wants to run any danger to his own segment of the economy, or to the social welfare measures upon which he has come to depend. Polanyi did indeed recognize that, if people came to love security too much, the proper operation of economic policy based upon Keynesian views would be endangered and chronic inflation might ensue. What he apparently did not foresee was the extent to which the use of these policies might help to fan the ardor for security over other social goods.

However, there is perhaps another and more permanent source for the increased pursuit of security which Polanyi generally ignored, along with, I might say, most classical economists—with a few exceptions, such as Henry Simons.[4] It is not that they are unaware of this factor; they simply seem to ignore its long-term contributions to chronic inflation, as well as to widespread disaffection from the free enterprise system. This abiding source for the inordinate love of security is identical with the tendency, already clearly noted by Adam Smith, of the producers in the market to try to achieve, through "combination," as great a control of their markets and prices as they can, and so to prevent the free market from operating in their own case.

It would be hopeless, it seems to me as I believe it did also to Polanyi, to try to remedy this problem by developing a business ethics that all producers would share which would restrain these natural desires. As Polanyi has astutely observed, there are no professional standards that guide business as there are in the learned professions, for there are no ideal purposes or "spiritual entities" in business which are pursued for their own sake, such as truth or justice. The immediate reason for engaging in business is to make profits, and the business professional knows that he can make them more surely if he has few (or better yet, no) competitors. Granted that it is in the best interests of society, of all of us, as consumers, that producers should have competitors; but the difficulty is that it is in the best short-run interest of each producer to have none. If all other producers are pursuing this interest, then any one given producer must pursue it also. And if no other producer is pursuing it, then it becomes even more profitable for any given one to do so. So we cannot expect any producer to subscribe to a voluntary ethical restriction that not only would curtail his profits but, quite conceivably, might also ruin him. Besides, it would certainly border on the immoral if not indeed be downright immoral, for the managers of a company to take such chances with someone else's money, that is the stockholder's. Therefore, if only for the reason that production is now carried on mainly by stockholder corporations rather than by individuals, an ethics restraining producers from seeking to gain control of their markets and their prices cannot develop.

But if commercial and industrial elements of the economy inevitably gravitate away from free markets to political jockeying to protect their sources of income from competitive markets, it is clear that all other elements in the economy will tend to follow. Whether or not they approved of it, they would, of course, be driven to it in order to protect themselves from the power of others. In the "state of nature" (which such a situation clearly resembles), as Hobbes pointed out, everyone is forced to seek power without limit. Thus labor unions, professional associations, welfare recipients, and all other elements of society also will organize, if they can, to protect their own interests—which means to acquire power to resist all downward pressure on what they are receiving for their goods and services and to push always in an upward direction by trying to remove their own interests as far as possible from determination by market forces.

The sum total of these almost universal efforts can only act as a constant, pervasive inflationary influence, since it exerts continual upward pressure on prices and wages, and downward pressure upon productivity. In order for this imbalanced system to continue, a continued increase in the money supply is essential, of course. There will be irresistible pressure from almost all sides upon politicians whenever any failure of the money supply to rise effects anyone's economic interest. But since people under these circumstances must continue to pay more and more, even in real money, for less and less (for this *is* inflation), they will not like this situation and so will insist, at the same time as they continue to desire an ever-increasing supply of money, that their politicians control inflation!

It would do no good, under these conditions, to educate and to plead for decency and reason in the economic demands that people make upon their government, as Polanyi advised. The framework in which they are forced to operate will preclude the effectiveness of such education. As in the case of political problems, if we wish to remedy such an unhealthy situation, institutions have to be developed which make use of self-interest in the solution of this economic problem. The insights of Polanyi and the classical economists were sound, I think, in maintaining that only a free market of competitors so numerous that no single one of them by his own actions could influence to any extent the quantity of goods brought to market was the sort of institution which would solve most of our economic problems without recourse to force or political action. As we have seen, Polanyi found only two exceptions to this. Maintaining a proper money supply, and providing for the just needs of all persons in the society to grow and develop as truly human beings, were two economic problems that he thought the market could not solve and which therefore required governmental operations of a nonmarket sort.

However, it seems to me these economists almost universally failed to see that at least one of the essential conditions for a free market—the existence of large numbers of competing units—also cannot be left to the operation of the "free" (meaning by this term only a nongovernment-influenced) market. In the face of the tremendous centralization that has taken place in our economy—the proliferation of vertical and horizontal integration, conglomerates of all sorts, oligopolies, and even real cartels—many of these economists still persist in saying that such associations in restraint of free competition tend to break up, if entrance to the market is formally free, i.e., not hampered by government, and so continue to blame these gigantic aberrations of the free market upon governmental actions!

It is true that Polanyi was one of those economists who emphasized that industries that could not be made competitive would have to be either publicly controlled or owned, as other classical economists have maintained. But to my knowledge he never addressed the question of how one could try to make such industries competitive, and of how and when we could know for certain that a particular industry could not be made competitive. To say, in the absence of any suggestion as to how we could make them competitive, that those which cannot be made competitive should be publicly controlled or owned is, under present-day conditions, practically to propose socialism—which, of course, Polanyi did not wish to do.

The real problem seems then again to be, if a free economy is truly important for us to maintain, to find some way to develop institutions that would maintain the conditions necessary for a free market. Or at least we should be able to propose such institutions.

There might be a number of ways to do this, if political economists would only put their minds to it. Unquestionably one of them is, as Simons long ago proposed,[5] to drastically reform our corporation laws so that the charters given to corporations to organize will set definite limits to their capitalization. These should also deny the firm power to acquire stock in any other functioning concerns.

It will be immediately obvious to everyone, I imagine, that the political problems are staggering in getting any such changes made in our corporation laws. Our ready recognition of this fact shows the extent to which we believe our institutions are neither adopted nor supported on the basis of our reasoned conceptualizations about what is most beneficial to a free society. One might almost be driven to say, in the face of such political obstacles, that any healthy fundamental economic changes as these could only come about by an incredibly fortunate accident—or by Providence, if one is religious.

But recognition of the enormous political difficulties of bringing about such changes is somewhat beside the point. If one wants to understand conceptually upon what grounds a free society can be based, we have to begin making hard, detailed, and realistic analyses of possible political and economic institutions. We need to figure out how they could be expected to work even when we cannot count on high, extensive moral dedication to the principles we need and which we hope these institutions might tend to embody. The city of man is not the city of God, as St. Augustine observed long ago, and must be designed to manage sinners as well as saints.

The political strategies to be used in trying to create sound institutions depend upon solving the practical problems we meet in seeking to take common action with others, not in what we individually think is sound. Indeed, frank recognition of what lies at the root of our endemic inflation and why politically it cannot be changed (if we come to that conclusion) might put us on the track of simply accepting continuous inflation. Then we would merely seek palliatives for its most unacceptable consequences (such as subsidies for persons on fixed incomes), rather than continually tossing the issue about like a political football and, from time to time, taking economically ineffective but potentially harmful measures to fight it, such as artifically raising interest rates.

Therefore, although Polanyi has brought to light many neglected truths about a free society and what is involved in it, I have to say that he committed a basic error in analogizing a free society to the self-governing community of (especially) scientists. He has failed to see the degree to which a propitious set of institutions, powered generally by self-interest rather than by free, intelligent, democratic discussion of the issues in the context of commonly shared ideals, operates in bringing things together in a society. We in America and everywhere in the world have only partially succeeded in developing such institutions, either in theory or in practice. And since we do not even in general understand the beneficial ways in which some of those work, we are in fact often busily engaged in destroying those we have accidentally developed in the past.

This brings us to a final criticism of Polanyi's efforts to treat the modern mind. Running throughout Polanyi's analysis is a continual assessment of where he thought we stood. Such an assessment is based on Polanyi's third set of principles in addition to the ontological and the methodological, namely, historical, empirical assumptions concerning our contemporary state of affairs, already mentioned in Chapter 16. As a "physician" Polanyi had to assess our present condition in order to advise our appropriate treatment. We can see that his assessment of the modern mind is indeed plausible. Our sciences of biology and of psychology do exhibit strong tendencies toward reductionism to "lower" ontological levels and this toward a downgrading of animistic and humanistic elements in our scientific view of life and of man. And we do seem often to be ennervated by the ambiguities involved in our view of the status of our values—moral, aesthetic, and religious—both in terms of their reality and of precisely what they demand of us.

We can also surely see that he may be quite right in maintaining that contemporary man is deeply—and possibly irremediably—involved in the industrial order that he cannot abandon. Since it cannot flourish with central planning it needs instead an economic system of spontaneous order. We have found, however, that Polanyi may have misjudged our present policital and economic situation: he did not see that the very existence of great masses of people in our modern societies might preclude the operation of simple democratic participation in political issues in a considered, intelligent manner. He did not understand that these might require instead a funneling of mass participation in government through a particular set of political institutions such that any public policies adopted would have to represent concurrent majorities of great numbers of special interests, rather than the will of anything like a simple majority of all persons or of their mass-elected representatives, presumably arriving at intelligent social policies through serious discussions of ways and means to implement them. We have seen that Polanyi also appears to have failed to note that the change in our economy to the preponderance of corporate enterprises may now demand certain changes in the corporation laws and the rest of the legal framework so that the mutual interaction of economic elements can generate the spontaneous order that would produce economic efficiency in the provision of wanted goods and services and their rational distribution among the various factors in the economy.

Nevertheless, in spite of these two deficiencies, which I believe somewhat inhibit the practical use of Polanyi's thought in improving the political and economic aspects of our societies, his work has deeply affected many educated people today in academic and professional circles. "Conversion" is perhaps the proper way to speak of what has occurred to them. Not religious conversion, it is true, nor conversion to a new charismatic leader nor to a social movement. Their conversion has been to the new epistemology of the "from–to"—the subsidiary–focal—way of understanding how we function as perceptual and cognitive beings and to the ontological hierarchy entailed in this understanding. This is truly a turn around, in that practically everything then appears to them in a new light. It is as if they have really seen and understood for the first time. Whatever their field, they have a new and firmer grasp of their discipline. The deep-set, gnawing inconsistencies in their thought and action in this discipline have disappeared.

These experiences that people have had, as well as the basic soundness we have found in his key concepts, as we have subjected them to serious critical scrutiny, are proofs that Polanyi's diagnosis, prescription, and treatment of the modern mind are reasonable and possible ways to handle at least part of our problem. Those who have followed the doctor's orders have recovered and know that he has been successful.

But, as we have seen, many have rejected his treatment—or remain ignorant of it. If it is an essential part of treatment by a physician that he (1) secure the attention of those needing treatment and (2) persuade them to allow him to treat them, then we have to say that Polanyi did not learn how to be successful in these aspects of his efforts to treat the ailments of our modern mind.

All analogies have limits, and we may have reached the limit of ours here. We do not ordinarily blame a physician if people reject his diagnosis, reject his prescriptions, or even refuse to allow him to treat them. But we do sometimes hold that a *philosopher* ought to be persuasive as well as correct. For the philosopher, the persuasion is indeed the treatment. A philosopher's position should be sound, but so should his rhetoric. Where this is possible but neglected, the philosopher is rightly blamed. Yet it is not always possible. We have noted that many philosophers have been too far ahead of their immediate contemporaries (in philosophy, at any rate) to be very influential in their own time.

Polanyi, as we have seen, innocently and on his own, outside the community of scholars in philosophy, made a discovery diametrically opposed to the going concerns of almost all his contemporaries in philosophy—and most of those in all other fields, as well. It is hard to imagine how he could have found a rhetoric that would soften this harsh contrast in the beginning, allowing it to insinuate itself into the going concerns of his contemporaries or making it palatable to them. Not being a philosopher by trade, Polanyi did not even realize what it was he had to do until the problem had already arisen. We cannot blame him for this failure to use a proper rhetoric to gain acceptance for his views.

His position, it seems to me, is basically sound. Were intellectuals to consider his proposals seriously and adopt most of their key elements, they would find most of the impasses and stultifications that bedevil contemporary thought could reach reasonable and satisfying resolutions. The gap between the "two cultures," which has bothered C. P. Snow and others, would certainly begin to narrow; fuller participation in many more aspects of our culture would be possible for people on both sides. At the same time such intellectuals no longer would be tempted by Utopian panaceas that entail destruction of many of the freedoms in our society. It would not, of course, solve all our problems: no philosophy could. But it could solve these particular ones.

Proceeding now beyond the aims that Polanyi set for himself in ushering in this new philosophy, let us complete our criticism by asking how his work stands up to the more timeless goals of philosophy. How sound is it as philosophy, not just as a way to help solve our present intellectual difficulties? This is too large a question to receive a definitive and final answer here. But I believe certain things can be said about it which would give his thought a respectable place in the pantheon of great philosophies.

Let us ask whether or not it is basically sound to hold his most fundamental contention—that all knowledge and thought must exhibit a tacit dimension. This inevitably means that personal commitments simply dwelt in uncritically toward the attainment of more explicit focal awareness and never themselves critically established as true and reliable—indeed never even focally or explicitly known—are always present. It was this radical contention that Polanyi himself seemed to believe distinguished his thought from every other philosophy.

The hardest test for this case must be, as he said, the "formal" sciences, mathematics and logic. He has shown us even these have tacit dimensions that consist of logical gaps across which we make intellectual leaps rooted in tacit grounds.

Since mathematics and formal logic make use of notations, the identification of these notations is not made on explicit grounds, nor in our judgment that their manipulation on a page satisfies our rules for mathematics and logic. As Kant put it, we cannot have rules for applying rules for applying rules ad infinitum. Somewhere we must simply see that what is present before us does satisfy our rule. We must judge tacitly that this which is before us is true. But why do we know that the statement that we cannot have an infinite series of rules for applying rules is true? Because the concept of an infinite series is not consistent with the concept of the completion of the series. We are brought face to face with relations between concepts, ideas, that we know must be true, because we know the nature and meaning of these concepts, and these relationships are part of that meaning. How else could Gödel know that his theorem is true? It could not be because it is part of a total logical system of consistent parts, for his theorem was simply that any such a system can always be known to be incomplete. That it is incomplete cannot be a part of the system, or else the system would, after all, be complete—by virtue of its being incomplete!

Thus we know more about a mathematical or logical system than is involved in its system of notations—i.e., more than we can tell. Yet this knowledge is not of the variable sort that Polanyi's "personal knowledge" is. Personal knowledge is variable, because what we have become committed to, what we dwell in, is dependent upon a myriad of factors, not the least of which is our own particular culture that we have absorbed into ourselves—even as a scientist does with the tradition followed by his discipline. The particular position in which this puts us is what Polanyi has called our "calling"—and it is not the same for everyone.

When we move from the tacit dimension to a focal object, we are engaging in what Polanyi called tacit inference. He regarded this as logic, though not explicit logic. There was indeed an explicit logic for

Polanyi that seems to entail spelling out certain inferences its terms—in their explicit sense—have for us. He did not deny that this sort of nontacit, explicit logic existed—that concepts really did have explicit implications. I asked him this question once and he replied that, of course, concepts had necessary explicit implications. It seemed clear that he held that only the application of formal, explicit logic required tacit elements.

Polanyi could therefore make a very real distinction between trans-natural and natural integrations on the gounds that the transnatural integrations were made by our imaginations from "incompatible" parts. These, he held, remained incompatible for us even after we had imag-inatively combined them. Their incompatibility seemed to be, as he presented examples of them, of the explicitly logical sort. They could never come to be compatible through our becoming used to them culturally. The depth in a painting and its flat surface must always remain explicitly incompatible for us. This continuing incompatibility was what made it essential for us to continue to see the painting as a transnatural work of our imagination and thus to continue to enjoy it as a work of art every time we viewed it. In natural integrations, by contrast, there was never such explicitly logical incompatibility (formal contradic-tion) between their parts.

Polanyi never gave very serious consideration to the problem raised by the existence of this sort of real, explicit logic for his basic position about the ubiquitous necessity for the tacit, personal dimension to knowledge. He could not give it a simple, linguistic resolution by nominally reducing concepts to words. Words were dwelt in, for him, toward meanings, some of which were concepts. Concepts and words were not the same. It was clearly not only words that had implications for him in their conventional usage in a language. Concepts as well seemed to really have implications, which was what made the logical relations between them so hard and fast and explicit.

Polanyi only dealt with the problem in an offhand manner, saying that "it is plausible to assume" that "explicit inferences" are based upon "fixed neural networks."[6] This explanation might account for the apparent transcendence of the explicit logical relations, and for their apparent universality as well, without moving them into the cognitive realm and so into the subsidiary–focal structure, where they would not, of course, fit very well.

But they do not fit very well as circuits in the brain either. If they were such circuits, they would lose their obvious normative character. Polanyi elsewhere rejects such neural circuits as an explanation of the way in which we think, precisely on the grounds that it could not account for the normative nature of our thought--its thrust toward "rightness."[7] If the rules of inference in explicit logic were neural circuits, we would simply have to think this way (as, for Kant, we *had* to perceive through the forms of space and time). But we do not, of course, have to think logically. Violations of *modus tollens* in people's actual thinking notoriously abound. People quite frequently affirm the antecedent from the truth of the consequent. The rules of an explicit logic function as norms, in the sense that we can come to see that we are wrong logically when we have slipped into logical errors. Logic, in both the tacit and explicit senses is, as Polanyi said, those principles of right thinking which get us from true grounds to true conclusions.[8] These logical principles become then normative principles for our thinking, not causal principles. Yet as circuits in the brain they could only be causal principles, and not normative.

So Polanyi can hardly be right that the basic logical principles are circuits in our brains. Yet what *are* they? For they seem also not to have a tacit dimension, and Polanyi avoids ever really attributing a tacit dimension to them.

What we see working here, it seems to me, are the inevitable limitations of a philosophy devoted entirely (to use Plato's terms) to the third level of his divided line figure the level of thought resting upon assumptions tested only by reference to empirical facts. Such problems as these are, it seems to me, evidence that a philosophy which denies any such dimension as Plato's fourth level the level of thought related only to ideas themselves, without reference to any assumptions or to empirical facts, (whether understood in Plato's terms or in some other) ultimately cannot be adequate as a philosophy.

In Plato's philosophy the problem is simply solved. There are eternal Ideas. When we think simply and purely of these eternal Ideas, we find they are related to each other in certain ways: inclusion, exclusion, etc. (as he showed us in examples in his *Sophist*). These are the basic logical relations and they have a timeless existence as the ways in which the eternal ideas are internally related to each other, because of what it is they each are in themselves, purely grasped at his fourth level of thinking, as Ideas or Forms, not as identified with objects in the world of experience or with words in language, as they are at his third level.

Sciences at the third level are ultimately empirical for Plato, since they must continually refer back to objects in our world of experience, due to the fact that our "sciences" at that level, observes Plato, all rest upon assumptions for which we have no good reasons except that the systems work out, using our experiences in the world of becoming as their touchstone. If there were no fourth realm, of Ideas, our knowledge would be limited to what we could do at the third level, and since here we can only inquire by means of hypotheses and there is no final truth about anything (since the world of becoming is always becoming something else) both our knowledge and our world can be conceived only as open-ended. There are no absolutes. Everything is relative to the circumstances that happen to prevail at any one moment. Knowledge at this level also, of course, can only be relative—both to the state of affairs that does prevail at any one time and to the assumptions from which we start. In short, the third level of Plato's world is almost identical with what is assumed to be the "real" world by contemporary thinkers—with the exception that Plato understands it as open, through the soul, to the eternal world of Forms and Ideas of his fourth level, whereas most contemporaries conceive such a notion to be either nonsense or else stultifying, and refuse to recognize anything that seems to bear at all on the eternal.

Although Polanyi's philosophy is definitely contemporary in its basic outlook and limitations, it does allow for that which bears upon eternity. To be sure, he specifically denied any intelligibility to Plato's world of Forms. He also confined the realities that exist independently of us to those dealt with by our natural sciences. These realities are all open-ended and fraught with temporality, in terms of the development both of their own further possibilities and of our knowledge of them. Our systems of knowledge, all significantly *articulate* for Polanyi, are grounded on assumptions which can never be proven—indeed some for him are irreducibly tacit. All such knowledge is rooted in the empirical, because it is all subject to verifiability.

But not only are art and religion excluded from this realm of the verifiable in experience, but mathematics as well. These are all subject only to validation. But these, he implied, do bear upon the eternal, and their attraction for man appears to be ineluctable. It is the pure intellectual beauty of mathematics that intrigues us, not its bearing upon our mundane concerns; the same seems true of art and religion. In addition, these latter two "carry us away," up and out of the chaos of our day-to-day lives, to meanings beyond the natural—meanings which become "transnatural." Indeed for Polanyi it is the whole noosphere in which we live which enables us to put one foot in the eternal. Thus a faint shadow, actually only a shade of a kind of Platonism, makes its appearance behind the backdrop on the stage of Polanyi's thought.

One of the participants with Polanyi at a symposium of the Colston Research Society actually accused him of Platonism (the classic putdown, apparently, for contemporary thinkers). Polanyi admitted that he could be so described—but, he insisted, as a Platonist without the Ideal Forms of Plato "laid up somewhere."[9] It is not clear just what sort of Platonist this could be, other than that of a mind incorrigibly contemporary, but with an incurable longing for the transcendent. Polanyi's stubborn refusal to give up either of these created somewhat of a problem for him, of course. But it has made his philosophy more interesting, and above all more true to the whole of the human situation.

Man's attraction to the eternal is difficult to incorporate into a philosophy striving to limit itself strictly to Plato's third level. The problem raised by a logical function, which apparently in formal logic has to have an identical but more general existence over and above its particular representation in any particular language—or even in any *system* of logic—is perhaps insurmountable for the contemporary mind. We are led to Ur-logics (and possibly Ur-languages, as someone like Chomsky apparently espouses) and then attempts are made to account for their existence by finding them to be grounded in psychological or even, as in Polanyi, in physiological causes. But this latter theory is surely falsified by the clearly normative role such logical functions appear to play, as we have seen.

However, if we are to remain staunchly non-Platonic and limit our understanding of cognitive enterprises strictly to the empirical, that is, to limits of the contemporary frame of mind, then in my opinion we could do no better than to embrace Polanyi's approach. His philosophy, in its basic positions, is the most adequate contemporary philosophy I know. Its systematic and coherent incorporation of a tacit dimension into our third-level cognitive enterprises puts it far ahead of its competitors and solves all sorts of enigmas engendered by the futile effort to generate wholly objective, explicit, detached—and so absolute—knowledge from the essentially relativistic knowledge derived from experience alone.

Not only this. But Polanyi, while remaining in the contemporary mode of empirical, third-level thinking, has managed to do so in such a way as to leave some room for the disclosure of things which "bear upon eternity." But he has not, like a magician, merely tricked us into thinking he has brought these rabbits out of his hat. It appears that he has actually produced them.

# Notes

CHAPTER ONE. INDICATIONS OF MALAISE

1  Michael Polanyi, "Why Did We Destroy Europe?" *Studium Generale*, 23 (Autumn 1970), pp. 911–12, and "Sixty Years in Universities," address to the Convocation of the University of Toronto, November 24, 1967, pp. 1–2 (unpublished), Michael Polanyi Papers, Box 38, Folder 10, Special Collections, University of Chicago Library.
2  Polanyi, *The Contempt of Freedom* (London, 1940), p. vi.
3  Polanyi, *Personal Knowledge* (New York, 1964), p. ix; see also "The Rights and Duties of Science," *Manchester School*, 10 (October 1939), republished as Occasional Pamphlet No. 2 of The Society for Freedom in Science (1945), pp. 1–26.
4  Polanyi, *The Logic of Liberty* (Chicago, 1951), pp. 3–90.
5  Ibid., pp. 91–200.
6  Polanyi, "The Value of the Inexact," *Philosophy of Science*, (April 3, 1936), pp. 233–34.
7  Ibid.


CHAPTER TWO. THE CAUSES

1  Polanyi, "The Growth of Thought in Society," *Economica*, 8 (November 1941), p. 454.

2   Ibid., pp. 454–55.
3   Ibid., p. 455.
4   Ibid., pp. 455–56.
5   "Sixty Years in Universities," p. 2 (from an early draft, deleted from final version).
6   Polanyi, *Knowing and Being* (Chicago 1969), p. 18.
7   "Growth of Thought in Society," pp. 455–56.
8   Polanyi, *Science, Faith, and Society* (Chicago 1964), pp. 78–79.
9   Polanyi, "Beyond Nihilism," *Encounter*, 14 (March 1960), p. 40. See also *Personal Knowledge* (Chicago 1958), pp. 227–33.
10  Polanyi, "Science and the Modern Crisis," *Memoirs and Proceedings of the Manchester Literary and Philosophical Society*, 86 (June 1945), pp. 107–16.
11  Polanyi, "The Logic of Liberty," *Measure*, 1 (Fall 1950), pp. 348–62.
12  *Knowing and Being*, pp. 4–5.
13  Ibid., p. 5.
14  Ibid.
15  Hilary Putnam, "What Theories Are Not," *Logic, Methodology and Philosophy of Science*, ed. Ernest Nagel, Patrick Suppes, and Alfred Tarski (Stanford 1962), p. 240.
16  Norwood Hanson, "Is There a Logic of Scientific Discovery?" *Current Issues in the Philosophy of Science*, ed. H. Feigl and G. Maxwell (New York 1961), pp. 20–35.
17  Paul Feyerabend, "Problems of Empiricism," *Beyond the Edge of Certainty*, ed. R. Colody (Englewood Cliffs, New Jersey, 1965), pp. 145–260.
18  Thomas Kuhn, *The Structure of Scientific Revolutions* (Chicago 1962).
19  Stephen Toulmin and J. Goodfield, *The Fabric of the Heavens*, (New York 1961).
20  Frederick Suppe, "Afterward," *The Structure of Scientific Theories*, 2nd ed. (Urbana, Illinois, 1977), pp. 717–23.
21  Ibid., p. 725. (Italics mine.)
22  Ibid., pp. 724–28.
23  Ibid., p. 724.
24  *Knowing and Being*, p. 5.
25  Ibid., p. 6.
26  Ibid.
27  Ibid.
28  Ibid., p. 10. See also *Personal Knowledge* (1958), p. 231.
29  *Knowing and Being*, p. 10.

CHAPTER THREE. THE PATHOGENESIS

1   *Logic of Liberty*, pp. 94–95.
2   Ibid., p. 97.
3   Ibid.
4   Ibid., p. 99.

5  Ibid., p. 95.
6  Ibid., p. 99.
7  Ibid., pp. 97–98.
8  Ibid., p. 99.
9  Ibid., pp. 99–100.
10 Ibid., p. 100.
11 Ibid.
12 Ibid., pp. 100–1. See also *Personal Knowledge* (1958), p. 239.
13 *Logic of Liberty*, pp. 101–2.
14 Ibid., p. 102.
15 Ibid., pp. 102–3.
16 Ibid., pp. 103–4.
17 Ibid., p. 104.
18 Ibid., pp. 106–7. See also Polanyi, "On the Modern Mind," *Encounter*, 24 (May 1965), p. 19.
19 *Logic of Liberty* (1958), pp. 104–5.
20 Ibid., pp. 105–6. See also *Personal Knowledge* (1958), pp. 235–37. In *History and Hope*, ed. K. A. Jelenski (New York 1962), "A Postscript," pp. 188–90, Polanyi answers some of the critics of his position on nihilism and Marxism. He defends himself against the suspicion that he may have invented his view of these movements in order to make it fit his diagnosis of the ills besetting the modern mind. He recounts for us many authors who have also seen something of the same thing.

Roger Calois, in his *Description du Marxisme*, says that Marx and Engels built up their theory in order to conceal from themselves and others that they were following the voice of their generous conscience, instilled by an education that their theory unmasked as fundamentally hypocritical. They transmuted their moral demands by uttering them in the form of scientific prediction.

J. Plamenatz also held that "Scientific socialism is . . . a myth, . . . the happy inspiration of two moralists who wanted to be unlike all moralists before them."

H. B. Acton has written that "The Marxist can derive moral precepts from his social science . . . to the extent that they already form, because of the vocabulary used, a concealed and unacknowledged part of it."

Carew Hunt indicates this derivation of moral precepts by quoting from Lenin: "Morality is what serves to destroy the old exploiting society." The struggle for power is seen here as the ultimate criterion of morality, seemingly justified by a moral condemnation of capitalism.

E. H. Carr, in his biography of Bakunin, shows how moral passions were first embodied in the revolutionary struggle for power. Nechayev, around 1870, took the final step of abandoning the romantic aspirations of the previous generation and raising revolution to the status of an absolute good, overriding any moral obligations. The internal contradiction ensuing from this step is analysed by Bochenski. Moral laws, he says, are appealed to and then their existence is denied.

Richard Lowenthal speaks of an "unconscious and indeed a fanatical hypocrisy—[a] ruthless immoralism justified by the subjectively sincere belief in the millenial rule of saints." Hannah Arendt finds that this denial of moral motivation or standards has become a "mainstay of Communist propaganda."

Why such professed immoralism should be so stable and seductive had been explained by E. E. Hirschmann. "We must realize that this disregard [of humanitarian idealism] has been a source of strength, not weakness. For because men in their moral professions have for so long not meant what they said, because the moral will has not seemed a reality which men could trust, therefore, by seeming to depend less on moral profession and moral will, they seemed the more to mean what they said and the more to rely upon realities." He also sees a kindred tendency underlying "the greatest self-conscious assault on humanitarian ideals yet seen in history, that of the Rome-Berlin-Tokyo axis."

Meinecke had interpreted the tragic failure of thought in the German Empire as due to the idea that the only true morality of a nation was immanent in its will to power.

The romantic nihilism first propounded by Nietzsche was likewise a moral protest against existing morality. In place of this hypocrisy he set the noble ideal of "something perfect, wholly achieved, happy, magnificently triumphant, something still capable of inspiring fear." He found it represented in Napoleon: "that synthesis of the brutish with the more-than-human."

Diderot in 1763, in *Le Neveu de Rameau*, already had justified his own work's immoralism by the hypocrisy of society. Then in his *Confessions* Rousseau had exhibited his vices as only nature's naked truth. And still later the Marquis de Sade had derived an intellectual and moral superiority for acts of cruelty and lust from a scientism that reduces man to a machine and a political theory that denounces the laws as the will of the stronger.

21  *History and Hope,* p. 192. (Italics Polanyi's.)
22  Ibid.
23  Ibid.
24  Ibid., p. 193.
25  "Sixty Years in Universities," p. 2.
26  Ibid.
27  Ibid., pp. 5–6. See also *Personal Knowledge* (1958), pp. 233–35.
28  Polanyi, "History and Hope," *Virginia Quarterly Review*, 38 (Spring 1962), pp. 194–95.

CHAPTER FOUR. A NEW EPISTEMOLOGY

1  *Personal Knowledge* (1958), p. 231.
2  See, for instance, *The Logic of Liberty*, pp. 15–25, and *Science, Faith and Society* (1964), pp. 21–41.

3  *Personal Knowledge* (1958), p. 231.
4  *Knowing and Being*, pp. 221–22.
5  Polanyi, *The Tacit Dimension*. Peter Smith, Publisher (Gloucester, Mass., 1983), p. x.
6  *Personal Knowledge* (1958), pp. 55–58, 97–98, 342.
7  *Knowing and Being*, p. 169.
8  *Knowing and Being*, p. 212, and Polanyi, "Logic and Psychology," *American Psychologist*, 23 (January 1968), p. 32. Copyright 1968 by the American Psychological Association. Reprinted by permission of the publisher.
9  *Knowing and Being*, pp. 169–70, and *Personal Knowledge* (1958), pp. 98–99.
10  Polanyi, "The Creative Imagination," *Chemical and Engineering News*, 44 (April 25, 1966), p. 87; "Logic and Psychology," p. 32; *Knowing and Being*, pp. 198–200.
11  *Knowing and Being*, p. 139. See also *Personal Knowledge* (1958), pp. 96–97.
12  *Tacit Dimension* (1983), p. 13.
13  Ibid., pp. 14, 15.
14  *Knowing and Being*, p. 139.
15  Ibid., pp. 139–40. See also *Personal Knowledge* (1958), pp. 55–56, 88.
16  *Knowing and Being*, p. 112, and Polanyi, "Tacit Knowing: Its Bearing on Some Problems of Philosophy," *Philosophy Today*, 6 (Winter 1962), p. 249.
17  *Knowing and Being*, p. 113.
18  Ibid., p. 165.
19  *Personal Knowledge* (1958), p. 97.
20  *Knowing and Being*, p. 165.
21  Ibid., p. 111. See also *Personal Knowledge* (1958), p. 38.
22  *Knowing and Being*, p. 111.
23  Ibid., p. 114. See also *Personal Knowledge* (1958), pp. 18, 73, 103–4, 132–33.
24  *Knowing and Being*, pp. 111–12. (Italics Polanyi's.)
25  "Logic and Psychology," p. 31.
26  *Tacit Dimension* (1983), p. 4. (Italics mine.)
27  *Logic of Liberty*, pp. 46–47; *Science, Faith and Society* (1964), pp. 70, 71. See also *Personal Knowledge* (1958), pp. 213–14, 242–43, 376–77.
28  *Logic of Liberty*, pp. 196–99.
29  *Tacit Dimension* (1983), p. 62.

CHAPTER FIVE. INDWELLING

1  *Tacit Dimension* (1983), pp. 7–8.
2  Polanyi, "The Logic of Tacit Inference," *Philosophy*, 41 (January 1966), p. 14.
3  *Personal Knowledge* (1958), p. 72.

Conrad Lorenz told a story about Pavlov's experiments that supports Polanyi's interpretation of what Pavlovian conditioning must in all strictness mean and why it is inadequate to the facts. He said:

A very strange story was told to me by Howard Lidell, a famous neurological specialist who was Pavlov's student in St. Petersburg. Lidell had conditioned a dog to salivate when a metronome accelerated. He asked himself, "What will happen if I release my dog from his harness?" Note that to perserve belief in the conditioned reflex the dog has to be tied up so that he can make use only of his salivary gland.

Lidell went ahead and unleashed the dog. What do you think the dog did? Though the metronome hadn't accelerated, he leaped toward the mechanism, pushed it with his nose, wagged his tail, and, while salivating furiously, asked the metronome to accelerate! What had previously been conditioned was quite simply the reaction of a beggar. The dog had formed the hypothesis that the metronome was the cause of his food. The great Pavlov was so furious that he forbade Lidell to divulge his experiment! Think of the complexity of what had happened and the simplism of the explanation. The conditioned reflex does exist, but it is not the only element of behavior.

Frederic de Towarnicki, "A Talk with Conrad Lorenz," tr. Stanley Hockman, *The New York Times Magazine*, 119, No. 41,070 (July 5, 1970), p. 29.

4  Polanyi and Harry Prosch, *Meaning* (Chicago 1975), pp. 69–70. See also *Knowing and Being*, pp. 192–93.

5  *Personal Knowledge* (1958), pp. 97–98.

6  "Talk with Conrad Lorenz," p. 29. Lorenz, in connection with his criticism of Pavlovian conditioning referred to above, also drew a conclusion from this which is similar to Polanyi's. He said: "As far as mass manipulators are concerned, the Pavlovian dog is the ideal citizen."

7  *Tacit Dimension* (1983), pp. 9–13.

8  Ibid., p. 9.

9  Ibid., p. 10.

10 "Creative Imagination," p. 86, and "Logic and Psychology," p. 31.

11 *Tacit Dimension* (1983), p. 10.

12 Ibid.

13 "Logic and Psychology," p. 29.

14 Ibid., p. 30

15 *Tacit Dimension* (1983), p. 11.

16 Ibid., pp. 11–12. (Italics Polanyi's.)

17 Polanyi, "What Is a Painting?" *British Journal of Aesthetics*, 10 (July 1970), pp. 227–31; *Meaning*, pp. 86–92.

18 *Personal Knowledge* (1958), pp. 261–64.

19 "Creative Imagination," p. 91.

20 "Logic and Psychology," pp. 30–31; *Knowing and Being*, pp. 181–82, 185–86.

21 *Tacit Dimension* (1983), p. 13. (Italics Polanyi's.)

22 Polanyi, "The Nature of Scientific Convictions," *Nineteenth Century*, 146 (July 1949), p. 18, where he said, "The moment we notice a thing . . . we perceive it as something."

23  *Tacit Dimension* (1983), pp. 32–33. See also *Knowing and Being*, pp. 119–20, 135, 168, and *Personal Knowledge* (1958), p. 147.

24  *Tacit Dimension* (1983), p. 15.

25  Ibid., pp. 12, 14. See also "Logic and Psychology," p. 30.

26  *Tacit Dimension* (1983), p. 12.

27  "Logic and Psychology," p. 39, and *Knowing and Being*, pp. 147, 162, 237.

28  *Tacit Dimension* (1983), pp. 18–21.

29  Ibid., p. 18.

30  Ibid., pp. 20–21; *Knowing and Being*, pp. 156, 160.

Chapter Six. Generalization

1   *Knowing and Being*, p. 156.

2   Ibid., p. 172.

3   *Science, Faith and Society* (1964), p. 38.

4   *Personal Knowledge* (1958), p. 169. See also Polanyi, "Scientific Beliefs," *Ethics*, 41 (October 1950), p. 27.

5   *Science, Faith and Society* (1964), p. 28.

6   Ibid., p. 29.

7   *Personal Knowledge* (1958), p. 169.

8   *Science, Faith and Society* (1964), pp. 42–45.

9   *Knowing and Being*, pp. 123–25.

10  *Personal Knowledge* (1958), p. 88.

11  Ibid.

12  Ibid., p. 89.

13  Ibid., pp. 82–83, 89.

14  Ibid., pp. 348–49.

15  "Logic and Psychology," p. 35.

16  *Tacit Dimension* (1983), p. 22.

17  *Personal Knowledge* (1958), p. 351.

18  Ibid.

19  *Knowing and Being*, p. 168. (Italics Polanyi's.)

20  "Logic and Psychology," p. 35.

21  *Knowing and Being*, p. 168.

22  Ibid., p. 195.

23  Ibid. (Italics mine.)

24  Ibid., p. 167.

25  Ibid., p. 170.

26  Ibid., pp. 170–71.

27  *Personal Knowledge* (1958), pp. 349–50.

28  Ibid., p. 350.

29  Ibid.

30  *Knowing and Being*, p. 171.

31  *Tacit Dimension* (1983), pp. 32–33.

32  *Personal Knowledge* (1958), p. 349.

33  Ibid., n3.
34  Ibid., p. 31.
35  *Knowing and Being*, p. 172.
36  *Personal Knowledge* (1958), p. 350.
37  Ibid., p. 351. (The quotation is from Pantin's "The Recognition of Species," *Science Progress*, 42 [1954], p. 587.)
38  Ibid., pp. 351–52. (The quotation is from Harland's "The Genetical Conception of the Species," *Cambridge Biological Review*, 11 [1936], pp. 83–112. Polanyi also cited later authors—1950 and 1954—as still concerned with this apparent begging of the epistemological question that taxonomy raises.)
39  Ibid., p. 352.
40  Ibid.
41  Ibid., pp. 352–53.
42  Ibid., p. 353.
43  Ibid., pp. 353–54. (The quotation is from Lorenz's *Physiological Mechanisms in Animal Behaviour*, Symposia of the Society for Experimental Biology, No. 4 [Cambridge, 1950], p. 235.)
44  Ibid., p. 354.
45  Ibid.
46  Ibid.
47  Polanyi, "Skills and Connoisseurship," *Atti del Congresso di Metodologia*, Turin, 1952, p. 391; Polanyi, "On the Introduction of Science into Moral Subjects," *Cambridge Journal*, 7 (January 1954), pp. 199–203; "Logic and Psychology," p. 42; *Personal Knowledge* (1958), pp. 18–20, 59–60, 261–67; Polanyi, "The Study of Man," *Quest*, 29 (April–June 1961), p. 29. *Knowing and Being*, p. 107.
48  Polanyi, "Genius in Science," *Encounter* 38 (January 1972), p. 48. (The reference is to Werner Heisenberg's "From a Life of Physics," a supplement of the *Bulletin of the International Atomic Energy Agency* (1970) [Vienna], pp. 36–37.)
49  Ibid. (Polanyi's reference is to Max Planck's *Positivismus und Reale Ausenwelt* [Leipzig, 1931], p. 21.
50  Ibid., p. 49. See also Polanyi, "The Stability of Beliefs," *British Journal for the Philosophy of Science*, 3 (November 1952), pp. 228–31.
51  "Genius In Science," p. 48.
52  Ibid., p. 49.
53  "Study of Man," p. 31.
54  Polanyi, "Science: Observation and Belief," *Humanitas* 1 (February 1947), pp. 13–14. See also "Skills and Connoisseurship," p. 393.
55  *Knowing and Being*, p. 167.

CHAPTER SEVEN. DISCOVERY

1  "Study of Man," pp. 28, 30, 33–34.
2  "Genius in Science," p. 49; *Science, Faith and Society* (1964), p. 24.

3   "Creative Imagination," p. 89; *Knowing and Being*, p. 118; *Personal Knowledge* (1958), p. 128.

4   Polanyi, "Science and Reality," *British Journal for the Philosophy of Science*, 18 (November 1967), pp. 185–87, 189; *Personal Knowledge* (1958), p. 146.

5   "Science and Reality," pp. 189–96.

6   *Science, Faith and Society* (1964), pp. 21–31.

7   *Logic of Liberty*, pp. 3–90.

8   Polanyi, "Knowing and Being," *Mind*, 70 (October 1961); "The Unaccountable Element in Science," *Transactions of the Bose Research Institute*, 24 (December 1961); "My Time with X-Rays and Crystals," *Fifty Years of X-Ray Diffraction*, ed. P. P. Ewald (Utrecht, 1962); "The Republic of Science, Its Political and Economic Theory," *Minerva* 1 (October 1962); "Tacit Knowing: Its Bearing on Some Problems," "Science and Religion: Separate Dimensions or Common Ground?" *Philosophy Today*, 7 (Spring 1963); "The Potential Theory of Adsorption," *Science*, 141 (September 13, 1963); "The Structure of Consciousness," *Brain*, 88, Part 4 (1965); "Creative Imagination"; "Logic of Tacit Inference"; "Science and Reality"; "Logic and Psychology"; "Science and Man," *Proceedings of the Royal Society of Medicine*, 63 (September 1970); "Genius in Science." My citations of *Knowing and Being* in this section of the Notes are references to some of these articles as reprinted there.

9   *Knowing and Being*, p. 156; "Genius in Science," p. 50.

10  *Knowing and Being*, p. 118.

11  *Tacit Dimension* (1983), p. 22.

12  *Knowing and Being*, p. 119.

13  *Tacit Dimension* (1983), pp. 23–24.

14  Ibid., pp. 24–25. (Italics mine.)

15  Ibid., pp. 24–25, 69.

16  Ibid., pp. 77–78; "Creative Imagination," p. 92; *Personal Knowledge* (1958), pp. 256, 266, 286, 303.

17  *Personal Knowledge* (1958), pp. 300 4, 324

18  Ibid., pp. 266–67; "The Outlook of Science: Its Sickness and Cure," lecture at Austin, Texas, November 1958, p. 11 (unpublished), Michael Polanyi Papers, Box 33, Folder 11, Special Collections, University of Chicago Library.

19  *Personal Knowledge* (1958), p. 303.

20  Ibid., pp. 299–308, 324.

21  *Tacit Dimension* (1983), p. 25.

22  *Personal Knowledge* (1958), p. 403; "Genius in Science," p. 45.

23  *Tacit Dimension* (1983), p. 79. (Italics Polanyi's.)

24  Ibid.

25  "Logic and Psychology," p. 41.

26  Ibid.

27  Ibid.

28  Ibid.

29  "Science and Reality," p. 189.

30 "Genius in Science," p. 43.
31 Ibid.
32 Ibid.
33 Ibid., pp. 43–44.
34 "Logic and Psychology," p. 41.
35 Ibid., pp. 41–42.
36 "Creative Imagination," p. 88.
37 Ibid. Polanyi, "Problem Solving," *British Journal for the Philosophy of Science*, 8 (August 1957), p. 99.
38 "Creative Imagination," p. 89.
39 Ibid., p. 91. (Italics Polanyi's.)
40 Ibid.
41 Ibid.
42 Ibid., p. 92.
43 Polanyi, Comments on Thomas S. Kuhn's "The Function of Dogma in Scientific Research," *Scientific Change*, ed. A. C. Crombie (New York 1963), pp. 378–79; *Personal Knowledge* (1958), pp. 266–67.
44 "Creative Imagination," p. 89; *Tacit Dimension* (1983), pp. 80–81.
45 "Creative Imagination," p. 92.

CHAPTER EIGHT. VERIFICATION

1 *Knowing and Being*, p. 54.
2 *Personal Knowledge* (1958), p. 21; *Logic of Liberty*, p. 16; *Science, Faith and Society* (1964), pp. 22–23.
3 *Knowing and Being*, pp. 53–54.
4 *Logic of Liberty*, p. 39; *Knowing and Being*, p. 119.
5 *Logic of Liberty*, pp. 55–57; *Science, Faith and Society* (1964), pp. 12–16.
6 *Tacit Dimension* (1983), p. 80.
7 *Logic of Liberty*, pp. 26–27, 32–40, 49–57.
8 Ibid., pp. 53–57; *Knowing and Being*, pp. 49–51.
9 *Logic of Liberty*, pp. 13–15.
10 *Knowing and Being*, pp. 87–95.
11 Polanyi, "Scientific Beliefs," *Ethics*, 41 (October 1950), pp. 35–36.
12 Polanyi, "Science, Tacit and Explicit," paper presented at the International Congress for the Philosophy of Science, Jerusalem, August 1964, p. 3 (unpublished), Michael Polanyi Papers, Box 37, Folder 13, Special Collections, University of Chicago Library; "Logic and Psychology," p. 42; "Problem Solving," pp. 101–3. See also "Creative Imagination," p. 85.
13 *Science, Faith and Society* (1964), p. 30.
14 Ibid.; *Knowing and Being*, p. 105.
15 *Science, Faith and Society* (1964), p. 31; *Personal Knowledge* (1958), pp. 292–93.
16 *Science, Faith and Society* (1964), p. 31.
17 "Creative Imagination," p. 90.

18 "Logic and Psychology," pp. 36–37.

19 "Logic and Psychology," p. 37.

20 "Science, Tacit and Explicit," pp. 1–2.

21 Ibid., p. 2.

22 "Logic and Psychology," p. 42.

23 *Personal Knowledge* (1958), p. 258.

24 Ibid., pp. 287–94.

25 *Science, Faith and Society* (1964), pp. 67, 81–82.

26 Ibid., pp. 25–26.

27 Ibid., p. 81.

28 *Personal Knowledge* (1958), p. 256.

29 "Science and Reality," p. 189; "Logic and Psychology," p. 28.

30 "Logic and Psychology," pp. 28–29; "Science: Observation and Belief," p. 11; "Scientific Beliefs," p. 35; *Tacit Dimension* (1983), pp. 64–65.

31 "Logic and Psychology," pp. 29–30.

32 Ibid., pp. 30–33, 40–42; "Creative Imagination," pp. 86–88, 92.

33 "Logic and Psychology," pp. 33–34.

34 Although, as we have seen, there really is no wholly impersonal knowledge, according to Polanyi. But the degree of personal involvement in this sort of knowledge is low enough to appear to many to be absent, at least by contrast.

35 See as a very good example Albert Camus' *The Rebel*.

Chapter Nine. Ontological Hierarchies

1 Polanyi, "Science and Man's Place in the Universe," *Science as a Cultural Force*, ed. Harry Wolf (Baltimore, 1964), pp. 68, 69; *Meaning*, p. 105.

2 Polanyi, "Expanding the Range," lecture, 1971, pp. 1, 2, 4–6 (unpublished), Michael Polanyi Papers, Box 41, Folder 9, Special Collections, University of Chicago Library; *Meaning*, pp. 165–68.

3 Polanyi, "Life Transcending Physics and Chemistry," *Chemical and Engineering News*, 45 (August 1967), pp. 65–66; *Knowing and Being*, p. 232; *Tacit Dimension* (1983), pp. 41–42; *Meaning*, p. 168; Polanyi, "Letter to Professor Charles C. Gillespie," *Forum for Correspondence and Contact*, June 30, 1966, pp. 25–26.

4 "Life Transcending Physics and Chemistry," pp. 57–59; *Tacit Dimension* (1983), pp. 38–40; *Meaning*, pp. 168–69; *Study of Man* (Chicago, 1959), pp. 46–52; *Personal Knowledge* (1958), pp. 328–32; *Knowing and Being*, pp. 225–26; "Science and Man," p. 970; "Science and Man's Place," pp. 66–68.

5 "Logic and Psychology," pp. 34–35; *Personal Knowledge* (1958), pp. 328–44, 399, 402; "Life Transcending Physics and Chemistry," pp. 65–66; *Study of Man*, pp. 53–54; *Tacit Dimension* (1983), pp. 44, 50–51; *Knowing and Being*, pp. 227–28; "Science and Man's Place," p. 68; *Meaning*, pp. 169–71. See also C. F. A. Pantin, *The Relations between the Sciences* (Cambridge, 1968), pp. 35–45, 53, 74, 124, 140–41.

6   *Personal Knowledge* (1958), p. 389; *Meaning*, p. 170.

7   *Knowing and Being*, pp. 108–109, 228–29; *Personal Knowledge* (1958), pp. 34–40; *Meaning*, p. 171; "Life Transcending Physics and Chemistry," pp. 62–64.

8   *Knowing and Being*, pp. 228–29; *Meaning*, pp. 171–72; "Life Transcending Physics and Chemistry," p. 62.

9   *Knowing and Being*, p. 229; "Life Transcending Physics and Chemistry," p. 62; *Meaning*, p. 172; "Science and Man," pp. 970–71. The word "linguistic" is Professor Howard H. Pattee's word for the nondynamic aspects of DNA in "Dynamic and Linguistic Modes of Complex Systems," *International Journal of General Systems*, 3 (1977), pp. 259–66.

10  "Expanding the Range," p. 4; *Meaning*, p. 172.

11  *Personal Knowledge* (1958), pp. 38, 384–86, 389, 398, 400, 402; "Science and Man's Place," pp. 68–76; *Tacit Dimension* (1983), p. 91; Polanyi, "Science and Religion," pp 12–14; *Meaning*, pp. 172–73; Polanyi, "Thought in Society," lecture, 1964, p. 23 (unpublished), Michael Polanyi Papers, Box 37, Folder 2, Special Collections, University of Chicago Library.

12  *Tacit Dimension* (1983), pp. 88–89; *Meaning*, pp. 173, 175.

13  *Tacit Dimension* (1983), p. 90; *Knowing and Being*, p. 219; *Personal Knowledge* (1958), pp. 382–85, 400–1; *Meaning*, pp. 175–77.

14  *Tacit Dimension* (1983), p. 89; *Meaning,* p. 176.

15  *Tacit Dimension* (1983), p. 88; *Meaning,* pp. 177–78.

16  "Study of Man," pp. 28–29; *Knowing and Being*, pp. 178–79; *Personal Knowledge* (1958), p. 342; *Tacit Dimension* (1983), p. 20.

17  *Personal Knowledge* (1958), pp. 390–95; "Life Transcending Physics and Chemistry," p. 57.

18  Polanyi, "On the Modern Mind," pp. 14–15; *Tacit Dimension* (1983), pp. 34–37; *Meaning*, pp. 49–51; *Knowing and Being*, p. 238; "Science and Man's Place," pp. 70–71; "Life Transcending Physics and Chemistry," p. 59; *Personal Knowledge* (1958), p. 382.

19  *Knowing and Being*, pp. 139, 142, *Tacit Dimension* (1983), pp. 8–15; "Logic and Psychology," p. 31.

20  *Tacit Dimension* (1983), p. 34; *Meaning*, p. 37; "Study of Man," p. 31; "Tacit Knowing: Its Bearing on Some Problems," pp. 240–41; Polanyi, "Clues to an Understanding of Mind and Body," *The Scientist Speculates*, ed. I. J. Good (New York, 1962), p. 72.

21  *Knowing and Being*, p. 154; *Tacit Dimension* (1983), pp. 33–35, 41, 55; "Science and Man's Place," p. 20; *Meaning*, pp. 50, 176.

22  *Knowing and Being*, pp. 236–37; *Tacit Dimension* (1983), pp. 50–51; *Personal Knowledge* (1958), pp. 385–86; "Study of Man," p. 59; Polanyi, "Transcendence and Self-Transcendence," *Soundings*, 53 (Spring 1970), p. 91.

CHAPTER TEN. PERSONAL PARTICIPATION

1   *Personal Knowledge* (1958), pp. 388–89; *Tacit Dimension* (1983), pp. 16–18; *Knowing and Being*, pp. 126–27, 160, 237; "Science and Man's Place," p. 71.

2 *Knowing and Being*, pp. 181–82, 185–86; "Logic and Psychology," p. 30.

3 *Meaning*, pp. 100–1, 106–7, 125, and passim; *Personal Knowledge* (1958), p. 46; *Knowing and Being*, pp. 82, 199–201.

4 *Tacit Dimension* (1983), pp. 69, 77–79; *Meaning*, pp. 194–96.

5 *Personal Knowledge* (1958), pp. viii, 64, 117, 147, 189, 396; *Knowing and Being*, pp. 119–20, 168; "Science and Reality," p. 191.

6 *Personal Knowledge* (1958), pp. 143–53; *Tacit Dimension* (1983), p. 69; Polanyi, "From Copernicus to Einstein," *Encounter*, 5 (September 1955), pp. 54–63.

7 *Personal Knowledge* (1958), pp. 201–202; "On the Modern Mind," p. 20; *Meaning*, pp. 66–68, 101–2, 104, 194–95; *Tacit Dimension* (1983), pp. 76–79; "Creative Imagination," p. 92.

8 *Tacit Dimension* (1983), pp. 69, 77–79; *Meaning*, pp. 194–96.

9 *Tacit Dimension* (1983), pp. 32–33; *Knowing and Being*, pp. 135–36, 151, 168.

10 *Tacit Dimension* (1983), p. 41; *Knowing and Being*, p. 135. See also *Personal Knowledge* (1958), pp. 385–90.

11 *Personal Knowledge* (1958), pp. 379–82, 386.

12 Ibid., pp. 229–31, 237–40; *Meaning*, pp. 12–28, 106–7; "Sixty Years in Universities," pp. 3–6; *Logic of Liberty*, pp. 97–110.

13 *Personal Knowledge* (1958), pp. 347–48.

14 Ibid., p. 259.

15 Ibid., p. 258.

16 Ibid., p. 118.

17 Ibid.

18 Ibid., p. 125.

19 Ibid., pp. 127–28.

20 Ibid., p. 131.

21 Ibid., pp. 260–61.

22 Ibid., pp. 259–60.

23 Ibid., p. 187.

24 Ibid., pp. 188–89.

25 Ibid., p. 189.

26 Ibid., p. 302.

27 Ibid., p. 262.

28 Ibid., pp. 364, 399.

29 Ibid., p. 364.

30 Ibid., pp. 370–71; *Knowing and Being*, pp. 152, 169, 215–16; *Meaning*, p. 47; "Logic and Psychology," pp. 35, 37; "Study of Man," p. 65; "Clues to an Understanding," pp. 73–74; "Science and Man's Place," pp. 65–66.

31 *Personal Knowledge* (1958), p. 344.

32 Ibid., pp. 344–46, 359–67.

33 Ibid., p. 363.

34 Ibid., pp. 363–64. "Science and Man's Place," p. 71; *Knowing and Being*, p. 136; "Science and Religion," p. 12.

35 *Personal Knowledge* (1958), pp. 363, 404. (Italics Polanyi's.)

36 Ibid., pp. 377–78; *Knowing and Being*, pp. 151–52; "Study of Man," p. 34.

37 *Personal Knowledge* (1958), p. 378.

38   Ibid., pp. 378–79; "Creative Imagination," p. 92.
39   *Personal Knowledge* (1958), p. 380; "Science and Man's Place," p. 68.
40   *Personal Knowledge* (1958), pp. 197–202.


CHAPTER ELEVEN. THE ARTS

1    *Meaning*, pp. 69–70.
2    Ibid., p. 70.
3    Ibid.
4    Ibid., p. 71.
5    Ibid. (Italics Polanyi's.)
6    Ibid.
7    Ibid., pp. 71, 73. (Italics Polanyi's.)
8    Ibid., p. 72. (Italics Polanyi's.)
9    Ibid.
10   Ibid., pp. 72–73, 75; "What Is a Painting?" pp. 232–33.
11   *Meaning*, p. 73.
12   Ibid., p. 76.
13   Ibid., p. 77.
14   Ibid., p. 78.
15   Ibid. (Italics mine.)
16   Ibid.
17   Ibid.
18   Ibid., pp. 78–79.
19   Ibid., p. 78.
20   Ibid., pp. 78–79.
21   Ibid., p. 79.
22   Ibid., pp. 80, 81.
23   Ibid., p. 80.
24   Ibid., pp. 80–81; "What Is a Painting?" pp. 231–32. See also *Personal Knowledge* (1958), p. 199, for an earlier hint of this.
25   *Meaning*, pp. 83, 125; "What Is a Painting?" pp. 232–33; *Personal Knowledge* (1958), p. 200.
26   *Meaning*, pp. 83–84.
27   Ibid., p. 90.
28   Ibid., pp. 91–92; "What Is a Painting?" pp. 225–27.
29   *Meaning*, pp. 91–92.
30   Ibid., pp. 110–15.
31   Ibid., p. 115.
32   Ibid., pp. 101, 104, 108, 109, 146; "What Is a Painting?" pp. 225–27; *Personal Knowledge* (1958), pp. 196, 202.
33   *Meaning*, p. 102; *Personal Knowledge* (1958), p. 201.
34   *Meaning*, pp. 103–4.

CHAPTER TWELVE. RELIGION

1 *Meaning*, p. 117.
2 Ibid.
3 Ibid., pp. 117–18. See also *Personal Knowledge* (1958) for the "negation of familiar meaning" in an "eternal, never to be consummated hunch," p. 199.
4 *Meaning*, p. 118. (Polanyi quotes his own translation of Helmut Kuhn, *Wesen und Wirken des Kuntswerks* (Munich, 1970), pp. 67, 68.)
5 Ibid.
6 Ibid., p. 119.
7 Ibid.
8 Ibid., pp. 122–23.
9 Ibid., pp. 123–24.
10 Ibid., p. 124.
11 Ibid., pp. 124–25. (Italics Polanyi's.)
12 Ibid., p. 125. See also *Personal Knowledge* (1958), pp. 198–99, 280–81, for "tensions" in the Christian religion which Polanyi was later to grasp as transnatural unions of incompatibles.
13 *Meaning*, p. 129. See also *Personal Knowledge* (1958), pp. 197–98.
14 *Meaning*, pp. 132–33.
15 Ibid., pp. 134–35.
16 Ibid., p. 136. See also *Personal Knowledge* (1958), pp. 287–94.
17 *Meaning*, pp. 137–38.
18 Ibid., p. 138. (Italics Polanyi's.)
19 Ibid., pp. 138–39.
20 Ibid., p. 139.
21 Ibid., pp. 144–45.
22 Ibid., pp. 146–47. (Polanyi's quotation is from Mircea Eliade, *Images and Symbols* [London, 1961], p. 59.)
23 Ibid., p. 147. See also *Personal Knowledge* (1958), pp. 280, 286.
24 *Meaning*, p. 147; *Personal Knowledge* (1958), pp. 284–85.
25 *Meaning*, pp. 154–56; *Personal Knowledge* (1958), pp. 198, 281.
26 *Personal Knowledge* (1958), pp. 198, 286; *Meaning,* p. 156.
27 *Meaning*, pp. 156–57; *Personal Knowledge* (1958), pp. 198, 286, 324; Polanyi, "Faith and Reason," *Journal of Religion*, 41 (October 1961), pp. 246–47.
28 *Meaning*, p. 155.
29 Ibid., pp. 158–59; *Personal Knowledge* (1958), p. 200.
30 *Meaning*, pp. 159–60.
31 Ibid., p. 160.
32 See also "Science and Religion," especially pp. 4 and 11, and *Personal Knowledge* (1958), pp. 404–5, for earlier statements on how he thought his theory of knowledge might bear upon religious beliefs.
33 *Personal Knowledge* (1958), p. 183n.

CHAPTER THIRTEEN. THE FREE SOCIETY

1   *Personal Knowledge* (1958), pp. 219–20. Polanyi here indicated that he was
    only, in *Personal Knowledge*, casting a cursory glance at provinces of thought
    other than science—such as the humanities, arts, and religions.
2   *Meaning*.
3   *Personal Knowledge* (1958), p. 202.
4   *Logic of Liberty*, pp. 26–27, 33–40, 154–59, 162–65, 193, 198.
5   Ibid., p. 158.
6   Ibid., pp. 44, 47, 97–98, 193.
7   *Personal Knowledge* (1958), p. 252.
8   *Logic of Liberty*, pp. 25, 28–31, 44–45, 47, 193, 198.
9   Ibid., p. 198.
10  In addition to presenting public lectures and publishing essays, Polanyi also
    was active during the 1940s and 50s in proposing and supporting the Society
    for Freedom in Science, *Civitas*, a new quarterly journal published by The
    Manchester Literary and Philosophical Society (1945), the journal *Humanitas*
    (1947), the Congress for Cultural Freedom in Milan (1955) and in Berlin
    (1960), and the Committee on Science and Freedom.
11  *Logic of Liberty*, pp. 111–92.
12  Ibid., pp. 126–33; Polanyi, *Full Employment and Free Trade* (Cambridge,
    1945), pp. 142–44.
13  *Logic of Liberty*, pp. 125, 133–38.
14  Ibid., pp. 133–37, 147–48, 150–53; *Full Employment and Free Trade*, pp. 96–
    97.
15  *Logic of Liberty*, pp. 122–26.
16  See as an example his film *Unemployment and Money*, produced in 1938 (copy
    at The Museum of Modern Art, New York City).
17  Polanyi, "Visual Presentation of Social Matters," 1937, p. 12 (unpublished),
    Michael Polanyi Papers, Box 25, Folder 9, Special Collections, University
    of Chicago Library.
18  Ibid., pp. 12–15.
19  *Full Employment and Free Trade*, pp. 146–47; Polanyi, "Economics by Mo-
    tion Symbols," *Review of Economic Studies*, 8 (October 1940), pp. 16–17.
20  Polanyi, "Extract from a Letter of 27th June, 1941" (unpublished), courtesy
    of Michael Polanyi.
21  *Full Employment and Free Trade*, ch. 1; Polanyi, "The Power of Social
    Illusions," *The New Leader*, 36 (November 16, 1953), pp. 15–17.
22  *Full Employment and Free Trade*, pp. 43–44.
23  Ibid., p. 45.
24  Ibid., p. 103.
25  Ibid., p. 141.
26  Ibid., p. 93.
27  Ibid., p. 92.

28  Ibid., pp. 92–93.

29  Ibid., p. 93; "Economics by Motion Symbols," p. 18.

30  *Full Employment and Free Trade*, p. 96. (Italics Polanyi's.)

31  Ibid., p. 97.

32  Ibid.; Michael Polanyi, "Popular Education in Economics," Notes for a Political Society Lecture, November 22, 1937, p. 13 (unpublished), Michael Polanyi Papers, Box 25, Folder 9, Special Collections, University of Chicago Library.

33  "Visual Presentation of Social Matters," pp. 25–26. (Italics mine.)

34  Ibid., pp. 11, 26–27; "Economics by Motion Symbols," p. 18.

35  *Full Employment and Free Trade*, pp. 149–50.

36  Polanyi, "It has been forcibly stated . . . ," February 2, 1939, p. 3 (unpublished), Michael Polanyi Papers, Box 26, Folder 1, Special Collections, University of Chicago Library.

37  "Visual Presentation of Social Matters," p. 7.

38  Ibid., p. 8.

39  Ibid., pp. 3–4, 6.

40  "Popular Education in Economics," pp. 4–5.

41  Ibid., p. 6.

42  Ibid., pp. 6–9.

43  Polanyi, "Suggested Headings for Memorandum to the Harris Committee," 1943?, p. 3 (unpublished), Michael Polanyi Papers, Box 28, Folder 3, Special Collections, University of Chicago Library. (Italics Polanyi's.)

44  *Logic of Liberty*, pp. 169, 149.

45  Ibid., p. 187.

46  Ibid., p. 149.

47  Ibid., pp. 148–49, 189, 191–92.

48  Ibid., p. 148.

49  Ibid., pp. 194–95n; *Meaning*, pp. 208–10.

50  *Personal Knowledge* (1958), p. 215; *Tacit Dimension* (1983), pp. 85–86; *Meaning*, pp. 208–10.

51  *Personal Knowledge* (1958), p. 245; *Meaning*, pp. 213–14.

52  *Personal Knowledge* (1958), p. 245.

53  *Tacit Dimension* (1983), p. 92.

54  *Personal Knowledge* (1958), p. 404; see also p. 109.

55  *Tacit Dimension* (1983), p. 92.

56  *Meaning*, pp. 156–57, 215.

57  Polanyi, "Science and Faith," *Question*, 5 (Winter 1952), p. 45.

58  *Logic of Liberty*, pp. 192–93; *Meaning*, p. 200.

CHAPTER FOURTEEN. RATIONALE FOR AN EVALUATION.

1  See footnote 20, Chapter 3.

CHAPTER FIFTEEN. CAN "FROM–TO" AWARENESS BE UBIQUITOUS?

1   Rom Harré, "The Structure of Tacit Knowledge," *Journal of the British Society for Phenomenology*, 8 (October 1977), pp. 172–73.
2   Ibid., p. 173.
3   Ibid.
4   Ibid.
5   Ibid.
6   Ibid.
7   Ibid., p. 175.
8   "Faith and Reason," pp. 239–40; "Life's Irreducible Structure," *Science*, 160 (June 21, 1968), p. 1311.
9   Harré, "Structure of Tacit Knowledge," p. 173. (Italics mine.)
10  Ibid.
11  Ibid.
12  Ibid., p. 174.
13  Ibid.
14  Ibid., pp. 174–75.
15  Ibid., p. 177.
16  Ibid., p. 176. (Italics Harré's.)
17  Ibid., p. 177.
18  Ibid., p. 176.
19  Ibid., p. 177.
20  Ibid., p. 176. (Italics Harré's.)
21  Thomas S. Kuhn, *The Structure of Scientific Revolutions* (Chicago, 1970), p. 192.
22  "Structure of Tacit Knowledge," p. 177.
23  Marjorie Grene, "Tacit Knowing: Grounds for a Revolution in Philosophy," *Journal of the British Society for Phenomenology*, 8 (October 1977), p. 168.
24  W. V. Quine, *Ontological Relativity and Other Essays* (New York, 1969), pp. 86–87.


CHAPTER SIXTEEN. IS EPISTEMOLOGICAL ANTIREDUCTIONISM SUFFICIENT?

1   Grene, "Tacit Knowing: Grounds for a Revolution," pp. 168–69. (Italics Grene's.) Her quotation is presumably a paraphrase of "Though rooted in the body, the mind is free in its actions—exactly as our common sense knows it to be free," on p. 40 of Polanyi.
2   Ibid., p. 168. Her quotation "stratified universe" is from p. 50 of *Tacit Dimension* (1983).
3   Ibid., p. 171.
4   Ibid., p. 170.
5   *Tacit Dimension* (1983), pp. 9–13.
6   Ibid., p. 13. (Italics Polanyi's.)

7   Ibid., p. 14. (Italics Polanyi's.)
8   Grene, "Tacit Knowing: Grounds for a Revolution," pp. 165–67.
9   *Tacit Dimension* (1983), pp. 33–34. (Italics Polanyi's.)
10  Ibid., p. 34.
11  Ibid., p. 45.
12  Ibid., pp. 36–37.
13  Ibid., p. 37.
14  Pattee, "Dynamic and Linguistic Modes of Complex Systems," p. 259.
15  Ibid., p. 260.
16  Ibid.
17  Ibid., pp. 260–62.

Chapter Seventeen. The Problem of Polanyi's Divarication

1   See Richard C. Gelwick, *The Way of Discovery* (New York, 1977), especially
    pp. 101, 109, 130, 134.
2   Thomas F. Torrance, "The Integration of Form in Natural and in Theologi-
    cal Science," *Science, Medicine and Man*, ed. Peter J. M. McEwan, 1 (Ox-
    ford, 1973), pp. 143–47. (Italics Torrance's.)
3   Ibid., pp. 148–49. (Italics mine.)
4   Ibid., pp. 153–54. (Italics Torrance's.)
5   Ibid., pp. 149, 158, 160.
6   Ibid., p. 152.
7   Ibid., p. 154.
8   Ibid.
9   Ibid., pp. 154–55. (Italics mine.)
10  Ibid., p. 155. (Italics Torrance's.)
11  Ibid., p. 158.
12  Ibid., pp. 162–66.
13  Torrance, *Theological Science* (London, 1969), p. 29n. (Italics Torrance's.)
14  Ibid., p. 30. (Italics Torrance's.)
15  Ibid., p. 30n. (The quotation is from Polanyi, *Personal Knowledge*, p. 37.)
16  Ibid., p. 30. (Italics Torrance's.)
17  Ibid., pp. 30, 31, and 30n.
18  Ibid., p. 32n.
19  Ibid., p. 33. (Italics Torrance's.)
20  Ibid., pp. 264–65. (Italics Torrance's.)
21  Ibid., p. 268n.
22  Torrance, "The Integration of Form," p. 164.
23  *Theological Science*, p. 104.
24  Ibid., p. 299.
25  Ibid., pp. 299–300. Torrance's quotation is from Polanyi, *Personal Knowl-
    edge* (1958), p. 284.
26  Torrance, "The Integration of Form," pp. 165–66, 169; *Theological Science*,
    p. 52; and see also pp. 302, 351, and *passim*. (Italics Torrance's.)
27  Torrance, "The Integration of Form," p. 162.

Chapter Eighteen. Polanyi Contra Torrance

1   *Personal Knowledge* (1958), p. 283. (Italics Polanyi's.)
2   Ibid., pp. 283–84.
3   Ibid., p. 279.
4   Ibid., p. 133.
5   Ibid., p. 311. (Italics Polanyi's.)
6   Ibid., p. 202.
7   Ibid., p. 189. (Italics mine.)
8   Ibid., p. 302.
9   Ibid., p. 201.
10  Ibid., p. 202. (Italics Polanyi's.)
11  Ibid., p. 280.
12  Ibid., p. 281.
13  Ibid.
14  Ibid.
15  Ibid., p. 283n. (Polanyi's quotation is from Paul Tillich, *Systematic Theology*, 1 [London, 1953], p. 144.)
16  Ibid., p. 284.
17  Ibid.
18  Ibid., pp. 284–85.
19  Ibid., p. 283n.
20  Ibid. (Polanyi's quotation is from Tillich, *Systematic Theology*, p. 144.)
21  Polanyi, "Meaning," lecture, 1970, pp. 19–20 (unpublished), Michael Polanyi Papers, Box 41, Folders 1–2, Special Collections, University of Chicago Library.
22  Polanyi, "Acceptance of Religion," lecture 1969, p. 12 (unpublished), Michael Polanyi Papers, Box 40, Folder 1, Special Collections, University of Chicago Library.
23  Terence Kennedy, *The Morality of Knowledge* (Rome, 1979), pp. 138–40.
24  Ibid., p. 139n.
25  Ibid., pp. 171–72.
26  Ibid., pp. 193–94.


Chapter Nineteen. Can Dualism Be Avoided?

1   Sheldon Richmond, "On Making Sense: Some Comments on Polanyi's and Prosch's *Meaning*," *Philosophy of the Social Sciences*, 9 (1979), p. 215.
2   Ibid., pp. 216–17.
3   Ibid., p. 217.
4   Ibid.
5   Ibid. Richmond, on pages 217–19, actually has a few reservations about Polanyi's success in this task. They are not, however, of telling importance, in my opinion.
6   Ibid., pp. 211–12, 210, 213.

7   Ibid., p. 214.
8   Ibid., p. 216.
9   Ronald L. Hall, "Michael Polanyi on Art and Religion: Some Critical Reflections on *Meaning*," *Zygon*, 17 (1982), p. 15.
10  Ibid., pp. 12–13.
11  Ibid., p. 13.
12  Ibid.
13  Ibid., p. 14.
14  Ibid.
15  Ibid., p. 15.
16  Ibid., p. 16.
17  Ibid., p. 18.
18  Ibid., p. 17.
19  Ibid., p. 18.
20  Ibid., p. 17.
21  *Personal Knowledge* (1958), p. 18.

CHAPTER TWENTY. AND SUB SPECIE AETERNITATIS

1   Polanyi, "Meaning: A Project," 1969, p. 1 (unpublished), Michael Polanyi Papers, Box 39, Folder 6, Special Collections, University of Chicago Library.
2   *Personal Knowledge* (1958), p. 109. Polanyi pointed out here that he was attempting in this book "to resolve by conceptual reform the apparent self-contradiction entailed in believing what I might conceivably doubt."
3   Carl J. Friedrich, "A Review of *Personal Knowledge*," *Natural Law Forum*, 7 (1962), pp. 132–48.
4   Henry C. Simons, *Economic Policy for a Free Society* (Chicago, 1948).
5   Ibid., pp. 52, 57–62. Simons, of course, advocates a coherent, integrated set of important changes in our economic institutional framework, especially in his second essay, "A Positive Program for Laissez-Faire."
6   Polanyi, "The Structure of Consciousness," p. 806.
7   *Personal Knowledge* (1958), pp. 33, 340–41, 369.
8   Polanyi, "The Mind–Body Relation," *Man and the Science of Man*, ed. William R. Coulson and Carl R. Rogers (Columbus, Ohio, 1968), pp. 86–87; "Tacit Knowing: Its Bearing on Some Problems," p. 256; "Logic and Psychology," p. 33.
9   Polanyi, "Beauty, Elegance and Reality in Science," *Observation and Interpretation*, ed. S. Korner (New York, 1957), p. 118.

# Bibliography of Michael Polanyi's Publications

BOOKS BY MICHAEL POLANYI

*A Békeszerzökhöz*, Benko Gyula Cs. És Ker (Budapest: 1917)
*Atomic Reactions*, Williams and Norgate (London: 1932)
*U.S.S.R. Economics*, Manchester University Press (Manchester: 1936)
*General Physics*, with P. Debye, F. Simon, M. Wiersma, C. V. Raman, and B. van der Pol, Herman (Paris: 1938)
*The Contempt of Freedom*, C. A. Watts (London: 1940)
*Full Employment and Free Trade*, Cambridge University Press (London: 1945)
*Science, Faith and Society*, Oxford University Press (London: 1946)
*The Logic of Liberty*, The University of Chicago Press (Chicago: 1951)
*Personal Knowledge,* The University of Chicago Press (Chicago: 1958)
*The Study of Man*, The University of Chicago Press (Chicago: 1959)
*Beyond Nihilism*, Cambridge University Press (London: 1960)
*Jenseits des Nihilismus*, D. Reidel (Dordrecht: 1961)
*Ciencia, Fe y Sociedad*, Taurus Ediciones (Madrid: 1961)
*Personal Knowledge*, with a new Preface by the author, Harper (New York: 1964)
*Science, Faith and Society*, with a new Introduction by the author, The University of Chicago Press (Chicago: 1964)
*The Tacit Dimension*, Doubleday (Garden City: 1966) (reprint, Peter Smith (Gloucester, Mass., 1983)
*El Estudio del Hombre*, Editorid Paidos AAICF (Bucnos Aircs: 1966)
*Knowing and Being, Essays by Michael Polanyi*: ed. Marjorie Grene, The University of Chicago Press (Chicago: 1969)

*Scientific Thought and Social Reality, Essays by Michael Polanyi*: ed. Fred Schwartz, *Psychological Issues*, 8, Monograph 32, International Universities Press (New York, 1974)
*Meaning*, with Harry Prosch, The University of Chicago Press (Chicago, 1975)

## SCIENTIFIC PAPERS BY MICHAEL POLANYI★

★Permission has been kindly granted by Routledge and Kegan Paul, Ltd.., to list here Michael Polanyi's scientific publications from *The Logic of Personal Knowledge, Essays Presented to Michael Polanyi on his Seventieth Birthday 11th March 1961.* Routledge and Kegan Paul (London: 1961), pp. 239–47.

### 1910

1   Chemistry of the Hydrocephalic Liquid. *Magyar ord. Archiv.*, N.F. 11, p. 116 (1910).

### 1911

2   Investigation of the Physical and Chemical Changes of the Blood Serum during Starvation. *Biochem. Z.*, 34, p. 192 (1911).
3   Contribution to the Chemistry of the Hydrocephalic Liquid. *Biochem. Z.*, 34, p. 205 (1911).

### 1913

4   With J. Baron, On the Application of the Second Law of Thermodynamics to Processes in the Animal Organism, *Biochem. Z.*, 53, p. 1 (1913).
5   A New Thermodynamic Consequence of the Quantum Hypothesis. *Verh. deut. phys. Ges.*, 15, p. 156 (1913).
6   New Thermodynamic Consequences of the Quantum Hypothesis. *Z. phys. Chem.*, 83, p. 339 (1913).

### 1914

7   Adsorption and Capillarity from the Standpoint of the Second Law of Thermodynamics. *Z. phys. Chem.*, 88, p. 622 (1914).
8   Adsorption, Swelling and Osmotic Pressure of Colloids. *Biochem. Z.*, 66, p. 258 (1914).
9   On the Derivation of Nernst's Theorem. *Verh. deut. phys. Ges.*, 16, p. 333 (1914).
10   On Adsorption from the Standpoint of the Third Law of Thermodynamics. *Verh. deut. phys. Ges.*, 16, p. 1012 (1914).

1915

11 On the Derivation of Nernst's Theorem. *Verh. deut. phys. Ges.*, 17, p. 350 (1915).

1916

12 Adsorption of Gases by a Solid Non-Volatile Adsorbent. *Verh. deut. phys. Ges.*, 18, p. 55 (1916).
13 New Procedure to Save Washing Materials. Vegyeszeti Lapok 12 (1916).

1917

14 Adsorption of Gases by a Solid Non-Volatile Adsorbent. *Ph. D. Thesis, Budapest* (1917).
15 On the Theory of Adsorption. *Magyar Chem. Folyoirat*, 23, p. 3 (1917).

1919

16 With L. Mandoki, On the Causes of the Conductivity of Casein Solutions. *Magyar Chem. Folyoirat*, 25 (1919).
17 Conductivity-Lowering and Adsorption in Lyophilic Colloids. *Magyar Chem. Folyoirat*, 25 (1919).

1920

18 Reaction Isochore and Reaction Velocity from the Standpoint of Statistics. *Z. Elektrochem.*, 26, p. 49 (1920).
19 On the Absolute Saturation of Attractive Forces Acting between Atoms and Molecules. *Z. Elektrochem.*, 26, p. 261 (1920).
20 On the Problem of Reaction Velocity. *Z. Elektrochem.*, 26, p. 228 (1920).
21 Correction to the Paper "Reaction Isochore and Reaction Velocity from the Standpoint of Statistics." *Z. Elektrochem.*, 26, p. 231 (1920).
22 On Adsorption and the Origin of Adsorption Forces. *Z. Elektrochem.*, 26, p. 370 (1920).
23 On the Nonmechanical Nature of Chemical Processes. *Z. Physik*, 1, p. 337 (1920).
24 On the Theory of Reaction Velocity. *Z. Physik*, 2, p. 90 (1920).
25 Adsorption from Solutions of Substances of Limited Solubility. *Z. Physik*, 2, p. 111 (1920).
26 On the Origin of Chemical Energy. *Z. Physik*, 3, p. 31 (1920).
27 With R. O. Herzog and W. Jancke, X-Ray Spectroscopic Investigations on Cellulose, II. *Z. Physik*, 3, p. 343 (1920).
28 Studies on Conductivity-Lowering and Adsorption in Lyophilic Colloids. *Biochem. Z.*, 104, p. 237 (1920).

29    With L. Mandoki, The Origins of Conductivity in Casein Solutions. *Biochem. Z.*, 104, p. 257 (1920).

30    Advances in the Theoretical Explanation of Adsorption. *Chem. Ztg.*, 44, p. 340 (1920).


*1921*

31    On the Adsorption of Gases on Solid Substances. *Festschr. Kaiser Wilhelm Ges. Zehnjahr. Jub.*, p. 171 (1921).

32    Fibrous Structure by X-Ray Diffraction. *Naturwiss.*, 9, p. 337 (1921).

33    On the Current Resulting from the Compression of a Soldered Joint. *Z. phys. Chem.*, 97, p. 459 (1921).

34    On Adsorption Catalysis. *Z. Elektrochem.*, 27, p. 142 (1921).

35    With E. Ettisch and K. Weissenberg, Fibrous Structure of Hard-Drawn Metal Wires. *Z. phys. Chem.*, 99, p. 332 (1921).

36    With K. Becker, R. O. Herzog, and W. Jancke, On Methods for the Arrangement of Crystal Elements. *Z. Physik*, 5, p. 61 (1921).

37    The X-Ray Fibre Diagram. *Z. Physik*, 7, p. 149 (1921).

38    With M. Ettisch and K. Weissenberg, On Fibrous Structure in Metals. *Z. Physik*, 7, p. 181 (1921).

39    On the Nature of the Tearing Process. *Z. Physik*, 7, p. 323 (1921).

40    With E. Ettisch and K. Weissenberg, X-Ray Investigation of Metals. *Physik. Z.*, 22, p. 646 (1921).


*1922*

41    The Reinforcement of Monocrystals by Mechanical Treatment. *Z. Elektrochem.*, 28, p. 16 (1922).

42    Reflection on Mr. A. Euchen's Work: *On the Theory of Adsorption Processes. Z. Elektrochem.*, 28, p. 110 (1922)

43    Determination of Crystal Arrangement by X-Ray Diffraction. *Naturwiss.*, 10, p. 411 (1922).

44    With K. Weissenberg, The X-Ray Fibre Diagram. *Z. Physik*, 9, p. 123 (1922).

45    With K. Weissenberg, The X-Ray Fibre Diagram. *Z. Physik*, 10, p. 44 (1922).

46    With H. Mark and E. Schmid, Processes in the Stretching of Zinc Crystals. I. General Description of the Phenomena and Research Methods. *Z. Physik*, 12, p. 58 (1922).

47    With H. Mark and E. Schmid, Processes in the Stretching of Zinc Crystals. II. Quantitative Consideration of the Stretching Mechanism. *Z. Physik*, 12, p. 78 (1922).

48    With H. Mark and E. Schmid, Processes in the Stretching of Zinc Crystals, III. Relationship between the Fibre Structure and Reinforcement. *Z. Physik*, 12, p. 111 (1922).

*1923*

49    With K. Weissenberg, Röntgenographic Investigations on Worked Metals. *Z. tech. Physik*, 4, p. 199 (1923).

50    With E. Schmid, "Discussion of the Sliding Friction Dependence on Pressure Normal to the Sliding Plane. *Z. Physik*, 16, p. 336 (1923).

51    On Structural Changes in Metals through Cold Working. *Z. Physik*, 17, p. 42 (1923).

52    With H. Mark, Lattice Structure, Sliding Directions and Sliding Planes of White Tin. *Z. Physik*, 18, p. 75 (1923).

53    With R. O. Herzog and W. Jancke, On the Structure of the Cellulose and Silk Fibre. *Z. Physik*, 20, p. 413 (1923).

54    With G. Masing, Cold Working and Reinforcement. *Erg. exakt. Naturw.*, 2, p. 177 (1923).

55    Structural Analysis by Means of X-Rays. *Physik. Z.*, 24, p. 407 (1923).

56    With H. Mark and E. Schmid, Investigations of Monocrystalline Wires of Tin. *Naturwiss.*, 11, p. 256 (1923).


*1924*

57    With H. Mark, Correction to the Paper "Lattice Structure, Sliding Directions and Sliding Planes of White Tin." *Z. Physik*, 22, p. 200 (1924).

58    With E. Schiebold and K. Weissenberg, On the Development of the Rotating Crystal Method. *Z. Physik*, 23, p. 337 (1924).

59    With E. Ewald, Plasticity and Strength of Rock Salt under Water. *Z. Physik*, 28, p. 29 (1924).

60    With G. Masing, On the Increase of Tensile Strength of Zinc by Cold-Working. *Z. Physik*, 28, p. 169 (1924).

61    Osmotic Pressure, Pressure of Swelling, and Adsorption. *Z. phys. Chem.*, 114, p. 387 (1924).

62    With E. Schmid, On the Structure of Worked Metals. *Z. tech. Physik*, 5, p. 580 (1924).

63    With A. Schob, Stretching Experiments with Soft Vulcanized Rubber at the Temperature of Liquid Air. *Mitt. Materialprüfungsamt*, 42, p. 22 (1924).


*1925*

64    Deformation of Monocrystals. *Z. Krist.*, 61, p. 49 (1925).

65    Moulding of Solid Bodies from the Standpoint of Crystal Structure. *Vortr. Dresden. Tag.Ges.angew. Math.Mech.*, 5, p. 125 (1925).

66    An Elongating Apparatus for Threads and Wires. *Z. tech. Physik*, 6, p. 121 (1925).

67    With E. Ewald, On the Form Strengthening of Rock Salt in Bending Experiments. *Z. Physik*, 31, p. 139 (1925).

68    With E. Ewald, Remarks on the Work of A. Joffe and M. Levitzky, "On the Limits of Strength and Elasticity of Natural Rock Salt." *Z. Physik*, 31, p. 746 (1925).

69   With E. Schmid, Strengthening and Weakening of Sn Crystals. *Z. Physik*, 32, p. 684 (1925).

70   With E. Wigner, Formation and Decomposition of Molecules. *Z. Physik*, 33, p. 429 (1925).

71   With G. Sachs, On Elastic Hysteresis and Internal Strains in Bent Rock–Salt Crystals. *Z. Physik*, 33, p. 692 (1925).

72   With M. Fischenich, The Origins of Conductivity in Casein Solutions. *Kolloid-Z.*, 36, p. 275 (1925).

73   With H. Beutler, Chemiluminescence and Reaction Velocity. *Naturwiss.*, 13, p. 711 (1925).

74   Crystal Deformation and Strengthening. *Z. Metallkunde*, 17, p. 94 (1925).

75   With G. Sachs, On the Release of Internal Strains by Annealing. *Z. Metallkunde*, 17, p. 227 (1925).


### 1926

76   With H. Beutler and S. v. Bogdandy, On Luminescence of Highly Dilute Flames. *Naturwiss.*, 14, p. 164 (1926).

77   With S. v. Bogdandy, Ejection of Atoms from Solids by Chemical Attack on the Surface. *Naturwiss.*, 14, p. 1205 (1926).

78   Moulding of Metal Crystals, and the Moulded State. *Werkstoff ausschuss Bericht*, No. 85, p. 1 (1926).

79   With S. v. Bogdandy and J. Boehm, On a Method of Producing Molecular Mixtures. *Z. Physik*, 40, p. 211 (1926).

80   Behaviour of Neutral Sodium Caseinogate in Membrane Hydrolysis. *Biochem. Z.*, 171, p. 473 (1926).

81   With G. Sachs, Elastic Hysteresis in Rock Salt. *Nature*, 116, p. 692 (1926).


### 1927

82   With R. L. Hasche and E. Vogt, Spectral Intensity Distribution in the D-line of the Chemiluminescence of Sodium Vapour. *Z. Physik*, 41, p. 583 (1927).

83   The Structure of Matter and X-Ray Diffraction. *Z. Ver. deut. Ing.*, 71, p. 565 (1927).

84   With S. v. Bogdandy, Rapid Analysis of Brass. *Z. Metallkunde*, 19, p. 164 (1927).

85   With S. v. Bogdandy, Chemically-Induced Chain Reaction in Detonating Gas. *Naturwiss.*, 15, p. 410 (1927).

86   Theory of Wall Reactions. *Chem. Rund. Mitteleuropa Balkan*, 4, p. 160 (1927).

87   With S. v. Bogdandy, Rapid Brass Analysis. *Metal Ind.* (London), 30, p. 195 (1927).

88   With S. v. Bogdandy, Chemically Induced Chain Reactions in Mixtures of Halogens, Hydrogen and Methane. *Z. Elektrochem.*, 33, p. 554 (1927).

## 1928

89   Reply to the Letter of O. L. Sponster, "Erroneous Determination of the Cellulose Space Lattice." *Naturwiss.*, 16, p. 263 (1928).

90   Deformation, Rupture and Hardening of Crystals. *Naturwiss.*, 16, p. 285 (1928).

91   Theoretical and Experimental Strength. *Naturwiss.*, 16, p. 1043 (1928).

92   With F. Goldmann, Adsorption of Vapours on Carbon and the Thermal Dilation of the Interface. *Z. phys. Chem.*, 132, p. 321 (1928).

93   With K. Welke, Adsorption, Heat of Adsorption and Character of Attachment between Small Amounts of Sulphur Dioxide and Carbon. *Z. phys. Chem.*, 132, p. 371 (1928).

94   With W. Heyne, Adsorption from Solutions. *Z. phys. Chem.*, 132, p. 384 (1928).

95   With L. Frommer, On Heterogeneous Elementary Reactions. I. Action of Chlorine on Copper. *Z. phys. Chem.*, 137, p. 201 (1928).

96   Application of Langmuir's Theory to the Adsorption of Gases on Charcoal. *Z. phys. Chem.*, A 138, p. 459 (1928).

97   With E. Wigner, On the Interference of Characteristic Vibrations as the Cause of Energy Fluctuations and Chemical Changes. *Z. phys. Chem.*, A 139, p. 439 (1928).

98   With H. Beutler, On Highly Dilute Flames, I. *Z. phys. Chem.*, B 1, p. 3 (1928).

99   With S. v. Bogdandy, On Highly Dilute Flames, II. Nozzle Flames. Increase of Light Emission with Increasing Partial Pressure of Sodium Vapour. *Z. phys. Chem.*, B 1, p. 21 (1928).

100  With G. Schay, On Highly Dilute Flames. III. Sodium-Chlorine Flame. Evidence for and Analysis of the Reaction and Luminescence Mechanism. Both Reaction Types. Survey of the Whole Work. *Z. phys. Chem.*, B 1, p. 30 (1928).

101  With G. Schay, Correction to the Work, "On Highly Dilute Flames, III." *Z. phys. Chem.*, B 1, p. 384 (1928).

102  On the Simplest Chemical Reactions. *Réunion Intern. Chim., Phys.*, p. 198 (1928).

103  With H. Beutler, On Highly Dilute Flames, I. *Z. Physik*, 47, p. 379 (1928).

104  With G. Schay, Chemiluminescence between Alkali Metal Vapours and Tin Halides. *Z. Physik*, 47, p. 814 (1928).

105  Deformation, Rupture and Hardening of Crystals. *Trans. Faraday Soc.*, 24, p. 72 (1928).

106  The Inhibition of Chain Reactions by Bromine. *Trans. Faraday Soc.*, 24, p. 606 (1928).

## 1929

107  Principles of the Potential Theory of Adsorption. *Z. Elektrochem.*, 35, p. 431 (1929).

108   Consideration of Activation Processes at Surfaces. *Z. Elektrochem.*, 35, p. 561 (1929).
109   With E. Schmid, Problems of Plasticity. Deformation at Low Temperatures. *Naturwiss.*, 17, p. 301 (1929).

### 1930

110   On the Nature of the Solid State. *Metallwirt.*, 9, p. 553 (1930).
111   With L. Frommer, On Gas Phase Luminescence in a Heterogeneous Reaction. *Z. phys. Chem.*, B 6, p. 371 (1930).
112   With H. v. Hartel, On Atomic Reactions Possessing Inertia. *Z. phys. Chem.*, B 11, p. 97 (1930).
113   With W. Meissner and E. Schmid, Measurements with the Aid of Liquid Helium, XII: Plasticity of Metal Crystals at Low Temperatures. *Z. Physik*, 66, p. 477 (1930).
114   With H. Eyring, On the Calculation of the Energy of Activation. *Naturwiss.*, 18, p. 914 (1930).
115   With F. London, The Theoretical Interpretation of Adsorption Forces. *Naturwiss.*, 18, p. 1099 (1930).
116   With E. Schmid, Problems of Plasticity: Deformation at Low Temperatures. *Mitt deut. Materialprüfungs Anst. Sonderheft*, 10, p. 101 (1930).
117   The Nature of the Solid State. *Umchau*, 34, p. 1001 (1930) and *Mitt. deut. Materialprüfungs Anst. Sonderheft*, 13, p. 113 (1930).

### 1931

118   With H. Eyring, On Simple Gas Reactions. *Z. phys. Chem.*, B 12, p. 279 (1931).
119   With E. Cremer, Estimation of Molecular Lattice Dimensions from Resonance Forces. *Z. phys. Chem.*, B 14, p. 435 (1931).
120   With E. Cremer, Decrease of Fundamental Frequency as the First Stage of Chemical Reaction. *Z. phys. Chem. Bodenstein Festband*, p. 720 (1931).
121   With P. Beck, Recovery of Recrystallizing Ability by Reformation. *Z. Elektrochem.*, 37, p. 521 (1931).
122   With P. Beck, Recovery of Recrystallizing Power by Reformation. *Naturwiss.*, 19, p. 505 (1931).
123   Atomic Reactions. *Z. angew. Chem.*, 44, p. 597 (1931).

### 1932

124   With H. Ekstein, Note on the Mechanism of the Reaction $H_2 + I_2 \rightarrow 2\,HI$ and of Similar Reactions at Surfaces. *Z. phys. Chem.*, B 15, p. 334 (1932).
125   With E. Horn and H. Sattler, On Highly Dilute Flames of Sodium Vapour with Cadmium Halides and Zinc Chloride. *Z. phys. Chem.*, B 17, p. 220 (1932).

126 With H. v. Hartel and N. Meer, Investigation of the Reaction Velocity between Sodium Vapour and Alkyl Chlorides. *Z. phys. Chem.*, B 19, p. 139 (1932).

127 With N. Meer, Comparison of the Reactions of Sodium Vapour with Other Organic Processes. *Z. phys. Chem.*, B 19, p. 164 (1932).

128 With E. Cremer, Test of the "Tunnel" Theory of Heterogeneous Catalysis: the Hydrogenation of Styrene. *Z. phys. Chem.*, B 19, p. 443 (1932).

129 Developments in the Theory of Chemical Reactions. *Naturwiss.*, 20, p. 289 (1932).

130 With D. W. G. Style, On an Active Product of the Reaction between Sodium Vapour and Alkyl Halides. *Naturwiss.*, 20, p. 401 (1932).

131 *Atomic Reactions.* Williams & Norgate, (London, 1932).

132 Theories of the Adsorption of Gases. A General Survey and Some General Remarks. *Trans. Faraday Soc.*, 28, p. 316 (1932).

133 The Theory of Chemical Reactions. *Uspekhi Khim.*, 1, p. 345 (1932).


*1933*


134 With S. v. Bogdandy and G. Veszi, On a Method for the Preparation of Colloids and for Hydrogenation with Atomic Hydrogen. *Angew. Chem.*, 46, p. 15 (1933) and *Chem. Fabrik*, 6, p. 1 (1933).

135 With E. S. Gilfillan, Micropycnometre for the Determination of Displacements of Isotopic Ratio in Water. *Z. phys. Chem.*, A 166, p. 254 (1933).

136 With E. Bergmann and A. Szabo, The Mechanism of Simple Substitution Reactions and the Walden Inversion. *Z. phys. Chem.*, B 20, p. 161 (1933).

137 With J. Curry, On the Reaction between Sodium Vapour and Cyanogen Halides. *Z. phys. Chem.*, B 20, p. 276 (1933).

138 With E. Cremer, The Conversion of o- into p-Hydrogen in the Solid State. *Z. phys. Chem.*, B 21, p. 459 (1933).

139 With E. Horn and D. W. G. Style, On the Isolation of Free Methyl and Ethyl by the Reaction between Sodium Vapour and Methyl and Ethyl Bromides. *Z. phys. Chem.*, B 23, p. 291 (1933).

140 With E. Cremer and J. Curry, On a Method for the Determination of the Velocity of Gaseous Reactions of Atomic Hydrogen. *Z. phys. Chem.*, B 23, p. 445 (1933).

141 A Note on the Electrolytic Separation of Heavy Hydrogen by the Method of G. N. Lewis. *Naturwiss.*, 21, p. 316 (1933).

142 With E. Bergmann, Autoracemization, and Velocity of Electrolytic Dissociation. *Naturwiss.*, 21, p. 378 (1933).

143 Adsorption and Capillary Condensation. *Phys. Z. Sowjetunion*, 4, p. 144 (1933).

144 A Method for the Measurement of Gaseous Reactions. *Nature*, 132, p. 747 (1933).

145 With J. Horiuti, A Catalysed Reaction of Hydrogen with Water. *Nature*, 132, p. 819 (1933).

146 With J. Horiuti, Catalyzed Reaction of Hydrogen with Water, and the Nature of Over-voltage. *Nature*, 132, p. 931 (1933).
147 Atomic Reactions. *Uspekhi Khim.*, 2, p. 412 (1933).


*1934*

148 With E. Horn, On the Isolation of Free Phenyl Radicals by the Reaction of Sodium Vapour with Bromobenzene. *Z. phys. Chem.*, B 25, p. 151 (1934).
149 With E. Horn and D. W. G. Style, The Isolation of Free Methyl and Ethyl by the Reaction between Sodium Vapour and Methyl and Ethyl Bromides. *Trans. Faraday Soc.*, 30, p. 189 (1934).
150 With A. L. Szabo, On the Mechanism of Hydrolysis. The Alkaline Saponification of Amyl Acetate. *Trans. Faraday Soc.*, 30, p. 508 (1934).
151 With L. Frommer, A Net Method for Measuring the Rate of High Velocity Gas Reactions. *Trans. Faraday Soc.*, 30, p. 519 (1934).
152 With J. Horiuti and G. Ogden, Catalytic Replacement of Haplogen by Diplogen in Benzene. *Trans. Faraday Soc.*, 30, p. 663 (1934).
153 With J. Horiuti, Exchange Reaction of Hydrogen on Metal Catalysts. *Trans. Faraday Soc.*, 30, p. 1164 (1934).
154 With R. A. Ogg, Jr., The Mechanism of Ionogenic Reactions. *Mem. Proc. Manchester Lit. Phil. Soc.*, 78, p. 41 (1934).
155 With J. Horiuti, On the Mechanism of Ionisation of Hydrogen at a Platinum Electrode. *Mem. Proc. Manchester Lit. Phil. Soc.*, 78, p. 47 (1934).
156 On a Form of Lattice Distortion that May Render a Crystal Plastic. *Z. Physik*, 89, p. 660 (1934).
157 Reaction Rates of the Hydrogen Isotopes. *Nature*, 133, p. 26 (1934).
158 With J. Horiuti, Catalytic Hydrogen Replacement, and the Nature of Over-voltage. *Nature*, 133, p. 142 (1934).
159 With B. Cavanaugh and J. Horiuti, Enzyme Catalysis of the Ionisation of Hydrogen. *Nature*, 133, p. 797 (1934).
160 With J. Horiuti, Catalytic Interchange of Hydrogen between Water and Ethylene and between Water and Benzene. *Nature*, 134, p. 377 (1934).
161 With J. Horiuti, Direct Introduction of Deuterium into Benzene. *Nature*, 134, p. 847 (1934).
162 With R. A. Ogg, Jr. and L. Werner, Optical Inversion by Negative Substitution. *Chem. and Ind.*, 53, p. 614 (1934).
163 Discussion on Heavy Hydrogen. *Proc. Roy. Soc. (London)*, A 144, p. 14 (1934).
164 Discussion on Energy Distribution in Molecules. *Proc. Roy. Soc. (London)*, A 146, p. 253 (1934).
165 With W. Heller, Quantitative Studies of Atomic Reactions. *Compt. rend.*, 199, p. 1118 (1934).
166 Discussion of Methods of Measuring and Factors Determining the Speed of Chemical Reactions. *Proc. Roy. Soc. (London)*, B 116, p. 202 (1934).

*1935*

167  With R. A. Ogg, Jr., Substitution of Free Atoms and Walden Inversion. The Decomposition and Racemisation of Optically Active sec-Butyl Iodide in the Gaseous State. *Trans. Faraday Soc.*, 31, p. 482 (1935).

168  With R. A. Ogg, Jr., Mechanism of Ionic Reactions. *Trans. Faraday Soc.*, 31, p. 604 (1935).

169  With M. G. Evans, Some Applications of the Transition State Method to the Calculation of Reaction Velocities, Especially in Solution. *Trans. Faraday Soc.*, 31, p. 875 (1935).

170  With R. A. Ogg, Jr., Diabatic Reactions and Primary Chemiluminescence. *Trans. Faraday Soc.*, 31, p. 1375 (1935).

171  Heavy Water in Chemistry. *Nature*, 135, p. 19 (1935).

172  With J. Kenner and P. Szego, Aluminum Chloride as a Catalyst of Hydrogen Interchange. *Nature*, 135, p. 267 (1935).

173  With G. H. Bottomley and B. Cavanagh, Enzyme Catalysis of the Exchange of Deuterium with Water. *Nature*, 136, p. 103 (1935).

174  Adsorption and Catalysis. *J. Soc. Chem. Ind.*, 54, p. 123 (1935).

175  Heavy Water. *J. Soc. Dyers Colourists*, 51, p. 90 (1935).

176  With J. Horiuti, Principles of a Theory of Proton Transfer. *Acta Physicochim. U.S.S.R.*, 2, p. 505 (1935).

*1936*

177  With W. Heller, Reactions between Sodium Vapour and Volatile Polyhalides, Velocities and Luminescence. *Trans. Faraday Soc.*, 32, p. 663 (1936).

178  With E. Bergmann and A. L. Szabo, Substitution and Inversion of Configuration. *Trans. Faraday Soc.*, 32, p. 843 (1936).

179  With M. G. Evans, Further Considerations on the Thermodynamics of Chemical Equilibria and Reaction Rates. *Trans. Faraday Soc.*, 32, p. 1333 (1936).

180  With D. D. Eley, Catalytic Interchange of Hydrogen with Water and Alcohol. *Trans. Faraday Soc.*, 32, p. 1388 (1936).

181  With M. Calvin and E. G. Cockbain, Activation of Hydrogen by Phthalocyanine and Copper Phthalocyanine, I. *Trans. Faraday Soc.*, 32, p. 1436 (1936).

182  With M. Calvin and D. D. Eley, Activation of Hydrogen by Phthalocyanine and Copper Phthalocyanine, II. *Trans. Faraday Soc.*, 32, p. 1443 (1936).

183  With M. G. Evans, Equilibrium Constants and Velocity Constants. *Nature*, 157, p. 530 (1936).

184  With C. Horrex, Atomic Interchange between Water and Saturated Hydrocarbons. *Mem. Proc. Manchester Lit. Phil. Soc.*, 80, p. 33 (1936).

### 1937

185  With M. G. Evans, On the Introduction of Thermodynamical Variables into Reaction Kinetics. *Trans. Faraday Soc.*, 33, p. 448 (1937).
186  The Transition State in Chemical Reactions. *J. Chem. Soc.*, p. 629 (1937).
187  The Transition State in Chemical Kinetics. *Nature*, 139, p. 575 (1937).
188  Catalytic Activation of Hydrogen. *Sci. J. Roy. Coll. Sci.*, 7, p. 21 (1937).
189  Colours as Catalysts. *J. Oil Col. Chem. Assoc.*, Buxton Conf. No. 3 (1937).

### 1938

190  With M. G. Evans, Inertia and Driving Force of Chemical Reactions. *Trans. Faraday Soc.*, 34, p. 11 (1938).
191  On the Catalytic Properties of Phthalocyanine Crystals. *Trans. Faraday Soc.*, 34, p. 1191 (1938).
192  The Deformation of Solids. Report Reunion Int. Phys. Chim. Biol., (1938).
193  With P. Debye, F. Simon, M. Wiersma, C. V. Raman, and B. van der Pol, *General Physics*, Hermann & Cie, Paris (1938).

### 1939

194  With M. G. Evans, Notes on the Luminescence of Sodium Vapour in Highly Dilute Flames. *Trans. Faraday Soc.*, 35, p. 178 (1939).
195  With C. Horrex and R. K. Greenhalgh, Catalytic Exchange of Hydrogen. *Trans. Faraday Soc.*, 35, p. 511 (1939).
196  With R. K. Greenhalgh, Hydrogenation and Atomic Exchange of Benzene. *Trans. Faraday Soc.*, 35, p. 520 (1939).

### 1940

197  With A. R. Bennett, Influence of Acidity on Catalytic Exchange of Hydrogen and Water. *Trans. Faraday Soc.*, 36, p. 377 (1940).
198  With E. T. Butler, Influence of Substitution on Organic Bond Strength. *Nature*, 146, p. 129 (1940).
199  With E. C. Baughan, Energy of Aliphatic Carbon Linking. *Nature*, 146, p. 685 (1940).

### 1941

200  With E. C. Baughan and M. G. Evans, Covalency, Ionisation and Resonance in Carbon Bonds. *Trans. Faraday Soc.*, 37, p. 377 (1941).
201  With E. C. Baughan, Activation Energy of Ionic Substitution. *Trans. Faraday Soc.*, 37, p. 648 (1941).
202  With M. G. Evans, Effect of Negative Groups on Reactivity. *Nature*, 148, p. 436 (1941).

*1942*

203   With A. G. Evans, Calculation of Steric Hindrance. *Nature*, 149, p. 608 (1942).

*1943*

204   With E. T. Butler, Rates of Pyrolysis and Bond Energies of Substituted Organic Iodides, I. *Trans. Faraday Soc.*, 39, p. 19 (1943).
205   Resonance and Chemical Reactivity. *Nature*, 151, p. 96 (1943).
206   With A. G. Evans, Steric Hindrance and Heats of Formation. *Nature*, 152, p. 738 (1943).

*1945*

207   With E. T. Butler and E. Mandel, Rates of Pyrolysis and Bond Energies of Substituted Organic Iodides. II. *Trans. Faraday Soc.*, 41, p. 298 (1945).

*1946*

208   With A. G. Evans, D. Holden, P. H. Plesch, H. A. Skinner, and M. A. Weinberger, Fricdel-Crafts Catalysts and Polymerization. *Nature*, 157, p. 102 (1946).
209   Activation of Catalysts in Olefine Reactions. *Nature*, 157, p. 520 (1946).
210   With A. G. Evans and G. W. Meadows, Friedel-Crafts Catalysts and Polymerization. *Nature*, 158, p. 94 (1946).

*1947*

211   With A. G. Evans, Polymerization of iso-Butene by Friedel-Crafts Catalysts. *J. Chem. Soc.*, 1947, p. 252.
212   With P. H. Plesch and H. A. Skinner, The Low Temperature Polymerization of iso-Butene by Friedel-Crafts Catalysts. *J. Chem. Soc.*, 1947, p. 257.
213   With A. G. Evans and M. G. Evans, Mechanism of Substitution at a Saturated Carbon Atom. *J. Chem. Soc.*, 1947, p. 558.
214   With A. G. Evans and G. W. Meadows, Friedel-Crafts Catalysts and Polymerization. *Rubber Chem. and Technol.*, 20, p. 375 (1947).
215   With A. G. Evans and G. W. Meadows, Polymerization of Olefines by Friedel-Crafts Catalysts. *Nature*, 160, p. 869 (1947).

*1948*

216   Polymerization at Low Temperatures. *Angew. Chem.*, 60 A, p. 76 (1948).

*1949*

217   Mechanism of Chemical Reactions. *Endeavour*, 8, p. 3 (1949).

218 Experimental Proofs of Hyperconjugation. *J. Chim. Phys.*, 46, p. 235 (1949).

PUBLISHED ARTICLES, ESSAYS, REVIEWS, AND FILMS BY MICHAEL POLANYI

### 1935

"U.S.S.R. Economics—Fundamental Data, System, and Spirit." *The Manchester School of Economic and Social Studies*, 6 (November 1935), pp. 67–89. Published also as the third essay in *The Contempt of Freedom*, 1940.

### 1936

"The Value of the Inexact." *Philosophy of Science*, 3 (April 1936), pp. 233–34.
"The Struggle between Truth and Propaganda." *The Manchester School of Economic and Social Studies*, 7 (October 1936), pp. 105–18. Published also as the fourth essay in *The Contempt of Freedom*, 1940.

### 1937

"Congrés du Palais de la Découverte." *Nature*, 140 (October 23, 1937), p. 710.

### 1938

*Unemployment and Money*. Film with Handbook, Science Film Limited (London: 1938).
"The 'Settling Down' of Capital and the Trade Cycle." *The Manchester School of Economic and Social Studies*, 9 (November 1938), pp. 153–69.

### 1939

"The Rights and Duties of Science." *The Manchester School of Economic and Social Studies*, 10 (October 1939), pp. 175–93. Published also 1945, and in *The Contempt of Freedom*, 1940.
Review of *A Critique of Russian Statistics*, by Colin Clark. *The Manchester School of Economic and Social Studies*, 10 (October 1939), pp. 202–3.

### 1940

"Science in the U.S.S.R." *The New Statesman and Nation*, 19 (February 10, 1940), p. 174.
"Economics on the Screen." *Documentary News Letter* (August 1940), pp. 5–6.
"Economics by Motion Symbols." *The Review of Economic Studies*, 8 (October 1940), pp. 1–19.

## 1941

"Cultural Significance of Science." *Nature*, 147 (January 25, 1941), p. 119.

"The Growth of Thought in Society." *Economica*, 8 (November 1941), pp. 428–56. [Similar to "Economic and Intellectual Liberties," 1950, and to Chapter 10 of *The Logic of Liberty*, 1951.]

## 1942

"Decline and Revival of Acid-Base Catalysis Theory," Review of *Acid-Base Catalysis*, R. P. Bell. *Nature*, 149 (January 24, 1942), p. 103.

"Modern Theory of Chemical Reactions," Review of *The Theory of Rate Processes*, by Samuel Glasstone, Keith J. Laidler, and Henry Eyring. *Nature*, 149 (May 9, 1942), pp. 509–10.

"The Revaluation of Science." *The Manchester Guardian*, November 7, 1942, p. 6.

## 1943

"Jewish Problems." *The Political Quarterly*, 14 (January–March 1943). pp. 33–45.

"The Autonomy of Science." *Memoirs and Proceedings of the Manchester Literary and Philosophical Society*, 85 (February 1943), pp. 19–38. Published also 1945 and 1974 [same], and as Chapter 4 of *The Logic of Liberty*, 1951 [substantially the same].

"Economics of Full Employment." *The Manchester Guardian*, February 13, 1943, p. 4.

"Research and Planning." *Nature*, 152 (August 21, 1943), pp. 217–18.

"The Hungarian Opposition." *The New Statesman and Nation*, 26 (October 2, 1943), pp. 216–17.

"The English and the Continent." *The Political Quarterly*, 14 (October–December 1943), pp. 372–81. Published also as "England and the Continent," 1944 [substantially the same].

## 1944

"Science—Its Reality and Freedom." *The Nineteenth Century*, 135 (February 1944), pp. 78–83.

"England and the Continent." *Fortune*, 29 (May 1944), pp. 155–57, 178, 182, 185. Published also as "The English and the Continent," 1943 [substantially the same].

"Science and the Decline of Freedom." *The Listener*, June 1, 1944, p. 599.

"Patent Reform." *The Review of Economic Studies*, 11 (Summer 1944), pp. 61–76.

"Reflections on John Dalton." *The Manchester Guardian*, July 22, 1944, pp. 4 and 6. Published also as "Dalton's Theory," 1952.

Review of *The Economics of Peace*, by Kenneth E. Boulding. *The Manchester School of Economic and Social Studies*, 14 (September 1946), pp. 81–86.

*1945*

Review of *What Is Life?* by Erwin Schrodinger. *The Manchester Guardian*, January 26, 1945, p. 3.

"The Autonomy of Science." *The Scientific Monthly*, 60 (February 1945), pp. 141–50. Published also 1943 and 1974 [same], and as Chapter 4 of *The Logic of Liberty*, 1951 [substantially the same].

"The Rights and Duties of Science." *Society for Freedom of Science*. Occasional Pamphlet No. 2. (Oxford: June 1945). Published also 1939 and in *The Contempt of Freedom*, 1940.

In *Science, the Universities and the Modern Crisis*, from *Memoirs and Proceedings of the Manchester Literary and Philosophical Society*, 86, 1943–45 Sessions. (Manchester: June 1945). "Science and the Modern Crisis," pp. 107–16. Published also 1974 [substantially the same]. "Preface," p. viii. "Postscript," pp. 61–63.

Review of *Mission of the University*, by José Ortega y Gasset. *The Manchester Guardian*, June 1, 1945, p. 3.

Review of *Science and the Planned State*, by J. R. Baker. *The Manchester Guardian*, June 27, 1945, p. 3.

"Reform of the Patent Law in Britain." *Nature*, 156 (July 14, 1945), p. 54.

"The Planning of Science." *The Political Quarterly*, 16 (October–December, 1945), pp. 316–28. Published also 1946 [same], and as Chapter 5 of *The Logic of Liberty*, 1951 [substantially the same].

"The Value of Pure Science." *Time and Tide*, 26 (December 15, 1945), pp. 1054–55.

*1946*

Review of *Soviet Economic System*, by Alexander Baykov. *The Manchester Guardian*, March 27, 1946, p. 3.

"The Social Message of Pure Science." *The Advancement of Science*, No. 12 (April 1946), pp. 288–90. Published also 1974 [same], and as Chapter 1 of *The Logic of Liberty*, 1951 [substantially the same].

"Soviets and Capitalism: What Is the Difference?" *Time and Tide*, 27 (April 6, 1946), p. 317.

"Social Capitalism." *Time and Tide*, 27 (April 13, 1946), pp. 341–42.

"Can Science Bring Peace?" *The Listener*, April 25, 1946, pp. 531–32. Published also 1948.

"Why Profits?" *The Plain View*, July 1946, pp. 197–208, and in *Humanitas*, 5 (1946), pp. 4–13. Published also as Chapter 9 of *The Logic of Liberty*, 1951 [substantially the same].

"Rededication of Science in Germany." *Nature*, 158 (July 13, 1946), p. 66.

"Policy of Atomic Science." *Time and Tide*, 27 (August 10, 1946), p. 749.

"The Foundations of Freedom in Science." *The Bulletin of the Atomic Scientists*, 2 (December 1, 1946), pp. 6–7. Published also 1947 [substantially the same].

"Free Trade through Full Employment." *University Liberal*, 3 (December 1946), pp. 1–2.

"The Planning of Science." Society for Freedom in Science Occasional Pamphlet No. 4 (Oxford: 1946). Published also 1945 [same], and as Chapter 5 of *The Logic of Liberty*, 1951 [substantially the same].

### 1947

"Old Tasks and New Hopes." *Time and Tide*, 28 (January 4, 1947), pp. 5–6.

"Science: Observation and Belief." *Humanitas*, 1 (February 1947), pp. 10–15.

"The Foundations of Freedom in Science." *The Nineteenth Century*, 141 (March 1947), pp. 163–67. Published also 1946 and in *Physical Science and Human Values*, ed. E. P. Wigner. Princeton University Press (Princeton, N. J.: 1947), pp. 124–32 [substantially the same]. Also, discussion, pp. 61–62.

"The Foundations of Academic Freedom." *The Lancet*, May 3, 1947, pp. 583–86. Published also in Society for Freedom in Science Occasional Pamphlet No. 6 (Oxford: September, 1947), pp. 3–18, and as Chapter 3 of *The Logic of Liberty*, 1951 [substantially the same].

"Organization of Universities, I." *Time and Tide*, 28 (July 19, 1947), p. 777.

"Organization of Universities, II." *Time and Tide*, 28 (July 26, 1947), pp. 802–803.

Review of *Russlands Volkswirtschaft unter dem Sowjets*, by S. N. Prokopovicz. *Economica*, 14 (May 1947), pp. 156–58.

"What Kind of Crisis?" *Time and Tide*, 28 (October 4, 1947), pp. 1056–58.

"Russian Science," Review of *Scientist in Russia*, by Eric Ashby. *The Manchester Guardian*, October 24, 1947, p. 3.

Reply to Eric Ashby's Letter to the Editor. *The Manchester Guardian*, November 1, 1947, p. 4.

"Humanitas." *Humanitas*, 2 (Autum 1947), p. 1.

"Science: Academic and Industrial." *Universities Quarterly*, 2 (November 1947), pp. 71–76. [Different from 1961 article of same title.]

### 1948

"The Universities Today." *The Adelphi*, 24 (January–March 1948), pp. 98–101.

"Power Politics," Review of *Scientific Man versus Power Politics*, by Han J. Morgenthau. *The Manchester Guardian*, February 24, 1948, p. 3.

"The Free Society." *Time and Tide*, 29 (March 13, 1948), pp. 265–66.

Review of *Man's Last Choice*, by E. M. Friedwald. *Discovery*, March 1948, pp. 94–95.

"The Place of Universities in the Community." *The Advancement of Science*, 5 (April 1948), pp. 13–15. (A report of Polanyi's position on this question in a discussion.)

"Ought Science To Be Planned? The Case for Individualism." *The Listener*, September 16, 1948, pp. 412–13. Published also as "The Case for Individualism," 1949 and as Chapter 6 of *The Logic of Liberty*, 1951 [substantially the same].

"Planning and Spontaneous Order." *The Manchester School of Economic and Social Studies*, 16 (September 1948), pp. 237–68. Published also as Chapter 8 of *The Logic of Liberty*, 1951 [substantially the same].

Review of *Reflections on the Revolution of Our Time*, by Harold J. Laski. *The Manchester Guardian*, October 8, 1948, p. 3.

Obituary for Professor Kornél de Körösy. *Nature*, December 18, 1948, pp. 953–54.

"Profits and Private Enterprise." *Economic Problems in a Free Society*, Lecture 4 Central Joint Advisory Committee on Tutorial Classes (London: 1948), pp. 50–62.

"Can Science Bring Peace?" *The Challenge of Our Time*, ed. Grace Wyndham-Goldie Percival Marshall (London: 1948), pp. 41–55. Published also 1946.


1949


"The Case for Individualism." *The Bulletin of the Atomic Scientists*, 5 (January, 1949), pp. 19–20. Published also as "Ought Science To Be Planned?" 1948 and as Chapter 6 of *The Logic of Liberty*, 1951 [substantially the same].

"Social Adjustment," Review of *Alternative to Serfdom*, by John Maurice Clark, *The Manchester Guardian Weekly*, February 17, 1949, p. 12.

Review of *Planning and the Price Mechanism*, by J. E. Meade. *Economica*, 16 (May 1949), pp. 169–70.

"Mr. Koestler," Review of *Insight and Outlook*, by Arthur Koestler, *The Manchester Guardian*, June 28, 1949, p. 4.

"The Nature of Scientific Convictions." *The Nineteenth Century*, 146 (July 1949), pp. 14–27. Published also 1974 [same], and as "Scientific Convictions and the Free Society," 1950, and as Chapter 2 of *The Logic of Liberty*, 1951 [substantially the same].

"Research," Review of *The Principles of Scientific Research*, by Paul Freedman. *The Manchester Guardian*, August 9, 1949, p. 4, and *The Manchester Guardian Weekly*, August 18, 1949, p. 11.

Review of *Individualism and Economic Order*, by F. A. Hayek. *Economica*, 16 (August 1949), pp. 267–68.

"The Authority of the Free Society." *The Nineteenth Century*, 146 (December 1949), pp. 347–60.


1950


"Scientific Convictions and the Free Society." *The Bulletin of Atomic Scientists*, 6 (February 1950), pp. 38–42. Published also as "The Nature of Scientific Convictions," 1949, 1951, and 1974 [substantially the same].

"Freedom in Science." *The Bulletin of Atomic Scientists*, 6 (July 1950), pp. 195–98 and 224. [In part the same as "Die Freiheit der Wissenschaft" and "Autorität und Freiheit in der Wissenschaft," 1951]

"Scientific Beliefs," *Ethics*, 61 (October 1950), pp. 27–37. Published also 1974, and as "Der Glaube an die Wissenschaft," 1950.

"Der Glaube an die Wissenschaft," *Physikalische Blätter*, 6 (October 1950), pp. 337–49. Published also as "Scientific Beliefs," 1950 and 1974.

Review of *Scientific Autobiography and Other Papers*, by Max Planck. *The Manchester Guardian*, October 6, 1950, p. 4.

Review of *Testament for the Social Sciences*, by Barbara Wooten. *The Manchester Guardian*, November 28, 1950, p. 4.

"The Logic of Liberty: Perils of Inconsistency," *Measure*, 1 (Fall 1950), pp. 348–62. Published also as Chapter 7 of *The Logic of Liberty*, 1951.

"Economic and Intellectual Liberties," *Zeitschrift für die Gesamte Staatswissenschaft*, 106 (1950), pp. 411–47. Published also as Chapter 10 of *The Logic of Liberty*, 1951 [substantially the same]. [Similar to "The Growth of Thought in Society," 1941.]

## 1951

"Planning for Freedom," Review of *Freedom, Power, and Democratic Planning*, by Karl Mannheim. *The Manchester Guardian*, July 3, 1951, p. 4.

"Totalitarianism," Review of *Origins of Totalitarianism*, by Hannah Arendt. *Time and Tide*, 32 (August 25, 1951), pp. 801–2.

"Marx and the Peasant," Review of *Marx Against the Peasant*, by David Mitrany. *The Manchester Guardian*, December 21, 1951, p. 3.

"Die Freiheit der Wissenschaft," *Physikalische Blätter*, 7 (1951), pp. 49–55. [In part the same as "Freedom in Science," 1950.]

"Autorität und Freiheit in der Wissenschaft," *Physikalische Blätter*, 7 (1951), pp. 97–102. [In part the same as "Freedom in Science," 1950.]

## 1952

Review of *Science and Humanism*, by Erwin Schrödinger. *The Manchester Guardian*, January 18, 1952, p. 4.

"The Hypothesis of Cybernetics." *The British Journal for the Philosophy of Science*, 2 (February 1952), pp. 312–15.

"Why? What for?" Review of *Conspiracy of Silence*, by Alex Weissberg. *The Manchester Guardian*, March 28, 1952, p. 4.

"Russell on War and Peace," Review of *The Impact of Science on Society*, by Bertrand Russell. *The Manchester Guardian*, May 16, 1952, p. 4.

"Some British Experiences." *The Bulletin of the Atomic Scientists*, 8 (October 1952), pp. 223–28.

"The Stability of Beliefs," *The British Journal for the Philosophy of Science*, 3 (November 1952), pp. 217–32.

"Mannheim's Historicism," Review of *Essay in the Sociology of Knowledge*, by Karl Mannheim. *The Manchester Guardian*, December 9, 1952, p. 4.

"Skills and Connoisseurship." *Atti del Congresso di Metodologia*. F. de Silva (Turin: 1952), pp. 381–95.

"Science and Faith." *Question*, 5 (Winter 1952), pp. 15–36. Published also as "Science and Conscience," 1953 [substantially the same]. Also, discussion, pp. 37–45.

"Dalton's Theory." *L. Farkas Memorial Volume*, ed. Adalbert Farkas and E. P. Wigner (Government Printers of Israel, Jerusalem: 1952), pp. 13–15. Published also as "Reflections on John Dalton," 1944.

## 1953

"Scientism," Review of *The Counter Revolution in Science*, by F. A. Hayek. *The Manchester Guardian*, January 2, 1953, p. 3.

"Marx and St. Paul," Review of *Marxism: An Interpretation*, by Aladair C. MacIntyre. *The Manchester Guardian*, March 17, 1953, p. 4.

"Social Illusions." *Christian News-Letter*, April 1953, pp. 77–82. [Almost identical to "The Power of Social Illusions," 1953.]

"Scholarship," Review of *Sociology of Communism*, by Jules Monnerot. *The Manchester Guardian*, May 26, 1953, p. 2.

"America and Europe," Review of *The Estrangement of Western Man*, by Robert Strausz-Hupé. *The Manchester Guardian*, July 28, 1953, p. 3.

"Applied Sociology," Review of *Science and the Social Order*, by Bernard Barber. *The Manchester Guardian*, October 27, 1953, p. 4.

"The Power of Social Illusions." *The New Leader*, 36 (November 16, 1953), pp. 15–17. [Almost identical to "Social Illusions," 1953.]

"Protests and Problems." *Time and Tide*, 34 (July 25, 1953), pp. 984–85. Published also in *The Bulletin of the Atomic Scientists*, 9 (November 1953), pp. 322 and 340.

"Pure and Applied Science and Their Appropriate Forms of Organization." Society for Freedom in Science Occasional Pamphlet No. 14. (Oxford: December 1953). Published also 1955, 1956 [same].

"Science and Conscience." *Religion in Life*, 23 (Winter 1953–54), pp. 47–58. Published also as "Science and Faith," 1952 [substantially the same].

## 1954

"On the Introduction of Science into Moral Subjects." *The Cambridge Journal*, 7 (January 1954), pp. 195–207. Published also 1974.

"Foundations of Morality," Review of *Realms of Value*, by Ralph Barton Perry. *The Manchester Guardian*, October 1, 1954, p. 4.

"Hide and Seek," Review of *The Invisible Writing*, by Arthur Koestler. *Time and Tide*, 35 (July 3, 1954), pp. 886–87. Published also as "Koestler's Inner Struggle," 1954.

"Koestler's Inner Struggle," Review of *The Invisible Writing*, by Arthur Koestler. *The New Leader*, 37 (October 11, 1954), pp. 18–19. Published also as "Hide and Seek," 1954.

"Physics and Philosophy," Review of *Science and the Common Understanding*, by J. Robert Oppenheimer. *The Manchester Guardian*, October 12, 1954, p. 4.

"A Letter from the Chairman." *Science and Freedom, A Bulletin of the Committee on Science and Freedom*, 1 (Oxford: November 1954), p. 7.

"Sociology Surveyed," Review of *Science and Social Action*, by W. J. H. Sprott. *The Manchester Guardian Weekly*, December 16, 1954, p. 10.

### 1955

"Logic of Stalinism," Review of *The Appeals of Communism*, by Gabriel A. Almond. *The Manchester Guardian*, March 8, 1955, p. 4.

"On Liberalism and Liberty." *Encounter*, 4 (March 1955), pp. 29–34.

"From Copernicus to Einstein," *Encounter*, 5 (September 1955), pp. 54–63. Published also 1974.

"Words, Conceptions and Science." *The Twentieth Century*, 157 (September 1955), pp. 256–67.

In *Science and Freedom*. Congress for Cultural Freedom (Boston: 1955). "Pure and Applied Science and Their Appropriate Forms of Organization." pp. 36–46. Published also 1953, 1956. "Preface," pp. 9–11. Discussion, passim, pp. 47–56.

### 1956

"This Age of Discovery." *The Twentieth Century*, 159 (March 1956), pp. 227–34. Published also as "Our New Age of Discovery," 1956.

"Our New Age of Discovery." *The New Leader*, 39 (May 7, 1956), pp. S26–S30. Published also as "This Age of Discovery," 1956.

"Passion and Controversy in Science," *The Lancet*, 270 (June 16, 1956), pp. 921–25. Published also 1957. [very similar].

"The Magic of Marxism," *The Bulletin of the Atomic Scientists*, 12 (June 1956), pp. 211–15, 232. Published also in *A Special Supplement to the Bulletin of the Committee on Science and Freedom*, November 1956, pp. 4–20, in *Encounter*, 7 (December 1956), pp. 5–17, and as "Die Magie des Marxismus," 1958 [very similar].

"Ethics and the Scientist." *The Bulletin of the Institute of Physics*, July 1956, pp. 1–21. Edited discussions by Polanyi, pp. 9–14, 16, 19, and 20.

"Pure and Applied Sciences and Their Appropriate Forms of Organization." *Dialectica*, 10 (September 15, 1956), pp. 231–42. Published also 1953, 1955.

"What Is Truth?" Review of *Society and Knowledge*, by V. G. Childe. *The Manchester Guardian*, October 26, 1956, p. 8.

"The Next Stage of History." *A Special Supplement to the Bulletin of the Committee on Science and Freedom*, November 1956, pp. 21–24. Also, "Preface," p. 3.

### 1957

Letter to the Editor *The Bulletin of the Atomic Scientists*, 13 (January 1957), p. 40.

"Scientific Outlook: Its Sickness and Cure." *Science*, 125 (March 15, 1957), pp. 480–84.

"Oscar Jaszi and Hungarian Liberalism." *Science and Freedom*, 1 (April, 1957), p. 7.

"Passion and Controversy in Science." *The Bulletin of the Atomic Scientists*, 13 (April 1957), pp. 114–19. Published also 1956 [slightly different].

"Problem Solving." *The British Journal for the Philosophy of Science*, 8 (August 1957), pp. 89–103.

"The Foolishness of History: November, 1917–November, 1957." *Encounter*, 9 (November 1957), pp. 33–37.

"Beauty, Elegance and Reality in Science." *Observation and Interpretation*, ed. S. Korner. Academic Press (New York: 1957), pp. 102–6. Also, discussion throughout. Reprinted from *Colston Papers: Proceedings of the Ninth Symposium of the Colston Research Society*, 9 University of Bristol (Bristol: 1957).

### 1958

"On Biased Coins and Related Problems." *Zeitschrift für Physikalische Chemie*, 15 (April 1958), pp. 290–96.

"The Committee on Science and Freedom and Apartheid." *Science and Freedom*, 10 (June 1958), pp. 9–11.

"Editorial." *Science and Freedom*, 11 (June, 1958), pp. 5–8.

"The Impact of Science." *Quest* (Bombay), 19 (October–December 1958), pp. 32–35.

"Die Magie des Marxismus." *Der Monat*, 11 (December 1958), pp. 3–15. Published as "The Magic of Marxism," 1956 [substantially the same].

### 1959

"Tyranny and Freedom, Ancient and Modern." *Quest* (Bombay), 20 (January–March 1959), pp. 9–18.

"A Philosophy of Perception," Review of *The Nature of Experience*, by Sir Russell Brain. *Brain*, 82 (June 1959), pp. 292–93.

"Darwin and His Evolution," Review of *Darwin and the Darwinian Revolution*, by G. Himmelfarb. *The New Leader*, August 31, 1959, pp. 24–25.

"The Two Cultures." *Encounter*, 13 (September 1959), pp. 61–64. Published also 1969.

"The Organization of Science and the Claim to Academic Freedom." *Science and Freedom*, 13 (November 1959), pp. 135–43.

### 1960

"An Epic Theory of Evolution," Review of *The Phenomenon of Man*, by Pierre Teilhard de Chardin. *Saturday Review*, 43 (January 30, 1960), p. 21.

Acceptance Speech of LeComte du Nouy Foundation Award to Michael Polanyi. *The Christian Scholar*, 43 (March 1960), pp. 57–58.

"Beyond Nihilism." *Encounter*, 14 (March 1960), pp. 34–43. Published also 1962, 1969 [substantially the same].

Closing Address of the Tenth Anniversary of the General Assembly of the Congress, Berlin, June 22, 1960. Congress for Cultural Freedom (Calcutta: 1960).

"Towards a Theory of Conspicuous Production." *Soviet Survey*, 34 (October–December 1960), pp. 90–99. [Somewhat similar to "Conspicuous Production," 1964.]

"Morals—A Product of Evolution," Review of *The Ethical Animal*, by C. H. Waddington. *The New Scientist*, December 22, 1960, pp. 1666–67.


## 1961

"The Study of Man." *Quest* (Bombay), 29 (April–June 1961), pp. 26–35.

"Faith and Reason." *The Journal of Religion*, 41 (October 1961), pp. 237–47. Published also 1974 [same], and as "Scientific Revolution," 1961 [substantially the same].

"Knowing and Being." *Mind*, 70 (October 1961), pp. 458–70. Published also 1969.

"The Unaccountable Element in Science." *Transactions of the Bose Research Institute*, 24 (December 1961), pp. 175–84. Published also 1962, 1969, and as "Experience and the Perception of Pattern," 1963. [substantially the same].

"Science—Academic and Industrial." *Journal of the Institute of Metals*, 89 (1961), pp. 401–6. [Different from 1947 article of same title.]

"Scientific Revolution." *The Student World*, 54 (1961), pp. 287–302. Published also as "Faith and Reason," 1961, 1974 [substantially the same].

Comments on Adolph Grünbaum's "The Genesis of the Special Theory of Relativity." *Current Issues in the Philosophy of Science*, ed. Herbert Feigl and Grover Maxwell. Holt, Rinehart and Winston (New York: 1961), pp. 53–55.


## 1962

"The Unaccountable Element in Science." *Philosophy*, 37 (January 1962), pp. 1–14. Published also in *Philosophy Today*, 6 (Fall 1962), pp. 171–82. Published also 1961, 1969 [same], and as "Experience and the Perception of Pattern," 1963 [substantially the same].

"History and Hope: An Analysis of Our Age." *The Virginia Quarterly Review*, 38 (Spring 1962), pp. 177–95.

"The Republic of Science, Its Political and Economic Theory." *Minerva*, 1 (October 1962), pp. 54–73. Published also 1968, 1969.

"Tacit Knowing: Its Bearing on Some Problems of Philosophy." *Reviews of Modern Physics*, 34 (October 1962), pp. 601–16. Published also in *Philosophy Today*, 6 (Winter 1962), pp. 239–61. Published also 1969.

In *History and Hope*, ed. K. A. Jekenski, A. Praeger (New York: 1962):
  "Beyond Nihilism." pp 17–35. Published also 1960, 1969 [substantially the same].
  "A Postscript," pp. 185–96.

"Clues to an Understanding of Mind and Body." *The Scientist Speculates*, ed. I. J. Good, Basic Books (New York: 1962), pp. 71–78.

"My Time with X-Rays and Crystals." *Fifty Years of X-Ray Diffraction*, ed. P. P. Ewald. Oosthoek (Utrecht: 1962), pp. 629–36. Published also 1969.

### 1963

"Science and Religion: Separate Dimensions or Common Ground?" *Philosophy Today*, 7 (Spring 1963), pp. 4–14.

"The Potential Theory of Adsorption." *Science*, 141 (September 13, 1963), pp. 1010–13. Published also 1969.

"Experience and the Perception of Pattern." *The Modeling of Mind*, ed. Kenneth M. Sayer and Frederick J. Crossen. Notre Dame University Press (South Bend, Ind.: 1963), pp. 207–20. Published also as "The Unaccountable Element in Science," 1961, 1962, 1969 [substantially the same].

Comments on Thomas S. Kuhn's "The Function of Dogma in Scientific Research." *Scientific Change*, ed. A. C. Crombie, Basic Books (New York: 1963), pp. 375–80.

### 1964

"The Feelings of Machines." *Encounter*, 22 (January 1964), pp. 85–86.

"Conspicuous Production." *Quest* (Bombay), 41 (April–June, 1964), pp. 16–21. [Somewhat similar to "Towards a Theory of Conspicuous Production," 1960.]

"Science and Man's Place in the Universe," *Science as a Cultural Force*, ed. Harry Wolf. Johns Hopkins Press (Baltimore: 1964), pp. 54–76.

### 1965

"On the Modern Mind." *Encounter*, 24 (May 1965), pp. 12–20. Published also 1974.

"The Structure of Consciousness." *Brain*, 88, Part 4 (1965), pp. 799–810. Published also 1969, in *Knowing and Being* [same] and *Anatomy of Knowledge* [substantially the same]. [Similar to "The Mind–Body Relation," 1968.]

### 1966

"The Creative Imagination." *Chemical and Engineering News*, 44 (April 25, 1966), pp. 85–93. Published also 1967, 1969 [substantially the same].

"Letter to Professor Charles C. Gillispie." *Forum for Correspondence and Contract*, June 30, 1966, pp. 23–27.

"Polanyi's Logic." *Encounter*, 27 (September 1966), p. 92.

"The Logic of Tacit Inference." *Philosophy*, 41 (January 1966), pp. 1–18. Published also 1969, 1970.

"Continuity and Contract: A Discussion between D. M. Mackinnon, R. H. S. Crossman, K. B. Smellie and M. Polanyi." *Ideas and Beliefs of the Victorians*, BBC Third Programme Broadcasts, 1948. E. P. Dutton (New York: 1966), pp. 433–45.

"The Message of the Hungarian Revolution." *American Scholar*, 35 (Autumn 1966), pp. 661–76. Published also 1969.

## 1967

"Life Transcending Physics and Chemistry." *Chemical and Engineering News*, 45 (August 1967), pp. 54–66.

"The Growth of Science in Society." *Minerva*, 5 (Summer 1967), pp. 533–45. Published also 1968, 1969.

"Sense-Giving and Sense-Reading." *Philosophy*, 42 (October 1967), pp. 301–25. Published also 1968, 1969.

"Science and Reality." *The British Journal for the Philosophy of Science*, 18 (November 1967), pp. 177–96.

"The Creative Imagination." *Tri-Quarterly*, 8 (Winter 1967), pp. 111–23. Published also 1966, 1969 [substantially the same].

## 1968

"Wider die Skepsis des modernen Denkens." *Gehört Gelesen*, January 1968, pp. 28–40.

"Logic and Psychology." *The American Psychologist*, 23 (January 1968), pp. 27–43.

"A Conversation with Michael Polanyi," Interviewer Mary Harrington Hall. *Psychology Today*, 1 (May 1968), pp. 20–25, 65–67.

"Life's Irreducible Structure." *Science*, 160 (June 21, 1968), pp. 1308–12. Published also 1969.

In *Criteria for Scientific Development, Public Policy, and National Goals*, ed. Edward Shils. Massachusetts Institute of Technology (Cambridge, Mass.: 1968):
"The Republic of Science," pp. 1–20. Published also 1962, 1969.
"The Growth of Science in Society," pp. 187–99. Published also 1967, 1969, and in *Man and the Science of Man*, 1968.

In *Man and the Science of Man*, ed. William R. Coulson and Carl R. Rogers. Charles E. Merrill (Columbus, Ohio: 1968):
"The Growth of Science in Society," pp. 11–26. Published also 1967, 1969 and in *Criteria for Scientific Development, Public Policy, and National Goals*, 1968.
Discussion, pp. 27–29.
"The Mind–Body Relation," pp. 85–102 [similar to "The Structure of Consciousness," 1965, 1969].
Discussion, pp. 103–12.
"Polanyi's Oral Response to Bar-Hillel," pp. 120–23.

"Letter to Bar-Hillel," pp. 124–27.

"Excerpts from the Discussion," pp. 135–47, 154–65, and 174–88.

"A Dialogue" (with Carl R. Rogers), pp. 193–201.

"Sense-Giving and Sense-Reading." *Intellect and Hope*, ed. Thomas A. Langford and William H. Poteat. Duke University Press (Durham, N.C.: 1968), pp. 402–31. Published also 1967, 1969.

## 1969

"On Body and Mind." *The New Scholasticism*, 43 (Spring 1969), pp. 195–204.

"The Determinants of Social Action." *Roads to Freedom*, ed. Erich Streissler. Augustus M. Kelly (New York: 1969), pp. 165–79.

"The Creative Imagination." *Toward a Unity of Knowledge*, ed. Marjorie Grene. (Psychological Issues, 6, 1969, Monograph 22), pp. 53–70. And discussions including Polanyi throughout. Main essay published also 1966, 1967 [substantially the same].

In *The Anatomy of Knowledge*, ed. Marjorie Grene. Routledge & Kegan Paul (London: 1969):

"The Message of the Hungarian Revolution," pp. 149–64. Published also 1966 and in *Knowing and Being*, 1969.

"The Structure of Consciousness," pp. 315–28. Published also 1965 and in *Knowing and Being*, 1960 [substantially the same]. [Similar to "The Mind-Body Relation," 1968.]

In *Knowing and Being, Essays by Michael Polanyi*, ed. Marjorie Grene. Routledge & Kegan Paul (London: 1969), consisting of edited versions of:

"Beyond Nihilism." Published also 1960, 1962 [substantially the same].

"The Message of the Hungarian Revolution." Published also 1966 and 1969.

"The Two Cultures." Published also 1959.

"The Republic of Science." Published also 1962, 1968.

"The Growth of Science in Society." Published also 1967, 1968.

"The Potential Theory of Adsorption." Published also 1963.

"My Time with X-Rays and Crystals." Published also 1962.

"The Unaccountable Element in Science." Published also 1961, 1962, and as "Experience and the Perception of Pattern," 1963.

"Knowing and Being." Published also 1961.

"The Logic of Tacit Inference." Published also 1966, 1970.

"Tacit Knowing: Its Bearing on Some Problems in Philosophy." Published also 1962.

"Sense-Giving and Sense-Reading." Published also 1967, 1968.

"The Structure of Consciousness." Published also 1965 [same] and in 1969 [substantially the same]. [Similar to "The Mind-Body Relation," 1968.]

"Life's Irreducible Structure." Published also 1968.

*1970*

"Transcendence and Self-Transcendence." *Soundings*, 53 (Spring 1970), pp. 88–94. Published also 1971.

"What Is a Painting?" *The British Journal of Aesthetics*, 10 (July 1970), pp. 225–36. Published also in *The American Scholar*, 39 (Autumn 1970), pp. 655–69.

"Science and Man." *Proceedings of the Royal Society of Medicine*, 63 (September 1970), pp. 969–76.

"Why Did We Destroy Europe?" *Studium Generale*, 23 (Autumn 1970), pp. 909–16.

"The Logic of Tacit Inference." *Human and Artificial Intelligence*, ed. Frederick J. Crosson. Appleton-Century-Crofts (New York: 1970), pp. 219–40. Published also 1966, 1969.

"Foreward." *Optics, Painting and Photography*, M. H. Pirenne. Cambridge University Press (Cambridge: 1970), pp. xv–xix.

*1971*

Review of *Approaches to a Philosophical Biology*, by Marjorie Grene. *British Journal for the Philosophy of Science*, 22 (1971), pp. 307–8.

"Transcendence and Self-Transcendence." *Science et Conscience de la Société*, ed. Jean-Claude Casanova. Colmann-Levy (France: 1971), pp. 101–8. Published also 1970.

*1972*

"Genius in Science." *Encounter*, 38 (January 1972), pp. 43–50. Published also in *De la Méthode*. Office International de Librairie (Brussels: 1972), pp. 12–25.

*1973*

"Tacit Knowing." *Essays in Theory*, ed. E. Graham Wood and James Moffett. Houghton Mifflin (Boston: 1973); pp. 171–93. Same as Part One of *The Tacit Dimension*, 1966, 1983.

*1974*

In *Scientific Thought and Social Reality: Essays by Michael Polanyi*, ed. Fred Schwartz, *Psychological Issues*, 8, Monograph 32. International Universities Press (New York: 1974), pp. 1 and 15–149, consisting of:
"Foreward."
"The Autonomy of Science." Published also 1943, 1945 [same], 1951 [substantially the same].

"Science and the Modern Crisis." Published also 1945 [substantially the same].

"The Social Message of Pure Science." Published also 1946 [same], 1951 [substantially the same].

"The Nature of Scientific Convictions." Published also 1949 [same], 1951 [substantially the same].

"Scientific Beliefs." Published also 1950.

"On the Introduction of Science into Moral Subjects." Published also 1954.

"From Copernicus to Einstein." Published also 1955.

"Faith and Reason." Published also 1961.

"On the Modern Mind." Published also 1965.


*1975*

"Truths in Myths," (with Harry Prosch), *Cross Currents*, 25 (Summer 1975), pp. 149–62. Published also as Chapter 9 of *Meaning*, 1975.

# Index